PLYMOUTH
HAYWARD
CALIFORNIA
YJR 013

THE ENCYCLOPEDIA OF AMERICAN MUSCLE CARS

BELVEDERE
GTX
426
Radial T/A

THE ENCYCLOPEDIA OF
AMERICAN MUSCLE CARS

JIM CAMPISANO

MetroBooks

MetroBooks

An Imprint of the Michael Friedman Publishing Group, Inc.

Library of Congress Cataloging-in-Publication Data

Campisano, Jim.
Encyclopedia of American muscle cars / Jim Campisano.
p. cm.
ISBN 1-58663-317-1
Includes bibliographical references and index.
1. Muscle cars—United States—History. 2. Muscle cars—United States—Encyclopedias.
I. Title.

TL23 .C365 2002
629.222'0973—dc21

2002024406

Editors: Ann Kirby-Payne and Rosy Ngo
Art Director: Kevin Ullrich
Designer: Dan Lish
Photo Editors: Jami Ruszkai and Paquita Bass
Production Manager: Richela Fabian Morgan

Color separations by Bright Arts Graphics
Printed in China by CS Graphics Shanghai

1 3 5 7 9 10 8 6 4 2

For bulk purchases and special sales, please contact:
Michael Friedman Publishing Group, Inc.
Attention: Sales Department
230 Fifth Avenue
New York, NY 10001
212/685-6610 FAX 212/685-3916

Visit our website:
www.metrobooks.com

Pages 8–9: When GM vice president Bill Mitchell conceived the idea for the Buick Riviera, he wanted it to be "a cross between a Ferrari and a Rolls-Royce." First introduced in 1963, this is a 1965 Gran Sport model, which had the dual-quad 425 engine as standard equipment.

Dedication

This book is dedicated to my two sons, Sam and Luke, the most wonderful kids a guy could ask for. Both saw their first organized drag race before the age of three, and I look forward to a lifetime of cruisin' with them.

It's also for the legendary designer Larry Shinoda and moto-journalist Steve Collison, two friends who threw their last earthly powershifts too soon.

Acknowledgments

A work like this doesn't happen without the help of many people. First and foremost, I'd like to thank Diego Rosenberg. I first met Diego in the early 1990s when I was the editor of *MuscleCars* magazine and he was an intern. Not only does he own a genuine 1970 Oldsmobile 4-4-2 W-30 convertible, but he voluntarily and enthusiastically compiled the list of production numbers in the appendix. A Herculean task, he did so while flatly refusing to take a penny for his efforts. His passion and dedication to muscle cars is unparalleled and I'm grateful to be able to call him a friend.

Dan Foley, owner of a magnificent '67 Dodge Coronet R/T and a longtime buddy, never flinched no matter how many Mopar-related questions I threw at him, regardless of the time, day or night.

Same goes for Andrew Hinckley. When I had a COPO, Yenko, or other 427 Chevy question, he took the time to point me in the direction of all the right people.

Tom DeMauro, my colleague at Primedia, editor of *High Performance Pontiac* magazine and author of *Original Pontiac GTO* and *The Restorer's Guide, 1960–1974*, is himself an encyclopedia of Pontiac knowledge and he didn't hesitate to share it with me.

O. John Coletti, chief engineer for Ford Special Vehicle Engineering and owner of a restored '68 AMX, is also one of the good guys. He came up with a comprehensive list of people for me to use as references for this encyclopedia. Plus, he keeps the muscle car flame burning today—the 2000 Cobra R, supercharged F-150 Lightning, and the 2003 "Terminator" Cobra are proof that the muscle car is alive and well in the new millennium.

Mopar historian, number-cruncher, and journalist extraordinaire Al Kirschenbaum was once again a big help. I hope this book inspires him to get that '70 'Cuda on the road again. Or at least ship it to me.

Then there is the staff at MetroBooks. Ann Kirby-Payne, my editor on two previous hardcover books, approached me about doing this tome and convinced me I was the right person for the job. So what if it was eighty thousand words and I had a day job as editor of *Muscle Mustangs & Fast Fords* magazine, a position that on a good week consumes fifty hours of my time? So what if she quit shortly after I signed the contract?

Working with a new editor is always scary, but Rosy Ngo stepped in and helped make this book happen. She put my caffeine-fueled prose into coherent English, offered plenty of encouragement and never threatened my life, despite repeated blown deadlines. Rosy, I hope I rewarded your patience with the kind of book you were looking for.

Contents

Riviera
Gran Sport

Introduction

It happened so fast that it was over almost before some knew it had started. The American muscle car era began in 1960, picked up steam with the introduction of the Pontiac GTO in 1964, and peaked in 1970. By the end of 1974 it was pretty much dust, with only the Super Duty 455 Pontiac Trans Am surviving with its big-inch engine intact. A total of fifteen model years came and went in the blink of an eye, but left an indelible mark on the automotive landscape. More milestone cars were produced during this time than perhaps any other era before or since.

When I started saving money for my first car, my parents couldn't understand why I was so obsessed with buying an old muscle car. "Why do you want someone else's headache?" they pleaded. "Wait until you can buy a new car."

Why would I? I got my license in 1978 and there wasn't a single new car worth having. Choked by emissions regulations, grossly overweight and underpowered, the few remnants left from the '60s were mere shells of their former selves. The good engines were all gone and there was nothing left but garish tape stripes and oversized bumpers. As a kid, I had lusted after the sleek machines that dotted my neighborhood—a '69 GTO Judge, a '70 Superbird, and a '71 340 'Cuda were just three of the classics that I drooled over every day while pedaling my bicycle. What was I going to buy, a Mustang II Cobra II whose 302 2-barrel V8 wheezed out 130 horsepower? No chance.

The muscle car era began in earnest in 1960 when Chevy, Ford, and Pontiac started really kicking it into gear with big-inch, high-compression, multiple carburetor–equipped mills. Meanwhile, organized drag racing started skyrocketing in popularity and stock car racing was getting bigger every day. At the time, many of the classes in both types of motorsports, especially the National Association for Stock Car Auto Racing (NASCAR), dictated that you use only factory stock parts. This prodded the factories to come up with high-performance parts—often disguised as "export" or "police" parts to trick the sanctioning bodies—in order to be competitive. Before you knew it, road-going showcases for this hardware were being built: 406 and 427 Fords, 413 and 426 Mopars, 409 and 427 Chevrolets, among others.

Then came the Pontiac GTO of 1964. General Motors issued a corporate ban on motor sports participation in 1963 and it couldn't have come at a worse time for Pontiac. This division had come from also-ran status in sales to number three behind only Chevrolet and Ford, thanks in large part to its success in NASCAR and NHRA (National Hot Rod Association) drag racing. Its product was youthful, exciting, stylish, and quite often very fast (as proven on racetracks across the country).

Pontiac's solution was to produce high-image machines that had the muscle of the earlier "super stocks," but in a more compact, street-friendly package. The GTO had a 389-cubic-inch engine, remarkably good looks, and all the goodies baby boomers and enthusiasts wanted: bucket seats, multiple carburetors, four-on-the-floor shifters, redline tires, and so on. The GTO was successful beyond anything its creators imagined, selling more than six times what they'd predicted for the first year alone, then doubling sales the following year.

In 1975, just a year past the GTO's demise, David E. Davis Jr., former editor of *Car and Driver*, perfectly summed up this high-strung intermediate: "My first ride in a GTO left me with a feeling like losing my virginity, going into combat and tasting my first draft beer all in about seven seconds.

"I remember that the GTO slammed out of the hole like it was being fired from a catapult, that the tach needle flung itself across the dial like a windshield wiper, that the noise from three 2-throat carburetors on that heavy old 389 cubic inch Pontiac V8 sounded like some awful doomsday Hoover-God sucking up sinners."

It was a car that spawned a host of imitators and inspires automotive lust to this day. All it takes is one ride. My first GTO experience came as a teenager in the mid '70s. I was working in a gas station and became acquainted with an older kid, Billy Becker, who had a ratty '69 with a 400-cubic-inch engine and a 4-speed transmission. Sliding into the passenger bucket, I was flipping: mesmerized by the uncivilized staccato beat coming out from the Thrush mufflers, yet at the same time amazed at the comfort of the bucket seats. I was ready for action.

Billy pulled out onto the street next to the gas station, revved the big Poncho mill, and dumped the clutch. The oversized rear tires howled, smoking to show their disapproval. I was pinned to the seat. With perfect timing, he kicked the clutch and yanked the big Hurst shifter back into second, never lifting the throttle off the floor (my first powershift!). The back tires screamed again and the Goat rocketed ahead like a locomotive from hell.

Third gear was made just like second and a traffic light was coming up quickly. We slowed, turned off, and headed back to the gas station. I had been hooked on muscle cars long before this, but it still took weeks to wipe the grin off my face.

The muscle car era was one hell of a ride. But what really caused its demise? Most magazine article and books blame the unholy trio of emissions controls, exorbitant insurance rates, and the first oil crisis of 1973. But there are other factors that I've never seen explored that I feel contributed mightily towards the era's death.

First was the Vietnam War. An unwelcome letter from the draft board forced many enthusiasts to put their dreams on hold—sometimes permanently. At the war's peak there were about a million American service men stationed all over the world and the closest they could get to a GTO or Road Runner was through a subscription to *Hot Rod* magazine. These men had been prime customers for Detroit's wildest beasts. The kids with the college deferments, for the most part, couldn't care less. They were too busy driving VW Beetles and Microbuses. The motorheads were getting shot at in the jungle.

Reliability and comfort were other factors that played a part in the demise of American muscle cars. Many customers just bought the most powerful car they could find and expected it to idle like a family sedan and require nothing more than semi-regular oil changes and tune-ups. An engine with multiple carburetors, a dual-point distributor, and (for good measure) a solid-lifter camshaft required more maintenance and attention to keep in peak tune than an ordinary Dodge Coronet. In many instances, this was more than the average Joe bargained for. Heavy-duty suspensions, stiff clutches, steep drag-oriented gear ratios, and exhaust systems that were louder than the radio could get monotonous quickly for the borderline enthusiast.

The popularity of personal luxury cars like the Chevy Monte Carlo, Pontiac Grand Prix, and Chrysler Cordoba in the mid-'70s is testimony that customers still wanted distinctive and stylish transportation, but without the tuning hassles. (Note: *stylish* is a term I use loosely here. I'm not an advocate of rich Corinthian leather. I also believe the proliferation and popularity of these same mid-'70s cars is evidence of the excesses of an era that gave us polyester leisure suits and disco music.)

As you read this encyclopedia, please keep a couple of things in mind. Whenever production numbers are considered, remember that a volatile labor force and/or the vagaries of the economy often had a deleterious effect on sales. The United Auto Workers union was constantly striking in the late '60s and '70s. Extended work stoppages nearly put the Camaro and Firebird out of production permanently in the early '70s.

Without getting too involved in an economics debate, a recession can put a real dent in sales. Few people recall it now, but the '57 Chevy, the quintessential American favorite, was not a great seller—not when compared to the '55 and '56 models—and one reason for this was that there was a downturn in the economy that year. There's no doubt that the Arab oil embargo of 1973, the insurance industry, and environmental issues played a key role in the demise of the great American muscle car, but there were other factors at work, too.

You will also find in this book extensive quoting of period road tests. This was something I felt necessary, but included with a sense of unease. I tried to refer to those tests that I believed had a moderate chance of being indicative of a car's performance. Journalists who were around during the muscle car apex have clued me in on what it was like to bang gears in the first Boss Mustang or a Baldwin-Motion car. Testing methods varied widely back in the '60s, as they do today. Some magazines did comprehensive instrumented tests of all facets of a car's performance. Others did quarter-mile testing at the drag strip and wrote about how they performed on the street

With Ford taking over production, Shelby Mustang's emblems became more ornate as the muscle car era progressed. This is the steering wheel emblem off a 1969 GT500.

Right: The last year for the Boss Mustang and the only year for the Boss 351 was 1971. It marked the end of the line for high-compression Ford small-blocks.

Pages 14–15: The most popular character on the television show *The Dukes of Hazzard* might have been the "General Lee," a '69 Dodge Charger painted with a confederate flag on the roof and numbers on the side. It spawned a host of imitators, including the '68 you see here.

(sometimes in illegal street races). In the early days, some of this testing was less than scientific—a guy in the passenger seat worked a stopwatch. I've heard firsthand that, for some annuals, performance numbers were fabricated.

Car Life usually ran its battery of tests with a driver, a passenger, and a full tank of fuel, which would have a very negative impact on performance. Other magazines like *Car Craft* and *Super Stock & Drag Illustrated* had experienced drag racers on staff who would treat each test like the final round of the U.S. Nationals; near-empty fuel tanks, full-throttle powershifts, and other tricks could make their times a half-second or more quicker than others.

Then there was the chicanery on the part of the manufacturers. The Big Three automakers knew good print in a popular buff book could help make or break a car. In his autobiography, former Pontiac ad executive Jim Wangers pretty much admitted that every Pontiac test car had, at a minimum, a Royal Bobcat performance tune-up. Since the engines looked virtually identical, many a 389 GTO test car actually held a 421-cubic-inch engine.

According to Martyn L. Schorr, who was editor of *High Performance Cars* and *Cars* magazines in the '60s and '70s, some brands cheated on road tests more than others. "Pontiac was the worst," he recalled, "but Ford was pretty bad, too.

Chevrolets were usually stock. Chevy was moving so many cars back then it didn't need to cheat. It just didn't matter."

While holed up in my home office writing this, I felt it necessary to put myself in a '60s state of mind. No, I didn't burn incense or turn on a lava lamp, but surrounded by an ever-growing collection of vintage car magazines and automotive books, I burned the midnight oil listening to my favorite '60s music—the Beatles, pre-*Pet Sounds* Beach Boys, the Rolling Stones, the Byrds, plus Rhino Records' *Hot Rods & Custom Classics* CD box set of car songs. I imagined what it must have felt like cruising in a 409 Chevy and hearing the Beach Boys sing its praises back in '63 when it was still a new car. I thought back to the warm summer nights I spent endlessly burning up gas in my friends' Super Bees, GTXs, Challengers, and my own '71 Barracuda ragtop and later a '69 Corvette. And then I just let the words flow. I concentrated on delivering a book that's not only informative and free of mistakes, but fun to read as well.

I hope you enjoy *The Encyclopedia of American Muscle Cars* for years to come. I also hope it inspires you to drive your favorite piece of Detroit iron more often. If you don't have one, may it prod you into buying one. Trust me, you won't regret it.

—Jim Campisano

01

The Engines

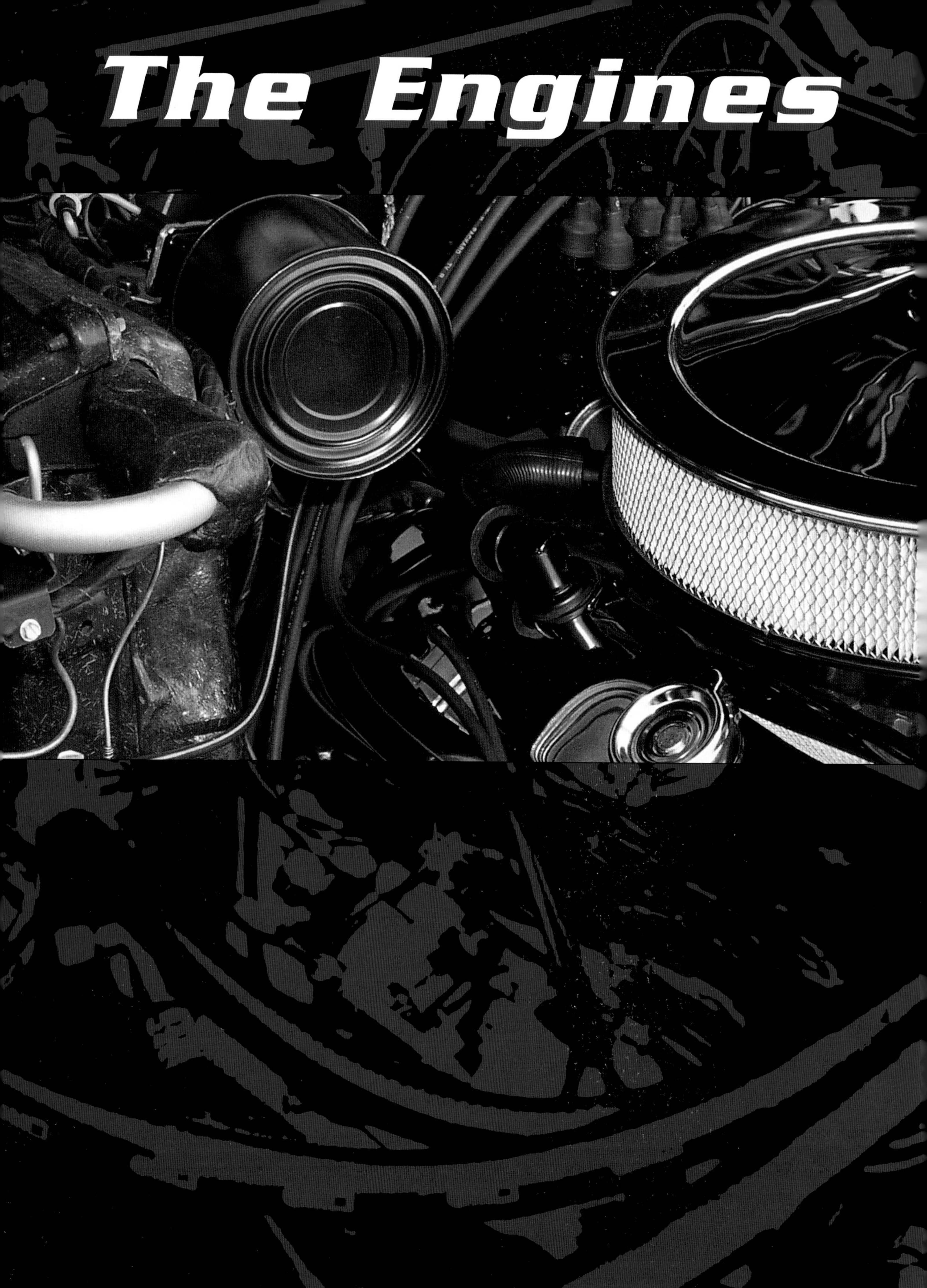

PART ONE
454
TURBO-JET

AMERICAN MOTORS ENGINE SPECIFICATIONS

1969 Hurst SC/Rambler	
Cu. In.	390
Bore (in.)	4.17
Stroke (in.)	3.57
Compression	10.20:1
Induction	1x4 bbl.
Horsepower/rpm	315/4600
Torque (lbs.-ft.)/rpm	425/3200

1969 Hurst AMX/SS	
Cu. In.	390
Bore (in.)	4.17
Stroke (in.)	3.57
Compression	12.30:1
Induction	1x4 bbl.
Horsepower/rpm	340/NA
Torque (lbs.-ft.)/rpm	NA

1970 Rebel Machine	
Cu. In.	390
Bore (in.)	4.17
Stroke (in.)	3.57
Compression	10.0:1
Induction	1x4 bbl.
Horsepower/rpm	340/5100
Torque (lbs.-ft.)/rpm	430/3600

The functional ram air hood on this 1970 AMX helped boost output on the optional 390 V8 to 340 horsepower. Without the ram air option and with the scoops sealed, it was rated at 325. This model has the optional "Shadow Mask" blackout paint treatment.

American Motors Corporation V8

In 1966 the American Motors introduced its last modern V8, a lightweight 290-cubic-inch engine designed by David Potter (who had come to AMC from Packard). With many excellent features, this V8 had just 200 horsepower and was designed as a common people mover, but before the muscle car era ended, versions of it powered legends like the AMX and Javelin, and won three Trans-Am racing championships.

The first iteration had a 3.75-inch (95mm) bore and a 3.25-inch (83mm) stroke, 9.0:1 compression, and hydraulic lifters. With an AMC 2-barrel carburetor in base form, it made no performance pretensions. There was, however, a 4-barrel option to liven things up. The V-8 enging was compact, which allowed AMC to fit it into the compact Rambler Rogue lineup. Things got better with the birth of the Javelin ponycar and two-seat AMX in 1968.

A higher-output version of this V8 family was the 343, which was optional in both of the aforementioned cars and produced 280 horsepower. Midway through 1968, coinciding with the introduction of the AMX, the 315-horsepower 390 was born. It was a bored and stroked 343 with big-valve cylinder heads (compression for both engines was rated at 10.2:1).

When the American Motors Corporation decided to go Super Stock drag racing in 1969, it had the Hurst Corporation build a limited number of specially prepared AMXs. Each car had a 390 equipped with an Edelbrock cross-ram, dual 4-barrel intake manifold, a pair of 650-cfm carbs, Doug Thorley headers, and 12.3:1 compression. Rated at 340 horsepower, just more than fifty of these cars were produced.

By 1970, the 390 engine was rated at 325 horsepower, despite a slight drop in compression to an even 10.0:1. When equipped with a functional hood scoop, the AMX and Javelin were rated at 340 ponies, the most powerful street engine AMC would ever offer. (For the record, this 340-horse engine was also used in the one-year-only Rebel Machine.)

A lengthened stroke in the 343 produced a new displacement engine in 1970, the 360, and it was an AMC staple for years to come. Like the 390, the 360 had a 10.0:1 compression ratio. It produced 290 horsepower and 395 lbs.-ft. of torque—quite a decent performer when used in the light AMX or Javelin. The biggest change to the engine was the redesigned cylinder heads, which now featured dog-leg ports.

AMERICAN MOTORS AMX AND JAVELIN ENGINE SPECIFICATIONS

1968

Cu. In.	343	390
Bore (in.)	4.08	4.17
Stroke (in.)	3.28	3.57
Compression	10.20:1	10.20:1
Induction	1x4 bbl.	1x4 bbl.
Horsepower/rpm	280/4800	315/4600
Torque (lbs.-ft.)/rpm	365/3000	425/3200

1969

Cu. In.	343	390	
Bore (in.)	4.08	4.17	
Stroke (in.)	3.28	3.57	
Compression	10.20:1	10.20:1	12.30:1*
Induction	1x4 bbl.	1x4 bbl.	2x4 bbl.
Horsepower/rpm	280/4800	315/4600	340
Torque (lbs.-ft.)/rpm	365/3000	425/3200	not rated

*AMX S/S only

1970

Cu. In.	360	390
Bore (in.)	4.08	4.17
Stroke (in.)	3.34	3.57
Compression	10.00:1	10.00:1
Induction	1x4 bbl.	1x4 bbl.
Horsepower/rpm	290/4800	325/5000
Torque (lbs.-ft.)/rpm	395/3200	420/3200

1971

Cu. In.	360	401
Bore (in.)	4.08	4.17
Stroke (in.)	3.34	3.68
Compression	8.50:1	9.50:1*
Induction	1x4 bbl.	1x4 bbl.
Horsepower/rpm	285/4800	330/5000
Torque (lbs.-ft.)/rpm	390/3200	430/3400

*Early production had 10.20:1 c.r.

1972

Cu. In.	360	401
Bore (in.)	4.08	4.17
Stroke (in.)	3.34	3.68
Compression	8.50:1	8.50:1
Induction	1x4 bbl.	1x4 bbl.
Horsepower/rpm	220/4400	255/4600
Torque (lbs.-ft.)/rpm	315/3100	345/3300

1973

Cu. In.	360	401
Bore (in.)	4.08	4.17
Stroke (in.)	3.34	3.68
Compression	8.50:1	8.50:1
Induction	1x4 bbl.	1x4 bbl.
Horsepower/rpm	220/4400	255/4600
Torque (lbs.-ft.)/rpm	315/3100	345/3300

1974

Cu. In.	360	401
Bore (in.)	4.08	4.17
Stroke (in.)	3.34	3.68
Compression	8.50:1	8.50:1*
Induction	1x4 bbl.	1x4 bbl.
Horsepower/rpm	220/4400	255/4600
Torque (lbs.-ft.)/rpm	315/3100	345/3300

*Lowered to 8.25 early in model year.

AMC's V8s always had large valves, but the new exhaust ports increased flow by 50 percent. To gear up for unleaded fuel, the 360 lost 1.5 points in compression for '71, although peak power was down only 5 horsepower.

The year 1971 was also when AMC increased the stroke on the 390 from 3.57 to 3.68 inches (91 to 93mm) to create the 401. Initially, the 401 retained the 390's 10.0:1 compression ratio, but fell to 9.5:1 partway through the model year. The increase in cubes helped offset the drop in compression, and the first 401-4V was rated at 330 horsepower and 430 lbs.-ft. of torque, both figures up 5 from 1970's base 390. If you ordered the AMX, a fiberglass cowl induction hood was optional. This undoubtedly picked up the pony count, but the rating stayed the same.

Compression was lowered another full point on the 401 in '72, and horsepower was switched to the more conservative net rating system, which put its output at 255 horses. The 360 stayed at 8.5:1 compression, and its output was listed as 220 horsepower. These ratings remained until the end of the '74 model year, when AMC pulled the plug on the Javelin and AMX. That was the end of the high-performance era at AMC.

Buick

Two basic engine designs carried Buick throughout the muscle car era. Its first muscle machine, the 1965 Skylark Gran Sport, was powered by a 401-cubic-inch version of the nailhead (or nail valve) V8, so nicknamed for its relatively small valves and vertical valve layout. But this version, combined with

Buick produced the torquiest muscle car of all time in 1970, the Stage 1 455 with 510 lbs.-ft. of torque at 2600 rpm. It also made 360 horsepower. Front and rear spoilers shown were standard on the GSX.

BUICK ENGINE SPECIFICATIONS

1965

Cu. In.	401	425*
Bore (in.)	4.19	4.31
Stroke (in.)	3.64	3.64
Compression	10.25:1	10.25:1
Induction	1x4 bbl.	2x4 bbl.
Horsepower/rpm	325/4400	360/4400
Torque (lbs.-ft.)/rpm	445/2800	465/2800

*Optional Riviera GS only

1966

Cu. In.	401
Bore (in.)	4.19
Stroke (in.)	3.64
Compression	10.25:1
Induction	1x4 bbl.
Horsepower/rpm	325/4400
Torque (lbs.-ft.)/rpm	445/2800

1967

Cu. In.	340	400
Bore (in.)	3.75	4.04
Stroke (in.)	3.85	3.90
Compression	10.25:1	10.25:1
Induction	1x4 bbl.	1x4 bbl.
Horsepower/rpm	260/4200	340/5000
Torque (lbs.-ft.)/rpm	365/2800	440/3200

1968

Cu. In.	350	400
Bore (in.)	3.80	4.04
Stroke (in.)	3.85	3.90
Compression	10.25:1	10.25:1
Induction	1x4 bbl.	1x4 bbl.
Horsepower/rpm	280/4600	340/5000
Torque (lbs.-ft.)/rpm	375/2800	440/3200

1969

Cu. In.	350	400	400*
Bore (in.)	3.80	4.04	4.04
Stroke (in.)	3.85	3.90	3.90
Compression	10.25:1	10.25:1	10.25:1
Induction	1x4 bbl.	1x4 bbl.	1x4 bbl.
Horsepower/rpm	280/4600	340/5000	350/5000
Torque (lbs.-ft.)/rpm	375/2800	440/3200	440/3200

*Stage 1

1970

Cu. In.	350	455	455*
Bore (in.)	3.80	4.31	4.31
Stroke (in.)	3.85	3.90	3.90
Compression	10.25:1	10.00:1	10.50:1
Induction	1x4 bbl.	1x4 bbl.	1x4 bbl.
Horsepower/rpm	285/4600	350/4600	360/4600
Torque (lbs.-ft.)/rpm	375/3200	510/2600	510/2600

*Stage 1

1971

Cu. In.	350	455	455*
Bore (in.)	3.80	4.31	4.31
Stroke (in.)	3.85	3.90	3.90
Compression	8.50:1	8.50:1	8.50:1
Induction	1x4 bbl.	1x4 bbl.	1x4 bbl.
Horsepower/rpm	260/4600	315/4600	345/5000
Torque (lbs.-ft.)/rpm	360/3200	450/2600	460/3000

*Stage 1

1972

Cu. In.	455	455*
Bore (in.)	4.31	4.31
Stroke (in.)	3.90	3.90
Compression	10.00:1	10.50:1
Induction	1x4 bbl.	1x4 bbl.
Horsepower/rpm	260/4400	270/4400
Torque (lbs.-ft.)/rpm	380/2800	390/3000

*Stage 1

Opposite: By 1970, the Stage 1 engine in the Buick GS had grown to 455 cubic inches, making a record 510 lb.-ft. of torque.

Left: These foam blocks sealed the air cleaner to the functional hood scoops on the 1970 Gran Sport, directing cold air directly to the Rochester carburetor. The system worked well, even though the actual hood scoops were rather understated. Stage 1 powerplants utilized a specially prepared carburetor, a high-lift hydraulic cam, and a low-restriction dual exhaust. All GS455s and Stage 1s shared the same size intake and exhaust valves.

the large displacement, helped the engine make a prodigious amount of torque. By the time it found its way into the GS, it was already an old engine and a modern replacement was on the drawing board. The replacement was not ready by 1965, however, and the 401, whose roots could be traced directly to the 322 of 1953, motivated the GS for two years.

According to corporate edict at the time, the 401 was 1 cubic inch too large to be installed in the intermediate Skylark body—400 cubes was the limit. But the only smaller version of the engine that Buick had was just 300 cubic inches, way too small for a muscle car, and the 401 was in truth just a hair less than 401 cubic inches, so Buick brass signed off on it.

The 401 was a variation of the Buick Wildcat V8. In order to put the engine in the Skylark chassis, the exhaust manifolds had to be modified to fit into the frame. Also, the intake manifold was altered, and the starter needed a special shield to protect it from the heat of the exhaust system. The oil sump and pan were unique to the GS as well.

A single Carter 4-barrel carburetor, 10.25:1 compression, and dual exhausts completed the package. It was rated at 325 horsepower and 445 lbs.-ft. of torque, and was dubbed the Wildcat 445 because of its torque production. For those looking for more power, there was a dealer-installed dual quad intake manifold, which was standard on the Riviera GS. With it, horsepower increased to 338 and torque to 465 lbs.-ft.

To make the engine breathe better and overcome the too-small exhaust valve, a cam with a lot of overlap was used. This opened the valve a little early and held it open longer. In its ads, Buick called the 401 GS "A Howitzer With Windshield Wipers."

If you ordered a Riviera GS in '65, you got a 425-cid nailhead with a pair of Carter AFB 4-barrels on an alloy intake, a 0.439/0.441-inch (11.1/11.2mm) lift camshaft, finned alloy valve covers, and a chrome dual-snorkel air filter. It produced 360 horsepower.

The year 1966 was basically a carryover for the GS, although you could order a 340-horsepower version of the 401 (still rated at 445 lbs.-ft. of torque). The difference was that the higher-output motor was equipped with a version of the new Rochester Quadrajet 4-barrel carburetor.

An all-new 400-cubic-inch V8 replaced the venerable nailhead in 1967. It featured a more traditional wedge-shaped combustion chamber. Nothing was interchangeable; the only thing that remained the same was the 10.25:1 compression ratio. It used a 4.04-inch (103mm) bore and 3.90-inch (99mm) stroke, 18 percent larger valves on the intake side, 56 percent larger valves on the exhaust, water jackets in the cylinder heads that were carried around the spark plug holes, a better-breathing intake manifold, and improved exhaust manifolds.

The new engine offered significantly better breathing and had scads more potential. In its maiden season, it produced 340 horsepower at 5000 rpm and 440 lbs.-ft. of torque at 3200. These weren't major improvements on paper, but the car it was placed in, now known as the GS400, was significantly quicker. In addition to the 400, Buick brought out a small version, a 340. It was an undersquare engine, meaning that the stroke was larger than the bore (3.85 versus 3.75 inches [98 versus 95mm]), and produced a junior supercar, the GS340, which had just 260 horsepower at 4200 rpm and 365 lbs.-ft. of torque at 2800.

Buick completely redesigned its intermediate car line for 1968 and shook up the powerplants a bit as well. An increase in bore on the 340 to 3.8 inches (97mm) created the 350 (as well as the GS350 model). Horsepower rose to 280 at 4600 rpm and torque to 375 at 2800. The 400 was carried over virtually unchanged, but for drag racers Buick quietly announced the first of its Stage engine packages, called Stage 2 (strange as it was, the Stage 2 preceded the Stage 1). Known at the time to only a small group of Buick engineers and a handful of drag racers, it was conservatively rated at 350 horsepower and had 11.0:1 pistons, a special camshaft and valvetrain, and assorted internal components. To make it legal for class drag racing, Buick filed its specifications with the NHRA as the Heavy Duty Stage 2 option on Skylarks.

The year 1969 saw the advent of the Stage 1 engine option, which, unlike the Stage 2 parts, was factory-installed. For the Stage 1, a specially prepared Rochester Quadrajet carb was set up so that the secondaries would open quicker. It was fed by a functional cold-air hood. There was a unique high-lift camshaft and 2.25-inch (57mm) exhaust pipes.

Horsepower was rated at 350 at 5000 rpm, and 440 lbs.-ft. of torque were produced at 3200 rpm. The package came with a 3.64:1 rear standard—3.42:1 if you ordered air conditioning. It was produced for only one model year (it was superseded by the 455 Stage 1 for 1970) and just 1,256 were built. It was good for 14.70-second ETs (elapsed time) in the quarter mile at about 92.5 mph (148kph).

When General Motors relented and allowed its divisions to install engines larger than 400 cubic inches in intermediate cars in 1970, Buick wasted no time in ditching the 400s in the GS lineup. GM bored out the 400 to 4.31 inches (109mm), resulting in a torque-monster 455 engine. Compression actually went down, to 10.0:1 from 10.25:1. Power on the GS455 was underrated at 350 ponies, but the torque was not—510 lbs.-ft. was recorded, the pinnacle for any muscle car engine. The Stage 1 kept that torque rating, but added 10 horsepower thanks to its special carburetor, high-lift hydraulic cam, and lower-restriction dual exhaust.

All 455s shared cast-aluminum alloy pistons, forged rods, and a nodular iron crankshaft. Both

versions of the 455 relied on a Quadrajet carburetor, but as in '69, the Stages were tweaked at the factory to bolster performance. Similarly, the GS455 and Stage 1 shared 2.125-inch (54mm) intake valves and 1.750-inch (44mm) exhaust valves. Lift on the Stage 1 cam was 0.490 inches (12mm), with 319-degree advertised duration.

For 1970, the Stage 2 package was again available in extremely limited numbers to drag racers. It now provided special D-port cylinder heads, a hotter cam, an Edelbrock manifold, 12.0:1 compression, and special racing headers, though casting problems early on killed the heads after only a few sets were produced.

It never got this good again. Buick, like the rest of GM's divisions, dropped compression to 8.5:1 on both 455s in '71, killing 35 horsepower on the base GS455 and 15 on the Stage 1. A switch to more conservative net power ratings in 1972, along with leaned-out carburetors and other emissions-related measures, caused the horsepower figures to drop to 260 for the GS455 and 270 for the Stage 1.

When the second-generation Camaro was introduced midway through the 1970 model year, the Z/28 lost its unique 302 engine. It now shared the solid-lifter 350 LT-1 with the Corvette. That engine was rated at 360 horsepower in the Camaro, 10 less than the Corvette thanks to a more restrictive exhaust system. The car pictured features the optional RS package, which included the split front bumper.

Chevrolet (Small-Blocks)

Chevrolet's high-performance reputation could be traced back to 1954 when chief engineer Ed Cole and project engineer and assistant chief engineer Harry F. Barr developed Chevrolet's first overhead valve V8. When it arrived in the fall of '54 for use in the all-new '55 Chevy, it was compact, small, and light—lighter than the Chevrolet 6-cylinder by almost 40 pounds (18kg). Before it went out of production in the 1990s, the new engine changed the entire face of the automotive industry.

The first version used a 3.75-inch (95mm) bore and 3-inch (76mm) stroke, giving it 265 cubic inches. The short stroke allowed it to be a high revver, and its revolutionary rocker arm system allowed it to rev quickly. Chevy's overhead valve V8 used a thin-wall casting technique (called the green sand process) to ensure its light weight. A forged steel crankshaft was standard. Hollow pushrods allowed oil to splash the rocker arms, eliminating the need for external oil lines. The cylinder heads were interchangeable, which greatly reduced cost and aided simplicity.

Perhaps the greatest innovation of the small-block Chevy (which it shared with the Pontiac V8 introduced that same year) was its use of stamped steel rocker arms that pivoted around a ball on their own stud. The brainchild of Clayton P. Leach (who later became assistant chief engineer at Pontiac), this innovation eliminated the heavy rocker arm shaft used on most engines and reduced the number of valvetrain parts.

Chevrolet Motor Division introduced the small-block V8 in its 1955 Chevrolets, including the Corvette. In that fiberglass sports car, the new engine reduced the 0-to-60-mph (96.5kph) time by three full seconds (to eight seconds flat) compared to the Blue Flame 6-cylinder the Corvette had been using. Top speed was up to 120 mph (193kph) and fuel economy improved from 17 to 20 miles per gallon (27 to 32km per 3.8L).

There were some teething pains early on, including excessive oil consumption, but these were fixed rather quickly. By '56, a higher-lift cam was used and the other Power Pack options became available (the inaugural season offered a 4-barrel

CHEVROLET ENGINE SPECIFICATIONS

1964			
Cu. In.	409		
Bore (in.)	4.31		
Stroke (in.)	3.50		
Compression	10.00:1	11.00:1	
Induction	1x4 bbl.	1x4 bbl.	2x4 bbl.
Horsepower/rpm	340/5000	400/5800	425/6000
Torque (lbs.-ft.)/rpm	420/3200	425/3600	425/4200

1965	
Cu. In.	327
Bore (in.)	4.00
Stroke (in.)	3.25
Compression	11.00:1
Induction	1x4 bbl.
Horsepower/rpm	350/5800
Torque (lbs.-ft.)/rpm	360/3600

1965 (cont.)		
Cu. In.	396	
Bore (in.)	4.094	
Stroke (in.)	3.76	
Compression	10.25:1	11.00:1
Induction	1x4 bbl.	1x4 bbl.
Horsepower/rpm	325/4800	425/6400
Torque (lbs.-ft.)/rpm	410/3200	415/4000

1965 (cont.)		
Cu. In.	409	
Bore (in.)	4.31	
Stroke (in.)	3.50	
Compression	10.00:1	11.00:1
Induction	1x4 bbl.	1x4 bbl.
Horsepower/rpm	340/5000	400/5800
Torque (lbs.-ft.)/rpm	420/3200	425/3600

1966	
Cu. In.	327
Bore (in.)	4.00
Stroke (in.)	3.25
Compression	11.00:1
Induction	1x4 bbl.
Horsepower/rpm	350/5800
Torque (lbs.-ft.)/rpm	360/3600

1966 (cont.)			
Cu. In.	396		
Bore (in.)	4.094		
Stroke (in.)	3.76		
Compression	10.25:1		11.00:1
Induction	1x4 bbl.		1x4 bbl.
Horsepower/rpm	325/4800	360/5200	375/5600
Torque (lbs.-ft.)/rpm	410/3200	420/3600	415/3600

1966 (cont.)		
Cu. In.	427	
Bore (in.)	4.25	
Stroke (in.)	3.76	
Compression	10.25:1	11.00:1
Induction	1x4 bbl.	1x4 bbl.
Horsepower/rpm	390/5200	425/5600
Torque (lbs.-ft.)/rpm	470/3600	460/4400

1967	
Cu. In.	327
Bore (in.)	4.00
Stroke (in.)	3.25
Compression	11.00:1
Induction	1x4 bbl.
Horsepower/rpm	350/5800
Torque (lbs.-ft.)/rpm	360/3600

1967 (cont.)			
Cu. In.	396		
Bore (in.)	4.094		
Stroke (in.)	3.76		
Compression	10.25:1		11.00:1
Induction	1x4 bbl.		1x4 bbl.
Horsepower/rpm	325/4800	350/5200	375/5600
Torque (lbs.-ft.)/rpm	410/3200	415/3400	415/3600

1967 (cont.)			
Cu. In.	427		
Bore (in.)	4.25		
Stroke (in.)	3.76		
Compression	10.25:1		11.00:1
Induction	1x4 bbl.	3x2 bbl.	3x2 bbl.
Horsepower/rpm	390/5400	400/5400	435/5800
Torque (lbs.-ft.)/rpm	460/3600	460/3600	460/4000

1968		
Cu. In.	327	
Bore (in.)	4.00	
Stroke (in.)	3.25	
Compression	10.00:1	11.00:1
Induction	1x4 bbl.	1x4 bbl.
Horsepower/rpm	300/5000	350/5800
Torque (lbs.-ft.)/rpm	360/3400	360/3600

1968 (cont.)			
Cu. In.	396		
Bore (in.)	4.094		
Stroke (in.)	3.76		
Compression	10.25:1		11.00:1
Induction	1x4 bbl.		1x4 bbl.
Horsepower/rpm	325/4800	350/5200	375/5600
Torque (lbs.-ft.)/rpm	410/3200	415/3400	415/3600

1968 (cont.)			
Cu. In.	427		
Bore (in.)	4.25		
Stroke (in.)	3.76		
Compression	10.25:1		
Induction	1x4 bbl.		3x2 bbl.
Horsepower/rpm	385/5200	390/5400	400/5400
Torque (lbs.-ft.)/rpm	460/3400	460/3600	460/3600

1968 (cont.)		
Cu. In.	427*	
Bore (in.)	4.25	
Stroke (in.)	3.76	
Compression	12.50:1	11.00:1
Induction	1x4 bbl.	3x2 bbl.
Horsepower/rpm	430/5200	435/5800
Torque (lbs.-ft.)/rpm	450/4400	460/4000

*L-88

1969		
Cu. In.	350	
Bore (in.)	4.00	
Stroke (in.)	3.48	
Compression	10.25:1	11.00:1
Induction	1x4 bbl.	1x4 bbl.
Horsepower/rpm	300/4800	350/5600
Torque (lbs.-ft.)/rpm	380/3200	380/3600

1969 (cont.)			
Cu. In.	396		
Bore (in.)	4.094		
Stroke (in.)	3.76		
Compression	10.25:1		11.00:1
Induction	1x4 bbl.		1x4 bbl.
Horsepower/rpm	325/4800	350/5200	375/5600
Torque (lbs.-ft.)/rpm	410/3200	415/3400	415/3600

1969 (cont.)			
Cu. In.	427		
Bore (in.)	4.25		
Stroke (in.)	3.76		
Compression	10.25:1		
Induction	1x4 bbl.		3x2 bbl.
Horsepower/rpm	335/4800	390/5400	400/5400
Torque (lbs.-ft.)/rpm	470/3200	460/3600	460/3600

1969 (cont.)			
Cu. In.	427*		
Bore (in.)	4.25		
Stroke (in.)	3.76		
Compression	12.50:1	11.00:1	11.00:1
Induction	1x4 bbl.	3x2 bbl.	1x4 bbl.
Horsepower/rpm	430/5200	435/5800	425/5600
Torque (lbs.-ft.)/rpm	450/4400	460/4000	460/4000

*L-88

1970			
Cu. In.	350		
Bore (in.)	4.00		
Stroke (in.)	3.48		
Compression	10.25:1	11.00:1	
Induction	1x4 bbl.	1x4 bbl.	
Horsepower/rpm	300/4800	350/5600	370/6000
Torque (lbs.-ft.)/rpm	380/3200	380/3600	380/4000

1970 (cont.)		
Cu. In.	402	
Bore (in.)	4.126	
Stroke (in.)	3.76	
Compression	10.25:1	11.00:1
Induction	1x4 bbl.	1x4 bbl.
Horsepower/rpm	350/4800	375/5600
Torque (lbs.-ft.)/rpm	415/3400	415/3600

1970 (cont.)			
Cu. In.	454		
Bore (in.)	4.25		
Stroke (in.)	4.00		
Compression	10.25:1		11.25:1
Induction	1x4 bbl.		1x4 bbl.
Horsepower/rpm	360/4400	390/4800	450/5600
Torque (lbs.-ft.)/rpm	500/3200	500/3400	500/3600

1971	
Cu. In.	350
Bore (in.)	4.00
Stroke (in.)	3.48
Compression	9:00:1
Induction	1x4 bbl.
Horsepower/rpm	330/5600
Torque (lbs.-ft.)/rpm	360/4000

1971 (cont.)	
Cu. In.	402
Bore (in.)	4.126
Stroke (in.)	3.76
Compression	8.50:1
Induction	1x4 bbl.
Horsepower/rpm	300/4800
Torque (lbs.-ft.)/rpm	400/3200

1971 (cont.)		
Cu. In.	454	
Bore (in.)	4.25	
Stroke (in.)	4.00	
Compression	8.50:1	9.00:1
Induction	1x4 bbl.	1x4 bbl.
Horsepower/rpm	365/4800	425/5600
Torque (lbs.-ft.)/rpm	465/3200	475/4000

1972	
Cu. In.	350
Bore (in.)	4.00
Stroke (in.)	3.48
Compression	9:00:1
Induction	1x4 bbl.
Horsepower/rpm	255/5600
Torque (lbs.-ft.)/rpm	280/4000

1972 (cont.)	
Cu. In.	402
Bore (in.)	4.126
Stroke (in.)	3.76
Compression	8.50:1
Induction	1x4 bbl.
Horsepower/rpm	240/4400
Torque (lbs.-ft.)/rpm	345/3200

1972 (cont.)	
Cu. In.	454
Bore (in.)	4.25
Stroke (in.)	4.00
Compression	8.50:1
Induction	1x4 bbl.
Horsepower/rpm	270/4400
Torque (lbs.-ft.)/rpm	390/3200

As automobile weights continued to escalate, the need for horsepower grew, too. Big-block engines offered the extra punch that could not be squeezed out of a small-block. In 1970, Chevy offered the LS6 454 in the midsize Chevelle. It was rated at 450 horsepower, tying the early 427 Corvette of 1966 for the highest output of a Chevrolet street engine (late '66 427 Vettes were down-rated to 425 horsepower). The air filter assembly was sealed directly ito the functional cowl-induction hood on the Chevelle. The only downside to the LS6 was the use of the Corvette's low-rise intake manifold, which hampered performance somewhat.

carb and dual exhausts). Regular Production Option (RPO) 410 added a higher compression ratio (9.25:1) and raised horsepower from 180 to 205. Later that year, RPO 411 was introduced, which added dual quads and increased horsepower to 225. This option was available in full-size cars and the Corvette, although the RPO numbers were different on the Vette.

The first increase in displacement came in 1957, when the bore was opened up to 3.875 inches (98mm), resulting in 283 cubic inches. The oiling system was further improved, but hot rodders cared only that horsepower was up. "Ram's horn" exhaust manifolds greatly improved exhaust scavenging. This was also the year in which fuel injection became an option on the small-block.

Engineered by two automotive legends, Zora Arkus-Duntov and John Dolza, the system carefully metered fuel and greatly increased horsepower. The 283 with this system, 10.5:1 compression, and a high-performance solid-lifter camshaft was rated at 283 horsepower, allowing it to meet the magical "1 horsepower per cubic inch" plateau. The cam, designed by Duntov, became known as the Duntov cam and was used in the highest-output Chevy small-blocks for years.

(Duntov told this author that the actual output of the injected 283 was really 290 horsepower, at which the engine would be rated the following year, but for marketing purposes in 1957 the 283 rating was deemed better.)

Fuel injection cut the 0-to-60-mph (96.5kph) time down to 5.7 seconds in the '57 Vette. Other carbureted engines were rated at 245 and 270 horsepower in the Corvette. There was even a fuel-injected engine later with a hydraulic cam. Fuel injection was an expensive option—about $500 on the full-size Chevy, which was a pretty hefty price for a $2,500 car.

Unfortunately, the fuel injection system could be temperamental and was very sensitive to dirty fuel. Few mechanics or dealer technicians could repair or service it properly, and many customers replaced the injection units with carburetors and normal intake manifolds. Fuel injection lasted until 1965 in the Corvette but only until 1959 in the regular Chevrolets. The fuelie (fuel-injected) engine was rated at 315 horsepower in 1960 when it still displaced 283 cubic inches.

With automobile weights increasing and electrical equipment becoming commonplace, Chevrolet decided to increase the displacement of the small-block again in 1962. Bore and stroke increased to 4 inches (102mm) and 3.25 inches (83mm), respectively, giving Chevy the 327-cid engine.

CHEVROLET CAMARO ENGINE SPECIFICATIONS

1967

Cu. In.	302	327	350
Bore (in.)	4.00	4.00	4.00
Stroke (in.)	3.00	3.25	3.48
Compression	11.00:1	10.00:1	10.25:1
Induction	1x4 bbl.	1x4 bbl.	1x4 bbl.
Horsepower/rpm	290/5800	275/4800	295/4800
Torque (lbs.-ft.)/rpm	290/4200	355/3200	380/3200

1967 (cont.)

Cu. In.	396	
Bore (in.)	4.094	
Stroke (in.)	3.76	
Compression	10.25:1	11.00:1
Induction	1x4 bbl.	1x4 bbl.
Horsepower/rpm	325/4800	375/5600
Torque (lbs.-ft.)/rpm	410/3200	415/3600

1968

Cu. In.	302	327	350
Bore (in.)	4.00	4.00	4.00
Stroke (in.)	3.00	3.25	3.48
Compression	11.00:1	10.00:1	10.25:1
Induction	1x4 bbl.	1x4 bbl.	1x4 bbl.
Horsepower/rpm	290/5800	275/4800	295/4800
Torque (lbs.-ft.)/rpm	290/4200	355/3200	380/3200

1968 (cont.)

Cu. In.	396		
Bore (in.)	4.094		
Stroke (in.)	3.76		
Compression	10.25:1	11.00:1	11.00:1
Induction	1x4 bbl.	1x4 bbl.	1x4 bbl.
Horsepower/rpm	325/4800	350/5200	375/5600
Torque (lbs.-ft.)/rpm	410/3200	415/3400	415/3600

1969

Cu. In.	302	350
Bore (in.)	4.00	4.00
Stroke (in.)	3.00	3.48
Compression	11.00:1	10.25:1
Induction	1x4 bbl.	1x4 bbl.
Horsepower/rpm	290/5800	300/4800
Torque (lbs.-ft.)/rpm	290/4200	380/3200

1969 (cont.)

Cu. In.	396		
Bore (in.)	4.094		
Stroke (in.)	3.76		
Compression	10.25:1	11.00:1	11.00:1
Induction	1x4 bbl.	1x4 bbl.	1x4 bbl.
Horsepower/rpm	325/4800	350/5200	375/5600
Torque (lbs.-ft.)/rpm	410/3200	415/3400	415/3600

1970

Cu. In.	350	402	
Bore (in.)	4.00	4.126	
Stroke (in.)	3.48	3.76	
Compression	11.00:1	11.00:1	11.00:1
Induction	1x4 bbl.	1x4 bbl.	1x4 bbl.
Horsepower/rpm	360/6000	350/5200	375/5600
Torque (lbs.-ft.)/rpm	380/4000	415/3400	415/3600

1971

Cu. In.	350	402
Bore (in.)	4.00	4.126
Stroke (in.)	3.48	3.76
Compression	9.00:1	9.00:1
Induction	1x4 bbl.	1x4 bbl.
Horsepower/rpm	330/5600	300/4800
Torque (lbs.-ft.)/rpm	360/4000	360/4000

1972

Cu. In.	350	402
Bore (in.)	4.00	4.126
Stroke (in.)	3.48	3.76
Compression	9.00:1	8.50:1
Induction	1x4 bbl.	1x4 bbl.
Horsepower/rpm	255/5600	240/4400
Torque (lbs.-ft.)/rpm	280/4000	345/3200

It was at this size that the engine became a staple of the muscle car movement, winning races in everything from Corvettes and Chevelles to Chevy IIs and Camaros—though it did a hell of a job in the Impala SS, too. In fact, it would take a separate book to cover every high-output version of the small-block Chevy of the period covered in this encyclopedia; hence we'll touch on only the highlights.

By '65, you could get the 327 with 11.0:1 compression, a hot hydraulic-lifter cam, and a single 4-barrel carb with 350 horsepower in the Chevelle and Corvette. The following year, this engine found its way into the Chevy II Nova, and that car dominated Super Stock drag racing.

That same year, Corvette lovers could get a 327 with a solid-lifter cam, a single 4-barrel carb, and 365 horsepower (375 horses with injection). At this point, however, the introduction of the powerhouse 396 big-block was making the high-winding small-blocks somewhat superfluous. The fuelie was the first casualty, disappearing soon after the 396 appeared in 1965.

The next great small-block was the 1967 302 Z/28 engine, which was used for the Camaro's foray into Trans-Am competition and limited displacement to 305 cubic inches. By using a 327 block with a 283 crankshaft, displacement was 302 cubes, and the engine was offered in a car that became known by only its RPO: Z/28. Combined with 11.0:1 compression, a hot solid-lifter cam, a single 780-cfm Holley, and dual exhaust, it made a robust 290 horsepower at 5800 rpm and 290 lbs.-ft. of torque at 4200. In the hands of Mark Donohue, the Z/28 won the Trans-Am series championship in 1968 and 1969.

Opposite: Production of the 1969 Camaro continued into the 1970 model year thanks to a United Auto Workers strike. The car was available in a variety of different configurations, including the RS/SS (shown) with fake hood vents, hideaway headlamps, and fender stripes.

Left & Below: This is the only 1968 Z/28 Camaro convertible ever produced. It was built for Chevrolet general manager Pete Estes, who was an open-car aficionado. It is equipped with the optional dealer-installed cross-ram dual 4-barrel intake manifold, a functional cowl-induction hood, and tubular exhaust headers.

(A couple of side notes: Chevy had actually built a 302 with fuel injection, the Duntov cam, and fuelie heads back in the 1950s. It never made production but was reportedly way ahead of the 283 powerwise. Also, Chevy reversed the formula of the 302 in 1968 when it combined the 283 block and 327 crank to create the 307, one of its more pedestrian powerplants, fated to live as a hassle-free mover of the masses.)

Also in 1967, Chevrolet redesigned the small-block in an attempt to increase its displacement to 350 cubic inches. This was done to improve torque in its ever-more-portly passenger cars. Stroke was increased to 3.48 inches (88mm), which required a little work in the block. Among other things, the crankshaft-journal diameters were increased, as were the main-journal diameter and rod-journal diameter. The webs in the cylinder block were cast larger and machined to provide clearance for the rotating members. High-performance versions got 4-bolt mains.

The engine was first used in the SS350 Camaro in 1967, which produced 295 horsepower. It was a decent engine, but there was a lot more power coming down the pike. A number of high-performance versions of the 350 arrived starting in 1969. A 350-horsepower 350 was introduced in the Corvette that year. Dubbed the L46, it supplanted the old L79 327/350. It used 11.0:1 compression, a forged

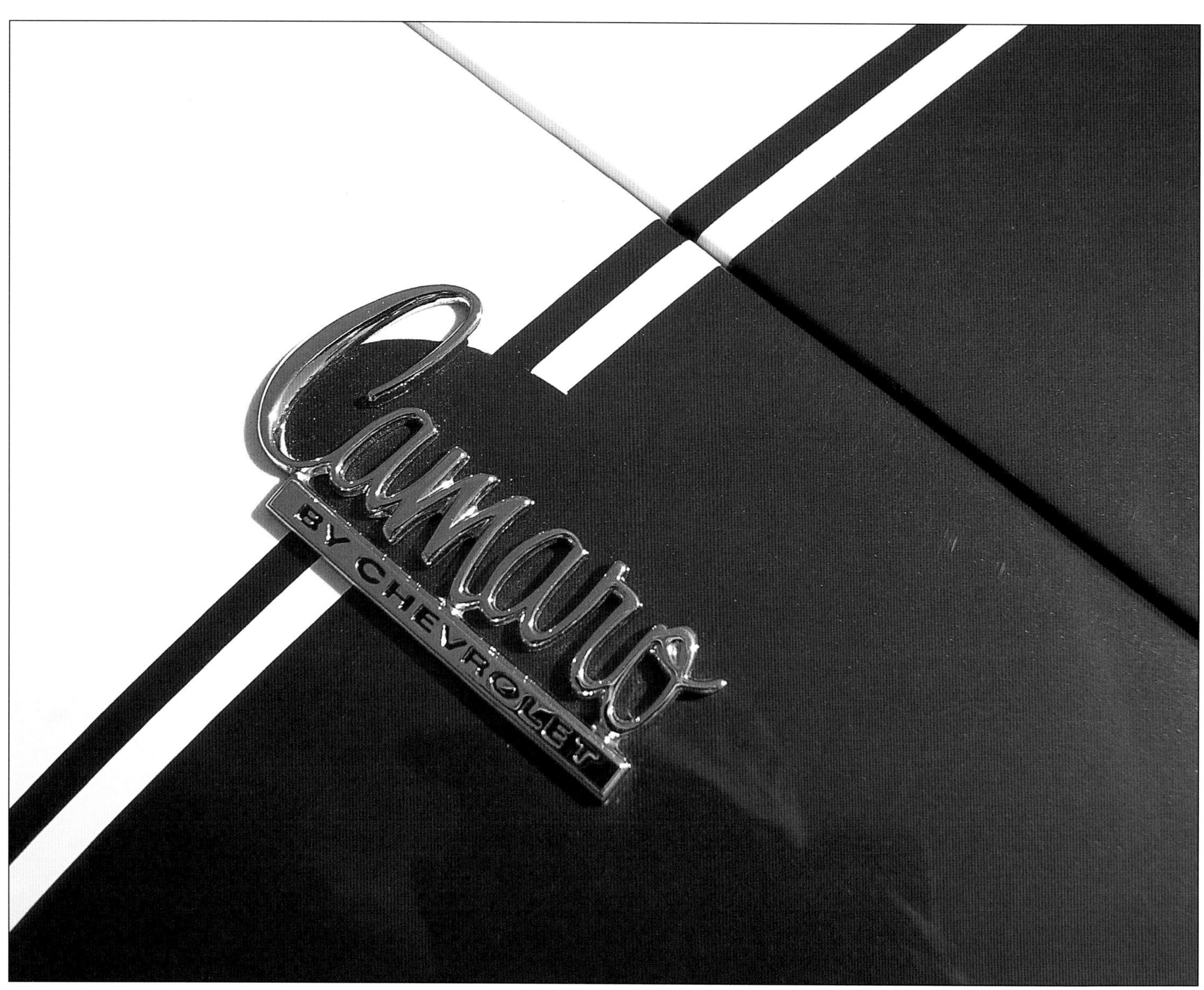

The Z/28 option, first introduced in January 1967, was the sole recipient of the 290-horsepower, 302-cubic-inch engine. A close-ratio 4-speed manual transmission and 3.73:1 gears were standard, as were special paint stripes on the hood and decklid.

crankshaft, 4-bolt mains, a mild hydraulic-lifter cam, big-valve fuelie cylinder heads, and a Rochester carb on an iron intake manifold. The 350 was a great engine, providing gobs of horsepower and more torque than the 327 was capable of delivering.

The following year, perhaps Chevrolet's best small-block ever arrived: the LT-1. The engine was designed for use in the Corvette and Z/28 Camaro, and all stops were pulled. It had many of the internal goodies of the L46, including the 2.02/1.60 heads, but added forged steel rods and a high-lift (0.458-inch [12mm]) solid-lifter cam with 317/346-degree duration, plus the heads featured screw-in rocker arm studs and hardened steel pushrod guides.

Up top, a cast-aluminum intake aided breathing and took a ton of weight off the nose of the car. It was fed by a 780-cfm Holley 4-barrel. Corvettes got an open-element air cleaner and "Ram's horn" exhaust manifolds, while the Z/28 got a dual-snorkel air cleaner and log-type manifolds, which accounted for the fact that the Vette version was rated at 370 horsepower, 10 higher than the Camaro.

The LT-1 lived for three years, although compression dropped two points in 1971. It was replaced by the L82, a low-compression, hydraulic-lifter 350 that actually performed well for a smog-motor. The 350 continued to be updated throughout the '70s and '80s, getting throttle-body fuel injection in '82 and direct-port injection in '85. When installed in the '85 Corvette, top speed reached 152 mph (245kph), the first time it passed the century-and-a-half mark in more than a dozen years. The engine underwent its first major redesign in 1992, when it was reborn as the LT1 (no longer hyphenated). The small-block Chevy was finally put out to pasture in 1997, when GM introduced the LS1, though even that engine incorporated some of the design features first seen by the public in the fall of 1954.

All in all, the Chevy small-block had a pretty good run.

Chevrolet (Big-Blocks)

Recognizing the ever-increasing size of its cars in the 1950s, Chevrolet went to work on a powerplant that was physically larger than the small-block, one it hoped would have more torque and be more capable of producing huge power numbers. No one knew how much displacement would be needed to propel the cars of the '60s, so work began on a completely new overhead valve V8, even though the small-block was still in its infancy. (This was true of most manufacturers, not just Chevrolet or GM.)

Introduced in 1958, the first big-block for Chevrolet was the 348 W engine, so called because of the shape of its cylinder heads. Much of the credit for its design goes to Zora Arkus-Duntov and Richard "Dick" Keinath. The 348 W engine was used in both trucks and passenger cars and proved itself to be very dependable. The 348 grew into the 409 in 1961 and enjoyed a fair amount of success on the racetrack, but it was an unconventional design that eventually limited its potential.

The 348's combustion chamber was its biggest drawback. It was a machined chamber partially in the block, so the top of the block was not square with the top of the piston or the centerline of the bore. This improved with the larger bore that was used to create the 409, but the problem never really went away.

When the 348 was introduced to the public in 1958, its most potent version made 280 horsepower, and that was with three 2-barrel carbs. The first great 348 appeared in 1960, the dawn of the muscle car era. It used 11.25:1 compression, big-port cylinder heads, Tri-Power, and a solid-lifter cam, the specs of which were similar to that of Chevy's small-block Duntov cam—no surprise given who helped design the 348.

The following year saw horsepower climb to 340 and then 350 in the 348. But its days were numbered, as 1961 was the first year of the "real fine" 409. It was essentially a punched-out 348 (4.31-inch [109mm] bore versus 4.13 inches [105mm]), but the stroke was actually lengthened from 3.35 to 3.50 inches (85 to 89mm). Mostly, the cylinder heads, cam, crank, rods, and so on were carried over from the high-output 348; the big difference was the new dual-plane aluminum intake manifold, which held a new 650-cfm Carter AFB carburetor, the largest 4-barrel carb available in 1961.

Above: The longer stroke of the 350 made the 1970 Z/28 much torquier than the defunct 302, but the engine still loved to rev.

Below: Unlike the previous model, the 396 big-block engine was readily available in the '66 midsize Chevelle, and the top-rated version had 375 horsepower.

The 375-horse 396 big-block made the compact Nova SS nose-heavy, but it was a fast automobile. Two 396s were available in the Nova from 1968–1970, a hydraulic-lifter model with 350 horsepower and the solid-lifter engine seen here. In 1970 the engine actually grew to 402 cubic inches, but it was still marketed as the Turbo-Jet 396.

While only 142 409s were delivered that first year (in part because of production problems), by 1962 sales of the 409 exploded to 15,019. A new aluminum dual-plane intake was optional and it held not one but two 650 AFBs. The cylinder heads had ports that were 0.25-inch (6.5mm) higher, and the intake valve diameter increased from 2.07 to 2.20 inches (53 to 56mm). This combo was good for 409 horsepower at 6000 rpm—remarkable revving ability for a large-displacement engine of the era. There was also a special single 4-barrel version with 380 horsepower. Both versions were rated at 420 lbs.-ft. of torque, though at different rpm ratings.

When NASCAR and the NHRA both decided to limit displacement to 7 liters (427.5 cubic inches) in 1963, Chevy (as well as Ford, Pontiac, and Chrysler) pushed its top powerplants to that. For racing purposes only, the 409 grew to 427 cid in what was known as the Z-11 package. Under the package's aluminum front sheet metal, the 409's bore was increased to 4.41 inches (112mm). The cars were legal only for NHRA's A/FX (Factory Experimental) class or match races and were underrated at 430 horsepower and 430 lbs.-ft. of torque.

The hottest 409 on the street was now rated at 425 horses with dual quads and 400 ponies with a single 4-barrel carb, thanks to better cylinder heads and a more aggressive camshaft profile.

Even before the Z-11 hit the track, the replacement for the W engine series was on Keinath's drawing board. The concept was to build a new race engine, even though technically GM was still adhering to the 1957 Automobile Manufacturers Association (AMA) ban on motorsports participation. Development on the Mk II and Mk IIS engine family (more commonly known by the public as the Mystery Motor) began as early as the summer of 1962, and remarkable engines were built, tested, and competing at the Daytona 500 in the winter of 1963.

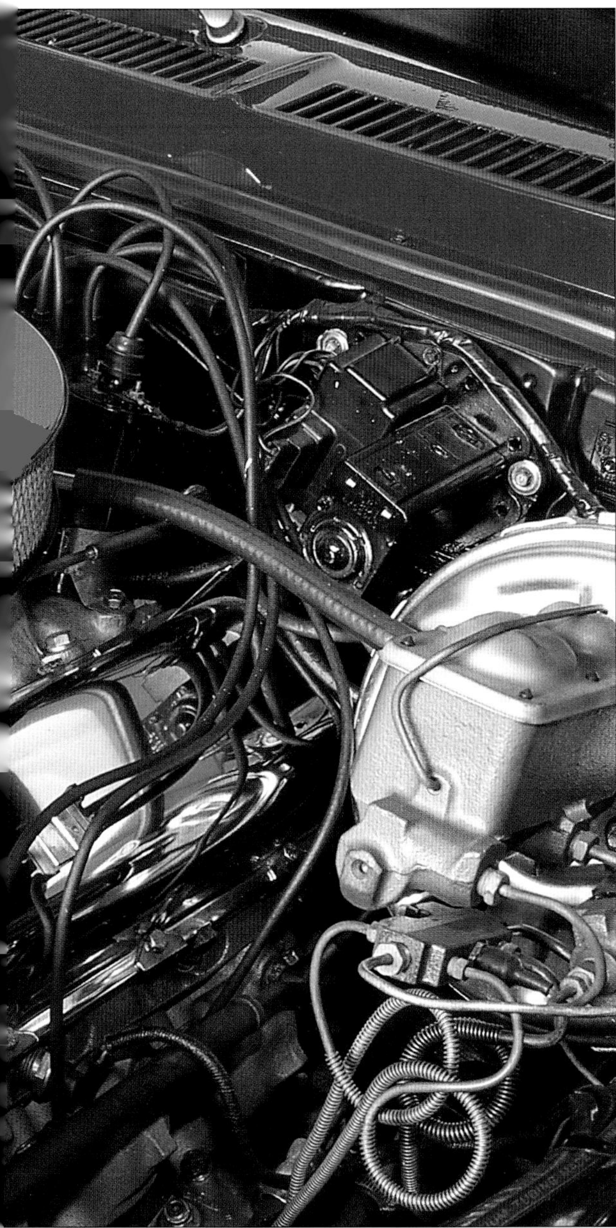

Starting with the 409's bore centers, Keinath designed a more conventional engine, with the combustion chambers completely in the cylinder head and the pistons square in the bore (they were angled on the W engines). For the cylinder heads, he went all-out. The valves were angled and the chamber itself was a semi-Hemi design, meaning that the valves were not laid out side by side but nor were they opposed as in a Hemi.

The engine was completely new, though the Mk II (Mk stood for Mark, which is a European-style designation) shared the 409's displacement. The S in Mk IIS stood for "stroked." Final displacement was 427 cubic inches, and when the Mk IIS debuted at Daytona, it stole the show. Junior Johnson's '63 Chevrolet was 10 mph (16kph) faster than the nearest Ford. Unfortunately for Chevy fans, that six-month gestation period reared its head when the engine dropped a valve through the piston.

It was around this time that GM recommitted itself to the "no racing" edict, which couldn't have come at a worse time. Not only did it cause a number of projects to be stillborn, but Ford was committing itself to its "Total Performance" theme, which meant it was out to dominate every form of motorsports worldwide. Like Chrysler, Ford could care less about the AMA ban.

As a race engine, the Mk IIS was a dead player. For Keinath, this meant developing it fully for use as a passenger car engine. Next up was the Mk III, which used a different bore center, but that didn't work out. The Mk IV went back to the Mk II's bore centers and incorporated a number of compromises for both cost-effectiveness and ease of production. The stroke on the production engine ended up longer than the engineers wanted and the bore was smaller, plus the ports were altered and the roof of the combustion chamber was higher than what would have been preferred for a race engine.

The bottom line, however, was that when the Mk IV 396 was introduced in 1965 in the Corvette, it made as much horsepower as the dual quad 409 (425) with only one carburetor and 13 cubic inches less displacement. In the Chevelle, a hydraulic-lifter version was rated at 375 horsepower.

In '66, Chevy bored out the 396 to create the 427 in the Corvette and its full-size cars (the Chevelle retained the 396 through 1970). Initially, it was rated at 450 horsepower, but this attracted too much heat from the insurance industry and it was quickly downrated back to 425 horses. Chevy produced the first Corvettes capable of sub-13-second quarter-mile times. *Car and Driver* reported a 12.8-second ET at 112 mph (180kph) in a '66 Sting Ray roadster, not to mention a top speed of 155 mph (249kph).

Numerous versions of the 427 and 396 were popping up, from 325 horsepower to 425. The top Chevelle (and later Camaro) engine until 1970 was the L78 396, which produced 375 horsepower. Beginning in 1967, you could even option the 427 with aluminum cylinder heads in the Corvette, not to mention the 396 in the Camaro and Chevelle.

The first full-race 427 was introduced in '67 as well. Dubbed the L88, it used the iron block from the 435-horsepower street Corvette fitted with 12.5:1 compression pistons, Magnafluxed rods, aluminum closed-chamber cylinder heads, a special solid-lifter cam, a high-rise aluminum intake manifold, and an 830-cfm Holley double-pumper 4-barrel carburetor. A high-volume oil pump ensured a supply of the slippery stuff, which was needed since the engine was designed for continuous use at 6800 rpm. The 427 required 103-octane fuel.

Above: Three versions of the 396 were available in the 1968 Camaro, rated from bottom to top at 325, 350, and 375 horsepower. Aluminum cylinder heads were available for the most powerful variant, but they were very expensive at $868.95 and only 272 cars were so equipped.

For racing purposes, the engine was rated at 430 horsepower at 5200 rpm—5 horsepower less than the street 427 with Tri-Power. Those ratings fooled no one in the race-sanctioning bodies. It's not that the engine didn't make 430 horses at 5200 rpm. GM just didn't rate it at its peak. Output was actually around 560 horsepower at 6600 rpm. Only a handful of Corvettes were ever equipped with this engine from 1967 to 1969, and no other Chevy got it, but it proved popular with racers as an over-the-counter piece.

As good as the L88 was, Chevy trumped it in 1969 with the introduction of the all-aluminum ZL-1 427 race engine, which was installed in Camaros and Corvettes. Designed for all-out competition, this engine had aluminum cylinder blocks and heads, and weighed 160 pounds (72.5kg) less than the all-iron big-blocks. The engine was based on the competition-only L88, but the heads were unique to the ZL-1 package and had larger exhaust ports that were round at the gasket face instead of square. The heads were worth about 20 horsepower more than the units on the L88. The combustion chambers were also opened up under the spark plug to more closely resemble an open Hemi chamber. Weight was roughly equivalent to a small-block Chevy with an aluminum intake manifold.

Chevy also used a higher-lift cam (0.560/0.600-inch [14/15mm] lift, intake and exhaust), better valve springs, and a host of other valvetrain tricks to improve reliability. Engineers removed a section in the plenum chamber to improve flow. Chevrolet's testing revealed elapsed times of 11 secon\ds flat at 127 mph (204kph) with open headers, making this the quickest Chevy of all time.

Performance was a lot hotter than the Z/28 or the SS396/375. The late Roger Huntington, a noted automotive journalist of the era, tested a ZL-1 Camaro for *Cars* magazine in stock trim (except the muffler system). On stock tires with 4.10 gears, the ZL-1 ran a best of 13.16 seconds at 110.21 mph (177.5kph), the speed indicative of the car's true potential. Huntington noted that the car was actually fairly docile on the street, except for poor fuel economy (5–7 mpg [8–11.5km per 3.8L]). He also mentioned that prototypes set up just for racing were running in the low-10-second zone at 130 mph (209kph).

This was the last hurrah for the famed 427. In 1970, its stroke was lengthened to 4 inches (102mm), giving it 454 cubic inches. This was done to improve torque. Compression on most engines was down to 10.25:1, although the top-of-the-line LS6 had 11.25:1. The LS6 was installed in only the Chevelle and made 450 horsepower.

If there was one part that kept Chevy from making more LS6s, it was the low-rise aluminum intake manifold, which was designed to fit under the low hoodline of the Corvette. Still, one such car ran 13.44 at a speed faster than 108 mph (174kph) in a *Hot Rod* magazine test in pure-stock trim.

There was also an LS5 Chevelle in 1970, which used a hydraulic-lifter cam and 10.25:1 compression. It produced 360 horsepower. The top-of-the-line Corvette that year was the LS5, but in this application it was rated at 390 horsepower. Camaros were limited to the 396, which partway through the year was bored out to 402 cubic inches.

There was also supposed to be an LS7 available in the Corvette that year, which would have basically been a 454-cubic-inch version of the L88, but that never happened, either. The days of fire-breathing Rat motors (as Chevy big-blocks were affectionately termed) were coming to a close. In '71, the LS6 (now rated at 425 horsepower) was available in the Corvette but not the Chevelle. It had 9.0:1 compression and aluminum heads and could be ordered with an automatic transmission.

The Mark IV 454 lived on until the 1990s, where it was used as a truck engine. As a production car engine, it was never again a high-performance engine. But hot rodders love it to this day. Few engines have as much potential for making horsepower, and this goes back to its roots as a race car engine. Some compromises may have been made to bring it to a mass audience, but its place in the pantheon of performance will never be in doubt.

Dodge/Plymouth (Small-Blocks)

Chrysler Corporation introduced its first modern small-block in 1964, the 273-cubic-inch V8. Dimensionally, its block was the same as the old 318 polyspherical-head engine that was first introduced in the 1950s. But the 273 utilized a thin-wall casting design that helped the block weigh about 30 pounds (14kg) less than that of the older engine.

The 273 also used a lighter intake manifold and different cylinder heads, which made it even lighter than the 318 poly. This lack of weight (and its compact size) was necessary since one of its main applications was in the compact A-body lineup—the Dodge Dart, Plymouth Valiant, and Barracuda. This new engine was known as the LA engine series, not the A engine series, which is what the old poly engine was designated.

In that first year, the 273 was in no way, shape, or form a performance engine. It was a reliable little piece, with low compression and a hydraulic-lifter cam for smooth, silent operation. It was not until 1965 that the 273 grew a little hair on its chest.

That was the year in which Chrysler blessed it with 10.5:1 compression (up from 8.8:1), a more performance-oriented mechanical-lifter camshaft, a 4-barrel carburetor, and a high-flow single exhaust (there was no room for duals). This engine was exclusive to the Dart and Barracuda and put out 55 more horsepower and 20 extra lbs.-ft. of torque than the base 273, bringing the totals to 235 and 280, respectively. At the drag strip, it was worth about 8 mph (13kph) in trap speed and was quicker by about six-tenths of a second.

This higher-output 273 carried over basically unchanged through the end of 1967, when it was put to rest. In 1968, Chrysler Corp. bored the engine from 3.63 to 4.04 inches (92 to 103mm) while leaving the 3.31-inch (84mm) stroke alone. The combination of a large bore and short stroke gave the 273 the potential to be a strong high-performance engine, and topped with a set of fantastic new big-port cylinder heads, it was all that and more.

The 340 came only one way, and that was as a high-performance engine. High 10.5:1 compression, a 4-barrel carb, and dual exhausts were standard, as was a stout hydraulic camshaft. The 4-speed-equipped 340s came with a cam that had 0.445-inch (11.3mm) lift on the intake side and 0.455-inch (11.6mm) lift on the exhaust, with 60 degrees of overlap, plus 284- to 292-degree duration. The idle was too wild for use with an automatic transmission, so the engines teamed with that gearbox used a less radical cam.

The heads used 2.02-inch (51mm) intake valves and 1.60 inches (41mm) on the exhaust—same as the Corvette's legendary fuelie heads. This was serious hardware, and the valve sizing was

Below: The 340 was underrated at 275 horsepower and made for one of the sweetest running packages of the muscle car era.

not the least bit coincidental. When the engine was under development, the heads being tested didn't flow well, and time and money were running out. Bob Cahill, Chrysler's performance head, was quoted in the magazine *'Cudas and Challengers* as saying, "Early on, the power output wasn't there, the heads did not flow enough. Timing was late, so we told engineering to copy the small-block Chevy heads. In the end, the 340 engine performed better than we expected and was as good as the 350 Chevy, except for possibly the four head bolts for each cylinder [versus] Chevy's five."

The 340 was rated at 275 horsepower, could rev up to 6000 rpm, and, when installed in a light car like the Dart GTS or Swinger, could hit mid-14s at the strip at 97 mph (156kph). According to that same article, Cahill said the sales, not engineering, department came up with that horsepower number in an attempt to get it classified better for drag racing.

The next evolution of the 340 came in 1970, when a new package was derived to celebrate the coming of a pair of Trans-Am-inspired ponycars, the AAR 'Cuda and T/A Challenger. While the real race cars were limited to 305 cubic inches and a single 4-barrel carburetor, the AAR and T/A got 340s equipped with three 2-barrel carburetors (fed cold air by functional scooped fiberglass hoods). They also used dual exhausts that exited at the side of the car just before the rear tires.

On paper, this iteration of the 340 had the potential to be the greatest small-block yet and was factory rated at 15 horsepower more than the single 4-barrel 340, but emissions regulations and drive-by noise standards kept its output nearly the same in reality. The only way to get the carburetors to pass emissions standards was to lean them out, and they didn't run great in this tune. Combined they flowed about 990 cfm, which was also too much for only 340 cubic inches.

CHRYSLER/HURST HEMI DARTS & BARRACUDAS ENGINE SPECIFICATIONS

1968

Cu. In.	426
Bore (in.)	4.25
Stroke (in.)	3.75
Compression	12.50:1
Induction	2x4 bbl.
Horsepower/rpm	not rated
Torque (lbs.-ft.)/rpm	not rated

Left: The Dodge Dart Swinger (shown) was akin to a compact version of the Super Bee—rubber floor mats, sparsely equipped, and with few available options that didn't add horsepower.

The final blow was the side-exiting exhaust, which was too loud to meet drive-by noise standards because the exhaust dumped right in front of the microphone. Baffles were added to the mufflers to quiet them, but they were so restrictive that power was lost to the point where 6-barrel 340 engines really only made as much power as the 4-barrel 340 engine.

Both the T/A and AAR models were dropped after just one year, so the 275-horse 340 was the only high-output small-block for 1971. Compression fell two full points in '72, helping to bring the now-net power rating down to 240. In '74, the 340's stroke increased from 3.31 to 3.48 inches (84 to 88mm), bringing cubic inches up to 360, horsepower to 245, and torque from 295 lbs.-ft. to 320. Chrysler still uses a version of the 360 engine in its trucks to this day.

Dodge/Plymouth (Big-Blocks)

Chrysler Corporation tended to keep things simple back in the '60s and early '70s. It used two versions of the same basic family, and their parts interchangeability was an endearing quality. So was stump-pulling torque and race-winning horsepower. The big-block engines used by Dodge and Plymouth came in two basic forms, those using the lower-deck-height B engine (361, 383, and 400) and those using the RB, or raised-block, engine (413, 426, and 440).

These engines had their roots in the 1950s, but they powered a large percentage of Chrysler's muscle cars well into the 1970s. The first muscle cars from Dodge and Plymouth were the 383/340-horse long-ram V8s in 1960. Compression was a healthy 10.0:1, but the most astounding feature of this powerplant was its twin 4-barrel carburetors mounted opposite each other on the long-ram intake. Each carb sat on a plenum chamber and fed the cylinders on the opposite side of the engine. The ram intake runners were a remarkable 30 inches (76cm) long, the idea being to bounce suction waves on each intake stroke for more power.

The 383 engine made 340 horsepower at 5000 rpm and 460 lbs.-ft. of torque at just 2800. It was an early exercise in engine tuning via intake runner length, albeit an extreme one. It was expensive, too, costing more than $400 in 1960.

In '61, Dodge and Plymouth saw fit to install a similarly inducted 413 RB engine into the Dart and Fury, respectively. Previously, the 413 had been the domain of the expensive Chrysler letter cars. Bore and stroke on the 413 were 4.18×3.75 inches (106×95mm) and compression was 10.0:1. Horsepower was a respectable 350 with the single 4-barrel and eye-opening with the optional 375-horse long-ram dual quad setup.

DODGE/PLYMOUTH ENGINE SPECIFICATIONS

1960

Cu. In.	383		
Bore (in.)	4.25		
Stroke (in.)	3.38		
Compression	10.00:1		
Induction	2x4 bbl.		
Horsepower/rpm	340/5000		
Torque (lbs.-ft.)/rpm	460/2800		

1961

Cu. In.	383		413
Bore (in.)	4.25		4.18
Stroke (in.)	3.38		3.75
Compression	10.00:1		10.00:1
Induction	1x4 bbl.	2x4 bbl.	2x4 bbl.
Horsepower/rpm	325/4600	340/5000	375/5000
Torque (lbs.-ft.)/rpm	425/2800	460-2800	465/2800

1962

Cu. In.	413	
Bore (in.)	4.19	
Stroke (in.)	3.75	
Compression	11.00:1	13.51:1
Induction	2x4 bbl.	2x4 bbl.
Horsepower/rpm	410/5400	420/5400
Torque (lbs.-ft.)/rpm	460/4400	460/4400

1963

Cu. In.	426	
Bore (in.)	4.25	
Stroke (in.)	3.75	
Compression	11.00:1	13.51:1
Induction	2x4 bbl.	2x4 bbl.
Horsepower/rpm	415/5600	425/5600
Torque (lbs.-ft.)/rpm	470/4400	480/4400

1964

Cu. In.	383	426-S
Bore (in.)	4.25	4.25
Stroke (in.)	3.38	3.75
Compression	10.00:1	10.30:1
Induction	1x4 bbl.	1x4 bbl.
Horsepower/rpm	330/4600	365/4800
Torque (lbs.-ft.)/rpm	425/2800	470/3200

1964 (cont.)

Cu. In.	426		
Bore (in.)	4.25		
Stroke (in.)	3.75		
Compression	11.00:1	12.50:1	12.50:1*
Induction	2x4 bbl.	2x4 bbl.	2x4 bbl.
Horsepower/rpm	415/5600	425/5600	425/6000
Torque (lbs.-ft.)/rpm	470/4400	480/4400	480/4600

*Race Hemi

1965

Cu. In.	273	383	426-S
Bore (in.)	3.63	4.25	4.25
Stroke (in.)	3.31	3.38	3.75
Compression	10.50:1	10.00:1	10.30:1
Induction	1x4 bbl.	1x4 bbl.	1x4 bbl.
Horsepower/rpm	235/5200	330/4600	365/4800
Torque (lbs.-ft.)/rpm	280/4000	425/2800	470/3200

1965 (cont.)

Cu. In.	426
Bore (in.)	4.25
Stroke (in.)	3.75
Compression	12.50:1*
Induction	2x4 bbl.
Horsepower/rpm	425/6000
Torque (lbs.-ft.)/rpm	480/4600

*Race Hemi

1966

Cu. In.	273	383	426*
Bore (in.)	3.63	4.25	4.25
Stroke (in.)	3.31	3.38	3.75
Compression	10.50:1	10.00:1	10.25:1
Induction	1x4 bbl.	1x4 bbl.	2x4 bbl.
Horsepower/rpm	235/5200	325/4800	425/5000
Torque (lbs.-ft.)/rpm	280/4000	425/2800	490/4000

*Street Hemi

1967

Cu. In.	273	383
Bore (in.)	3.63	4.25
Stroke (in.)	3.31	3.38
Compression	10.50:1	10.00:1
Induction	1x4 bbl.	1x4 bbl.
Horsepower/rpm	235/5200	325/4800
Torque (lbs.-ft.)/rpm	280/4000	425/2800

1967 (cont.)

Cu. In.	426*	440
Bore (in.)	4.25	4.32
Stroke (in.)	3.75	3.75
Compression	10.25:1	10.00:1
Induction	2x4 bbl.	1x4 bbl.
Horsepower/rpm	425/5000	375/4600
Torque (lbs.-ft.)/rpm	490/4000	480/3200

*Street Hemi

1968

Cu. In.	340	383	426
Bore (in.)	4.04	4.25	4.25
Stroke (in.)	3.31	3.38	3.75
Compression	10.50:1	10.00:1	10.25:1
Induction	1x4 bbl.	1x4 bbl.	2x4 bbl.
Horsepower/rpm	275/5000	335/5200	425/5000
Torque (lbs.-ft.)/rpm	340/3200	425/3400	490/4000

1968 (cont.)

Cu. In.	440
Bore (in.)	4.32
Stroke (in.)	3.75
Compression	10.10:1
Induction	1x4 bbl.
Horsepower/rpm	375/4600
Torque (lbs.-ft.)/rpm	480/3200

1969

Cu. In.	340	383
Bore (in.)	4.04	4.25
Stroke (in.)	3.31	3.38
Compression	10.50:1	10.00:1
Induction	1x4 bbl.	1x4 bbl.
Horsepower/rpm	275/5000	335/5200
Torque (lbs.-ft.)/rpm	340/3200	425/3400

1969 (cont.)

Cu. In.	440		426
Bore (in.)	4.32		4.25
Stroke (in.)	3.75		3.75
Compression	10.10:1	10.50:1	10.25:1
Induction	1x4 bbl.	3x2 bbl.	2x4 bbl.
Horsepower/rpm	375/4600	390/4700	425/5000
Torque (lbs.-ft.)/rpm	480/3200	490/3200	490/4000

1970

Cu. In.	340	383
Bore (in.)	4.04	4.25
Stroke (in.)	3.31	3.38
Compression	10.50:1	9.50:1
Induction	1x4 bbl.	1x4 bbl.
Horsepower/rpm	275/5000	335/5200
Torque (lbs.-ft.)/rpm	340/3200	425/3400

1970 (cont.)

Cu. In.	440		426
Bore (in.)	4.32		4.25
Stroke (in.)	3.75		3.75
Compression	9.70:1	10.50:1	10.25:1
Induction	1x4 bbl.	3x2 bbl.	2x4 bbl.
Horsepower/rpm	375/4600	390/4700	425/5000
Torque (lbs.-ft.)/rpm	480/3200	490/3200	490/4000

1971

Cu. In.	340	383
Bore (in.)	4.04	4.25
Stroke (in.)	3.31	3.38
Compression	10.50:1	8.50:1
Induction	1x4 bbl.	1x4 bbl.
Horsepower/rpm	275/5000	300/4800
Torque (lbs.-ft.)/rpm	340/3200	410/3400

1971 (cont.)

Cu. In.	440		426
Bore (in.)	4.32		4.25
Stroke (in.)	3.75		3.75
Compression	9.70:1	10.50:1	10.25:1
Induction	1x4 bbl.	3x2 bbl.	2x4 bbl.
Horsepower/rpm	370/4600	385/4700	425/5000
Torque (lbs.-ft.)/rpm	480/3200	490/3200	490/4000

1972

Cu. In.	340
Bore (in.)	4.04
Stroke (in.)	3.31
Compression	8.50:1
Induction	1x4 bbl.
Horsepower/rpm	240/4800
Torque (lbs.-ft.)/rpm	290/3600

1973

Cu. In.	340
Bore (in.)	4.04
Stroke (in.)	3.31
Compression	8.50:1
Induction	1x4 bbl.
Horsepower/rpm	240/4800
Torque (lbs.-ft.)/rpm	295/3600

1974

Cu. In.	360
Bore (in.)	4.00
Stroke (in.)	3.58
Compression	8.40:1
Induction	1x4 bbl.
Horsepower/rpm	245/4800
Torque (lbs.-ft.)/rpm	320/3600

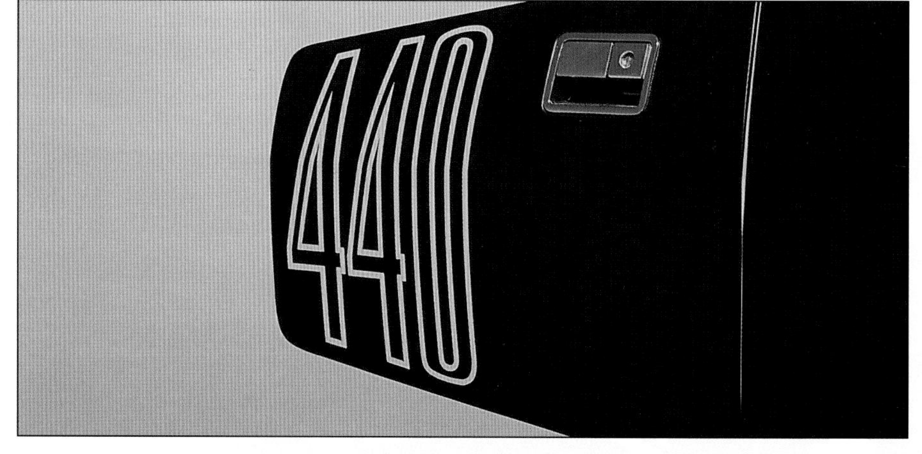

With the muscle car wars further escalating, Dodge and Plymouth pulled out the stops. This was the year they introduced the street and strip versions of the Max Wedge 413. Made of heavy cast iron, these unique headers flowed into 3-inch-(76mm) diameter pipes featuring dump tubes that could be opened for competition in minutes. Street versions of the 413 Super Stock had 11.0:1 compression ratios, required premium fuel, and were rated at 410 horsepower at 5400 rpm, while the "competition" model had 13.5:1 compression, ran only on race fuel, and produced 420 horsepower at 5400 rpm. An 8.75-inch (22cm) rear end with a 3.91:1 Sure-Grip differential was standard. A 300-degree mechanical-lifter camshaft with heavy-duty springs was used in both. These were radical rides, borne out by their 1200-rpm idle speeds.

Transmission choices were limited to a Warner T-85 3-speed manual or a specially prepared 3-speed

Opposite: Plymouth used Billboard stripes for 1971 only, and just on the 'Cuda, to announce engine displacement to the police or your competition.

Above: The race version of the 426 Hemi (shown) debuted in 1964, supplanting the 426 Max Wedge as the top high-performance engine from Chrysler. When the Street Hemi arrived in 1966, it shared many of the same parts as the Race Hemi.

Left: Rare was the 425-horsepower Hemi in a convertible. Chrysler's intermediate convertibles would go away forever after 1970. This one has a non-stock battery.

DODGE CHALLENGER/PLYMOUTH 'CUDA ENGINE SPECIFICATIONS

1965

Cu. In.	273
Bore (in.)	3.63
Stroke (in.)	3.31
Compression	10.50:1
Induction	1x4 bbl.
Horsepower/rpm	235/5200
Torque (lbs.-ft.)/rpm	280/4000

1966

Cu. In.	273
Bore (in.)	3.63
Stroke (in.)	3.31
Compression	10.50:1
Induction	1x4 bbl.
Horsepower/rpm	235/5200
Torque (lbs.-ft.)/rpm	280/4000

1967

Cu. In.	273	383
Bore (in.)	3.63	4.25
Stroke (in.)	3.31	3.38
Compression	10.50:1	10.00:1
Induction	1x4 bbl.	1x4 bbl.
Horsepower/rpm	235/5200	280/4200
Torque (lbs.-ft.)/rpm	280/4000	400/2400

1968

Cu. In.	340	383
Bore (in.)	4.04	4.25
Stroke (in.)	3.31	3.38
Compression	10.50:1	10.00:1
Induction	1x4 bbl.	1x4 bbl
Horsepower/rpm	275/5000	300/4400
Torque (lbs.-ft.)/rpm	340/3200	400/2400

1969

Cu. In.	340	383	440
Bore (in.)	4.04	4.25	4.32
Stroke (in.)	3.31	3.38	3.75
Compression	10.50:1	10.00:1	10.10:1
Induction	1x4 bbl.	1x4 bbl.	1x4 bbl.
Horsepower/rpm	275/5000	330/4400	375/4600
Torque (lbs.-ft.)/rpm	340/3200	425/3400	480/3200

1970

Cu. In.	340		383
Bore (in.)	4.04		4.25
Stroke (in.)	3.31		3.38
Compression	10.50:1		9.50:1
Induction	1x4 bbl.	3x2 bbl.	1x4 bbl.
Horsepower/rpm	275/5000	290/5000	335/5200
Torque (lbs.-ft.)/rpm	340/3200	340/3200	425/3400

1970 (cont.)

Cu. In.	440		426
Bore (in.)	4.32		4.25
Stroke (in.)	3.75		3.75
Compression	9.70:1	10.50:1	10.25:1
Induction	1x4 bbl.	3x2 bbl.	2x4 bbl.
Horsepower/rpm	375/4600	390/4700	425/5000
Torque (lbs.-ft.)/rpm	480/3200	490/3200	490/4000

1971

Cu. In.	340	383
Bore (in.)	4.04	4.25
Stroke (in.)	3.31	3.38
Compression	10.50:1	8.50:1
Induction	1x4 bbl.	1x4 bbl.
Horsepower/rpm	275/5000	300/4800
Torque (lbs.-ft.)/rpm	340/3200	410/3400

1971 (cont.)

Cu. In.	440		426
Bore (In.)	4.32		4.25
Stroke (in.)	3.75		3.75
Compression	9.70:1	10.50:1	10.25:1
Induction	1x4 bbl.	3x2 bbl.	2x4 bbl.
Horsepower/rpm	370/4600	385/4700	425/5000
Torque (lbs.-ft.)/rpm	480/3200	490/3200	490/4000

1972

Cu. In.	340
Bore (in.)	4.04
Stroke (in.)	3.31
Compression	8.50:1
Induction	1x4 bbl.
Horsepower/rpm	240/4800
Torque (lbs.-ft.)/rpm	290/3600

1973

Cu. In.	340
Bore (in.)	4.04
Stroke (in.)	3.31
Compression	8.50:1
Induction	1x4 bbl.
Horsepower/rpm	240/4800
Torque (lbs.-ft.)/rpm	295/3600

1974

Cu. In.	360
Bore (in.)	4.00
Stroke (in.)	3.58
Compression	8.40:1
Induction	1x4 bbl.
Horsepower/rpm	245/4800
Torque (lbs.-ft.)/rpm	320/3600

These pages: The last year for the 'Cuda (opposite) was the first for the 360 (left), the newest version of the powerful and reliable LA engine family. Using a revised bore and longer stroke, horsepower was up by 5, but torque by 25.

TorqueFlite Chrysler automatic. The automatic was not only quicker than the stick shift model (an industry first), but it employed Chrysler's now-infamous push-button gear selector, which was mounted on the dash.

These Plymouths were built in very limited numbers—no more than 150 total—but their impact was felt on both the nation's drag strips and stock car tracks. With the dump tubes open and special racing tires fitted, the 420-horsepower models were capable of elapsed times in the 13.3-second range at 109 mph (175.5kph).

For 1963, displacement of the Max Wedge engine increased to 426 cubic inches because of an increase in cylinder bore. Horsepower was up to 415 in the street version and 425 for the racing variation. This was basically a carryover engine with the exception of the bore, though it did have an improved oiling system and slightly larger ports for the heads.

To take full advantage of the 7-liter displacement limits instituted by both the NHRA and NASCAR, Chrysler Corp. engineers punched out the 413 to 426 cubic inches via a 4.25-inch (108mm) bore. The basic engines stayed the same for the Ramcharger 426 (Dodge) and Super Stock 426 (Plymouth), though improved oiling systems and slightly larger ports in the heads aided reliability and power. Horsepower was up to 415 and torque to 470 lbs.-ft. on the street job, with 425 horsepower and 480 lbs.-ft. of torque on the race version.

On July 23, 1963, Chrysler announced the introduction of the Stage II Max Wedge engine. Heads, cam, springs, carbs, and other essential parts were upgraded to bring the 426 to this specification, although the power ratings remained unchanged. Further relief machining in the combustion chambers around the valves improved airflow, while undervalve bowl areas in the inlet passage were enlarged and relieved to aid flow. A new cam with more lift and duration was used, and new Carter carbs had more venturi area.

Most street enthusiasts in 1964 opted for the 383 or the new 426-S (for Street Wedge). The new engine used the bore and stroke of the 426, but instead of the Max Wedge induction hardware, it used the 383's heads, cam, intake, and carburetor. It was rated at 365 horsepower.

As powerful (and dominant at the drag strip) as the Stage II was, Chrysler was not finished with the Max Wedge. In 1964, it introduced the Stage III version. This one had extensive cylinder head modifications, including an open combustion chamber designed to lower compression (12.5:1 on the race version). The exhaust valves decreased in diameter as well. Stiffer valve springs and a more radical camshaft drove the actual power way up, though it was rated the same.

Development and the history of the 426 Hemi is discussed in the next section, but it bears mentioning here that in '64, Chrysler built fifty-five of its new race engines for NASCAR and drag teams.

By the time the Challenger arrived on the scene in 1970, the muscle car market had peaked, and this hurt Challenger's sales. It was the right car at the wrong time, competing at the high end of the ponycar market against the Mercury Cougar.

The Hemi was so good that it made the Max Wedge 426 virtually obsolete. The Max Wedge was discontinued after 1964, although it continues to dominate certain drag racing classes to this day.

While the Race Hemi was the big story for '64 and '65 and the introduction of the Street Hemi garnered most of the attention in '66, the next big step for the average enthusiast was the introduction of the 440 Magnum (Dodge) and Super Commando (Plymouth) in '67. The big 440 retained the 3.75-inch (95mm) stroke of the 426 Hemi and Max Wedge, but the bore was enlarged to 4.32 inches (110mm). All those cubic inches helped the 440 develop 480 lbs.-ft. of torque, which made it a favorite on the street.

The 440s in the letter cars—Dodge R/T and Plymouth GTX—were fitted with large-port heads, hot hydraulic camshafts, beefed-up bottom ends, and split-port exhaust manifolds that garnered quite a reputation for their efficiency. They even came equipped with an exhaust system H-pipe for improved torque. Valves measured 2.08 inches (53mm) on the intake and 1.74 inches (44mm) on the exhaust. Lift was 0.450/0.465 inches (11.4/11.8mm) and duration was 268/284 degrees. Up top, a Carter AFB carburetor on an iron intake delivered the mixture.

In '68, Chrysler fit all the induction goodies from the 440 Magnum and Super Commando (and the exhaust manifolds) and installed them on the 383 for use in the budget supercars known as the Dodge Super Bee and Plymouth Road Runner (they now used the Carter AVS carburetor). On the 383, this made for a quick revver good for high 14s at 98 mph (158kph) in the quarter mile on the junk tires of the day. All told, it kicked out 335 horsepower at 5200 rpm and 425 lbs.-ft. at 3400.

When it was felt that there was too much of a discrepancy between the 383 and optional Hemi in the Road Runner/Super Bee, Chrysler developed a new induction package for the 440—three Holley 2-barrels on an aluminum Edelbrock intake manifold. Chrysler stuffed the whole thing into those cars under a fiberglass hood with the industry's largest air scoop. Compression was bumped up from 10.1:1 to 10.5:1. A special cam, valves, springs, and rockers rounded out the engine package. It came in at 390 horsepower and 490 lbs.-ft. of torque.

For 1970, Chrysler cast the 440 Six-Pack's intake out of iron and dropped the compression on the 335-horse 383 to 9.5:1. Unlike General Motors, though, Chrysler held the line on compression ratios until 1972, though the ratios on the hotter engines did start going down slightly in '71. The Six-Pack's squeeze was reduced to 10.3:1, while the Magnum slid to 9.5:1—not optimal, but not a huge drop, either.

That big drop in compression came in '72, when the 440s and the new 400 (a bored and destroked 383) clocked in at 8.2:1. You could still get either of these engines in a Charger or Road Runner as late as 1974, but by that time the best the 440 could do was 275 net horsepower.

Dodge/Plymouth Hemi

Chrysler engineers knew in 1963 that the limits were being pushed on the powerful Max Wedge engine. Chrysler's involvement with drag and stock car racing was at the point where it practically needed to guarantee victories. With the competition from Ford getting tougher all the time, Chrysler felt the time was right to bring back an engine with a hemispherical combustion chamber.

What exactly is a Hemi? In a conventional engine, the intake and exhaust valves are arranged side by side inside the combustion chamber. In a Hemi, they are opposite each other, usually on an angle. This allows the use of much larger valves and improves the combustion and exhaust processes.

Chrysler had plenty of experience with Hemi engines. Chrysler had used Hemi engines extensively in the 1950s, but they were expensive to manufacture, and wedge-engine technology was to the point that engineers could get similar power for less money. On the other hand, Chrysler knew in the '60s how much horsepower they needed to be competitive in racing and (to a lesser extent) on the street. Chrysler felt the Hemi would blow the other cars off the track while costing considerably less money.

And Chrysler was correct.

When the modern Hemi returned, it was built on a 426-cubic-inch RB block. Part of the reason for this was the 7-liter displacement limit imposed by NASCAR. The Hemi was also very cost-effective because it shared many of the parts with the 440 and other big-blocks.

What it did not share were those incredible Hemi heads. Intake valves measured a whopping 2.25 inches (57mm) and exhaust 1.94 inches (49mm). The ports were huge, which hampered street performance somewhat, but the Hemi was magnificent at the racetrack. The Race Hemi actually showed up first, in 1964, and was outlawed by NASCAR in '65 unless Chrysler could build a minimum of five hundred copies for the street. This was not going to happen, so the only competition the Hemi saw was at the drag strip, where it was cleaning house.

To get the engine homologated for NASCAR, Chrysler detuned the Race Hemi, and for 1966, the Street Hemi was born. The two engines were remarkably similar, considering how much horsepower the race engine made. Compression for the Street Hemi was a modest 10.25:1 instead of 12.5:1, and the engine used cast-aluminum domed pistons. The heads and intake were cast iron instead of aluminum and magnesium like the parts the racers used. The valve springs were softer and a less radical solid-lifter camshaft was used, but that was about it for the differences.

A pair of Carter AFB carburetors, rather than the single 4-barrel mandated by NASCAR, supplied the fuel. The cam specs were 0.460-inch (11.7mm) lift and 276-degree duration—fairly hot but not overly radical, especially compared to what had been in the Max Wedge. The engine was rated at 425 horsepower at 5000 rpm and 490 lbs.-ft. of torque at 4000. It was very underrated by the factory, both for insurance purposes and perhaps to get a more favorable weight break at the drag strip.

But it fooled no one. With the Hemi heads, 8-barrel induction, solid lifters, and dual-point distributor, it could easily pull higher than the 6000-rpm limit on the factory tachometer. *Popular Hot Rodding* made a number of runs with a '66 Hemi Satellite and it made numerous 13-second passes, wavering between 13.25 and 13.75, with the best speed being 109.89 mph (177kph).

The basic specifications on the Street Hemi were unchanged for most of its life. For ease of maintenance, it switched to a hydraulic cam in 1970. But despite the commonality of parts with the other big-blocks, it was still expensive to manufacture and painfully expensive to insure. The combination of dual points, solid lifters, and multiple carbs was more than most Hemi customers could handle, and the car required constant maintenance.

The other factor working against the Hemi was the onslaught of crushing emissions regulations. These were helping to eliminate many of the muscle cars as engineering dollars were spent to meet the government's many mandates. The last Street Hemi rolled off the assembly line in 1971 and the car became an instant collectible.

In an effort to tame the beast, the Hemi received a hydraulic-lifter cam in 1970. One magazine called the Plum Crazy Hemi Challenger "Ghengis Grape."

FORD ENGINE SPECIFICATIONS

1960			
Cu. In.	352		
Bore (in.)	4.00		
Stroke (in.)	3.50		
Compression	10.60:1		
Induction	1x4 bbl.		
Horsepower/rpm	360/6000		
Torque (lbs.-ft.)/rpm	380/3400		

1961			
Cu. In.	390		
Bore (in.)	4.05		
Stroke (in.)	3.78		
Compression	10.60:1		
Induction	1x4 bbl.	3x2 bbl.	
Horsepower/rpm	375/6000	401/6000	
Torque (lbs.-ft.)/rpm	427/3400	430/3500	

1962			
Cu. In.	390	406	
Bore (in.)	4.05	4.13	
Stroke (in.)	3.78	3.78	
Compression	10.50:1	11.40:1	
Induction	1x4 bbl.	1x4 bbl.	3x2 bbl.
Horsepower/rpm	340/5000	385/5800	405/5800
Torque (lbs.-ft.)/rpm	430/3200	444/3400	448/3500

1963			
Cu. In.	390	406	
Bore (in.)	4.05	4.13	
Stroke (in.)	3.78	3.78	
Compression	10.50:1	11.40:1	
Induction	1x4 bbl.	1x4 bbl.	3x2 bbl.
Horsepower/rpm	330/5000	385/5800	405/5800
Torque (lbs.-ft.)/rpm	427/3200	444/3400	448/3500

1963 (cont.)			
Cu. In.	427		
Bore (in.)	4.23		
Stroke (in.)	3.78		
Compression	11.00:1		
Induction	1x4 bbl.	2x4 bbl.	
Horsepower/rpm	410/5600	425/6000	
Torque (lbs.-ft.)/rpm	476/3400	480/3700	

1964			
Cu. In.	289		
Bore (in.)	4.00		
Stroke (in.)	2.87		
Compression	10.50:1		
Induction	1x4 bbl.		
Horsepower/rpm	271/6000		
Torque (lbs.-ft.)/rpm	312/3400		

1964 (cont.)			
Cu. In.	390	427	
Bore (in.)	4.05	4.23	
Stroke (in.)	3.78	3.78	
Compression	10.00:1	11.00:1	
Induction	1x4 bbl.	1x4 bbl.	2x4 bbl.
Horsepower/rpm	330/5000	410/5600	425/6000
Torque (lbs.-ft.)/rpm	427/3200	476/3400	480/3700

1965			
Cu. In.	289		
Bore (in.)	4.00		
Stroke (in.)	2.87		
Compression	10.50:1		
Induction	1x4 bbl.		
Horsepower/rpm	271/6000		
Torque (lbs.-ft.)/rpm	312/3400		

1965 (cont.)			
Cu. In.	390	427	
Bore (in.)	4.05	4.23	
Stroke (in.)	3.78	3.78	
Compression	10.00:1	11.00:1	
Induction	1x4 bbl.	1x4 bbl.	2x4 bbl.
Horsepower/rpm	330/5000	410/5600	425/6000
Torque (lbs.-ft.)/rpm	427/3200	476/3400	480/3700

1966			
Cu. In.	289	390	
Bore (in.)	4.00	4.05	
Stroke (in.)	2.87	3.78	
Compression	10.50:1	11.00:1	
Induction	1x4 bbl.	1x4 bbl.	
Horsepower/rpm	271/6000	335/4800	
Torque (lbs.-ft.)/rpm	312/3400	427/3200	

1966 (cont.)			
Cu. In.	427		428
Bore (in.)	4.23		4.13
Stroke (in.)	3.78		3.98
Compression	11.00:1		10.50:1
Induction	1x4 bbl.	2x4 bbl.	1x4 bbl.
Horsepower/rpm	410/5600	425/6000	360/5400
Torque (lbs.-ft.)/rpm	476/3400	480/3700	459/3200

1967			
Cu. In.	289	390	
Bore (in.)	4.00	4.05	
Stroke (in.)	2.87	3.78	
Compression	10.50:1	10.50:1	
Induction	1x4 bbl.	1x4 bbl.	
Horsepower/rpm	271/6000	320/4800	
Torque (lbs.-ft.)/rpm	312/3400	427/3200	

While NASCAR long ago made the Hemi illegal, it continues to dominate just about every class of drag racing, from Top Fuel and Funny Car on down to Super Stock.

Ford/Mercury (Small-Blocks)

In the late 1950s, Ford had two V8 engine families: the FE (Ford Engine) big-block (which included the 352 and 390) and the Y-block (which replaced the flathead V8 in 1954). While the FE had a good design, the engine was too large and heavy to be installed in Ford's upcoming Fairlane, an intermediate-size car.

A lot was riding on the Fairlane, and V8s had been a part of the Ford tradition since the first flathead in 1932. It was deemed that the Fairlane would have an optional V8. The difficulty was that the Y-block was proving itself to be problematic, with oiling and other mechanical issues, and it just wasn't a great design. Ford needed something else in a hurry.

Work began on a more compact, lighter V8, and in 1962, the 221-cubic-inch small-block Ford V8 was born. Unlike the small-block Chevy, which featured siamese exhaust valves for the middle two cylinders, the Ford small-block used the more traditional layout of intake/exhaust/intake/exhaust. Variations of the small-block-powered Ford vehicles were produced in North America until 1999, when they were replaced by the 4.6 "modular" V8 family. (The V8 small-block survived in Australia until 2001.)

With a bore of 3.50 inches (89mm) and a short, 2.87-inch (73mm) stroke, the 221 was not exactly a powerhouse. It made only 145 horsepower, and engineers were soon looking for more oats to feed the horses. Enlarging the bore later that year to 3.80 inches (97mm) added 19 horsepower, but it wasn't until the 289 was released in 1970 (4-inch [102mm] bore, 2.87-inch [73mm] stroke) that the small-block started making serious power. With a 2-barrel carb it was nothing great, but in 1963 Ford fit it with high-compression pistons, small-chamber cylinder heads, and a high-lift cam, creating the High Performance 289. This engine, equipped with a 480-cfm Autolite carburetor on a revised intake manifold, made 271 horsepower at 6000 rpm.

It was first used in the full-size Fords and the Fairlane, and in June of '64 it became available in the Mustang, where it was a great match to that car's light weight. The 289 even found its way into a few '65 Falcons in Canada (seven is believed to be the correct number). It was a staple of Ford high performance through the end of 1967, when it was phased out.

Carroll Shelby took this basic engine and modified it further for use in his Cobra sports car and eventually in the GT350 Shelby Mustang. In the 1965–1967 GT350s, the 289 made 306 horsepower thanks to a large 715-cfm Holley carburetor on an aluminum high-rise intake manifold, tri-Y exhaust

1967 (cont.)

Cu. In.	427		428
Bore (in.)	4.23		4.13
Stroke (in.)	3.78		3.98
Compression	11.00:1		10.50:1
Induction	1x4 bbl.	2x4 bbl.	1x4 bbl.
Horsepower/rpm	410/5600	425/6000	360/5400
Torque (lbs.-ft.)/rpm	476/3400	480/3700	459/3200

1968

Cu. In.	390	427	428
Bore (in.)	4.05	4.23	4.13
Stroke (in.)	3.78	3.78	3.98
Compression	10.50:1	10.90:1	10.60:1
Induction	1x4 bbl.	1x4 bbl.	1x4 bbl.
Horsepower/rpm	335/4800	390/4600	335/5200
Torque (lbs.-ft.)/rpm	427/3200	460/3200	445/3400

1969

Cu. In.	351
Bore (in.)	4.00
Stroke (in.)	3.50
Compression	10.70:1
Induction	1x4 bbl.
Horsepower/rpm	290/4800
Torque (lbs.-ft.)/rpm	385/3200

1969 (cont.)

Cu. In.	390	428
Bore (in.)	4.05	4.13
Stroke (in.)	3.78	3.98
Compression	10.50:1	10.60:1
Induction	1x4 bbl.	1x4 bbl.
Horsepower/rpm	320/4600	335/5200
Torque (lbs.-ft.)/rpm	427/3200	445/3400

1970

Cu. In.	351*
Bore (in.)	4.00
Stroke (in.)	3.50
Compression	11.00:1
Induction	1x4 bbl.
Horsepower/rpm	300/5400
Torque (lbs.-ft.)/rpm	380/3400

***Cleveland engine**

1970 (cont.)

Cu. In.	428	429	429*
Bore (in.)	4.13	4.36	4.36
Stroke (in.)	3.98	3.59	3.59
Compression	10.60:1	10.50:1	11.30:1
Induction	1x4 bbl.	1x4 bbl.	1x4 bbl.
Horsepower/rpm	335/5200	360/4600	370/5400
Torque (lbs.-ft.)/rpm	445/3400	480/3400	450/3400

***Cobra Jet**

1970 (cont.)

Cu. In.	429*
Bore (in.)	4.36
Stroke (in.)	3.59
Compression	11.30:1
Induction	1x4 bbl.
Horsepower/rpm	375/5600
Torque (lbs.-ft.)/rpm	450/3400

***Super Cobra Jet**

1971

Cu. In.	351*
Bore (in.)	4.00
Stroke (in.)	3.50
Compression	10.70:1
Induction	1x4 bbl.
Horsepower/rpm	385/5400
Torque (lbs.-ft.)/rpm	370/3400

***Cleveland engine**

1971 (cont.)

Cu. In.	429		
Bore (in.)	4.36		
Stroke (in.)	3.59		
Compression	11.30:1		
Induction	1x4 bbl.		
Horsepower/rpm	360/4600	370/5400*	375/5600**
Torque (lbs.-ft.)/rpm	480/3400	450/3400	450/3400

***Cobra Jet**
****Super Cobra Jet**

headers, and glasspack mufflers. As you were less limited when ordering a Cobra or GT350, there were extra power-boosting engine options not available on a regular-production Mustang, including a Paxton supercharger starting in 1966.

When Ford axed the High Performance 289, there was no replacement for '68. Mustangs equipped with the 390 big-block proved far more popular in '67 and were less of a hassle to work on thanks to their hydraulic-lifter cams. Plus, Ford had the 428 Cobra Jet coming. The 289 had outlived its usefulness—that is, except for road racing, where the new 302 was getting demolished by the similarly displaced Camaro Z/28 in the Sports Car Club of America's (SCCA's) Trans-Am series. Ford increased the stroke on the 289 to 3 inches (76mm) to arrive at the new displacement. With a 4-inch (102mm) bore, it should have been a natural high-output engine, but Ford didn't see fit to use a proper set of cylinder heads, cam, or high compression on the 289.

This lack of success—combined with the fact that Chevrolet walked away with the Trans-Am title in '68—led to the development of the Boss 302 in 1969. Ford had a new engine in development for 1970, a derivation of the small-block but with free-flowing canted-valve cylinder heads. Engineer Bill Barr grabbed those heads and fitted them to a 302, and the Boss engine was born.

Realistically, the Boss heads that were pirated from the yet-to-be-released 351-Cleveland used valves that were way too large for a 302-cubic-inch engine. It made decent power on the racetrack, but it was not that great a performer on the street. The intake valves alone were 2.19 inches (56mm) in diameter, the exhausts 1.71 inches (43mm). Velocity was nonexistent in the heads. Ford shrunk them down in 1970 and the result was a much more responsive street engine.

For the two years it was offered, the Boss 302 was rated at 290 horsepower at 5800 rpm and was used exclusively in the Mustang and the Mercury Cougar. It used a hydraulic-lifter cam and had 10.5:1 compression.

So now Ford had a 302 with wedge-style heads and another with canted-valve heads. In '69, Ford introduced the first redesign of the small-block, the 351. Instead of the 302's 8.2-inch (21cm)

Above: The solid-lifter cam-equipped High Performance 289 was a beautiful mating to the intermediate Fairlane and the lightweight Mustang. High-compression pistons, small-chamber cylinder heads, and a high-lift cam were responsible for most of the extra power.

FORD MUSTANG/MERCURY COUGAR ENGINE SPECIFICATIONS

1965

Cu. In.	289
Bore (in.)	4.00
Stroke (in.)	2.87
Compression	10.50:1
Induction	1x4 bbl.
Horsepower/rpm	271/6000
Torque (lbs.-ft.)/rpm	312/3400

1966

Cu. In.	289
Bore (in.)	4.00
Stroke (in.)	2.87
Compression	10.50:1
Induction	1x4 bbl.
Horsepower/rpm	271/6000
Torque (lbs.-ft.)/rpm	312/3400

1967

Cu. In.	289	390
Bore (in.)	4.00	4.05
Stroke (in.)	2.87	3.78
Compression	10.50:1	10.50:1
Induction	1x4 bbl.	1x4 bbl.
Horsepower/rpm	271/6000	320/4800
Torque (lbs.-ft.)/rpm	312/3400	427/3200

1968

Cu. In.	390	427	428
Bore (in.)	4.05	4.23	4.13
Stroke (in.)	3.78	3.78	3.98
Compression	10.50:1	10.90:1	10.70:1
Induction	1x4 bbl.	1x4 bbl.	1x4 bbl.
Horsepower/rpm	325/4800	390/4600	335/5600
Torque (lbs.-ft.)/rpm	427/3200	460/3200	445/3400

1969

Cu. In.	302	351	390
Bore (in.)	4.00	4.00	4.05
Stroke (in.)	3.00	3.50	3.78
Compression	10.50:1	10.70:1	10.50:1
Induction	1x4 bbl.	1x4 bbl.	1x4 bbl.
Horsepower/rpm	290/5800	290/4800	320/4600
Torque (lbs.-ft.)/rpm	290/4300	385/3200	427/3200

1969 (cont.)

Cu. In.	428	429
Bore (in.)	4.13	4.36
Stroke (in.)	3.98	3.59
Compression	10.60:1	10.50:1
Induction	1x4 bbl.	1x4 bbl.
Horsepower/rpm	335/5200	375/5200
Torque (lbs.-ft.)/rpm	440/3400	450/3400

1970

Cu. In.	302	351
Bore (in.)	4.00	4.00
Stroke (in.)	3.00	3.50
Compression	10.50:1	11.00:1
Induction	1x4 bbl.	1x4 bbl.
Horsepower/rpm	290/5800	300/5400
Torque (lbs.-ft.)/rpm	290/4300	380/3400

1970 (cont.)

Cu. In.	428	429
Bore (in.)	4.13	4.36
Stroke (in.)	3.98	3.59
Compression	10.60:1	10.50:1
Induction	1x4 bbl.	1x4 bbl.
Horsepower/rpm	335/5200	375/5200
Torque (lbs.-ft.)/rpm	440/3400	450/3400

1971

Cu. In.	351	351*
Bore (in.)	4.00	4.00
Stroke (in.)	3.50	3.50
Compression	10.70:1	11.00:1
Induction	1x4 bbl.	1x4 bbl.
Horsepower/rpm	285/5400	330/5400
Torque (lbs.-ft.)/rpm	370/3400	370/4000

* Boss

1971 (cont.)

Cu. In.	429	
Bore (in.)	4.36	
Stroke (in.)	3.59	
Compression	11.30:1	
Induction	1x4 bbl.	
Horsepower/rpm	370/5400	375/5600
Torque (lbs.-ft.)/rpm	450/3400	450/3400

1972

Cu. In.	351	
Bore (in.)	4.00	
Stroke (in.)	3.50	
Compression	8.60:1	8.80:1
Induction	1x4 bbl.	1x4 bbl.
Horsepower/rpm	266/5400	275/6000
Torque (lbs.-ft.)/rpm	301/3600	286/3800

1973

Cu. In.	351
Bore (in.)	4.00
Stroke (in.)	3.50
Compression	8.60:1
Induction	1x4 bbl.
Horsepower/rpm	266/5400
Torque (lbs.-ft.)/rpm	301/3600

The extra torque and horsepower developed by the big-block 390 spelled doom for the 271-horse 289 in 1967. By '68, Ford wouldn't offer a high-output small-block in the Mustang or any other car. That would change with the introduction of the Boss 302 in 1969.

deck height, the 351 (which became known as the 351-Windsor [W] for its city of manufacture in Canada) had a 9.5-inch (24cm) deck height, which allowed it to use a much longer stroke. The heads on this engine were interchangeable with the 302, but the 302 never used them, which is too bad because they flowed quite well.

For 1970, Ford threw everyone a curve when its second 351—known as the Cleveland (C) for the city in which it was assembled—was released. This engine used a completely different deck height (9.2 inches [23.5cm]), and the heads did not interchange easily with the 302 or the 351-W. The Cleveland was the best of the lot. Like the 351-W, it had a 4-inch (102mm) bore and 3.5-inch (89mm) stroke, but the canted-valve heads really allowed it to breathe. This new engine produced 300 horsepower at 5800 rpm. Torque was a healthy 380 at 3400. The 351-C became a staple of Ford racing for the next decade.

In '71, Ford did away with the Boss 302 and replaced it with the Boss 351, which was a

high-output version of the 351-Cleveland (the engine itself was actually called the 351 HO in sales literature). It may have been the best engine Ford ever released. Standard, it carried a 4-bolt main block, large-port cylinder heads with big valves, a high-lift solid-lifter camshaft, 11.0:1 compression, and aluminum valve covers. It revved like nobody's business, made 330 horsepower, had 370 lbs.-ft. of torque, and could outmuscle the 429 Cobra Jet Mustang of the same vintage.

Ford shuffled its lineup again in 1972. There were two powerful small-blocks, the 351 HO and the 351 Cobra Jet. Both were based on the 351-C. The 351 HO was essentially a low-compression version of the Boss 351 and was rated at 275 net horsepower. Both small-blocks were produced for just one year and were pretty uncommon even then.

The Cobra Jet (CJ) 351, which was actually a very late 1971 introduction (it was released in May of that year and was rated at 280 horsepower and 345 lbs.-ft. of torque), now had less compression than the HO (8.6:1 versus 9.2:1). They shared the same cylinder heads—essentially 351-2V heads fitted with the larger valves from the 351-4V engine. Also, the HO still used the mechanical-lifter cam, while the Cobra Jet used hydraulics. The CJ produced 266 horsepower at 5400 and 301 lbs.-ft. of torque at 3600.

To improve velocity and make the 1970 Boss 302 more responsive on the street, Ford decreased the size of the intake valves. Shown is the 1970 Boss 302 (without the available Shaker hood scoop).

For 1961, the top option for engines in the Ford Galaxie was the 390 with three 2-barrel carburetors, rated at 401 horsepower. A single 4-barrel with 375 horsepower was a less expensive option.

The 351 CJ carried over for one last go-round in '73, after which the words "Ford" and "high performance" were mutually exclusive until the introduction of the 1982 Mustang GT.

Ford/Mercury (Big-Blocks)

As was the case with the Ford small-blocks, Ford had so many different big-block engines running around that it was hard to keep up with them. There were two basic families—the FE series (352, 390, 406, 427, and 428) and the 385 series (429 and 460)—but even within these ranks, there were variations like the single overhead cam (SOHC) 427 race engine and the Boss 429 semi-Hemi.

There were also differences on certain engines, like the 429 Cobra Jet and 429 Super Cobra Jet (SCJ), the 428 Cobra Jet and 428 Super Cobra Jet, the 427 medium-riser and 427 high-riser, and so on. It all makes for one rather convoluted tale. On the plus side, most of these engines ran like wild beasts. And in the supercar 1960s, that was what mattered most.

The FE family was born with the 332 and 352 in 1958. Neither of these had any sporting pretensions at first. But in 1960, the Ford 352 Special (or Interceptor) arrived with high performance in mind. Through the use of flat-top pistons and smaller combustion chambers in the heads, compression rose to 10.6:1. It used a fairly radical 306-degree solid-lifter camshaft with 0.480-inch (12mm) valve lift, and a 550-cfm Holley 4-barrel sat on an aluminum intake manifold. It also used unique split-flow iron exhaust manifolds, which worked almost as well as headers. The only downside were weak valve springs, which in early cars would cause the valves to float as low as 5000 rpm. Later cars had stiffer springs that would go to about 5800 rpm.

In '61, Ford upped the bore and stroke on the 352 from 4 and 3.5 inches to 4.05 and 3.78 inches (102 and 89mm to 103 and 96mm) to create the 390. It was a torquey mill even in its lowest forms, but there were two high-output versions to take the place of the 352 Special. The two 390s shared the basic hardware with the 352, but the

FORD/SHELBY MUSTANG ENGINE SPECIFICATIONS

1965

Cu. In.	289
Bore (in.)	4.00
Stroke (in.)	2.87
Compression	10.50:1
Induction	1x4 bbl.
Horsepower/rpm	306/6000
Torque (lbs.-ft.)/rpm	329/4200

1966

Cu. In.	289
Bore (in.)	4.00
Stroke (in.)	2.87
Compression	10.50:1
Induction	1x4 bbl.
Horsepower/rpm	306/6000
Torque (lbs.-ft.)/rpm	329/4200

1967

Cu. In.	289
Bore (in.)	4.00
Stroke (in.)	2.87
Compression	10.50:1
Induction	1x4 bbl.
Horsepower/rpm	306/6000
Torque (lbs.-ft.)/rpm	329/4200

1967 (cont.)

Cu. In.	427	428
Bore (in.)	4.23	4.13
Stroke (in.)	3.78	3.98
Compression	11.00:1	10.50:1
Induction	2x4 bbl.	2x4 bbl.
Horsepower/rpm	425/6000	355/5400
Torque (lbs.-ft.)/rpm	476/3400	420/3700

1968

Cu. In.	302	
Bore (in.)	4.00	
Stroke (in.)	3.00	
Compression	10.00:1	
Induction	1x4 bbl.	
Horsepower/rpm	250/4800	335/5200*
Torque (lbs.-ft.)/rpm	318/3200	325/3200

***With optional Paxton supercharger**

1968 (cont.)

Cu. In.	427	428	
Bore (in.)	4.23	4.13	
Stroke (in.)	3.78	3.98	
Compression	11.60:1	10.50:1	10.70:1
Induction	1x4 bbl.	1x4 bbl.	1x4 bbl.
Horsepower/rpm	400/5600	360/5400	335/5400
Torque (lbs.-ft.)/rpm	460/3200	420/3200	445/3400

1969/1970

Cu. In.	351	428
Bore (in.)	4.00	4.13
Stroke (in.)	3.50	3.98
Compression	10.70:1	10.70:1
Induction	1x4 bbl.	1x4 bbl.
Horsepower/rpm	290/4800	335/5400
Torque (lbs.-ft.)/rpm	385/3200	445/3400

extra cubic inches paid off. The single 4-barrel version kicked out 375 horsepower, and now there was a three-deuce option, rated at 401 horsepower. The 4-barrel 390s were rated at 427 lbs.-ft. of torque, the 6-barrel models at 430.

If these engines had any shortcomings, they were the cylinder heads and the bottom end. You could get only 2-bolt mains in the 352 and 390, which weren't optimal for an engine that would see severe duty, and the heads never breathed very well—a problem that lasted until the day the last one was built.

Both of these areas were addressed partway through the '62 model year with the introduction of the 406. It used the same stroke as the 390 and had a larger bore (from 4.05 to 4.13 inches [103 to 105mm]), but the block was significantly better. It used five mains for the crank, but the center three used cross-bolt caps. There was also more beef in the webbing and a much-improved oiling system.

To increase horsepower, compression was raised to 11.4:1, and the exhaust valves in the cylinder heads were made larger to improve flow. With Tri-Power, advertised horsepower was up to 405, just 4 more than the 390 (and 448 lbs.-ft. of torque), but it is considered that the 390 was somewhat overrated by the factory. With a single 4-barrel, the 406 was rated at 385 horses and 444 lbs.-ft. of torque.

The 406 started 1963 as the top powerplant, but later in the year the mighty 427 was introduced. Its displacement came via a 4.23-inch (108mm) bore and 3.78-inch (96mm) stroke. Compression was up a hair, to 11.5:1, over the 406. In its first year, the 427 used a cast-iron crank, but after '64 the cranks were all forged steel. The cylinder heads were much improved, and the Tri-Power option was shelved in favor of a pair of Holleys on a big-passage aluminum intake manifold. Power was 410 horsepower with a single Holley and 425 with the pair. The only thing working against the 427 was the weight of the cars in which it came—more than 2 tons (1.8t) with a driver.

The weight issue was addressed the following year, when Ford introduced the race-only Fairlane Thunderbolt equipped with a new version of the 427, the high-riser. This engine had raised intake ports (0.5 inch [13mm] higher than the other 427s) and needed a special intake manifold to feed them. It came only with dual quads, which sat 3 inches (76mm) higher than in a normal 427. They were fed cold air through ducting in the grille that picked up air where the inboard headlamps would have normally been on a street car. The valves had hollow stems and were light enough to allow 7000 rpm with the special high-lift cam used. The heads flowed far better than stock.

For racing purposes only, Ford produced its most radical engine of the 1960s, the 1965 SOHC 427. The valvetrain was laid out in a hemispherical pattern and the cams were chain-driven. The block was similar to that of the 427 wedge engine, but there were enough differences to accommodate the huge cylinder heads that not a lot of parts were interchangeable. Since the cams were mounted one apiece atop the cylinder heads, Ford had no way of turning the distributor, so it kept a dummy cam in the block, which was spun by the cam chains.

Naturally, a forged crankshaft was used in the SOHC Hemi, as were rods, the same ones found in the 427 wedge. Cap-screw-type connecting rods

After 1964, all 427s used forged steel crankshafts. This was a genuine race-bred engine with 11.1:1 compression, dual Carter 4-barrel carburetion, and 425 horsepower. A single 4-barrel was available to legalize the 427 for NASCAR.

and floating pistons were included, and compression was 12.0:1. A 7.5-quart (7L) pan held the oil. When NASCAR told Ford that the engine could not be used in competition unless five hundred similarly equipped street cars were built, Ford balked and shelved the program. The engine was quite successful in the Funny Car and Top Fuel ranks in drag racing in the '60s, but it was too expensive to produce and too few engines were built. For 1966, Chrysler's Hemi would soon dominate those classes, not to mention NASCAR, because Dodge and Plymouth offered the Street Hemi to homologate the race Hemi.

The big 427 survived in 410- and 425-horsepower trim through the end of 1967, but it was an expensive engine to build and sell. And it wasn't until 1966 that Ford used it in a midsize street car, the Fairlane. Big-block enthusiasts, for the most part, were stuck with the 390. Those who purchased '67 Shelby GT500 Mustangs were in for a treat, however. Shelby offered these cars with a 428 (a bored and stroked 390 first introduced in Ford's full-size cars in '66) with a dual 4-barrel intake manifold, which produced 355 horsepower. A handful of 427 GT500s were also said to be built, but the dual quad 428 was standard.

In 1968, Ford introduced the 428 Cobra Jet, which surprised everyone. This potent machine had the combination of the strong 428 bottom end with the race-developed, large-valve 427-style cylinder heads. The CJ had a slightly beefier block and a nodular iron crankshaft. Compression was a robust 10.7:1. Intake valve size was 2.097 inches (53mm) and the exhausts were 1.660 inches (42mm). The intake was virtually identical to that of the 428 Police Interceptor, except it was cast iron instead of aluminum. Topping it off was a 735-cfm Holley 4-barrel carb, which breathed through an air-filter lid with a flapper door to allow cool air to enter. Ford engineer Bill Barr said that it was the hottest street engine Ford ever built, despite its tame 335-horsepower rating. This engine made a big splash in the Mustang, winning class at the Winternationals in Pomona, California, in '68 (where it debuted). But it was also available in the Fairlane, Mercury Cyclone, and Cougar.

As a side note, Ford tamed the 427 for the street in '68, adding a hydraulic-lifter cam and limiting the customer to a single 4-barrel carb. It produced 390 horsepower and disappeared midway through the model year.

In '69, Ford quietly made a good package better. If you ordered your 428 Cobra Jet with the Drag Pack option, you automatically got an oil cooler for the engine, LeMans-style 427 cap-screw connecting rods, and a different crankshaft, flywheel, and damper.

There was a new big-block engine family born in 1968, the 385 series (the 385 referred to the 3.85-inch [10cm] stroke of the larger 460-cubic-inch version used in larger cars). At first it came in two sizes, 429 and 460, and was used in Ford's, Mercury's, and Lincoln's big luxobarges. Bore and stroke on the 429 were 4.36 and 3.59 inches (111 and 91mm), respectively; the 460 used the same bore. It wasn't until 1969 that the first high-output version was produced, and it was radically different from its Thunderbird and Lincoln counterparts. The engine was designed to take the place of the 427 in NASCAR competition, and very few parts interchanged with the more pedestrian 385-series engines.

Above: The 1965 Ford was all-new from the ground up. Its styling was quite reminiscent of 1963–64 full-sized Pontiacs, especially its use of stacked headlights. This one has a non-stock teardrop hood and Cragar S/S wheels, which were extremely popular in the '60s and '70s.

Following pages: *Hot Rod* magazine tested a '65 Galaxie fastback and called it the "biggest, boldest Ford street machine . . . and a strong contender for AA/Stock honors at the strip." Four-bolt mains, forged pistons, a high-lift solid cam, and heavy-duty adjustable rockers were all standard.

Dubbed the Boss 429, it used semi-hemi aluminum cylinder heads that used O-rings rather than traditional head gaskets to seal them to the block. The valves were tuliped for lighter weight. The block used 4-bolt main bearing caps in the number one, two, three, and four positions. The street engine used a rather mild hydraulic-lifter cam and small Holley carburetor, which really took a lot of the steam out of it. Granted, it was rated at 375 horsepower, but the carb used was smaller than the one on the Boss 302.

The engine was used only in a street car to homologate it for NASCAR, and as such, it was sold to the public only in 1969 and 1970—available solely in the Mustang both years.

In 1970 Ford built a "regular" high-performance version of the 429, and it too used the Cobra Jet and Super Cobra Jet nomenclature. The 429/460 family had a tremendous amount of potential for both size and horsepower. When it was designed, engineers had no idea how big and heavy the cars were going to get (some foresaw 5,000-pound [2,270kg] full-size cars, and if not for the Arab oil embargo in '73, it might have happened), and the 385 family was capable of easily exceeding 500 cubic inches with the correct bore and stroke.

Like the 351-Cleveland, the 429 Cobra Jet was based on the 385-series Ford engine, whereas the 428 Cobra Jet from the year before sprung from FE roots. The 429 CJ had large-port heads with canted valves, a high-output hydraulic cam, a high-rise intake manifold, 11.3:1 compression, and free-flowing iron exhaust manifolds. The engine produced 370 horsepower at 5400 rpm and 450 lbs.-ft. of torque at 3400.

To achieve Super Cobra Jet status, Ford used a more radical mechanical-lifter cam and a Holley 4-barrel (which required the use of a smog pump). Internally, the engine was treated to 4-bolt main caps, forged pistons, and a dual-entry oil pump. Since these cars all came with the Drag Pack option, an engine oil cooler was standard. The intake was the same as the Cobra Jet, but with a different bolt flange for use with the 780-cfm Holley carburetor. The engine was rated at 375 horsepower and 450 lbs.-ft. of torque. A 3.91:1 gear ratio was standard, with 4.30s optional.

The end of the muscle car era temporarily killed development of the 385-series engine as a high-performance unit, but incredibly in the 1990s it started making a comeback with drag racers. Ford, through its Ford Racing Performance Parts program (now-defunct Special Vehicle Operations), began offering cylinder heads and other high-output goodies, including complete engines ranging from 460 to 514 cubic inches. The rest of the aftermarket is following suit, and more than thirty years after its birth, the 385-series engine is finally reaching the potential its engineers designed into it.

FORD
MICHIGAN
BMT 231
GREAT LAKES

Oldsmobile used different camshafts in the 4-4-2's 400 in 1968, depending on whether you ordered a manual or automatic transmission. The one for manuals delivered an idle that was deemed too radical when used with an automatic. The difference between the two in performance was 25 horsepower, with the stick being rated at 350 horsepower versus 325.

Oldsmobile

Post–World War II America was a nation starved for new cars and new technology. Automobile production halted shortly after the attack on Pearl Harbor in 1941 and didn't resume until 1946. Against this backdrop, a group of Oldsmobile engineers went to work developing the division's first overhead valve V8 engine, one designed with high compression and high performance in mind.

Charles Kettering, the inventor of the self-starter, had been at Oldsmobile for three decades and was nearing retirement. He wanted to leave one last mark on the evolution of the automobile. With a team of hungry young engineers, he began working on what would become the Oldsmobile Rocket V8.

Kettering and his crew knew the L-head (valve-in-block) engine design was severely limited and, because of a small combustion chamber, could not sustain compression ratios higher than 8.0:1. It was Kettering who suggested moving the valves to the top of the cylinders, solving a host of structural problems that impeded high compression.

Chief draftsman Gilbert Burrell designed what was called SV-49 in January 1946, a 288-cubic-inch, 90-degree V8 with an integrally cast block. In less than a year, the first running prototype was on an engine stand.

Unfortunately, Cadillac was also working on a 90-degree V8, and since it wouldn't have been good politics to upstage the top division, Kettering and his crew were literally sent back to the drawing board. After attempting a few more designs, Burrell and associate E.M. "Pete" Estes proved that altering the V8 configuration to a 70- or 60-degree bank would produce a crankshaft imbalance that could not be corrected with counterweights. With this information, they went back to the GM brass, who gave the green light to the project. In March 1949, plans for putting SV-49 into production moved forward, which included building a new engine plant. Opened in 1948, the Kettering Engine Plant

OLDSMOBILE ENGINE SPECIFICATIONS

1964

Cu. In.	330
Bore (in.)	3.94
Stroke (in.)	3.39
Compression	10.25:1
Induction	1x4 bbl.
Horsepower/rpm	310/5200
Torque (lbs.-ft.)/rpm	355/3600

1965

Cu. In.	400
Bore (in.)	4.00
Stroke (in.)	3.975
Compression	10.25:1
Induction	1x4 bbl.
Horsepower/rpm	345/4800
Torque (lbs.-ft.)/rpm	440/3200

1966

Cu. In.	400	
Bore (in.)	4.00	
Stroke (in.)	3.975	
Compression	10.50:1	
Induction	1x4 bbl.	3x2 bbl.
Horsepower/rpm	350/5000	360/5000
Torque (lbs.-ft.)/rpm	440/3600	440/3600

1967

Cu. In.	400
Bore (in.)	4.00
Stroke (in.)	3.975
Compression	10.50:1
Induction	1x4 bbl.
Horsepower/rpm	350/5000
Torque (lbs.-ft.)/rpm	440/3600

1968

Cu. In.	350	400	
Bore (in.)	4.06	3.87	
Stroke (in.)	3.39	4.25	
Compression	10.50:1	10.50:1	
Induction	1x4 bbl.	1x4 bbl.	
Horsepower/rpm	325/5400	350/5000*	360/5400**
Torque (lbs.-ft.)/rpm	360/3600	440/3600	440/3600

***325 hp with automatic transmission**
****W-30 option**

1969

Cu. In.	350	400	
Bore (in.)	4.06	3.87	
Stroke (in.)	3.39	4.25	
Compression	10.50:1	10.50:1	
Induction	1x4 bbl.	1x4 bbl.	
Horsepower/rpm	325/5400	350/5000	360/5400*
Torque (lbs.-ft.)/rpm	360/3600	440/3600	440/3600

***W-30 option**

1970

Cu. In.	350	455	
Bore (in.)	4.06	4.12	
Stroke (in.)	3.39	4.25	
Compression	10.50:1	10.50:1	
Induction	1x4 bbl.	1x4 bbl.	
Horsepower/rpm	325/5400	365/5000	370/5200*
Torque (lbs.-ft.)/rpm	360/3600	500/3200	500/3600

***W-30 option**

1971

Cu. In.	455	
Bore (in.)	4.12	
Stroke (in.)	4.25	
Compression	8.50:1	
Induction	1x4 bbl.	
Horsepower/rpm	340/4600	360/4700*
Torque (lbs.-ft.)/rpm	460/3200	460/3200

***W-30 option**

1972

Cu. In.	350	455	
Bore (in.)	4.06	4.12	
Stroke (in.)	3.39	4.25	
Compression	8.50:1	8.50:1	
Induction	1x4 bbl.	1x4 bbl.	
Horsepower/rpm	180/4000	270/4400	300/4400*
Torque (lbs-ft.)/rpm	275/2800	370/3200	410/3200

***W-30 option**

produced Rocket V8s for forty years before giving way to the Quad 4 in 1988.

"The new high-compression 1949 Rocket engine in production at Oldsmobile is the most powerful and at the same time the most economical 8-cylinder powerplant ever manufactured by the division," said an Oldsmobile press release dated January 20, 1949. "Quiet, smooth and outstanding in its performance, it has a compression ratio of 7.25:1 and is rated at 135-hp."

While a compression ratio of 7.25:1 seems incredibly low today, that was extremely high by the standards of the day. That first Rocket V8 measured 303.7 cubic inches and made 135 horsepower at 3600 rpm and 263 lbs.-ft. of torque at 1800 rpm. It used a 3.75-inch (95mm) bore and 3.875 (98mm) stroke. A mere ten years later, it had been bored and stroked to 394 cubic inches and produced 314 horsepower at 4600 rpm and 435 lbs.-ft. of torque at 2800.

From the day the first one was installed in a car, the Rocket V8 was considered an engineering marvel, and from 1950 to 1953, Lee Petty, Fonty Flock, and Tim Flock drove Oldsmobiles to numerous victories in the fledgling NASCAR ranks.

Olds produced its first factory speed parts for the Rocket in 1951. In response to Hudson's introduction of a heavy-duty "export" suspension kit (remember that in its early years, NASCAR's Stock Cars had to truly be stock), Olds launched an export kit of its own, which included some engine parts, namely high-compression cylinder heads, a more radical cam, solid lifters, and a modified intake manifold.

HURST/OLDSMOBILE ENGINE SPECIFICATIONS

1968	
Cu. In.	455
Bore (in.)	4.12
Stroke (in.)	4.25
Compression	10.50:1
Induction	1x4 bbl.
Horsepower/rpm	390/5000
Torque (lbs.-ft.)/rpm	500/3600

1969	
Cu. In.	455
Bore (in.)	4.12
Stroke (in.)	4.25
Compression	10.50:1
Induction	1x4 bbl.
Horsepower/rpm	380/5000
Torque (lbs.-ft.)/rpm	500/3200

1972		
Cu. In.	455	
Bore (in.)	4.12	
Stroke (in.)	4.25	
Compression	8.50:1	
Induction	1x4 bbl.	
Horsepower/rpm	270/4400	300/4400*
Torque (lbs-ft.)/rpm	370/3200	410/3200

*W-30

In 1957, Olds released the J-2 Tri-Carb option, which used a trio of 2-barrel carburetors and 10.0:1 compression to raise horsepower to 300 (with 415 lbs.-ft. of torque). Olds also recommended dual exhausts and power brakes on J-2-equipped cars. It was versions of this Rocket V8 that powered Oldsmobiles throughout the muscle car years. Oldsmobile's next major evolutionary step came in 1962, when it installed a turbocharger in a 215-cubic-inch version in the Jetfire, a new intermediate. Maximum displacement at the time in an intermediate GM car was 330 cubic inches. The Olds engineers figured that the turbo would be the perfect way to move more air through the engine's combustion chambers. By placing the turbo, which runs off exhaust gases, on the inlet side, the engineers were able to increase the air charge over atmospheric pressure, thus enabling the engine to use more air and fuel to produce more power.

To prevent detonation, Olds injected a mixture—dubbed Turbo-Rocket Fluid—of methyl alcohol, corrosion inhibitor, and water into the engine when turbo boost measured 1 psi. The fluid allowed the engine to accept greater boost pressure without increasing its octane requirement.

The result was 215 horsepower and 310 lbs.-ft. of torque, enough to move the Jetfire in a pretty good hurry. Cubic inches were everything in the '60s, though, and the introduction of the 389 Pontiac GTO in 1964 meant that all bets were off. Olds engineers were developing the Police Apprehender package for the F-85 Cutlass series at the time, and this evolved into Olds' first muscle car, the '64 4-4-2. The 4-4-2 was an option package available on all F-85 models except the station wagon. It included suspension and brake upgrades, but the heart of the 4-4-2 was the 330-cubic-inch Rocket under the hood. With a 4-barrel carb and dual exhaust, horsepower was 310 at 5200 and torque was 355 at 3600. Compression was 10.25:1. A new cam gave more lift and overlap, while a dual-snorkel air cleaner fed more air to the carburetor.

In 1965, engineers redesigned the Rocket V8. It incorporated a taller deck height and a beefier bottom end, which allowed for much larger displacements and better durability. This raised-deck Rocket was physically larger, essentially giving Olds two similar but separate engines. When used in the 4-4-2, displacement was 400 cubic inches. Bore and stroke on the 400 was 4.00x3.975 inches (102x101mm), compression was 10.25:1. It was rated at 345 horsepower and 440 lbs.-ft. of torque and made the 4-4-2 much more competitive against the GTO. Like all Olds engines of the '60s, it used hydraulic lifters for ease of maintenance. (The smaller low-block that the 330 was based on grew to 350 cubic inches in '68.)

The introduction of the Rochester Quadrajet carburetor and an extra quarter point in compression in '66 helped boost horsepower in the 4-4-2 to 350. For those wanting more, the L69 Tri-Carb option, the first such setup since the J-2 of the '50s, was available. A trio of 2-barrel carbs increased horsepower to 360.

Those craving the ultimate 4-4-2 in '66 specified the W-30 option, which gave you the L69's three 2-barrel carbs plus enough other heavy-duty hardware to be competitive at any drag strip in the country. The carbs were covered with a special chrome air cleaner that was fed fresh air through 5-inch (13cm) flexible fabric hoses. The air was picked up by 7.75x3.5-inch (19.5x9cm) ducts located in the front bumper at the parking-light location (this required changes to the bumper and meant the parking lamps had to be placed further inboard in the bumper).

A radical 308-degree, 0.474-inch (12mm) hydraulic-lift cam offered a flat power curve, and the valves used improved springs; 1.6:1 rocker arms were part of the package, too. The valve size was 2.06 inches (52mm) on the intake side and 1.629 inches (41mm) on the exhaust. A different oil pump spring increased pressure.

A General Motors edict prohibiting multiple carburetion setups on passenger cars (except the Corvette) went into effect in 1967, which meant the end of L69 option. The 4-barrel 400 was the only induction choice available, though the W-30 fresh-air package could still be purchased. Bore on the 400 was 3.87 inches (98mm), while stroke increased to 4.25 inches (108mm). This undersquare configuration aided torque, though the peak rating remained the same. Compression was 10.5:1.

A new cylinder head design with modified ports was introduced at the same time. The 400 had a more performance-oriented camshaft and stiffer valve springs. If you ordered the manual transmission, the engine was rated at 350 horsepower. Automatics got a more conservative camshaft profile, which depleted the horsepower account by 25.

Force-Air induction was still optional with large 13×2-inch (33×5cm) scoops. If you ordered it, you also got a special cam, heat-treated valve springs, and a modified distributor, all good for 360 horsepower at 5400 rpm. The W-30 package consisted of a blueprinted version of the 400 with (among other things) cold-air induction, a radical cam with 328-degree duration, and 0.475-inch (12mm) lift.

The year 1968 was also when Olds chose to deliver its W-31 option, which was based on the 350. Like the 400, it had 10.5:1 compression, but it was an oversquare design with a 4.06-inch (103mm) bore and 3.39-inch (86mm) stroke. The Ram Rod 350 used small-port heads with larger-than-normal intake valves and a long-duration cam. (Engineers tried using the 400's heads, but they flowed too well for the smaller displacement mill.) It was designed for high-rpm duty and came standard with 3.91 rear end gears. The W-31 option cost $205 and was available only in the Cutlass.

For 1970, Olds adopted the 455 Rocket V8 as the standard 4-4-2 engine. The extra cubes came via an increase in the bore from 3.87 to 4.12 inches (98 to 105mm). It had a 10.5:1 compression ratio and carried high-performance cylinder heads; a 294/296-degree, 0.472-inch (12mm) lift camshaft; and special aluminum intake for its single 4-barrel carb. Valve diameters were now 2.077 inches (53mm) for the intake and 1.630 (41mm) for the exhaust.

A new connecting rod design improved durability, and positive valve rotators allowed for better seating and increased compression. Horsepower was up to 365 at 5000 rpm, and torque checked in at 500 lbs.-ft. at a low 3200 rpm. A functional fiberglass hood with a pair of molded-in scoops was optional (standard with W-30 cars).

Speaking of which, gone were the under-the-bumper scoops for which the W-30 package was famous. The fiberglass hood fed a sealed air cleaner through a vacuum-operated flip valve. This opened only at full throttle, so the engine could breathe warm underhood air while cruising. This was necessitated by emissions regulations, which required lean part-throttle carburetion that would cause stumbling and hesitation in very cold air. To improve performance, W-30 engines used a radical 308-degree camshaft with slightly more lift—0.475 inches (12mm). Valve size was shared with the base 455.

The wild W-31 returned and was still quite the screamer thanks to its favorable undersquare layout and radical camshaft (308-degree duration and 0.474-inch [12mm] lift). With 325 horsepower and 360 lbs.-ft. of torque, it was a fun ride.

That fun started to dissipate when GM cut compression in 1971. Olds' high-compression 455 lost two full points. The first casualty was the demise of the W-31 350. The second was a reduction in the base 455's horsepower (to 340 at 4600 rpm) and torque (460 lbs.-ft. at 3200). Finally, the W-30 was down to 360 ponies at 4700. Ever-tightening emissions regulations, which forced manufacturers to lean out or eliminate their high-performance carburetors and back off on ignition timing, hurt performance as well.

Top & Bottom: This is the very rare 1969 4-4-2 with the W-32 option. In 1969, when you ordered an Oldsmobile 4-4-2, the engine you received had a different camshaft depending on whether you ordered a manual transmission or an automatic. The 400 with a 4-speed was rated at 350 horsepower, while the automatic had 325. The W-32 option provided the stick shift engine/cam combination with the automatic transmission. Furthermore, the package included the W-30's under-the-bumper ram air induction system (but without the W-30's red inner fenders).

In '72, GM switched from gross to net horsepower ratings, which caused the numbers to plummet even further—to 270 for the 455 (which was now an option) and to 300 on the W-30. The 4-4-2 switched from a separate model to an option package, which it had been from 1964 to 1967. For the first time since '64, an engine smaller than 400 cubic inches was available, in this case a 180-horse 350.

Even with the drop in compression, the 455-powered 4-4-2s could still run, especially the W-30 cars. But that model was discontinued in 1973, and the muscle car era at Oldsmobile was over.

Pontiac

Long before Pontiac was the "excitement division" of General Motors, it was the producer of rather plain, reliable but otherwise uninteresting automobiles. It used a 6-cylinder engine in its lower lines and a flathead inline 8-cylinder in its better models.

Work on a modern overhead valve Pontiac V8 began in 1949 under the direction of general manager Harry J. Klinger but proceeded slowly, and it virtually ground to a halt when he was promoted and his successor, Arnold Lenz, was killed in a car/train crash in 1952. It was Lenz's replacement, R.M. Critchfield, who got the program back on track.

The all-new V8 debuted for the 1955 model year. It was a thoroughly modern design, especially its ball-stud rocker arm, which it shared with the new small-block Chevy V8. This design allowed the engine to rev higher than older shaft-mounted rocker systems, plus it cost less to manufacture.

Using a 3.75-inch (95mm) bore and a 3.25-inch (83mm) stroke, the new powerplant displaced 287.2 cubic inches. (In keeping with the 1950's space age

The 1970 4-4-2 came standard with 455 cubic inches. The top-of-the-line package was the 365-horsepower W-30. Gone were the under-the-bumper air scoops, replaced by a functional fiberglass hood.

PONTIAC ENGINE SPECIFICATIONS

1960

Cu. In.	389		
Bore (in.)	4.06		
Stroke (in.)	3.75		
Compression	10.75:1		
Induction	3x2 bbl.		
Horsepower/rpm	348/4800		
Torque (lbs.-ft.)/rpm	425/2800		

1961

Cu. In.	389		421
Bore (in.)	4.06		4.09
Stroke (in.)	3.75		4.00
Compression	10.75:1		11.00:1
Induction	1x4 bbl.	3x2 bbl.	2x4 bbl.
Horsepower/rpm	333/4800	348/4800	373*/5600
Torque (lbs.-ft.)/rpm	425/2800	430/2800	not rated

*Over-the-counter option only

1962

Cu. In.	389		
Bore (in.)	4.06		
Stroke (in.)	3.75		
Compression	10.75:1		
Induction	1x4 bbl.	3x2 bbl.	1x4 bbl.*
Horsepower/rpm	333/4800	348/4800	385/5200
Torque (lbs.-ft.)/rpm	425/2800	430/2800	430/3200

*Super Duty option

1962 (cont.)

Cu. In.	421*		
Bore (in.)	4.09		
Stroke (in.)	4.00		
Compression	11.00:1		
Induction	2x4 bbl.		
Horsepower/rpm	405/5600		
Torque (lbs.-ft)/rpm	425/4400		

*Super Duty option

1963

Cu. In.	421		
Bore (in.)	4.09		
Stroke (in.)	4.00		
Compression	10.75:1		12.00:1*
Induction	1x4 bbl.	3x2 bbl.	1x4 bbl.
Horsepower/rpm	353/5000	370/5200	390/5800
Torque (lbs.-ft.)/rpm	455/3400	460/3800	425/3600

*Super Duty option

1963 (cont.)

Cu. In.	421*		
Bore (in.)	4.09		
Stroke (in.)	4.00		
Compression	12.00:1	13.00:1*	
Induction	2x4 bbl.	2x4 bbl.	
Horsepower/rpm	405/5600	410/5600	
Torque (lbs.-ft.)/rpm	425/4400	435/4400	

*Super Duty option

1964

Cu. In.	389		
Bore (in.)	4.06		
Stroke (in.)	3.75		
Compression	10.75:1		
Induction	1x4 bbl.	3x2 bbl.	
Horsepower/rpm	325/4800	348/4800	
Torque (lbs.-ft.)/rpm	428/3200	428/3600	

1964 (cont.)

Cu. In.	421		
Bore (in.)	4.09		
Stroke (in.)	4.00		
Compression	10.50:1	10.75:1	
Induction	1x4 bbl.	3x2 bbl.	
Horsepower/rpm	320/4400	350/4600	370/5200
Torque (lbs.-ft.)/rpm	455/2800	454/3200	460/3800

1965

Cu. In.	389		421
Bore (in.)	4.06		4.09
Stroke (in.)	3.75		4.00
Compression	10.75:1		10.75:1
Induction	1x4 bbl.	3x2 bbl.	3x2 bbl.
Horsepower/rpm	335/5000	360/5200	376/5000
Torque (lbs.-ft.)/rpm	431/3200	424/3600	461/3600

1966

Cu. In.	389		421
Bore (in.)	4.06		4.09
Stroke (in.)	3.75		4.00
Compression	10.75:1		10.75:1
Induction	1x4 bbl.	3x2 bbl.	3x2 bbl.
Horsepower/rpm	335/5000	360/5200	376/5000
Torque (lbs.-ft.)/rpm	431/3200	424/3600	461/3600

1967

Cu. In.	400		
Bore (in.)	4.12		
Stroke (in.)	3.75		
Compression	10.75:1		
Induction	1x4 bbl.		
Horsepower/rpm	335/5000	360/5100	360/5400
Torque (lbs.-ft.)/rpm	441/3400	438/3600	438/3800

1967 (cont.)

Cu. In.	326	400	
Bore (in.)	3.72	4.12	
Stroke (in.)	3.75	3.75	
Compression	10.50:1	10.75:1	
Induction	1x4 bbl.	1x4 bbl.	
Horsepower/rpm	285/5000	325/5200	
Torque (lbs.-ft.)/rpm	359/3200	410/3600	

1968

Cu. In.	350	400	
Bore (in.)	3.88	4.12	
Stroke (in.)	3.75	3.75	
Compression	10.50:1	10.75:1	
Induction	1x4 bbl.	1x4 bbl.	
Horsepower/rpm	320/5100	330/4800	335/5000
Torque (lbs.-ft.)/rpm	380/3200	430/3300	430/3400

1969

Cu. In.	350	400	
Bore (in.)	3.88	4.12	
Stroke (in.)	3.75	3.75	
Compression	10.50:1	10.75:1	
Induction	1x4 bbl.	1x4 bbl.	
Horsepower/rpm	325/5100	330/4800	335/5000
Torque (lbs.-ft.)/rpm	380/3200	430/3300	430/3400

1969 (cont.)

Cu. In.	400		
Bore (in.)	4.12		
Stroke (in.)	3.75		
Compression	10.75:1		
Induction	1x4 bbl.		
Horsepower/rpm	345/5400		
Torque (lbs.-ft.)/rpm	440/3700		

1970

Cu. In.	400		
Bore (in.)	4.12		
Stroke (in.)	3.75		
Compression	10.00:1	10.25:1	10.50:1
Induction	1x4 bbl.	1x4 bbl.	1x4 bbl.
Horsepower/rpm	330/4800	335/4800	370/5500
Torque (lbs.-ft.)/rpm	445/2900	430/3000	445/3900

1971

Cu. In.	400	455	
Bore (in.)	4.12	4.15	
Stroke (in.)	3.75	4.21	
Compression	8.20:1	8.20:1	8.40:1
Induction	1x4 bbl.	1x4 bbl.	1x4 bbl.
Horsepower/rpm	300/4800	325/4400	335/4800
Torque (lbs.-ft.)/rpm	400/2400	455/3200	480/3600

1972

Cu. In.	400	455	
Bore (in.)	4.12	4.15	
Stroke (in.)	3.75	4.21	
Compression	8.20:1	8.40:1	
Induction	1x4 bbl.	1x4 bbl.	
Horsepower/rpm	250/4400	300/4000	
Torque (lbs.-ft.)/rpm	325/3200	415/3200	

1973

Cu. In.	400	455	
Bore (in.)	4.12	4.15	
Stroke (in.)	3.75	4.21	
Compression	8.00:1	8.00:1	8.40:1
Induction	1x4 bbl.	1x4 bbl.	1x4 bbl.
Horsepower/rpm	230/4400	250/4000	310/4000
Torque (lbs.-ft.)/rpm	325/3200	370/2800	390/3600

1974

Cu. In.	400	455	
Bore (in.)	4.12	4.15	
Stroke (in.)	3.75	4.21	
Compression	8.00:1	8.40:1	
Induction	1x4 bbl.	1x4 bbl.	
Horsepower/rpm	225/4400	290/4000	
Torque (lbs.-ft.)/rpm	330/2800	390/3600	

PONTIAC GTO ENGINE SPECIFICATIONS

1968			
Cu. In.	350	400	
Bore (in.)	3.88	4.12	
Stroke (in.)	3.75	3.75	
Compression	10.50:1	10.75:1	
Induction	1x4 bbl.	1x4 bbl.	
Horsepower/rpm	320/5100	350/5000	360/5100*
Torque (lbs.-ft.)/rpm	380/3200	445/3000	445/3600

*HO

1968 (cont.)	
Cu. In.	400
Bore (in.)	4.12
Stroke (in.)	3.75
Compression	10.75:1
Induction	1x4 bbl.
Horsepower/rpm	360/5400
Torque (lbs.-ft.)/rpm	445/3800*

*Ram Air II

1969			
Cu. In.	350	400	
Bore (in.)	3.88	4.12	
Stroke (in.)	3.75	3.75	
Compression	10.50:1	10.75:1	
Induction	1x4 bbl.	1x4 bbl.	
Horsepower/rpm	325/5100	350/5000	366/5100*
Torque (lbs.-ft.)/rpm	380/3200	450/3000	445/3600

*Ram Air III

1969 (cont.)	
Cu. In.	400
Bore (in.)	4.12
Stroke (in.)	3.75
Compression	10.75:1
Induction	1x4 bbl.
Horsepower/rpm	370/5500
Torque (lbs.-ft.)/rpm	445/3900*

*Ram Air IV

1970			
Cu. In.	400		
Bore (in.)	4.12		
Stroke (in.)	3.75		
Compression	10.00:1	10.25:1	10.50:1
Induction	1x4 bbl.	1x4 bbl.	1x4 bbl.
Horsepower/rpm	330/4800*	350/5000	366/5100**
Torque (lbs.-ft.)/rpm	445/2900	445/3000	445/3600

*Tempest only, automatic transmission only
**Ram Air III

1970 (cont.)		
Cu. In.	400	455
Bore (in.)	4.12	4.15
Stroke (in.)	3.75	4.21
Compression	10.50:1	10.25:1
Induction	1x4 bbl.	1x4 bbl.
Horsepower/rpm	370/5500	360/4300
Torque (lbs.-ft.)/rpm	445/3900*	500/2700

*Ram Air IV

1971			
Cu. In.	400	455	
Bore (in.)	4.12	4.15	
Stroke (in.)	3.75	4.21	
Compression	8.20:1	8.20:1	8.40:1
Induction	1x4 bbl.	1x4 bbl.	1x4 bbl.
Horsepower/rpm	300/5000	325/4400	335/4800*
Torque (lbs.-ft.)/rpm	430/3400	455/3200	480/3600

*455 HO

1972			
Cu. In.	400	455	
Bore (in.)	4.12	4.15	
Stroke (in.)	3.75	4.21	
Compression	8.20:1	8.20:1	8.40:1
Induction	1x4 bbl.	1x4 bbl.	1x4 bbl.
Horsepower/rpm	250/4400	250/3600	300/4000*
Torque (lbs.-ft.)/rpm	325/3200	475/3400	415/3200

*455 H.O.

1973		
Cu. In.	400	455
Bore (in.)	4.12	4.15
Stroke (in.)	3.75	4.21
Compression	8.00:1	8.20:1
Induction	1x4 bbl.	1x4 bbl.
Horsepower/rpm	230/4400	250/4000
Torque (lbs.-ft.)/rpm	325/3200	370/2800

1974	
Cu. In.	350
Bore (in.)	3.88
Stroke (in.)	3.75
Compression	7.60:1
Induction	1x4 bbl.
Horsepower/rpm	200/4400
Torque (lbs.-ft.)/rpm	295/2800

Part of the GTO's mystique in the early years was its Tri-Power induction. Mechanical carburetor linkage made its way onto 3x2/4-speed versions in 1965, also available was a dealer-installed Ram Air package.

theme, it was called the Strato-Streak V8.) The first change occurred in 1956, when it was bored out to 316.6 cubes. In 1957, its stroke was lengthened, making it a 347. That same year it was given higher compression and Tri-Power—three 2-barrel carburetors, a system it would retain and refine for ten years. Horsepower was way up, from a peak of 180 in 1955 to 290 or 317, depending on which Tri-Power engine you ordered.

That same year there was even a fuel-injected 347, and it was available only in the Bonneville (in which it was standard equipment). The 347 fuelie used a mechanical injection setup similar to the one used at Chevrolet, but it made 2 less horsepower than the top Tri-Power option and wasn't brought back for '58.

Remarkably, Pontiac bored the V8 again in '58, from 3.94 to 4.06 inches (100 to 103mm), bringing displacement to 370 (and the top horsepower rating to 330 at 5200 rpm). That same season, a NASCAR-certified 4-barrel engine was introduced. It had 10.5:1 compression, a higher-lift camshaft, the aforementioned induction system, and dual exhausts, good for 315 horsepower.

The engineers continued their tour de force in '59, stroking the 370 to 389 cubic inches, a displacement that it stuck with until 1967 (although a 421 would be added shortly). At the dawn of the muscle car era, Pontiac brought the Trophy 425-A engine to the game. It was, naturally, a three 2-barrel-carb engine, with 10.75:1 compression, a 288-degree cam, 4-bolt main caps, and special streamlined exhaust manifolds that fed a low-restriction dual exhaust. It made 348 horsepower and 425 lbs.-ft. of torque (hence the name).

The Trophy 425-A was basically a carryover powerplant in 1961, but to legalize a combination for NASCAR, a single 4-barrel engine was offered as well, producing 333 horsepower at 4800 rpm.

For those who needed more power, Mac McKellar led engineering developments for the Super Duty parts, which were sold through Pontiac dealers to help racers. This program was a direct offshoot of GM's adherence to the AMA's ban on participation in 1957. Without the help of the factory, the Pontiacs that had begun cleaning up on the nation's racetracks would have been out of luck, and their success was critical to general manager Bunkie Knudsen's plan to reinvent Pontiac as a sporty, young person's car.

By 1959, there were camshafts, high-flow exhaust manifolds, intake manifolds, and the like for serious hot rodders. By 1961, you could order the Super Duty (SD) parts to build a 373-horsepower 421 engine. The 421 was introduced that year, the product of a bore and stroke job on the 389. It was

CAUTION

a nearly square motor, with a 4.0937-inch (104mm) bore and a 4-inch (102mm) stroke.

If you had the money, you could order the necessary over-the-counter Super Duty hardware to put together a 373-horsepower 421. Pontiac took away the trouble of doing it yourself in 1962 with the release of two race engines. The 421 Super Duty came with a single 4-barrel carburetor, 385 horsepower, and 430 lbs.-ft. of torque for NASCAR applications; there was a dual-quad setup with 405 horsepower and 425 lbs.-ft. of torque for drag racers. At the time, you could race only what you sold. NASCAR didn't allow multiple carburetion; hence that version had only a single 4-barrel carburetor. The 421 Super Duty could be ordered in the Catalina and the Grand Prix.

New cylinder heads with larger valves and double valve springs, a new cam, and more compression (either 12.0:1 or 13.0:1) raised the stakes further in the Super Duty in 1963. The valve springs allowed the 421 SD's redline to increase from 6000 to 6400 rpm. Horsepower on the single 4-barrel SD (which carried 12.0:1 compression) was 390. If you ordered the dual 4-barrels you got either 405 (12.0:1 compression) or 410 (13.0:1 compression).

There was also a high-output 421 released for street cars in '63, with a more reasonable 10.75:1 compression and either a single 4-barrel carb or the famous Tri-Power setup. The engines were rated at 353 horsepower at 5000 rpm and 455 lbs.-ft. of torque at 3400 for the single 4-barrel, 370 horsepower at 5200 rpm and 460 lbs.-ft. at 3600 for the "trips." It should be noted that Pontiac redesigned its engine block that year so that it would be lighter.

When Pontiac released the intermediate-size GTO in 1964, it marked a turning point in the development of the muscle car. The full-size Super Stocks, like the Catalina, Chevy Bel Air, and Ford Galaxie, were suddenly going out of fashion. GM's renewed adherence to the AMA racing ban in 1963 caused its divisions to shift their emphasis away from race packages with little street value to "packaged" machines that offered plenty of showroom appeal, better drivability, and increased profits. That spelled doom for the fabled Super Duty cars.

When the GTO was unveiled, its 389 engine benefited greatly from what was learned on the racetrack. The 421 HO cylinder heads (with 1.92/1.66-inch [49/42mm] valves, intake/exhaust) flowed quite well. The GTO used a block with 2-bolt main caps and 10.75:1 compression. The 4-barrel version used a Carter carb and made 325 horsepower at 4800 rpm and 428 lbs.-ft. of torque at 3200, while the Tri-Power version utilized a trio of Rochester 2-barrels bringing the tally to 348 horsepower at 4800 revs and 428 lbs.-ft. at 3600. The engine ran primarily off the center carb; the end units opened via a vacuum diaphragm when the center 2-barrel was more than two-thirds open.

In '65, the GTO's 389 had reworked cylinder heads and intake manifold to produce more airflow. If you ordered Tri-Power and a 4-speed, you got a longer-duration camshaft, not to mention mechanical carburetor linkage. These changes helped increase horsepower to 335 on the base 4-barrel versions and to 360 for the Tri-Power cars. This was also the year Pontiac began selling an over-the-counter Ram Air (RA) setup so that owners could make the car's new hood scoop functional.

Not much changed for '66, although the Ram Air package got you a more radical camshaft as well. Late in the model year, it appears that a number of cars were produced on the factory assembly line with this package, beginning a legacy that lasted for years. This was, however, the last hurrah for Tri-Power as GM banned multiple carburetor induction systems on passenger cars for '67 (with the exception of the Corvette, which was considered a sports car). This was also the swan song for the venerable 389, which was superceded by the 400 in '67.

The 421, though never installed in the GTO, soldiered on as an option in the larger Pontiacs, such as the Catalina 2+2 and Grand Prix. Through '66, you could order a 421 HO with Tri-Power, good for 376 horsepower at 5000 rpm and 461 lbs.-ft. of torque at 3600.

Pontiac's Ram Air option in the GTO was a real screamer in '67. It came with a Quadrajet 4-barrel carb, a radical street camshaft, and D-port cylinder heads with dual valve springs (to prevent valve float). Those heads were bolted to a newly sized 400-cubic-inch engine, which was a 389 with a 0.060-inch (1.5mm) overbore. Incredibly, a set of 4.33:1 rear end gears were standard. It used an open-element air cleaner that it shared with the 400 HO, which was the middle high-performance engine in the lineup, sandwiched between the base 335-horse 4-barrel and the Ram Air V8. There was also a low-compression, 255-horse "economy" 400 2-barrel for those who wanted the GTO image with fewer trips to the gas station. Both the HO and the Ram Air 400 were rated at 360 horsepower, the former at 5100 rpm and the latter at 5400. The Ram Air engine was obviously underrated. The actual equipment that made the Ram Air system functional—the tub that went under the carburetor and foam that sealed it to the hood—was shipped in the trunk and installed by the dealer prior to delivery.

The cylinder heads also underwent a major redesign in '67. The valve entry angles were altered and larger 2.11/1.77-inch (54/45mm) (intake/exhaust)

This '65 GTO wears factory redline tires (U.S. Royal 7.75x14s) and aftermarket Hurst wheels.

valves were fitted. The 4-barrel manifold was redesigned for improved flow and was based on an early Super Duty part.

Best of all, the fantastic Ram Air GTO engine was available in somewhat detuned trim in the Firebird when it was introduced in February 1967. General Motors did not allow a car to be rated at more than 1 horsepower for every 10 pounds of vehicle weight, so the 400 was rated at 325 horsepower in the F-body. Internally, the engine was the same; the main differences were a more restrictive exhaust system and a kink in the linkage of the Quadrajet carb that kept the secondaries from opening fully. Straighten the linkage and you'd gain back much of the missing 35 horsepower. Ram Air was available on this 400 at extra cost, though the power rating was the same.

Another Firebird engine of note was the 326 HO, which used the 400's stroke but with a cylinder bore of just 3.72 inches (94mm). It had high compression (10.5:1) and made 285 horsepower and 359 lbs.-ft. of torque. It was the only Firebird V8 that year to use a Carter carburetor.

More horsepower arrived in '68. Though the heads had new combustion chambers for cleaner emissions, the base engine was rated at 350 horse,

The 1973–74 Super Duty 455 engine was the last salvo fired in the muscle car wars. Originally, the engine was to find a home in the GTO as well as the Firebird lineup, but the manufacturer of the connecting rods couldn't produce enough rods so Super Duty 455 became a Firebird exclusive.

15 more than the previous year. Also, the 360-horse HO carried over with 360. But the big news was the April 1 introduction of the Ram Air II V8. The new engine retained its 400 cubic inches, but the cylinder heads had larger intake and exhaust ports (the exhaust ports were now round). An even more radical camshaft was employed, one with 0.475-inch (12mm) lift and 308/320-degree duration. The valvetrain components were all heavy-duty and the valves were tulip-shaped for improved flow. (It is currently thought that automatic transmission–equipped versions got a less radical camshaft than 4-speed models.)

The 4-bolt-main block from the previous Ram Air engine was retained, but was now fitted with forged pistons. Even with all these changes, Pontiac rated it at only 366 horsepower and 445 lbs.-ft. of torque. Once again, the Ram Air hardware was shipped in the trunk and dealer-installed.

Gone from the Firebird was the 326 HO, replaced by a new 350 HO. It was the same engine block with a larger bore, but it also got new cylinder heads with larger valves. Horsepower was up to 320. It went up again the following year, when it borrowed the heads off the 400 with larger 2.11- and 1.77-inch (54 and 45mm) valves.

In '69, two new options made the scene with the 400, while the base mill got a hotter cam if you ordered a 4-speed (its horsepower rating remained 350, however). The Ram Air III became available with functional hood scoops. It had D-port heads, a cast-iron intake, and cast-iron headerlike exhaust manifolds. As in years past, it had a different cam for manual- and automatic-transmission versions. It was rated at 366 horsepower at 5100 rpm and 445 lbs.-ft. of torque at 3000. Essentially, it was 1968's 400 HO with a driver-controlled cold-air system.

But it was the Ram Air IV that caused the biggest stir. It replaced the Ram Air II as the top engine choice for the GTO. Supposedly named for a prototype four-scoop ram induction system that never made production, it had all the good stuff from the factory—round-port heads, an Arma steel crank and rods, forged pistons, a recalibrated

Quadrajet carb on an aluminum intake, and 4-bolt main caps.

For a cam, the RA IV got a 0.520-inch (13mm) lift stick with 308/320-degree duration (intake/exhaust). It was the most powerful GTO mill to date, with 370 horsepower at 5500 rpm and 445 lbs.-ft. at 3600. It was available with only 3.91 or 4.33:1 gears. Both the RA III and RA IV utilized 10.75:1 compression, and the scoops could now be opened or closed by the driver via a dash-mounted lever.

Pontiac was finally allowed to install engines larger than 400 cubic inches in its intermediate cars in 1970, but unlike Buick, Oldsmobile, and Chevrolet—which used 455-, 455-, and 454-cubic-inch mills, respectively, for their top performers—Pontiac took a different approach. The Ram Air IV 400 remained the most powerful engine in the lineup, while a 455 (a 400 with a larger bore and longer stroke) was available for those who preferred torque to all-out horsepower.

Dubbed the 455 HO, it was an undersquare engine with a bore of 4.15 inches (105mm) and a stroke of 4.21 inches (107mm). This prevented it from being much of a revver, one of the reasons Pontiac cited for not installing the Ram Air IV's free-breathing, high-rpm induction components. It used the D-port 400 heads with 2.11/1.77-inch (54/45mm) valves, a Ram Air III cam in 4-speed models, a dual-plane cast-iron intake, and a Rochester Quadrajet carb. Compression was just 10.25:1, half a point lower than the norm for a high-output GTO engine. (Actually, compression dropped to 10.0:1 on the base 400 when you ordered the automatic transmission and to 10.25:1 if you ordered the base motor and a stick. On all other optional 400s, it was also down, from 10.75:1 to 10.5:1.)

In its maiden season, the 455 HO produced 360 horsepower at a low 4600 rpm and 500 lbs.-ft. of torque at 3100, making it a good choice if you liked your GTOs laden with plenty of comfort-producing options. If you wanted a 455 HO in 1970, you had to order an intermediate. The big-inch motor was not available in the Firebird lineup until 1971.

Compression dropped further in 1971, to 8.2:1 for the 400s and 8.4:1 for the 455 HO. As the muscle car era began to wane, the hottest engines quickly disappeared. Gone were the Ram Air III and IV. The base 400 was down to 300 horsepower.

The good news for the GTO and Firebird was that Pontiac reversed itself and decided to install the round-port heads on the 455 HO, though the company used the standard 455 valvetrain parts. The 455 HO didn't have the Ram Air IV's radical camshaft, but it did still employ the good Ram Air II and III cam. Rated at 335 horsepower, this turned out to be one of the best-performing Pontiac street engines ever.

The 455 HO came back for '72, now quoted at 300 horsepower thanks to GM's change to net power ratings.

Remarkably, while other manufacturers were throwing in the proverbial towel, Pontiac unleashed one last great muscle car engine. In 1973, it unveiled the 455 Super Duty, reviving that great name from its fabled past. Unlike the engines of old, it had an emissions-friendly low compression ratio of 8.4:1.

Credit for the 455 SD is generally given to engineers Herb Adams and Tom Nell. The 455 SD was supposed to receive the Ram Air IV cam, but the engine would not pass emissions tests with it so a milder camshaft was chosen. The engine used unique cylinder heads. The intake ports were made 0.125 inch (3mm) wider by sleeving the pushrod holes with steel tubes and moving the port wall to the edge of the tube. They were also 0.125 inch (3mm) higher. On the exhaust side, the ports were recontoured. Both intake and exhaust were said to flow 20 percent better than any Pontiac head previously used.

To take advantage of the high-rpm capability (it would rev to 6200 rpm), the bottom end had to be reengineered. The main webs of the cylinder block were reinforced around the bulkheads, and 4-bolt bearing caps were used on all five mains. It used a cast crank, but it had forged connecting rods. It was topped with a single 4-barrel carb.

The 455 SD was rated at 310 net horsepower at an absurdly low 4000 rpm and 415 lbs.-ft. of torque at 3600 in 1973. What made this even more impressive is that it came out the same year in which federal emissions standards for hydrocarbons and carbon monoxide were considerably tightened and nitrogen oxide standards were introduced. The following year, the horsepower rating on the Super Duty was down to 290 net. But its birth in the same year as the 1973 Arab oil embargo was like a death sentence. Few people ordered Super Dutys—43 SD Formulas and 252 SD Trans Ams were built in the first year, and just 57 Formulas and 943 Trans Ams were sold the next. That accounted for every Super Duty ever sold to the public. The option was killed in 1975.

Ironically, the SD engine was never offered in the GTO. It was slated to be offered in that car in 1973 when it was still built on a midsize platform, but that plan fell through when the manufacturer of the connecting rods informed Pontiac that it wouldn't be able to supply them if the engine was offered in any other models.

The Cars

PART TWO

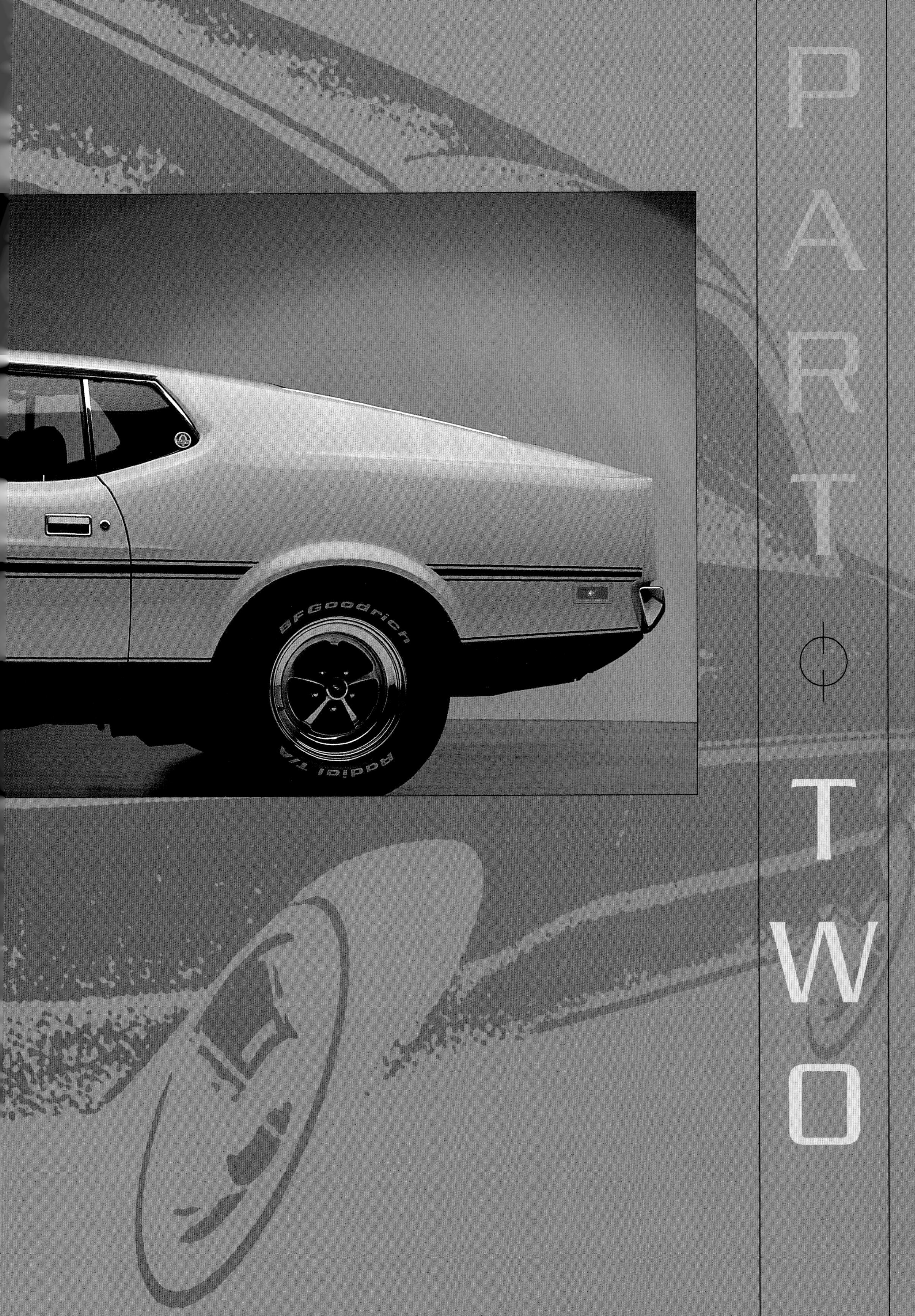

A-body (Chrysler Corporation)

This was Chrysler Corporation's internal code for the unibody platform upon which its lineup of compact cars was based. A-bodies included the Dodge Dart (1963–1976) and Demon, as well as the Plymouth, Barracuda (1964–1969), Duster, and Valiant.

A-body (General Motors)

This was the internal code for the platform upon which the midsize cars of General Motors were based during the muscle car era. A-bodies included the Pontiac GTO (as well as the Tempest and LeMans), the Chevelle (and Malibu), the Oldsmobile 4-4-2 (and Cutlass), and Buick Gran Sport (and Skylark). The A-body muscle cars utilized a 115-inch (292cm) wheelbase when they were introduced, beginning with the GTO in 1964, and were of traditional body-on-frame construction. The first major revamping of all of these cars occurred in 1968, and at that time the wheelbase was decreased to 112 inches (284.5cm). The last true intermediate GM supercars were the 1972 models, though much less powerful versions of the GTO and 4-4-2 were offered in 1973.

Sox & Martin

Ronnie Sox was called Mr. 4-Speed and was considered the quickest shifter in drag racing back in an era when race cars still used factory transmissions. He and partner Buddy Martin formed a team that devastated the competition from the early '60s to the early '70s.

Both Martin and Sox were running 409 Chevrolets in the very early days, and Sox was so good that Martin would often ask him to drive Martin's car. At the end of the '62 season, Martin told Sox that he was getting a '63 Z-11 427 Chevy and asked if Sox would like to drive it. That January, Sox won his first time out in the car. They finished '63 in the Chevy, even though the factory had pulled its support in February.

For '64, the pair secured a factory deal with Ford to drive a 427 A/FX Comet. In their first race, Sox used a holeshot, to beat the other factory Comet driven by "Dyno" Don Nicholson off of the line to win the race, even though Sox ran slower than his opponent. The team switched to Plymouth the following year, driving a radial Altered Wheelbase Hemi car. Though the NHRA disallowed them in competition, Sox & Martin (with engines built by Jake King) went on the match race circuit, where they made tons of money and won tons of races.

After one year in a Funny Car, Sox & Martin returned to the Super Stock ranks with much success. The team's level of professionalism elevated the entire class, and the pair won the Springnationals Super Stock title for three consecutive years.

When the NHRA formed the Pro Stock class in 1970, no one could beat Sox & Martin. They won three of the seven events in 1970, six more in '71, and had three world championships to their credit. So dominant were they that the NHRA eventually rewrote the rules so that the Fords and Chevrolets could be competitive.

The rules swung so far the other way that Sox & Martin were no longer competitive themselves, and in 1975 the team shut down. In 1998, the pair teamed up, for what was probably the last time, to run NHRA Pro Stock Truck.

Altered Wheelbase Mopars

Due to the limits of tire technology in the mid-1960s and the traction available on the starting line of the era's drag strips, harnessing the excessive horsepower produced by the supercharged and fuel-injected race engines of the day was problematic. Chrysler's engineers came up with a solution that involved altering the wheelbase of its race cars.

The first change involved moving the front and rear wheels forward by 2 percent, the maximum allowed under class rules at the time. These Dodges and Plymouths, of which a total of only four were built, appeared in late 1964 and became known as the Two Percent cars, or Two Percenters.

But the Two Percenters were just an interim solution. After the 1965 National Hot Rod Association (NHRA) Winternationals, Chrysler engineers took the concept one step further. By moving the rear wheels forward by 15 inches (38cm) and the front wheels by 10 inches (25.5cm), they created what came to be known as Chrysler's Altered Wheelbase cars.

Chrysler built six Dodge Coronets and six Plymouth Belvederes in this configuration, hoping that the NHRA would revise its rules against changing the wheelbase by more than 2 percent on its Factory Experimental cars. The NHRA did not, and the cars were relegated to running in the Altered classes. Their odd appearance helped coin the term "Funny Car," a class that exists to this day in NHRA competition.

American Motors Corporation (AMC)

AMC was founded in 1954 as the result of a merger between Nash-Kelvinator and Hudson, two long-standing but faltering automobile companies. Though Hudson Hornets had played a major role in the early days of NASCAR stock car racing, AMC was best known in the early 1960s for its spartan Rambler line of cars.

Roy Abernathy became AMC's president and chairman in 1962, replacing George Romney, who had resigned from AMC in order to run for governor of Michigan (he was successful in this endeavor). Abernathy was less wedded to AMC's traditionally conservative products, and the first public demonstration of this was at the Tarpon show car in 1964 with a fastback design based on a 106-inch- (269cm) wheelbase American chassis. That car would lead to AMC's first foray into the fringes of the youth market, the 1965 Marlin, which was actually built on the longer Classic chassis.

In 1966, the AMC badge replaced the Rambler tag on the Marlin and the full-size Ambassador line. AMC nearly went broke in 1967, forcing Abernathy to retire, but the sale of Kelvinator, the company subsidiary that made appliances, and the arrival of the Javelin ponycar in 1968 helped the company return to solvency. By 1968, the Rambler name applied only to its compact American/Rogue models. American Motors made up for lost time by introducing a slew of high-performance models by the end of the '60s and early '70s, including the AMX, the Hurst SC/Rambler, and the Rebel Machine. AMC sponsored a number of successful drag teams, including Shirley "The Drag-On Lady" Shahan. Craig Breedlove, well known for setting land speed records at Utah's Bonneville Salt Flats in the Spirit of America jet-powered car, was enlisted by AMC in February 1968 to drive an AMX at Goodyear's Texas test track. By the time he was finished, 106 new records had been set.

In the late 1960s and early 1970s, AMC branched out into both road racing and drag racing. Buoyed by its success in the Sports Car Club of America's Trans-Am road race series (which at the time was composed of production-based automobiles) in 1968 and 1969, AMC lured the dominant team of owner Roger Penske and driver Mark Donohue away from Chevrolet in 1970 to run AMC's Trans-Am racing efforts. Although the team of Penske and Donohue struggled in 1970, it won the Trans-Am championship in 1971 and 1972 running Javelins. AMC sponsored a handful of factory Gremlin and later Hornet Pro Stock drag racing teams as well, the success of which was mixed.

Eventually, in the 1980s, AMC and its Jeep subsidiary (purchased from Kaiser in 1970) merged with French automaker Renault, a less-than-successful venture. Chrysler Corporation, itself nearly out of business on numerous occasions, purchased AMC in the early 1990s, primarily for that highly profitable Jeep lineup. Chrysler kept Jeep alive, killed off American Motors, and sold AM General, maker of the Hummer military vehicle, to General Motors.

AMX (1968–1970)

In the 1950s, American Motors Corporation claimed in its advertising that the only race it was interested in was the human race. Just about ten years later, the AMX arrived on the scene to eradicate this corporate edict once and for all. Performance was in, and the AMX was AMC's flagship vehicle. This two-seat sports car was introduced midway though the model year in February 1968. It had been given the go-ahead for production by AMC chairman Robert Evans and rode on 97-inch (246cm) wheelbase. A stretched version of the AMX got a backseat and was produced as the Javelin, and the two cars shared many parts. The standard engine in the '68 AMX was the 290 V8, but it had more potent optional powerplants, including the 343 V8, which produced 280 horsepower, and the 390, which had 315 horsepower and 425 lbs.-ft. of torque.

Further fortification came in the form of the Go Package, which for a little more than $200 delivered either the 343- or 390-cubic-inch engine, E70×14-inch (35.5cm) tires on 6-inch (15cm) rims, a suspension that improved handling, power disc brakes, Twin-Grip differential, a heavy-duty cooling system, and racing stripes. Inside was a tachometer and a 140-mph (225.5kph) speedometer. Just less than 7,000 AMXs were built in this abbreviated model year (6,725, to be precise), enough to consider it a success.

For the most part, the 1969 AMX was a carryover vehicle, but AMC did combine with Hurst Corporation to build a limited-run (52 or possibly 53) of Hurst AMX S/S drag-only race cars. The S/S stood for Super Stock, which was a popular class in NHRA racing. The Hurst AMX S/S machines came with specially prepared 390 engines that had dual 650-cfm 4-barrel carburetors (as opposed to a single 4-barrel on the standard-production AMX 390) on

With its "Ramble Seat" and fastback roofline, the AMX concept car of 1966 whet the public's appetite for the production AMX and Javelin, which would arrive in 1968.

Right & Below: In 1969, American Motors teamed up with Hurst to produce the limited-production AMX S/S drag car. Just more than fifty were built with special high-performance 390 engines, and naturally, Hurst shifters for their transmissions.

Opposite inset: Dick Teague (left) poses with the still beautiful AMX/3 concept car. Only a handful of these cars were actually produced and it was Teague's crowning achievement in the design field.

a cross-ram aluminum Edelbrock intake manifold. Performance was further enhanced by higher-than-stock compression (12.3:1), Doug Thorley exhaust headers, and other modifications. The price was $5,994, quite a bit of money for the day, especially considering that the base AMX started at $3,297. Today, the Hurst AMX S/S cars that have survived are worth quite a bit, with top examples fetching more than $30,000—far more than any other American Motors product.

Another significant event in 1969 was the introduction of the Big Bad colors for the AMX and Javelin. Big Bad Blue, Big Bad Green, and Big Bad Orange were psychedelic hues more luminescent than anything that had been seen before. They were announced via press release on January 14 and lasted until 1971, when a handful of Jeeps were painted Big Bad Orange. A Hurst shifter became an option for the AMX's 4-speed Borg-Warner transmission that year as well. Thanks in part to positive press reports, production increased slightly, to 8,293 units, the highest total for the three-year run of two-place AMXs.

The year 1970 was the last for the AMX as a stand-alone model; for 1971 this was an option package on the four-place Javelin. The two-seat AMX received a minor face-lift for 1970. Its grille was redesigned and the hood received an effective front-facing and functional hood scoop. Under that hood, the 343 grew to 360 cubic inches, thanks to an increase in the length of its stroke. Horsepower was up by 10, to 290, for the 360, and the 390 was rated at 325. Torque was likewise up, from 365 to 395 lbs.-ft. The 390 remained virtually unchanged; it grew to 401 cubes the following year, again thanks to a lengthened stroke.

For 1970, the taillights on the AMX no longer wrapped around the car onto the body sides, instead ending just past the edges of the rear decklid. The popular Big Bad colors (sans painted bumpers) remained on the option sheets, as did the Go Package. Another interesting paint option, available in 1970, was the Black Shadow, alias the Shadow Mask, which for an extra $52 delivered a two-tone AMX with the hood, cowl, and tops of the front fenders painted black, among other perks. A total of 982 cars received the one-year-only Shadow Mask treatment.

AMX production slid to a mere 4,116 units, and although the decision to halt production had already been made (much to the dismay of loyalists), this figure shows that it was a sound business move.

AMX (concept car)

AMX stood for American Motors Experimental. This 1966 concept car was a preview of what American Motors would be offering in showrooms in 1968. Designed under the direction of styling boss Richard "Dick" Teague, it displayed the basic shape of AMC's upcoming production two-seat sports car (also called the AMX), but its back end design incorporated a rumble seat for extra passengers,

a portent of its four-place ponycar, the Javelin. Since it was from AMC, known then for its Rambler line of automobiles, this seat was dubbed a Ramble Seat. The concept car differed from the production 1968 AMX style-wise in that the rear end treatment had no bumpers, side exhaust pipes were utilized, and the front end carried rectangular headlamps, but it was a dead giveaway of the future to sharp-eyed viewers.

AMX II (concept car)

The AMX II was also shown in 1966, but it carried a more formal roofline than the AMX and sported hide-away headlights plus chrome bumpers. While the AMX concept car was nearly a dead ringer for the '68 AMX production car, the side body sculpturing of the AMX II was similar to the Ford Mustang and seemed strangely similar to the yet-to-be-introduced 1967 Mercury Cougar.

AMX/2 and AMX/3

Designed in-house by a team of staff members headed by AMC styling chief Dick Teague, the AMX/2 was a mid-engined two-seat sports car concept that was introduced in February 1969 at the Chicago Auto Show. It looked like it could have come from the finest coach builders in Italy. A revised version of this vehicle, the AMX/3, was built by Bizzarrini in Italy and introduced at the International Automobile Show in New York on April 4, 1970. Styled by Teague, the AMX/3 was powered by a midship-mounted, 340-horsepower 390 V8 engine and is still considered to be one of the most beautiful concept cars ever. Reaction to the AMX/3 was so positive that a small run of production cars (twenty-four annually) was planned. Unfortunately, U.S. government regulations and cost overruns killed the program after five (or possibly six) cars were built. AMC ordered these cars destroyed, though it is known that some survived.

Richard "Dick" Teague

"You gotta love automobiles and have gas in your blood," was Richard "Dick" Teague's motto. Having spent nearly fifty years in the automotive business, including twenty-three as head of styling at American Motors, he surely fit the description of his motto.

He started his formal career at General Motors and shortly thereafter moved to Packard, where he ended up as chief stylist when the person who hired him quit. Packard was not financially stable in the mid-1950s and eventually Teague left to go to Chrysler, where he stayed for just a year and a half.

In September 1959, Teague joined American Motors as the assistant director of styling. Within five years, he was vice president of AMC. His first memorable design was the Tarpon show car, a fastback sporty model. Unfortunately, the size of the car was not embraced by AMC

president Roy Abernathy, who decided to adapt the basic shape to the larger Rambler Classic. The result was the Marlin, a car that didn't translate well in its new size and was virtually ignored by the public.

The design that solidified Teague's reputation was the AMX show car, which was a short-wheelbase two-seater with a rumble seat that popped up in its fastback. The Mustang was a runaway success at this point and American Motors knew it had to respond. The company couldn't afford to build production versions of both the AMX and a stretched adaptation called the Javelin, so it went with the latter, a four-seater. When Robert Evans became chairman of AMC, he gave the go-ahead to build both for 1968 as long as the AMX and the Javelin shared a lot of common parts to keep costs down.

The 1968 AMX is considered a modern classic; the Javelin, while not as pure a design, was very successful. In its maiden season, the Javelin outsold the established Plymouth Barracuda and helped AMC turn a profit for the first time in years. The two-seat AMX design lasted for three years, after which it became a top-of-the-line model based on the four-place Javelin. Among Teague's later creations that caused a stir (for better or worse) were the gorgeous AMX/3 show car, a mid-engined sports car that never made production, and the Gremlin and Pacer, which (some would say unfortunately) did make production.

Dick Teague passed away on May 5, 1991.

These pages: This 1969 Baldwin-Motion SS427 Camaro had many options. It has both the SS and RS packages, Z/28 front and rear spoilers, and a 435-horse power 427 Corvette engine. A hood-mounted tachometer was also an option for this model.

Baldwin Chevrolet/Motion Performance

During the muscle car era, it was not uncommon for new car dealers to become heavily involved in racing, selling speed equipment, and sometimes even adding performance goodies to their new car offerings. Certain dealerships took this one step further, and Baldwin Chevrolet in Baldwin on Long Island, New York, was one of them. It teamed up with a young entrepreneur named Joel Rosen, whose speed shop was located just down the road on Sunrise Highway, to crank out some of the most outlandish automobiles of a truly outrageous era.

Rosen had opened his first speed shop in Brooklyn, New York, in the late 1950s and bounced around a bit until finally settling on Long Island in 1966. When his speed emporium was thriving, he approached Baldwin Chevrolet with a plan to allow customers to purchase cars from the dealership with all the popular go-fast parts of the day already installed; Baldwin Chevrolet would supply the cars and Rosen the know-how, cosmetics, parts, and wrenching. In 1967, the Baldwin-Motion cars were born when the two entities introduced the Fantastic Five, which consisted of modified big-block Camaros, Corvettes, Chevelles, Chevy IIs, and full-size Chevrolets (like the Biscayne).

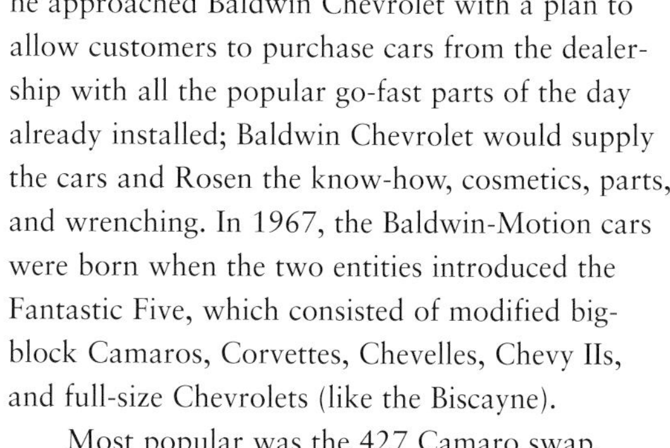

Most popular was the 427 Camaro swap. Because of a General Motors edict at the time, the individual divisions could not sell cars with engines larger than 400 cubic inches of displacement except for full-size models and Corvettes. The most potent Camaro engine option, therefore, was the 375-horsepower 396. Rosen took such a Camaro and swapped in a 425-horsepower 427 Corvette engine, which was available over-the-counter. With race headers, the modified Camaro rated at 450 horsepower.

And that was just the beginning. If you checked off the correct boxes, you could get a full-on 500-plus-horsepower, dyno-tuned Phase III L88 Camaro, which was guaranteed to run 11-second times at the drag strip or your money back. In fact, a 500-horsepower Phase III Camaro was tested by *High Performance Cars* magazine in the March 1968 issue and was clocked at 11.5 seconds in the quarter mile at 125 mph (201kph).

Later, Rosen offered the Z/30, which was a high-performance 350-powered Camaro. For $5,495, your factory Camaro got a special solid-lifter cam and kit, a dyno-jetted 850-cfm carburetor, a unique fiberglass hood, and traction bars, among other goodies. For another thousand dollars, you could order the Z/50, which was a Z/30 with a turbocharged engine.

The same corporate edict that limited the Camaro to engines smaller than 400 cubic inches also applied to the midsize Chevelle, and Rosen did not disappoint here, either. The radical powerplant offered in the Baldwin-Motion Camaro was also available in the Chevelle. In fact, the last Phase III car Motion ever produced was an L88-powered '73 Chevelle. The car was meant to be driven hard, and the engine was modified to produce more than 550 horsepower. It came with a 4-speed transmission with an aftermarket Hone overdrive unit for more relaxed cruising, a Motion Mallory ignition, Hooker headers with sidepipes, and a Lakewood blowproof bellhousing, but interestingly enough the original owner used it for years as a daily driver between his home in New Jersey and his job in Manhattan. It was the only Phase III Chevelle built that year and cost a staggering $12,030.

Even though you could purchase a 427 in a Corvette from the factory, the factory couldn't give you Rosen's special touch to the car. He added his own scoops and body work, which was similar in design to that of the Chevrolet Mako Shark II and Manta Ray concept cars. There were also plenty of engine modifications available to back up the super-tough looks. In its March 1969 issue, *Super Stock & Drag Illustrated* magazine tested a Phase III Vette, which sailed through the traps in 12 seconds flat at 115 mph (185kph).

Full-size Chevrolets got headers, dyno tunes, and special wheels and tires. But by the end of the '60s, there wasn't nearly as much interest in these models. They grew larger by the year, and there was more performance available for less money in smaller packages.

Before the supercar era ended and the EPA (Environmental Protection Agency) swooped down on Motion Performance with a cease-and-desist order, Motion unleashed on the streets unbelievable vehicles such as 427 Novas and 454 Vega compacts. It was the 454 Vega, Rosen said, that caused the EPA to threaten to close him down. Even though he maintained that these extreme vehicles were for off-road use only (they had been stripped of every emissions-control device mandated by law), the EPA felt that as long as they had headlights, wipers, and

other roadgoing equipment, they were street cars. The fines would have been enough to put Rosen out of business, so in 1974 he abandoned the new-car game to concentrate on selling aftermarket speed parts and fiberglass body panels, the bulk of his business today.

The collectors have not forgotten the Fantastic Five or Sensational Six (the sixth being the V8 Vega). Today, Baldwin-Motion cars are highly sought-after by collectors, and Rosen has the documentation to verify which cars are authentic and which are fakes. He charges $1,000 to document a car and has never revealed how many B-M automobiles were produced, though the number is believed to be less than five hundred.

Banshee

This name was applied to a couple of Pontiac concept cars produced in the early 1960s. At the time, Pontiac general manager John DeLorean had the idea for an economical two-seat sports car, one that would not compete with the Corvette but would provide fun transportation, nimble handling, and brisk acceleration. In 1963, he had two running prototypes built, both called the Banshee. One was a 6-cylinder coupe, the other a V8 roadster. Both featured beautiful styling and were designed to be sold at a cost less than $2,500.

In 1966, the name surfaced again on another two-seater, but General Motors wasn't about to give in to DeLorean's wishes. GM wanted no competition—real or imagined—for the Corvette, which had finally become profitable after the introduction of the 1963 Sting Ray model. DeLorean's bosses astutely argued that there was more of a market for a four-place ponycar that could go head-to-head with the Mustang.

When it was decreed that Pontiac would offer its own version of the Chevrolet Camaro for production in 1967 (despite DeLorean's objections), the car was originally supposed to be called Banshee—at least until someone found out that the word was defined as a Gaelic spirit that wailed about the approaching death of a family member. At this point, Pontiac culled a name from an earlier 1950s concept car, the Firebird.

The Banshee name would not go away forever, however. It resurfaced in the 1970s on two Pontiac show cars. The first was based on a 1973/1974 Super Duty 455 Trans Am, the second an updated version of the first with different wheels and taillights. At a glance, the profiles of both were similar to the 1975 Chevrolet Monza 2+2. Both also used the "window within a window" side glass that would later appear on the Lamborghini Countach and the Irish-built DeLorean DMC-12 sports car.

Barracuda

Few would have believed that, from its economy car roots, this compact Plymouth with the big, glass fastback window would eventually evolve into one of the elite—if not most desirable of all—muscle cars by 1970. The Barracuda was Plymouth's entry into the small specialty-car segment in the spring of 1964. While most people credit the Ford Mustang with single-handedly creating this niche, the Barracuda was rushed into production and beat the Mustang into the market by two weeks. (To be fair, sporty versions of Chevrolet's Corvair, most notably the turbocharged Spider, actually appeared years earlier, but neither car had the impact on the market that the Mustang did.)

The Barracuda was based on sound mechanicals, the sturdy A-body platform, which it would have in common with the Plymouth Valiant and Dodge Dart. While the Barracuda and Valiant would share a great number of parts (early Barracudas even had both Valiant and Barracuda emblems on them), the Barracuda was different in a number of ways, such as the grille, which was sportier and featured inboard round turn signals.

The interior of the Barracuda had bucket seats up front and fold-down rear seats, which allowed you to take advantage of the car's most distinctive styling element, its enormous fastback rear window. With the seats in the folded position, you had nearly as much room as in a small station wagon—an excellent feature for young families, but one that never really caught on with the baby boomers to which the car was marketed.

For '64, the car was little more than a gussied-up Valiant. It wasn't until 1965, when Plymouth introduced the exciting Formula S package, that the Barracuda began to show its teeth a bit. The Formula S option retailed for $258 and gave the purchaser an awful lot of quality equipment for the money. In addition to special trim, the package included an upgraded 273-cubic-inch V8 with an unusual, high-flow single exhaust system; a revised suspension with thicker torsion bars, a sway bar up front, and higher rate leaf springs in the rear; larger drum brakes; and 14×5.5-inch (35.5×14cm) wheels, available with Goodyear Blue Streak tires, which were considered cutting edge for sports cars at the time.

The engine itself was quite a bit stronger than the base 273, which came with only a 2-barrel carburetor. Compression was increased to 10.5:1 and a Carter AFB 4-barrel carb was employed, as were a high-output camshaft and low-restriction exhaust manifolds. Horsepower was rated at 235 at 5200 rpm, with 280 lbs.-ft. of torque at 4000. With 55 more horsepower than the low-performance 273,

a Formula S Barracuda could scoot through the quarter mile in the high-15- to mid-16-second range, a huge improvement.

Equally important was the fact that it handled extremely well, perhaps better, road testers of the day said, than its rival the Mustang GT. "More than the Mustang or the Corvair, the Barracuda—in its high-performance configuration—is a car that must be driven to be appreciated," noted *Car and Driver* magazine in its October 1964 issue. A front sway bar made a huge difference (in fact, a sway bar was not even available on the standard car), as did extra leaf springs in the rear, a total of six instead of four and a half.

The following year, the Barracuda received a nose job and, for better or worse, looked almost exactly like the low-line Valiant. Mechanically it was virtually a carryover, and sales fell by nearly a third. But there were big plans for 1967. The Barracuda remained on the A-body platform but received an all-new body and interior—three new bodies, actually. Like its competition from Dearborn (the Mustang), the 1967 Barracuda was available as a hardtop coupe, a fastback, and a convertible.

The styling of all three was remarkable devoid of gimmicks and excess chrome, prompting *Car and Driver* to dub it "unquestionably, the best-looking

For 1966, the hottest Barracuda available was the Formula S, which had a 235-horsepower 273 engine, a vastly improved handling suspension, and stripes that ran the length of the hood, roof, and deck. The one pictured here has a non-stock decal aft of the front wheels.

Right: The Rallye Instrument Panel Group was optional on the 1974 'Cuda and included a 150-mph (241.5kph) speedometer and 7000-rpm tach. A Pistol-Grip shifter was standard with the 4-speed. The optional console was not ordered on this car.

car out of Detroit in 1967." Plymouth's designers embraced the "longer, lower, wider" mantra prevalent at the time and produced a vehicle that was every bit as stylish as the Mustang, if not quite up to the standard set by the new Chevrolet Camaro and Pontiac Firebird.

Mechanically, the engine compartment was widened 2 inches (51mm), allowing engineers to shoehorn the excellent 383-cubic-inch big-block under the hood. Rated at 280 horsepower (45 less than the 383 available in midsize and larger Plymouths) at 4200 rpm and 400 lbs.-ft. of torque at just 2400, the new Barracuda (dubbed by media and car aficionados as simply the 'Cuda) was more than 1 second quicker at the drag strip than the 273 Formula S of 1965–1966 and capable of 92-mph (148kph) trap speeds. In fact, *Super Stock & Drag Illustrated* reported times as quick as 14.53 at 97 mph (156kph).

Of course, in the speed-crazed 1960s, no manufacturer could stand pat for very long, and 1968 saw Plymouth unleash all sorts of mayhem on the competition. For small-block fans, Chrysler delivered the 340, an updated, enlarged, and much-improved version of the 273/318 small-block (internal code: LA engine family). This came in only an underrated 275-horsepower configuration and was a perfect match for the reasonably light 'Cuda. In fact, it ran as quick as and sometimes quicker than the 383 Formula S.

As if the 340 weren't enough, Plymouth saw fit to upgrade the 383 to 300 horsepower. But the biggest blow to the competition was the Hurst-built Hemi 'Cuda (see *Hurst Hemi Barracudas and Darts* for complete details). This limited-production race car (and its Dodge cousin, the Hemi Dart) rewrote the NHRA record books and continues to dominate the track in Super Stock racing in the new millennium. In its April 1968 issue, *Car Craft* magazine tested a version set up for Super Stock A/Automatic, and at 3,000 pounds

Below: To commemorate Plymouth's latest entry into the SCCA's Trans-Am series, the AAR 'Cuda (for Dan Gurney's All American Racers team) was built.

Left: The AAR 'Cuda was a 1970-only model and featured 3M tape stripes running the entire length of both sides of the car.

(1,362kg), the Hurst 383 ran the quarter mile in 11 seconds at 130 mph (209kph).

When Plymouth put the 383 in the '67 Barracuda, many in the press wondered why Plymouth didn't just use the 440, which was similar externally (the block was raised) and made significantly more power. Chrysler Corporation did just that in 1969, with the largest displacement engine to that point ever offered in a ponycar. Two magazines on the West Coast tested 440 'Cudas: *Popular Hot Rodding*, which posted a 14.47 at 99.66 mph (160.5kph), and *Car Life*, which went 14.00 at 103.8 mph (167kph).

The year 1969 was also the first time that the 'Cuda name was officially used by Plymouth. Long the car's nickname on the street, Plymouth offered the 'Cuda Performance Package on coupes and fastbacks. At first, you could order either the 'Cuda 340 or 'Cuda 383, but later came the 'Cuda 440.

Despite these muscle car powerplants, 'Cuda, now in its third year of a styling cycle, suffered a sales setback, down to just about 27,000 units. The 'Cuda was in a tough position. It was facing an uphill battle in the ponycar market, taking on the likes of the Mustang, Camaro, Firebird, and AMC Javelin while struggling in its own showroom with the Plymouth Road Runner, which was a runaway success from the moment it was introduced in 1968. For comparison's sake, the Mustang outsold the Barracuda by more than ten to one in 1969, the Road Runner by three to one.

Optional Billboard stripes for 1971 boldly announced your engine displacement. The 'Cuda came standard with a 383 4-barrel V8 and high-intensity driving lights. A Shaker fresh air hood (shown) was optional. The '71 Barracuda was the last Plymouth convertible built in the 1970s.

There was, however, a mean school of fish swimming into town.

For 1970, Chrysler unveiled a pair of exciting ponycars, a new-from-the-ground-up 'Cuda and the appropriately named Dodge Challenger. Both cars were built on the E-body chassis, a modified version of the intermediate B-body. Styling of both cars was nothing short of spectacular, and the bigger, wider chassis allowed Plymouth to install the fabulous 426 Street Hemi in the 'Cuda on a factory assembly line.

The new 'Cuda was available in two body styles, a coupe and a convertible. Though riding on the same 108-inch (274.5cm) wheelbase, the 'Cuda was 3.3 inches (8.5cm) wider, 2.2 inches (5.5cm) lower, and 6.2 inches (15.5cm) shorter. It looked nothing like its predecessor and garnered rave reviews in the press. All 'Cuda models came with a nonfunctional twin-scooped performance hood as standard equipment; a functional Shaker scoop, mounted directly to the carburetor(s) and sticking up through the hood, was an option.

Among its other unusual features were optional Elastomeric bumpers, which were made of a durable, rubberlike material; a collapsible spare

tire; driving lights (fairly uncommon in 1970); and special soft-touch plastic door panels and interior trim. This last item, which was considered cutting-edge at the time, proved not to live up to its designers' hopes. Instead of the quality material they tried to achieve, the soft-touch plastic felt fairly hard and cheap.

Regardless, the 425-horsepower Hemi (now with hydraulic lifters) was optional, as was the 440 Six-Barrel from the Road Runner, making the 'Cuda one of the muscle car elite. *Car Craft, High Performance Cars,* and *Hot Rod* magazines all tested Hemi 'Cudas in 1970, and the results were among the best ever for a production car. *Car Craft* reported 13.10 at 107 mph (172kph), *High Performance Cars* 13.34 at 105 mph (169kph), and *Hot Rod* 13.39 at 108.17 mph (174kph).

A new model was added to the 'Cuda stable for 1970. Plymouth was making a big push into Trans-Am racing, a series for stock-bodied sedans that to this point had been dominated by the Mustang and Camaro. In honor of Dan Gurney's All American Racers team, Plymouth dubbed this sporty new car the AAR 'Cuda. The emphasis was handling (with a special suspension and the unusual feature of having different-size tires for the front and the rear), but the engine was not left alone, either.

Like its 440-inch, 6-barrel big brother, the AAR 'Cuda's 340-cubic-inch engine wore a trio of Holley 2-barrel carburetors on a special Edelbrock manifold. A reinforced block and different cylinder heads were unique to the AAR and its Dodge counterpart, the Challenger T/A. Side exhausts were also standard equipment, but they were very restrictive (in order to meet federal drive-by noise standards) and ended up cutting actual engine output. While the AAR rated at 290 horsepower (same as the Boss 302 Mustang and Z/28 Camaro), Chrysler engineers later said that actual output because of the exhaust was about the same as the single 4-barrel version of the 340, which was still 275.

The AAR 'Cuda wore unique striping on its sides, a blackout paint treatment on its hood and top of its front fenders, and an AAR-only fiberglass hood, which had a molded-in functional air scoop, as well as front and rear spoilers. Plymouth finished a disappointing fifth in the actual Trans-Am series in 1970, although the car did well in the sales department with 2,724 sold.

Barracuda sales surged compared to 1969, with more than fifty thousand units delivered, but the end was near. Increasing government regulations, the insurance industry, and other factors were beginning to take their toll on performance models. For '71, the 'Cuda got a sharp face-lift, with quad headlights, wild front fenders with four gills cut into them, and slightly different taillights. Gone, however, was the AAR, not to mention buyer interest. Sales plummeted to just more than eighteen thousand, a huge disappointment, even in a downturn sales year. For muscle car fanatics, this was the last year for the Hemi, the 440s, and the 383. Mopar convertibles also bit the dust this year.

For 1972, Plymouth revised the 'Cuda's grille, reverting to a single headlamp design reminiscent of the '70 model, but with the turn signals in the lower valence instead of the upper grille. Out back was the most unusual change—a switch to four round taillamps, which looked like they'd be more at home on a Corvette or a Camaro.

The top engine option for '72 was the 340, now producing 240 net horsepower. It was still capable of 14-second quarter-mile times, but it was a long way from the low 13s of the Hemi and 440 Six-Barrel monsters of the previous year. By 1974, the only "performance" engine was the 360 4-barrel, which produced 245 horsepower. Sales slumped further, to fewer than ten thousand, and this was the last year for the Barracuda.

B-body

This was the internal designation used by Chrysler Corporation for its intermediate-size lineup of automobiles. Introduced in 1962, cars with B-body platforms employed unibody construction, which meant that the body itself was a major component of the chassis. While not considered muscle cars by the later standards of the 1960s (they lacked pizzazz and styling panache), the downsized 1962 Dodges and Plymouths with 413 Max Wedge engine power were among the quickest running cars built during the supercar era. What held these cars back, sales- and image-wise, was their controversial styling, which was considered somewhat unusual to say the least.

In the B-body's favor, however, was its sound and, in many cases, advanced engineering. And by the mid-1960s, the styling started to come around as well. Chrysler based its most formidable street offerings on the B-body platform during the 1960s and 1970s, including the Dodge Charger, R/T, and Super Bee; and the Plymouth Road Runner, GTX, and Superbird. Dodge, being the more upscale division, built its B-bodies on a wheelbase 1 inch (2.5cm) longer than that of the Plymouth, 117 versus 116 inches (297 versus 295cm). The difference in wheelbase length was implemented more for marketing purposes than for any serious engineering principle.

Right & Below: With 409 horsepower, the 409 engine was tough to beat in 1962. The 409 was available in any full-sized Chevrolet including this Bel Air coupe. The coupe body was lighter than the hardtop.

Dave Strickler

A native of York, Pennsylvania, Dave Ziegler Strickler began racing a 348 Chevy Biscayne in 1959. One day at Lancaster Speedway in Pennsylvania, the Chevy was running a bit poorly and the steward at the track took a look at it. That man was Bill "Grumpy" Jenkins, who adjusted the tuning of the motor so well that the car ran better than ever. Soon the pair teamed up on a series of Chevy drag cars. However, in 1963 when the General Motors' renewed ban on auto racing left them without a factory sponsor, the pair campaigned a Dodge.

In 1960, when Strickler's racing budget got tight, he worked out a sponsorship deal with Ammon R. Smith Chevrolet in his hometown for the 1961 season. The result of that deal was a 409 Biscayne, the first car to sport the Old Reliable logo, which was the dealership's motto. The team of Strickler and Jenkins was quite successful as they traveled around the country match racing the Chevy.

For '62, Strickler and Jenkins took delivery of a 409-horse Bel Air, which became the Old Reliable II. They racked up almost 150,000 miles (241,350km) traveling the United States, winning races and setting records wherever they went.

Old Reliable III was one of the rare Z-11 aluminum front end Impalas, which put it in the B/Factory Experimental class. Even meaner than its predecessors was Old Reliable IV, which had the Z-11 lightweight sheet metal but also the special 427-cubic-inch version of the W engine. It used a 4-speed transmission, vented metallic brakes, a unique cowl with induction air cleaner, and Positraction. Old Reliable IV won about 90 percent of the two hundred races in which it ran.

After the GM racing ban, Strickler and Jenkins teamed up for one season in Mopars, a factory-backed '64 Dodge Max Wedge, and two lightweight Hemi sedans. In '65 the team split when Jenkins got his own ride, the Black Arrow Hemi Plymouth. Strickler's factory ride was an Altered Wheelbase Hemi '65 Coronet. By '66, Strickler was back driving Chevys, including Camaro Super Stocks. He even teamed up with Jenkins in '69 and '70 to produce a series of performance seminars and youth auto safety clinics at Chevy dealerships.

Strickler retired from drag racing after the 1974 season and died of a heart attack while mowing his lawn on June 6, 1985.

Bel Air and Biscayne

Although the Impala was the top dog in the Chevrolet performance car lineup in the early 1960s, the same muscle-bound engines available in the Impala could be ordered in the lower-priced Bel Air and Biscayne models. The Biscayne was the lowest of the low price-wise and was available only as a two- or four-door sedan, while the Bel Air was a step above and available as a hardtop.

The best news for 1960 was the availability of the 348-cubic-inch W engine, which was offered with up to 335 horsepower, not to mention a genuine 4-speed manual transmission. There were four versions of the 348 offered in the full-size Chevrolets that year (at this point in time, the only non-full-size cars offered were the Corvette sports car and the compact Corvair, neither of which got the 348), three of which were designed with high output in mind.

First on the list was the 305-horsepower version. It had 11.0:1 compression, a single 4-barrel carburetor, and dual exhausts, and it kicked out 350 lbs.-ft. of torque. Next up was the 320-horsepower version, which had a high-lift, solid-lifter camshaft, a single 4-barrel carb, dual exhausts, and even more compression (11.25:1).

For the ultimate hot Chevy in 1960, though, you ordered the 335-horsepower 348, which had all the goodies of the 320-horse engine but came with a trio of Rochester 2-barrel carbs on a special, free-breathing intake manifold. Off the showroom floor, there was little that could touch a 335-horse 348 Biscayne or Bel Air in 1960. In fact, from 1960 to 1962, a 348 Chevrolet won the B/Stock class championship at the NHRA Winternationals, as well as the U.S. Nationals in 1960 and 1961.

By 1961, the high-output 348, first introduced in 1958, had reached its pinnacle of development. It was now advertising 350 horsepower with Tri-Power carburetion. But the mighty 348 gave way later in the year to a new engine that would become a legend. The 348's block was redesigned to allow for a bigger bore and longer stroke, and born was the "real fine" 409, but only 142 were produced in 1961, all of which went into the sportier Impala model (see *Impala* for complete details).

While the 1961 Biscayne and Bel Air continued to ride on a 119-inch (302.5cm) wheelbase, the body on the car was all-new. The styling excesses of 1959 and 1960—excess chrome and bat-wing fins—gave way to a toned-down tour de force. Even the low-level Biscayne coupe was an attractive car.

But it was the Bel Air (and even more so the Impala) that came with what became known as a bubbletop hardtop roof, which set a styling standard for years to come. The interior was also new, and with a recessed, horizontal speedometer, a Corvette-style grab handle for the passenger-side dash, and plenty of bright colors available, the Bel Air was just as exciting on the inside.

Under the hood, the 348 was now available with 305, 340, or 350 horsepower, the last with three 2-barrel carburetion. The full-size Chevrolets continued to employ the same chassis design introduced in 1958.

By 1962, the hardworking 348 had been replaced entirely by the stronger 409, and you could get it into the Biscayne and the Bel Air

Chevrolet updated its styling every year, but since the '50s Bel Airs and Biscaynes got two taillights per side, and the upscale Impala got three. This is a '62 Bel Air.

without difficulty. The "base" 409 came with a single 4-barrel carburetor, dual exhausts, 11.0:1 compression, and churned out an impressive 380 horsepower at 5800 rpm and 420 lbs.-ft. of torque at 3200. *Car and Driver* tested such a Chevy and it registered 14.9 at 94 mph (151.5kph) at the drags, very impressive for the day.

A dual 4-barrel 409 was available as an extra cost option and produced 409 rated horsepower and 420 lbs.-ft. of torque. All 409s came with redesigned cylinder heads that had larger ports and valves, and both intake manifolds were new as well. At this point both 409s had solid-lifter camshafts, a sign that they were meant for high performance, as was the fact that only manual transmissions were available behind the 409, the 3-speed as standard with most opting for the 4-speed. To give its readers an idea of the potential of the dual quad 409, *Car Life* drag tested a dual quad Bel Air set up for NHRA Super Stock competition, and it went 12.2 seconds in the quarter mile at 115 mph (185kph).

As was the custom, styling was altered again for '62, and the entire lineup of full-size Chevrolets was slightly more formal. The fastback bubbletop roof of 1961 was now available only on the midline Bel Air. The Biscayne was still offered only as a two- or four-door sedan. The Impala had a more formal, squared-off roofline that was designed to look more like a convertible top.

The Bel Air was the favorite among drag racers and NASCAR Grand National pilots. The former liked it because it was lighter and carried fewer frills than the upscale Impala SS, while the latter preferred it for its more aerodynamic fastback roofline. The 409 was a major player that year at drag strips nationwide, with "Dyno" Don Nicholson, Dave Strickler, Butch Leal, and Hayden Profitt all enjoying a great deal of success. By the end of the season, a run of cars was built with aluminum body panels that pared 130 pounds (59kg) off the car. These parts could also be available over-the-counter.

As for NASCAR, Chevrolet experienced the thrill of victory quite often in 1962. It went to the winner's circle fourteen times that year, second only to Pontiac, which won twenty-two of fifty-three events.

The year 1963 saw another face-lift for the full-size Chevrolets, and gone was the pretty bubbletop. All models came with the formal roofline of the previous year's Impala. The solid-lifter 409 engines, while virtually identical to the '62s, were now rated at 400 and 425 horsepower (with single 4-barrel and two 4-barrel carburetion, respectively).

For those who wanted 409 power but without the headache of solid lifters and ultrahigh compression ratios, a new 340-horse model was available. This engine came with a smaller single 4-barrel carburetor, hydraulic-lifter camshaft, and 10.0:1 compression (which still required premium fuel). It came with a 3-speed manual as standard equipment. Optional was a wide-ratio 4-speed manual transmission or a heavy-duty Powerglide automatic.

In 1963, General Motors announced that it was getting all its divisions out of racing, adhering to the AMA ban first agreed to in 1957. This decimated a multitude of NASCAR and drag racing teams. Anyone serious about racing looked to Ford and Chrysler for support. This action also killed off some very promising engine, chassis, and suspension development. Overnight, the aluminum body panels, 427-cubic-inch W motors, and other developments were gone. Where Chevrolet won fourteen NASCAR races in 1962 alone, it won only eleven between 1964 and 1971—the height of the muscle car era.

The same 409 street engines were carried over into 1964, which saw the big Chevys wearing extremely conservative styling. The shift for the larger cars was moving ever increasingly away from performance, a trend that began in the mid-1950s with the Chevy Power Pack and fuel-injected small-blocks, and more toward comfort and luxury. The introduction of Pontiac's GTO in 1964 only accelerated this process. From here on, buyers were leaning more toward intermediates like the SS Chevelles and later the ponycars, like Ford's Mustang and Chevy's Camaro.

In 1965, the full-size Chevrolets were new from the ground up. The X-frame introduced in 1958 was gone, replaced by a full perimeter frame. The wheelbase remained 119 inches (302.5cm), but overall size and weight were up significantly, another move that hurt performance. Still, the 409 hung in there (minus the two 4-barrel version) until the midyear release of the all-new 396-cubic-inch big-block V8.

A descendent of the fabled Mark II Mystery Motor of 1963, it featured splayed valves, far superior breathing, and limitless potential.

Two variations of the Turbo-Jet 396 were offered in the full-size Chevrolets in 1965, a hydraulic-lifter version with 10.25:1 compression and 325 horsepower and a full-bore 425-horsepower variant with solid lifters and 11.0:1 compression. The combination of a strong national economy, extraordinary new styling (especially compared to the Ford of the same vintage), and increased luxury and performance made 1965 a banner year for Chevrolet's large cars. In fact, the division's total production was a record 2.3 million cars.

The following year, Chevrolet showed remarkable restraint, merely tweaking the styling of the big boats, but it bored the cylinders of the 396 from 4.09 to 4.25 inches (10.5 to 11cm), delivering a total of 427 cubic inches. This massive powerplant now delivered 390 horsepower in hydraulic-lifter trim and an underrated 425 with solids. A 4-speed transmission was still available in the Bel Air and Biscayne with the 427, and though they didn't sell extremely well, they could be real sleepers on the street.

The 425-horsepower L72 427, introduced in 1967, was available in the full-size Chevys through the end of 1969, but sales tapered off toward the end of the decade. *Super Stock & Drag Illustrated* got its hands on a 425-horsepower Biscayne for testing in 1968 and recorded a 13.65/105-mph (169kph) drag strip time. The emphasis had shifted away from full-size muscle cars. Chevrolet's new 454 (a stroked 427) was offered in 1970, but it wasn't a true performance engine.

Belvedere

When people think of muscle cars, the name Belvedere is rarely the first to come to mind, or even the last. But in 1962, this model from Plymouth was one of several to receive the magnificent 413 Super Stock engine (the others from Plymouth being models that shared the same basic body, unibody chassis, and interior, such as the low-buck stripper Savoy and the higher-end Fury and Sport Fury).

Below & Bottom: The 1967 Belvedere GTX was Plymouth's answer to the Pontiac GTO. It had the 375-horse 440 standard, and the only optional V8 was this 425-horse, dual quad 426 Hemi. Hemi convertibles were always rare.

Plymouth (and sister division Dodge) downsized all its cars for 1962, both believing that the public wanted smaller cars and mistakenly thinking that Ford and Chevrolet were going to be downsizing their full-size models. While the former might have been true to some extent, the latter wasn't the case, and Plymouth and Dodge ended up with their full-size cars being only slightly larger than their rivals' intermediates.

On the plus side, the Belvedere could accommodate the powerful B (383) and RB (413) Chrysler engines. The 413 Super Stock—also known as the Max Wedge—employed lots of hard-core racing hardware, including TRW forged aluminum pistons, a hardened crankshaft, and stronger-than-stock connecting rods. It used a radical camshaft, heavy-duty valve springs, big-port cylinder heads, and dual Carter AFB 4-barrel carburetors on a short-runner (15 inches [38cm]) cross-ram intake manifold.

The 1963 Max Wedge was basically a carryover engine, with the exception of the bore, though it did have an improved oiling system and slightly larger ports for the heads. But on July 23 of that year, things changed dramatically as Chrysler introduced the Stage II Max Wedge. The cylinder heads, cam, valve springs and carburetors (among other things) were upgraded for increased performance, although the official ratings never changed. See *Dodge/Plymouth (Big-Blocks)* in Part I for more details.

For the most hard-core enthusiasts, Plymouth offered aluminum front end panels in 1963. This package included fenders, fresh air scooped hood, splash shield, and aluminum bumper brackets, among other minor pieces. Plymouths so equipped were the only Super Stock cars to come with their batteries mounted in the trunk from the factory (for improved weight distribution and traction). Less than one hundred of these Max Wedge cars were built.

As strong as the Stage II cars were, Plymouth wasn't resting on its success. The following model year saw the unveiling of the Stage III Max Wedge and the legendary 426 Race Hemi. The Stage III had a radical new cam, stiffer valve springs, and extensive cylinder head refinements, even though it had the same horsepower rating as before. The hemispherical headed 426 was the first of its kind since the early Chrysler Hemis of the 1950s (which were among the fastest street and race cars of their era).

The new Hemi was a race-only piece and was available only in a lightweight or steel-bodied drag

A flip-open gas cap was standard on the '67 GTX, but the hood stripes, decklid stripes, and vinyl roof were options.

car or in a steel-bodied NASCAR stocker. Fifty-five Race Hemis were built for both Plymouth and Dodge in '64, and were quite underrated at 425 horsepower at 6000 rpm.

For 1965, Plymouth made things somewhat easier for its customers. Belvedere was now the name given to the entire line of Plymouth intermediates, rather than a trim level, and the Fury nameplate was attached to its new line of larger cars. The Savoy designation was history, as Belvedere I was now the cheapest of the cheap, right down to its blackwall tires. Belvedere II had more trim, carpeting on the floor as opposed to a rubber floor mat, special trim and upholstery, foam seat cushions, and backup lights.

The top-of-the-line Belvedere was now the Satellite. All Belvedere models were available with a total range of optional V8s: 318 polyspherical, 361, 330-horsepower 383, and the 426-S, which was essentially a long-stroke 383 rated at 365 horsepower. This engine was based on the Chrysler's B engine, not to be confused with the RB 426.

It is important to mention that while the 413 and 426 Belvederes get most of the notoriety, the 383-powered cars were very strong runners in their own right, capable of hanging with most muscle cars that had similar displacement. What they lacked in the public's eyes was the panache of a full-on GTO. The Belvederes lacked image enhancers like hood scoops, redline tires, and fancy wheels. The Belvedere name itself was rather bland, whereas Pontiac had stolen the GTO moniker from a Ferrari.

The most radical of all '65 Belvederes were the Altered Wheelbase Race Hemi models. A pair of Two Percent Plymouths debuted at the NHRA Winternationals in Pomona, California, that year by Al Eckstrand (Golden Commandos team car) and Tommy Grove ("the Melrose Missile"). While the length of their cars' wheelbase was the same as a stock Belvedere, the front and rear wheels were moved forward by 2 percent in an effort to improve traction. But these cars were nothing compared to those that came next, which were radically different (see *Altered Wheelbase Mopars* for complete details).

When the now-legendary 426 Street Hemi debuted in 1966, it was optional in any of the completely restyled Belvedere bodies except for the station wagon. Those looking for the most comfort or prettiest body would order the 425-horsepower Hemi in a Belvedere II or Satellite hardtop, while the savvy racer or hot rodder trying to sneak up on the competition would order that engine in the nondescript Belvedere I two-door sedan. With a rubber floor mat and minimal options, it looked like a taxi, but it was the lightest possible model in which to put the Hemi.

The Street Hemi was a $907.60 option package that gave you a detuned race engine with 10.25:1 compression. Included in the Street Hemi package were stiffer torsion bars and rear springs, metallic brake linings, and Goodyear Blue Streak tires, among other goodies. Mandatory was either the heavy-duty TorqueFlite automatic or the 4-speed manual transmission.

Car and Driver tested a Street Hemi Satellite when it first came out, and the car recorded a 13.8-second quarter-mile time at 104 mph (167.5kph). Top speed was 130 mph (209kph). Aided by the Hemi's 490 lbs.-ft. of torque, 60 mph (96.5kph) came up in 5.3 seconds.

For the record, there were approximately fifty Race Hemi Belvederes produced in 1966.

For 1967, Plymouth introduced its first "packaged" muscle car, the Belvedere GTX. Standard under the hood was the Super Commando 440 Wedge-style engine, which pumped out 375 horsepower at 4600 rpm and 480 lbs.-ft. of torque at 3200 rpm. This was the largest engine available in any intermediate muscle car except its Dodge R/T cousin, which shared the 440.

In 1960 the Bonneville could be ordered with the 318-horse 389.

The GTX came standard with a pair of non-functional scoops (optional were two hood stripes which ran the length of the body overhead). Inside, the GTX had a much-improved interior with handsome bucket seats (many were built with an optional console). Not surprisingly, the underpinnings were upgraded for improved handling.

A total of fifty-five special code Street Hemi cars were built to take the place of the Race Hemi, which was no longer available. The option code was RO23 for the Plymouths, and these had ram induction hoods with a seal for the carburetor in the trunk (along with a set of tubular exhaust headers), a distributor without a vacuum advance, retuned carburetors, and an intake manifold modified by racer Arlan Vanke. The cars were sold without a sound deadener or heaters for weight reduction.

Berger Chevrolet

Located in Grand Rapids, Michigan, Berger sold hundreds of specially prepared Camaros, Chevelles, Novas, and other Chevrolets at the height of the muscle car era. What makes it so interesting is that the company is still in business and owned by the Berger family after more than seventy-five years.

Berger, in fact, was still turning out specially prepared Camaros in 2001, and these cars featured some of the tricks made popular by the dealership a generation earlier—chambered exhaust, a "Prescribed Power by Berger" decal, a metal "by Berger" rear emblem, and custom wheels.

Bonneville

While the Bonneville name bespeaks luxury today, there was a short period of time in the early 1960s when this Pontiac could be equipped with real

muscle car engines. In the late 1950s, you could order a fuel-injected model, though this was exceedingly rare. In 1960, the same three 2-barrel-equipped 389 available in the Catalina, Ventura, and Star Chief (making 318 horsepower and 430 lbs.-ft. of torque) could be had in the big Bonnie.

Certainly not a muscle car in the strictest terms, the Bonneville could be ordered with as much as 348 horsepower in '61 and '62. In 1963, the 370-horsepower 421-cid engine (with 6-barrel carburetion) was released. It was a beautiful car with a lot of style—a true executive hot rod.

Bullitt Mustang

The movie *Bullitt*, starring the late Steve McQueen as San Francisco police detective Lt. Frank Bullitt, is notable for one of the most significant car chases in cinematic history. Driving a specially prepared 1968 Mustang GT with a 390-cubic-inch V8, McQueen rips through the streets of the hilly California city in pursuit of a pair of hit men in a black 1968 Dodge Charger. For nearly eight minutes, the two muscle cars careen through the city, literally flying through the air and skidding across major intersections before heading onto the highway.

The Bullitt Mustang (there were actually two used for the film) was modified by noted race car builder and driver Max Balchowski. Stronger springs, Koni shocks, and American Racing Torq-Thrust "D" rims with wider-than-stock tires improved cornering, while the 390 engine received enough tweaks that it could keep up with the Charger during filming.

After two weeks of shooting, the primary car was so severely damaged that it was sent to the crusher because of liability concerns. The backup car, less damaged but far from perfect, was sold to an employee of the Warner Bros. editing department. The movie and the '68 Mustang became such icons that, in 2001, Ford Motor Company introduced a specially prepared, limited-edition Bullitt Mustang, with a tricked-out suspension, unique 265-horsepower engine, and Bullitt-only interior appointments (including 1968-style Mustang gauges for the speedometer and tachometer) and trim. Each car was serialized with an underhood dash plaque and hidden identification marks to prevent forgeries.

Pete Brock

Today he is a highly regarded automotive journalist whose specialty is race reporting and especially race photography. But as a stylist in the 1950s and '60s, Pete Brock was the main player on two projects that would become legendary.

At nineteen, Brock was the youngest automotive designer ever at General Motors. He was hired by Chuck Jordan, who later became GM's head of styling. While at GM, Brock did design work on the Stingray sports racer, a car that set the tone for the '63 Corvette.

Brock's crowning achievement came when he worked at Shelby American. He was the main designer of the body for the Cobra Daytona Coupe, which won the FIA International Grand Touring World Championship. Though refined by Phil Remington, the basic shape was Brock's concept. Only six Daytona Coupes were ever built, all in 1964, and they are worth seven figures today.

Brock formed Brock Racing Enterprises in 1966, which built and campaigned Datsun 2000 roadsters and 510 sedans in sports car competition during the late 1960s and early 1970s. Both were wildly successful and are highly sought after today.

Camaro

For roughly two and a half years, Ford Motor Company had no real competition in the small specialty car segment, a niche that became known as the ponycar market because of the runaway success of the Mustang. That all changed with the introduction of the Chevrolet Camaro in the fall of 1966.

Unlike the Chevy Corvair, which was given a major overhaul in 1965 and maintained its rear-mounted, air-cooled engine, the Camaro was a conventional American car. The Camaro had a watercooled engine in front, its differential in the back, lots of power, and a ton of options—plus it had the long-hood, short-deck styling made popular by the Mustang. The Camaro may have been late to arrive on the scene, but it made a bold statement when it got there.

The Camaro was based on the Chevy II/Nova chassis, which combined unibody construction out back with a bolt-on subframe up front. It shared some of the Corvair's design cues on the interior, but there was no mistaking it for an economy car. Styling on the first-generation Camaro was under the direction of Henry Haga, and it is one of the cleanest-looking automobiles of the era. The Camaro was available in two body styles—a two-door hardtop and a convertible—and came standard with a modest 6-cylinder engine.

But that only tells part of the story. Taking a nod from the Mustang, the Camaro was available in a staggering number of models, colors, engines, and transmissions. You could also order virtually every option in the Chevrolet catalog—eighty-one, to be

Right: Chevrolet built 69 Camaros in 1969 with the all-aluminum 427 ZL-1 engine. The ZL-2 cowl-induction hood (shown) was standard on every 427 Camaro built that year.

precise—from power windows to automatic speed control. If that weren't enough, another forty-one dealer-installed options were available.

At first, muscle car fanciers were a little disappointed. The hottest engine was the new 350 4-barrel in the Camaro SS. This was the first use of the enlarged small-block and it produced a respectable 295 horsepower. It was good enough for high-14- to low-15-second ETs at the track, but when Ford announced it was putting the 390 in the Mustang, Chevy responded with the 325-horsepower 396. But that was only a stopgap measure. Late in the model year, the Chevelle's 375-horsepower, solid-lifter 396

Above: This 1967 Camaro has the RS option package, which consisted of (among other things) hideaway headlights, parking lights mounted in the front valence, body lower side moldings, and RS badging. This example sports an aftermarket tachometer on the steering column and aftermarket gauges under the dash.

This Dana 427 Camaro has SS and RS options. Its hood was unique to the Dana 427 Camaro.

finally became available, but it was fairly uncommon, with only 1,138 produced. Camaro 396s are highly prized by car collectors and Camaro enthusiasts alike.

The 396 didn't help the Camaro's already nose-heavy weight distribution, but it was a bona fide muscle machine. Tested in *Motor Trend* magazine, a 325-horsepower SS with a 4-speed transmission recorded a strong 14.5 quarter-mile time at 95 mph (153kph), although in stock trim the rear suspension wasn't up to the task of harnessing all that torque (410 lbs.-ft.) and horsepower. The 375-horsepower 396 (RPO code L78) was a true high-performance engine, with a Holley 4-barrel carb, solid-lifter camshaft, and 11.0:1 compression. Launching an L78 car, with 415 lbs.-ft. of torque on the stock tires of the day, was usually a lesson in futility, but 14-second quarter-mile times were possible.

Of all the option packages, the one that became a legend almost instantly was one that sold very few copies, at least initially. In order to compete in the SCCA's Trans-Am road race series, Chevrolet needed a powerful engine, but displacement was limited to 305 cubic inches. Using a trick made popular by hot rodders, Chevy engineers put a crankshaft from a 283 into a 327 block. Thus was born the 302-cubic-inch engine, and it would go in a car called Z/28.

Available on the coupe only, RPO Z/28 was more than just a strong engine (it was rated at 290 horsepower). This was a total package, with revised spring rates, quicker steering, and front disc brakes among the goodies. A set of 15×6-inch (38×15cm) wheels held 15×7.35-inch (38×18.5cm) red-stripe tires. The cooling system was also upgraded, dual deep tone mufflers gave a healthy exhaust note, and 3.73:1 gears were standard (Positraction recommended).

As with the 396, the Z/28 option was not available at the start of production. It was a midyear option and one that was not pushed heavily. Still, it garnered an instant reputation as a giant killer on the street. The high-winding 302 could propel the Z/28 to high-14-second ETs with the standard rear gearing, but it was the car's handling that got people's attention. Of the 1969 Z/28, *Hot Rod* stated, "The Z/28 can shame some rather expensive machinery without any chassis alteration. There're no suspension options for it; they are all standard."

The Z/28 proved its worth in the Trans-Am series as well. With Mark Donohue behind the wheel, the Camaro won the SCCA crown in 1968 and 1969. In fact, the team of Donohue and owner Roger Penske dominated the series in 1969, setting records that weren't broken for years. Camaro won ten of the thirteen Trans-Am races in '68, all with Donohue behind the wheel, and eight out of twelve in '69. With the addition of steeper rear end gears, open exhaust headers, and tuning tricks, the Z/28 could be a standout drag racer as well.

While the '67 Camaro had a nearly overwhelming choice of engines, the one that was missing, the one many enthusiasts cried out for, was the 427. Externally, it was nearly identical to the 396 and therefore fit the same, but it was more engine than corporate edict said was prudent for such a light passenger car. This opened the floodgates for numerous enterprising dealerships nationwide, such as Nickey Chevrolet in Chicago, Dana Chevrolet in southern California, and Yenko Chevrolet in Pennsylvania, to build and sell their own cars (see individual dealers' entries for complete details). Suffice to say they did pretty good business. And the 427 Camaros were superpotent performers, capable of 11-second quarter-mile times with slicks, gears, open headers, and other simple tricks.

Chevrolet sold a whopping 220,906 of its new Mustang fighters in 1967—including an unspecified number of Indy 500 pace car replicas, all-white RS/SS convertibles with blue interiors. Chevrolet wisely did not mess with the Camaro too much the following year. The side vent windows went away for good in 1968, replaced by what Chevrolet called Astro Ventilation, which drew air into the interior from grilles on the cowl.

Up front, there was a more pointed split in the center of the standard grille, and rectangular parking lights replaced the round units of '67. If you ordered the RS option, you still got hideaway headlamps, but they were now vacuum-operated instead of electric. For the first time a rear spoiler was available, and it made its way onto 15,520 vehicles. In a move to help traction and quell axle hop on non-327 V8 cars, the single leaf springs in the rear were replaced with multileaf springs and the rear shocks were staggered; the driver's-side unit was mounted ahead of the axle and the passenger-side shock behind it.

The muscle car engine lineup remained virtually unchanged, with two exceptions: a hydraulic-lifter, 350-horsepower 396 was added, and RPO L89 provided a 375-horsepower 396 with aluminum cylinder heads, which are the rarest 396s around.

Above: This is part of the factory's optional gauge cluster for 1968. The tach and clock were mounted in the dash, and the amp, water temperature, fuel level, and oil pressure gauges were affixed to the console.

Left: Aluminum heads were a $710.95 option on the '69 L78 396.

Perhaps the most beautiful Camaro ever was the 1970–1972 SS or Z/28 with the RS option. Part of the RS package was the split front bumper. This is a '72 SS/RS.

The former was moderately popular, popping up in 2,579 cars, while the latter, at $868.95, was pricey and found its way onto only 272 vehicles. *Popular Hot Rodding* tested a '68 L78 Camaro (sans aluminum heads), which ran 14.09 at 99 mph (159.5kph).

Sales of the RPO Z/28 exploded, increasing more than tenfold. A total of 7,199 '68 models were ordered, and the hardware was getting more interesting. A cold-air package and tubular exhaust headers were available but since GM was technically not racing, racing-type parts couldn't be installed on the assembly line, so they came loose with the car.

Things only got better for 1969. Styling was revised and while it echoed the original design themes, it was more broad-shouldered, more muscular. The grille cavity was much larger, and a functional cowl induction hood designed by noted Corvette stylist Larry Shinoda was optional under RPO ZL2. The fenders had pronounced body lines that streaked toward the rear of the car. If you went for the RS option, hideaway headlamps were still used but now appeared as three slits. Much of the sleekness and purity of the original design was gone, but it was a smash hit with the buying public. Thanks to an extended model year (due to a United Auto Workers [UAW] strike), sales of the '69 tallied a whopping 243,045. The '69 has become the most popular Camaro among enthusiasts, the benchmark by which all others are judged.

Among the unusual nonperformance RPOs were two one-year-only items: headlight washers (CE1), which were standard on the Rally Sport, and liquid tire chain (V75), which sprayed a traction compound on the rear tires to aid traveling in the snow. Only 188 people chose to spend the $23.20

for the tire chain, while the headlight washers proved even less desirable, making it onto only 116 non-RS Camaros.

More than anything, though, the 1969 Camaro was about mind-bending performance. All the heavy hitters from 1968 were back, though the 350 in the SS was now rated at 300 horsepower. A special cross-ram, dual 4-barrel intake and a fiberglass cowl hood were available as dealer-installed options. Four-wheel disc brakes became an RPO, making Camaro the only American car besides the Corvette to offer them.

This was also the year that Chevrolet finally relented and offered the 427 in the Camaro, albeit in limited quantities. The engine could not be found in the option books, but you could get one through a Central Office Production Order (COPO). If you wanted a 425-horsepower 427 with an iron block and heads, COPO 9561 was what you ordered. Yenko Chevrolet ordered 201 of them, and other dealers got in on the action as well (see *COPO* for complete details).

Of all the hell-raising engines installed in the Camaro, none was quite like the ZL-1 427. Because these cars were meant strictly for Super Stock drag racing and were produced in extremely limited numbers (sixty-nine were eventually built), Chevrolet never made a specific exhaust manifold for the oval-port heads. Racers would swap in tubular headers anyway, so the logic was why bother.

Cars magazine got a ZL-1 Camaro in pure street trim with closed exhausts and factory rubber to run 13.16 at more than 110.21 mph (177.5kph), though this was hardly indicative of the car's race performance. Cars set up for drag racing with blueprinted engines were moving 130 mph (209kph) in the 10s.

The price for all this excitement was $4,160 just for the engine. A full-on ZL-1 Camaro sold for about $7,800, which included a close-ratio 4-speed transmission, a fresh air cowl hood, and the Z/28 suspension.

When the 1970 Camaro was finally introduced in March of that year, it was similar under the skin, but the body was completely new. Only one body was available, a two-door coupe, and it was universally praised as one of the most beautiful designs ever out of Detroit. Once again, it was Henry Haga who was in charge of Camaro styling, under the direction of vice president of design Bill Mitchell. The car was only 2 inches (51mm) longer, but the passenger compartment was moved 3 inches (76mm) aft for better weight distribution. This created an even longer hood and shorter deck and improved weight transfer for drag racing.

Two grille designs were offered: a traditional full-width bumper and a split-bumper Endura nose if you ordered the Rally Sport (RS) option. Hideaway headlamps were no longer part of the package, but the RS was a brilliant execution that looked even more spectacular once the gigantic federally mandated 5-mph (8kph) bumpers began appearing on cars beginning in 1973. The roofline was 1.1 inch (28mm) lower than in 1969, but it appeared even sleeker thanks to the futuristic styling. At the tail were four round taillights, à la Corvette. The radio antenna was now hidden in the windshield glass.

The interior was totally revamped as well. Unlike the first-generation F-body, all gauges were

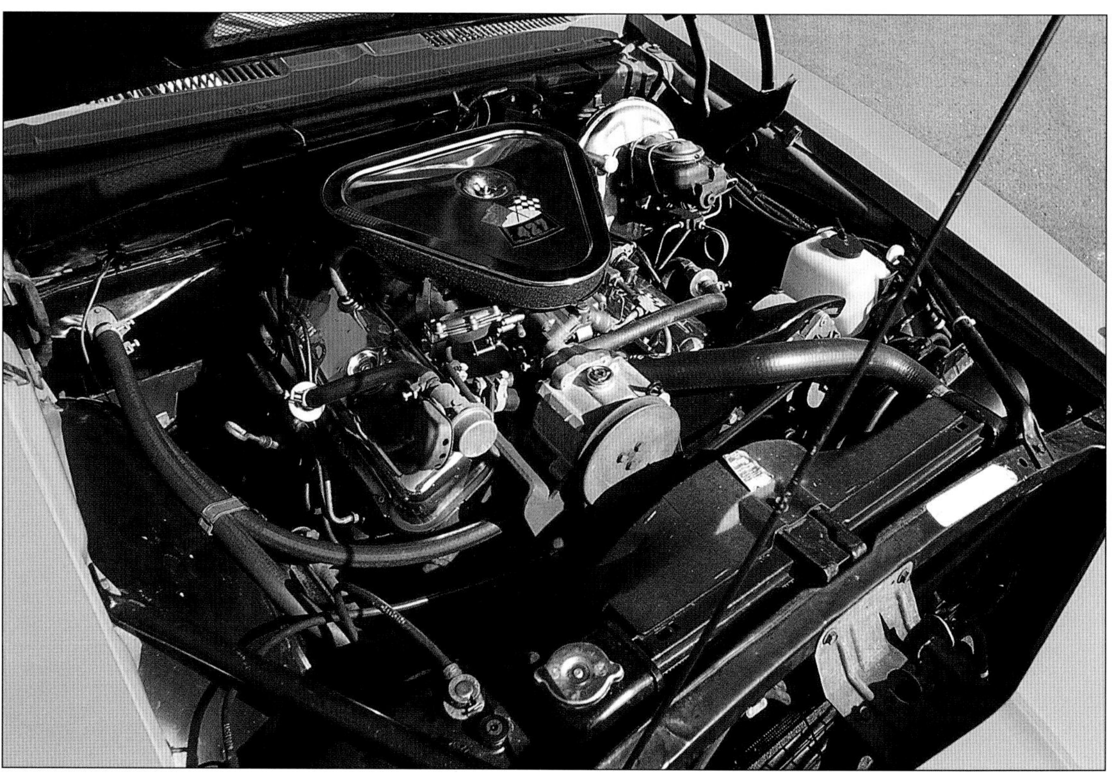

Above & Right: Because Chevy did not produce Camaros with 427 engines prior to 1969, Dana Chevrolet offered 1968 Camaros fitted with the Corvette 427 engine. The one shown here has three 2-barrel carburetors, which was an option above the single 4-barrel 427 conversion.

positioned directly in front of the driver. Overall, the cockpit felt more intimate, more Corvette-like. The view from the cockpit made the hood seem enormous, which it was, but it definitely made a statement. Contoured Strato-bucket seats with short, adjustable headrests were standard. Because the doors were so long, there was no longer a place for rear quarter windows. The longer doors made entering the rear seat somewhat easier, but made entering or exiting the front difficult in tight parking lots. Guard beams were used inside the doors for the first time and contributed to a car that was now about 200 pounds (91kg) heavier than before.

The year 1970 was the pinnacle of the muscle car era, and the Camaro was better in some ways and worse in others. The Z/28 got a new engine, the 360-horsepower LT-1 350 from the Corvette. Not only did it have 70 more horsepower than the year before, but torque was way up as well, from 290 to a whopping 370. This gave the '70 Z/28 a decided edge in straightline performance. *Car and Driver* reported a 14.2-second quarter-mile time at 100.3 mph (161.5kph) with an automatic-equipped version (this was the first year you could purchase an automatic transmission in the Z/28). *Car Craft* did even better with a 4-speed model, publishing a 14.11 at 102.73 mph (165.5kph). More telling was that the car modified with exhaust headers and slicks ran 12.93 at 108.76 mph (175kph).

How did things get worse? Well, the 454 engine was originally scheduled to be an option, but it never happened. There were no COPO big-block cars. The hottest big-block was once again the L78 396 with 375 horsepower. Aluminum heads were no longer available for it, and the 396 name itself was a misnomer. Thanks to a slight overbore, the engine now displaced 402 cubic inches. A mere six hundred were sold to the public, however road tests were not found to quantify their performance. The 350-horsepower SS396 also returned to the lineup.

On the sales front, the second-generation Camaro was nothing but successful in its maiden half-year. A total of 124,901 moved off showroom floors; the vast majority (112,323) had V8 engines, including 8,733 Z/28s.

That was the last hurrah for genuine big-block muscle in the Camaro. The following year, 1971, saw GM lower the compression ratios on all its engines across the board to get them ready for the lower-octane and low- and no-lead fuels that were being phased in. This not only appeased the Environmental Protection Agency, but the resultant loss in horsepower made the insurance industry smile. Cam timing and carburetion were also dialed back in 1971 to improve tailpipe emissions. The top-rated 396 had 8.5:1 compression instead of 11.0:1, the carb was now a Quadrajet instead of a big Holley, and the horsepower was now rated at only 300—gone forever was the solid-lifter L78.

Meanwhile, the Z/28's 350 was downgraded to 330 horsepower, thanks to a two-point drop in

Semon E. "Bunkie" Knudsen

If ever a person was destined for automotive greatness, it was Semon E. Knudsen. He was the son of Lt. Gen. William "Big Bill" Knudsen, who was the president of General Motors from 1937–1940. Legend has it that when Bunkie was fourteen, his father offered him a 1927 Chevrolet. When Bunkie went to pick it up, he found the car in one thousand pieces. Semon took two months to assemble it.

The junior Knudsen (who got his nickname, Bunkie, from the time he and his dad were bunk mates on a hunting trip) was a 1936 MIT graduate with a degree in engineering. He joined General Motors in 1939 as a tool engineer with Pontiac. He worked in the plants, setting up the assembly line. In 1950, Knudsen became director of GM's process development. When he rejoined Pontiac in 1956, this time as its general manager, his goal was to reinvent the division from a purveyor of dull cars to sporty, young-person's cars. Knudsen coined the phrase "You can sell an old man a young man's car, but you can't sell a young man an old man's car."

He arrived too late to exert much influence over the '57 Pontiac, but he made one move that shook up a lot of people—he stripped the car of its signature chrome "suspenders," two long strips of brightwork that ran from head to tail on the hood. Pontiacs had had them for years, and this was a symbol of the company's stodginess. Knudsen also got the division involved in racing, and a Pontiac won the first NASCAR race in which it was entered. When the AMA racing ban hit in 1957, it could have been a death blow to Knudsen's plan, but he clandestinely supported stock car and drag racing through the use of Pontiac's Super Duty parts program.

By 1959, Knudsen had completely reinvented Pontiac and brought it from number eight in sales to number three behind Chevrolet and Ford. The Wide-Track division was rife with sporty, luxurious cars—the Bonneville, Catalina, and Ventura. Knudsen was promoted to vice president of General Motors/general manager of Chevrolet in 1961, but his next (and last) great Pontiac had yet to hit the showrooms. It was the 1962 Grand Prix, and it became another grand slam.

Knudsen retained his position at Chevrolet until 1968, when he was passed over for the presidency of GM. He quit the company six days later to become president of Ford Motor Company, a move that rattled the auto industry. When Henry Ford II fired him about a year later, Knudsen's days as an auto executive were over.

Eventually, he moved on to White Trucks and became the national commissioner for NASCAR, a position he held until his death in 1998.

compression to 9.0:1. Performance of both the SS396 and Z/28 was way off. *Hot Rod* wrung out an SS396, and its best ET was a lackluster 14.827 at 96.30 mph (155kph), while *Car and Driver* reported a 15.1 at 94.50 mph (152kph) for a 4-speed-equipped Z/28. *Popular Hot Rodding* tested a Z/28 and reported 14.8 at 96.35 mph (155kph).

All was not lost, however, as *Road & Track* called the SS350 Camaro one of the ten best cars in the world in its August 1971 issue. Also, the three-piece tail spoiler that had been available as a COPO option the year before became a regular production option, and a larger front air dam, standard on the Z/28, became part of the same RPO.

Even though the Camaro had a full model year, sales slipped to 114,630. Sales got even worse in '72, thanks in part to a 117-day UAW strike. A piddling 68,651 were sold, only 930 of them SS396s. Now rated at 240 net horsepower, the SS396 went away at the end of the model year.

The Z/28 soldiered on until 1974, when Chevrolet put it on hold. In a rare bit of forthrightness, Chevrolet didn't want to denigrate the Z/28 name if the car could not live up to its image. By '73, the solid-lifter engines were gone entirely from the Chevy lineup. The top option was the hydraulic-lifter L82, which the Z/28 shared with the Corvette. It was rated at 245 horsepower in '73 and '74, 5 horsepower less than the flagship Stingray.

The handsome Rally Sport grille survived 1973 intact with structural modifications, but was relegated to history in '74. Camaro underwent its first face-lift since 1970, getting a sloped-back nose and more angular taillights. The only grille treatment had a monstrous bumper designed to meet the federal government's new 5-mph (8kph) crash standards and can be likened only to a chrome railroad tie.

The Z/28 also featured a cartoonish graphics package on the hood, three enormous stripes with Z/28 callouts at the leading edge. Surprisingly, Z/28 sales increased from 11,574 in 1973 (the year of the Arab oil embargo, which hurt sales of most performance cars) to 13,802 in '74. By this time, the Z/28—even in its emasculated form—was one of the best performing cars on the road. *High Performance Cars* tested both a manual-transmission model and an automatic, and they ran 14.82 at 93 mph (149.5kph) and 14.99 at 92.38 mph (149kph), respectively. Only the lighter Corvette, the Super Duty Pontiac Firebirds, and high-priced exotic Italian cars could perform better.

The Z/28 returned in 1977, but a long time passed before it could match the acceleration times of the earlier cars.

Catalina

The Catalina name appeared on a Pontiac model car in 1959, the first year for the division's Wide-Track advertising campaign. The car replaced the Chieftain series and may have been one of the first steps in general manager Semon E. "Bunkie" Knudsen's plan for ridding Pontiac of its American Indian nomenclature. The Catalina was the lowest line in the showrooms, but that meant it was the least burdened by optional equipment and excess weight.

In 1960, you could order a 389 Trophy 425-A V8 with a trio of 2-barrel carburetors and 10.75:1 compression, good for 348 advertised horsepower at 4600 rpm and 425 lbs.-ft. of torque at 2800 rpm.

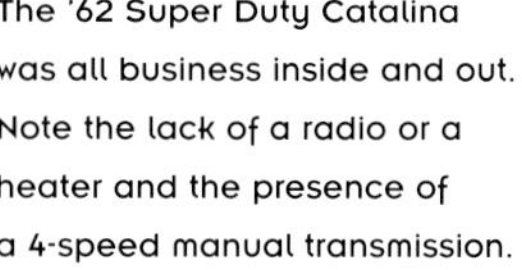
The '62 Super Duty Catalina was all business inside and out. Note the lack of a radio or a heater and the presence of a 4-speed manual transmission.

Left: Dual quads on the 421 Super Duty were legal only for NHRA competition. Versions of the 421 for NASCAR had a single 4-barrel carb.

Below: The lightweight version of the Catalina utilized an aluminum hood, front fenders, and front bumper. All sound deadening was deleted and the drag cars got aluminum exhaust headers.

The Wide-Track advertising theme was so successful in the '50s and '60s, Pontiac reverted to it in the 1990s and into the new millennium.

The engine could be teamed up with a Warner T-10 4-speed manual transmission. On Labor Day weekend in 1960, Jim Wangers won NHRA top-stock eliminator at Detroit Dragway in a 389 Catalina coupe, and Pontiacs were victorious seven times in NASCAR that same year.

A single 4-barrel version of the torquey Trophy engine was introduced for 1961, making slightly less horsepower (333 at 4800). The three-deuce 389 was a virtual carryover, and either could be had in the restyled Catalina. All of GM's full-size '61s got new looks, but the Pontiacs were the most stunning. They were fast, too. *Car Life* tested a Super Stock version of the Tri-Power Poncho and reported a 13.7 at 108 mph (174kph). Pontiac pretty much owned NASCAR in '61, with the team of Fireball Roberts and tuner Smokey Yunick making up the bulk of the division's thirty-one stock car victories that year.

With the muscle car era in high gear by '62, Pontiac unleashed two 421 Super Duty race engines that were factory-installed, one with a 4-barrel carb and intake that made 385 horsepower for NASCAR applications, the other a 405-horse dual quad version for drag racing. The latter came with lightweight aluminum exhaust manifolds, which flowed well but melted if they got too hot. The NASCAR versions got the same manifolds in cast iron.

For 1963, the 421 became available in the Catalina in both Super Duty and non–Super Duty trim. The street versions of the high-output 421 came with 10.75:1 compression, hydraulic camshafts, and your choice of either a single 4-barrel carb or three 2-barrels.

The Super Duty program ended in '63 when GM reiterated its stance supporting the AMA's racing ban. From this point forward, Pontiac's engines were nurtured with street-legal performance in mind, hence the evolution of the GTO in 1964.

Still, Pontiac stayed with its full-size brawlers till the end, though in a reduced role. The 421 could be ordered with 320 horsepower with a 4-barrel carb in the Catalina or two versions with Tri-Power, one producing 350 horsepower and 454 lbs.-ft. of torque, the other 370 ponies and 460 lbs.-ft. of torque. Pontiac even introduced a new option, the Catalina 2+2, which came standard with bucket seats, special trim, and a floor-mounted shifter with a console.

In 1965, The 2+2 was marketed as a full-size GTO, and the wheelbase had grown to 214 inches (5.5m). While this was only 1 inch (25mm) longer than the previous model, it seemed enormous. A 376-horsepower 421 with Tri-Power was available, as was a 4-speed gearbox. A heavy-duty suspension was standard. More than 11,500 2+2s were sold in '65, and more than 5,000 had stick shift transmissions. The year 1966 was the last in which you could order multiple carburetion in any GM car other than a Corvette; ergo it was the end of the line for the 376-horsepower 421 in the Catalina.

Things weren't all bad in 1967, however. The GTO was still garnering the lion's share of attention from the performance-minded buying public, and the new Firebird created a bit of a sensation in the ponycar segment, but Pontiac still built strong land-yachts. The hottest Catalina remained the 2+2, now completely restyled and using a 428-cubic-inch V8 with a single 4-barrel carburetor. It made 360 horsepower. A high-output 428 with more compression produced 376 horsepower and 462 lbs.-ft. of torque, but just 1,768 2+2s were sold. The show was over for the hot Catalina.

Challenger

This was an appropriately named ponycar. For years, Dodge didn't have an entry to compete with the Mustang or, later, the Camaro or Firebird. Plymouth had the Barracuda and wanted something its sister division didn't have. Similarly, Dodge had the wild Charger, a personal hot rod that it didn't have to share with Plymouth. Still, the ponycar market got too big for the Dodge division to ignore. Unfortunately, the timing for its introduction could not have been worse. By the time the Challenger arrived, its market segment was fragmented by six other entries and was shrinking as smaller and more practical cars like the Ford Maverick and Plymouth Duster came into vogue.

When the Challenger was first conceived, back in late 1966, it was supposed to compete with the

Left: The year 1971 was the last for the 440 Six-Pack in the Dodge Challenger. This example has the optional rear window louvers.

Below: The 340 4-barrel was the top small-block engine for 1971, thanks to the deletion of the T/A with tri-power. The interior of this Challenger is fitted out with the ultra-rare tape recorder option (note the microphone on the console).

new Mercury Cougar in the sports/luxury market and its top engine was going to be the 383. By the time it came out three years later, the Challenger was supposed to be everything from a 6-cylinder economy car to a Hemi-powered muscle machine. The desire to put the 440 and the 426 Street Hemi in the Challenger dictated that it be based on the intermediate B-body platform. It would be a larger car than many of its competitors.

But the Challenger had a lot going for it, including amazing good looks, more than sixty available options, and a choice of nine engines—everything from the frugal 225 Slant Six to the thundering 425-horse Hemi and 426 Hemi (also delivering 425 horsepower). There were two 340s (4-barrel and 6-barrel carburetion), two 383s (2-barrel and 4-barrel carburetion), and a pair of 440s (single 4-barrel or three Holley 2-barrels).

Since it was a Dodge, it had a longer wheelbase than the Barracuda, 110 versus 108 inches (279.5 versus 274.5cm). Only the Cougar, at 111 inches (282cm), had a longer wheelbase in the ponycar market. It was 5 inches (12.5cm) wider than a 1970 Mustang and 3 inches (7.5cm) wider than the same-vintage Camaro and Firebird. Since it was based on Chrysler's B-body platform, it was considerably heavier than most of its competitors, especially when powered by a 440 or the 426 Hemi.

Right: A twin-scooped Performance hood was standard on the Challenger R/T, optional on lesser models.

Below: Pictured is the functional and feared Shaker hood on a Challenger. Initially, the Shaker was supposed to be a 'Cuda-only option.

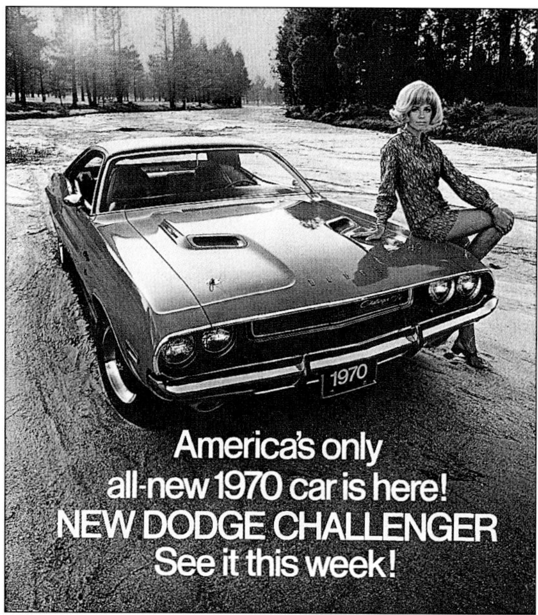

Styling was done under the direction of Dodge studio chief Bill Browlie, and the result was a car that outsold the Barracuda by more than twenty-seven thousand units. The final production number for the '70 Challenger was 83,032. Even though the Barracuda and Challenger looked quite similar, not a single body part was interchangeable. From a profitability standpoint this worked against them to a degree. In addition to the stretched wheelbase, the Challenger differed from the Barracuda in that the former had quad headlights, full-width taillights, and a sleeker profile in general. The 'Cuda looked more aggressive.

Inside, the Challenger was hamstrung by the same poor materials and manufacturing techniques as its Plymouth cousin, though the shapes in both cars were considered fairly forward thinking. The entire interior, from the instrument panel to the door panels and seats, was designed as one unit, and the gauges had a beautiful green lighting that seemed to come out of nowhere. In fact, it came from small bulbs that shone on the instruments from their mounting place in the rear of the dashpad.

Performance was typically quite strong. *Car Craft* reported a 13.62 at 104.28 mph (168kph) drag strip time in its test of a Challenger R/T equipped with a 440 Six-Pack engine and a TorqueFlite transmission. *Car and Driver* claimed 14.1 at 103.2 mph (166kph) in an R/T/SE model (with a column-mounted automatic transmission, no less). *Car and Driver* wrote glowingly of its "handsome" good looks but took Dodge to task for the Challenger's nearly 4,000 pounds (1,816kg)—3,890 pounds (1,766kg), to be precise—of curb weight.

When introduced, the Challenger was available in two body styles (coupe and convertible) and nine models. Midway through the year, a tenth model was added, the Challenger T/A, which was introduced to trumpet Dodge's entry in the SCCA's Trans-Am road race series. Mechanically, it was pretty much a clone of the AAR 'Cuda, complete with heavy-duty suspension, side-exiting exhaust trumpets, and 290-horsepower, 340 Six-Pack engine.

Like the 'Cuda, Challenger T/A came with a fiberglass hood with a unique scoop, a blackout treatment on the hood and sides, and different-size front and rear tires. *Super Stock & Drag Illustrated* got hold of a 4-speed model for its July 1970 issue and reported a 13.70 at 101.92 mph (164kph) in its drag test.

After its successful maiden campaign, the Challenger was only slightly revamped for its sophomore year. The grille was now split and the taillights were slightly revised, but there was no mistaking it for any other car from Dodge. This was the last hurrah for the Challenger convertible; none was produced with the R/T package. The T/A model was one year only; it was not brought back for '71, nor was Dodge's factory Trans-Am effort.

Under the hood, the first signs of trouble appeared. Thanks to a drop in compression, horsepower was considerably down in the 383 engine (300 with a 4-barrel carb). The mighty 440 Six-Pack was now rated at 385 horsepower. The 426 Hemi, the last true race engine available in a street car, disappeared after this year. In general, 1971 was a dismal one for supercars and the Challenger was not immune. Sales collapsed nearly 65 percent, to 29,883.

The Challenger got a fairly extensive face-lift for 1972. The grille still featured quad headlamps, but the opening looked less aggressive. Out back, the full-width taillamps had been replaced by four trapezoid-shaped lights encased in a wide panel.

Almost all the hot models vanished in 1972. Gone were the R/T, the Street Hemi, and all the big-blocks. The performance-oriented Challenger was now dubbed the Rallye, and while the horsepower was toned down, it was still an exciting machine. There were fake louvers with black tape stripes running down the side, and a twin-scooped hood was standard. The grille and tail panel were painted flat black.

The standard engine in the Rallye was the 318 2-barrel and the only optional mill was the 340 4-barrel, now rated at 240 "net" horsepower. Torque was 290 net at 3600 rpm. Compression was dropped to an anemic 8.5:1 so that the Rallye could run on low- or no-lead fuel.

The 340 Rallye survived one more season, still with 240 horsepower. It was replaced in '74 by the 360 Rallye, which was a 340 with a longer stroke. Horsepower crept up to 245 and torque to 280 lbs.-ft. It was a pleasant car to drive, if not the fire-breather it had been only a few years earlier. The basic hardware was there; you just had to do the work yourself. Either way, there was little interest from a consumer standpoint, and the Challenger passed into history after only five model years.

Charger

This flashy intermediate from Dodge was Chrysler's attempt at combining the brutal performance of a muscle car with the personality and style of a car like the Ford Thunderbird. The Charger name first appeared on a Dodge A/FX drag race car, not to mention a pair of futuristic concept cars in the early 1960s.

The Charger, though based on the Coronet's B-body platform, arrived on the scene with a host of distinctive touches, all of which made it impossible to forget once you saw it. Up front, hideaway headlights, still somewhat rare in 1966, rotated into place. Even more unusual was the fact that, once in place, the headlight buckets matched the rest of the grille, giving the Charger's nose an integrated look either way. The parking lights were placed at the outer edge of the grille and could barely be seen unless they were turned on.

In the rear, the Charger wore a full-width taillamp panel with the car's name spelled out in chrome letters. Of course, the Charger's most memorable design touch was its huge, sloping fastback roofline. Popular in the late 1940s and early '50s, fastbacks were out of fashion for a time, then started making a comeback in 1963 with the Corvette and the midyear Ford Galaxie 500. The AMC Marlin was the marriage of a

The Charger 500 used a flush grille and redesigned backlight in an attempt to be more competitive on the NASCAR circuit. When it didn't prove successful, Dodge created the outrageous Daytona. This 1969 Charger has a Hemi.

In 1971, two-door Dodge intermediates were called Chargers, and the R/T and Super Bee were optional models for it.

midsize Rambler and a sloping roof in 1965, the same year the Mustang 2+2, also with a fastback body style, was introduced.

The fastback Charger was important for three reasons: it promoted Dodge's sporty image, it gave the company an aerodynamic body style for NASCAR Grand National stock car racing, and it gave Dodge an exciting body style in which to showcase its awesome new Street Hemi engine. If nothing else, the Charger was a departure from the company's conservative lineup of Coronets and Darts. It also placated Dodge's dealer body, which had longed for a sporty car ever since Plymouth got the Barracuda in 1964.

All the glitz was not reserved for the exterior. Inside were four bucket seats, which could be divided by an optional full-length console. They also folded down for improved cargo capacity. The gauges, including a tachometer, were like pods growing out of the instrument panel, and their lighting almost appeared fluorescent.

The 318 polyspherical V8 was standard and the 361 was optional, but the true muscle car enthusiasts stepped up for the 325-horsepower 383 or the race-bred 426 Hemi. With 425 horsepower at 5000 rpm and 490 lbs.-ft. of torque at 4000, it was as close to a stock car engine you could buy for street use. "Beauty and the Beast" was how Dodge proclaimed the marriage of its sleek new Charger and the throbbing Street Hemi engine in one of its ads. "The Hemi has never been in better shape," said another.

The Hemi was a $907.60 option, and for this you got the engine, heavy-duty suspension and brakes, and Goodyear Blue Streak tires. If you wanted the Hemi engine, mandatory options were either a reworked TorqueFlite automatic ($206.30) or a 4-speed manual transmission ($184). In a 1967 road test in *Popular Hot Rodding*, a 4-speed Hemi Charger delivered a 13.85-second quarter-mile time at 102 mph (164kph). Top speed could be in the neighborhood of between 130 and 150 mph (209 and 241.5kph), depending on the rear end gear ratio.

Initial reaction from the public was positive. The Charger sold more than thirty thousand copies in its maiden season. It saw minimal changes for 1967, the second and final incarnation of its original design. Front fender–mounted turn signals became standard. The new 440 Magnum V8 with 375 horsepower, standard in the Coronet R/T, was optional in the Charger. It offered Hemi-like performance with the convenience and reliability of a single 4-barrel carburetor and a mild hydraulic-lifter cam. *High Performance Cars* got a 440/4-speed Charger to go 13.6 at 103.7 mph (167kph) in the quarter mile.

Perhaps because the Charger was designed to run on the NASCAR superspeedways, a special version was introduced in 1967 with a small rear spoiler to aid aerodynamics, although in truth the Charger never did well in Grand National racing.

"Even Custer couldn't muster a stampede like this," shouted the Charger's ads. But sales fell by less than 50 percent, to 15,788. Perhaps the car's styling was too avant-garde. It was certainly quirky. This scarcely mattered. An all-new Charger was introduced in the fall of 1967, one that became a new benchmark for passenger-car styling.

All Dodge and Plymouth intermediates got a major face-lift for 1968, but none was more radical or successful than the Charger. It retained its hide-away headlights, but now they were set in a deep grille cavity. The body was Coke bottle–shaped, very swoopy and curvy, but extremely muscular. It was a large car: 208 inches (528.5cm) long and

Part of the Charger's appeal remained its outstanding performance. Despite the car's ample curb weight, the Hemi and the 440 Magnum made the Charger scream. With just a 3.23 gear and an automatic transmission, *Car and Driver* claimed a 13.5 drag strip time at 105 mph (169kph). The numerically low gear ratio helped the car top out at 139 mph (223.5kph). Even the 440-equipped model could top 100 mph (161kph) in the quarter mile in factory trim.

For '69, Dodge did little to mess with the Charger—at least initially. It got fancy new taillights that, perhaps in tribute to the early models, ran nearly the full width of the rear fascia. The grille got a divider, but otherwise the graceful shape was left basically intact. For the first time, a 6-cylinder engine was available in the lineup, but only five hundred were built.

A flip-open fuel door was standard equipment on the Charger from 1968 through 1970. It was mounted on the top of the left rear fender.

76.6 inches (194.5cm) wide, and when equipped with a big-block V8, it tipped the scales at more than 2 tons (1.8t). This scarcely mattered. Bigger was better in the fuel-rich 1960s, and *Car and Driver* called the Charger the most beautiful new car of 1968. "The only 1968 car which comes close to matching the new Charger for styling accolades is the new Corvette," the magazine stated. This was high praise, as 1968 was a high watermark for styling in a decade that has become known for great designs. *Car and Driver* noted correctly that the Vette and the Charger shared many of the same styling features, including the taillights and flying buttress roofline. Gone was the Charger's signature fastback.

Buyers reacted to the new Charger by snapping up some ninety-six thousand of them, helping Dodge to a record sales year. This number is even more remarkable when the car's cost is taken into account: it had a base price of just more than $3,000, but options like the Hemi engine could push the window sticker to nearly $5,000.

When the Charger failed to perform as expected in NASCAR, it became apparent that aerodynamics were partly to blame. The deep grille cavity caught a lot of wind and slowed the car quite a bit. It also caused the front end to lift at high speeds. The recessed rear window didn't help, either. Worst of all, the car was about 3 mph (5kph) slower than the all-new '68 Fords and Mercurys on the superspeedways.

The solution was the Charger 500, a model released solely to legalize the car for stock car racing (580 cars were produced). The 500 had a flush grille with exposed headlights (taken from the '68 Coronet), and a completely reworked rear window and roofline in the C-pillar area. The glass was now flush with the roofline, which reduced drag. Even for the '60s this was a massive undertaking. This work was not done on an assembly line; it was farmed out to an outside contractor. Dodge expected to pick up 5 mph (8kph) on the high banks with these modifications. The new grille treatment was fairly awful, but as any racer will tell you, beauty is

Car and Driver magazine called the 1968 Charger the most beautiful new automobile of that year.

as beauty does. Functional is gorgeous; anything that slows you down is ugly.

When the Charger still didn't win races, Dodge went all-out to build a better replacement. To counter the 500, Ford Motor Company had introduced its own aero warriors, the Torino Talladega and the Mercury Cyclone Spoiler. They made short work of the 500. From this scenario, the Charger Daytona was born. It had a slippery sloping nose up front, the Charger 500's roofline treatment, chrome wind deflectors on the roof's A-pillars, and an enormous rear wing mounted to the back fenders.

The car's first race was the inaugural Talladega 500 in Alabama, NASCAR's newest and fastest superspeedway. When the Daytona arrived, it blew everyone's mind—especially after "Chargin'" Charlie Glotzbach qualified at an unprecedented 199.466 mph (321kph), a full 9 mph (14.5kph) faster than anyone had ever qualified before. That car won at Talladega, though not with Glotzbach behind the wheel. A strike by the drivers, who were concerned about tire failure due to the high speeds (and thus heat) at the track, resulted in mostly scab drivers. Richard Brickhouse drove car number 99 to victory that day.

Unfortunately, there isn't a magazine found that can provide a top-speed test of the Daytona, so its prowess as a street car remains strictly conjecture. The Daytona was a one-year-only model. Technically, the 500 was sold again in 1970, but it the same equipment as the base car from the year earlier and had nothing to do with the high-performance, aerodynamic race car it once was. Sales of all Chargers were still strong, with about ninety thousand finding homes.

The last year for the second-generation Charger was 1970, and once again Dodge stylists altered the grille. A chrome collar encircled the opening, and the divider from 1969 disappeared. Inside, superplush high-backed bucket seats with built-in headrests were available, as were conveniently placed map pouches on the doors.

Under the hood, the biggest news was the availability of the 440 Six-Pack engine, which thanks to its trio of 2-barrel carbs made 390 horsepower. This was also the year the Street Hemi got the more owner-friendly hydraulic-lifter camshaft. Emissions laws were starting to take their toll on performance, and the insurance industry was scaring off buyers of high-performance cars with usurious rates. Also, 1970 was a big year for sales of compact cars like the Dodge Dart and Ford Maverick. Combined with the fact that this was the third (and final) year of the body style, sales dipped dramatically, to less than fifty thousand.

When the 1971 Charger arrived on the scene, it had been repositioned in the marketplace. Previously, there were two-door and four-door Dodge Coronets and two-door Chargers. Beginning in 1971, all two-door Dodge intermediates were called Charger and the four-door models dubbed Coronet. Gone were the Coronet R/T and Super Bee; they were replaced by the Charger R/T and the newly minted Charger Super Bee. There was a 6-cylinder Charger offered, and the top-of-the-line model was the more luxurious SE (Special Edition).

Like the previous Coronet-based Super Bee, the Charger that bore this name was the budget supercar. A 300-horsepower 383, now designed to run on regular-grade fuel, was standard; optional were the 440 Six-Pack and the Hemi. As with the previous R/T, the standard engine was the powerful 440 Magnum, now rated at 370 horsepower (from 375). Available at extra cost were the 440 Six-Pack and the Hemi.

More telling was the success of the SE model. As tastes changed and midsize personal luxury cars like the Chevrolet Monte Carlo and Pontiac Grand Prix became more in vogue, the Charger SE outsold the R/T and Super Bee combined by almost two to one. Extroverted styling had been a Charger hallmark since day one and the third generation was no different, although it was the tamest yet. As was the case with the '68, the design of the '71 Charger was universally praised by the automotive media. *Cars* magazine wrote, "Its styling can best be described as tasteful.... Both the chrome loop bumper treatment or the optional color matched application works into the overall design." *Car and Driver* called it the "best styled new car for 1971."

This was the first year for Chrysler Corp.'s so-called fuselage styling for its intermediates. The Coke-bottle shape of the past remained but was less radical. Gone was the tunnelback roofline. And for the first time in Charger history, exposed headlights were standard equipment. Hideaway headlamps were standard on the upmarket SE and optional on the other five models, a nod to the car's changing role as a more mainstream automobile.

Sales were still flat, but they rebounded in 1972 to more than seventy-five thousand. Unfortunately, all the serious high-performance engines and models were gone—the Hemi, the R/T, and the Super Bee. Only a handful of the 440 Six-Packs trickled out in '72 and the only model that outwardly hinted at muscle was the Charger Rallye. The Rallye was available with either a 340, 400, or 440 V8. *Cars* magazine reported a 14.8 with a 440 Rallye, but this was a far cry from the brutal Hemis of just twelve months earlier.

The 440 stuck around until 1974, the last year for the third-gen Charger, but it was down to 275 net horsepower by then. On the high banks of NASCAR, Richard Petty was a dominant force for years in the third-generation Charger. In fact, he called it the best race car he ever had, more stable than the much ballyhooed Plymouth Superbird aero warrior.

Chevelle

In 1962, Ford introduced its first intermediate, the Fairlane, which was quite successful. Two years later Chevrolet countered. The car that took on the Fairlane was the Chevelle. Built on a 115-inch (292cm) wheelbase, it was a squareish design that was similar in some ways to the smaller Chevy II/Nova. (In fact, the Chevelle was marketed as a "senior compact.") A total of eleven models comprised the lineup, starting with the Chevelle 300 on the low end and peaking with the Chevelle Malibu SS.

While the SS was a very nice car with its bucket seat interior, there was little about it that was muscular. The standard engine was a small 194-cubic-inch 6-cylinder, and the first optional mill was a 230-cubic-inch 6-cylinder. Early in the model year, the largest engine offered was the 283. Thanks to a GM policy that limited engines in its intermediates to 326 cubic inches, the already legendary 327 was not offered at first. All that changed thanks to the success of the GTO. Pontiac bucked this edict and installed a hot 389 in its Tempest. When orders exceeded everyone's expectations, Oldsmobile unleashed the 330-cubic-inch 4-4-2 and Buick countered with the 401 Skylark Gran Sport. Chevy countered with a pair of 327s, one with 250 horsepower and another with 300. Neither of these set the world on fire, but it was a start.

The following year, Chevy had the Corvette's strong 350-horsepower 327 on the option sheet. For a while, this hydraulic-lifter engine was the hottest you could purchase in a Chevelle SS. A 4-speed transmission was standard; automatic was not offered. The rear axle came with a 3.31:1 cog, and Positraction was available. So equipped, the SS could turn in the neighborhood of 90 mph (145kph) in the quarter mile, but this still wasn't competitive with a Tri-Power GTO.

Right: With 450 horsepower, the 1970 LS6 454 Chevelle was the top-rated Chevelle muscle car of all time. Only the early '66 427 L72 Corvette could match that number.

Then came the midyear introduction of the 396 big-block. Chevrolet produced a limited run (201) of SS Chevelles with this engine, which was rated at 375 horsepower at 5600 rpm in the intermediate. Dubbed the Z-16 option, the first SS396 Malibu had distinctive features, including gold-stripe Firestone tires, an AM/FM radio, simulated 5-spoke wheel covers, a tach mounted atop the dash, and unique body moldings. A 160-mph (257.5kph) speedometer sat in the instrument cluster. Three colors were employed—red, yellow, or black—and most cars had vinyl tops. All were coupes.

The engine was very similar to the 425-horse versions, but it used a hydraulic-lifter cam. A Holley 4-barrel delivered the fuel mixture, and cast-iron

Above: The 1965 Z-16 SS396 Chevelle got a 375-horse "Rat" motor and a tachometer mounted atop the dash.

The SS396 Chevelle was one of the most popular muscle cars on the street in the late '60s. Three versions of the "Rat" motor were available, with 325, 350, and 375 horsepower. The 1969 models shown here have alternating black-and-red color schemes.

headers delivered burned fuel to a 2.25-inch (57mm) dual exhaust system. A 4-bolt main block was standard. Torque was rated at 420 lbs.-ft. at 3600 rpm. To handle all this power, a convertible-type frame was used. (Buick did the same thing a year earlier with its 401 Skylark GS.) Larger, 11-inch (28cm) brakes (with power assist) were standard, as were front and rear sway bars. Even on stock tires, Z-16 Chevelles could run in the 14-second zone at up to 100 mph (161kph). *Road & Track* and *Popular Hot Rodding* both tested these cars, with the former reporting a 14.7-second ET and the latter 14.6 at 100 mph (161kph).

From 1966–71, all Chevelle SS models had the 396 as standard equipment. For '66, the Chevelle was rebodied and the standard mill in the SS was the 325-horse 396, which produced 410 lbs.-ft. of torque. Next in line was option L34, the 360-horse version with 420 lbs.-ft. of torque. At the top of the heap was the 396/375, code L78, which now sported a solid-lifter camshaft and 11.0:1 compression. (Lesser 396s had 10.25:1 compression ratios.) A total of 3,099 of L78 Chevelles were built; the vast majority, 24,811, were of the 325-horse stripe.

If you preferred a hot small-block to the thumper 396, the 350-horse 327 (option L79) was available in non-SS Malibus. In road tests of the day, the 360-horsepower 396 was every bit the match for the '65 Z-16. *Popular Hot Rodding* went 14.42 at 100.22 mph (161kph), while *Car Life*, which tested with two passengers aboard, knocked off a 14.66 at 99.88 mph (160.5kph).

Very little was new for '67. There was a minor face-lift and the L34 was downrated to 350 horses, though it picked up 5 lbs.-ft. of torque. The L79 327 survived one more model year, but it was now advertised at 325 ponies.

Remarkably, in 1968, every company in the Big Three unveiled completely revamped intermediates. For Chevrolet, the hot ticket was its all-new Chevelle hardtop, which now rode on a 112-inch (284.5cm) wheelbase with a track that was 1 inch (2.5cm) wider. Styling was vastly improved over '67, with a sloping, near-fastback roofline; smart rear quarter windows, and a forward-slanting nose that was mean and conventional at the same time.

A more comfortable, more modern interior greeted passengers. Strato-bucket seats and a console were optional. Pushing you back in those seats was the same basic engine lineup as the previous model. The L78 was the top dog and easier than ever to order, as it was officially listed as an option.

While the Chevelle SS was priced to be Everyman's Muscle Car, the lack of development—not to mention cubic inches—under the hood was

SS
SS

beginning to make it an also-ran in the performance department. It simply could not keep up with the 440-powered Mopars of the day, and a 428 Ford could give it fits.

This carried over to 1969, although for the first time the SS396 was available on the low-line 300 Chevelle coupe. This may have been Chevy's way to both grab some business away from the Plymouth Road Runner, which was a budget supercar, and get more performance out of the Chevelle thanks to its lower weight. Either way, what the Chevelle SS really needed was the 425-horse 427 from the full-size Chevys. This only happened through select dealers like Baldwin Chevrolet in New York (through its deal with Motion Performance) or via the Central Office Production Order (COPO) connection. It should be noted here that four hundred Chevelles were ordered with the optional (L89) aluminum cylinder heads in '69.

It wasn't until 1970 that the Chevelle got its first serious injection of cubic performance since 1965. The new-for-1970 454 became available in the midsize model. The 396 actually grew to 402 cubes during the model year thanks to an enlarged cylinder bore, though the car was still marketed as the SS396.

These 402-propelled Chevelles were nothing compared to the optional 454s, however. General Motors had finally lifted its ban on engines larger than 400 cubic inches in its intermediate offerings, and Chevrolet made the most of it. The handwriting was on the wall for the muscle car era, and with the LS5 and LS6 454s, Chevrolet seemed intent on going out on top. The LS5 had hydraulic lifters and was rated at 360 horsepower and 500 lbs.-ft. of torque. It was good for high-13-second quarter-mile excursions.

But it was the LS6 that got everyone's heart beating faster. This was Chevy's ultimate muscle car, quicker than even the Corvette that year, which, although slated to get the LS6 (one rated at 460 horsepower), had to wait until 1971. Rated at 450 horsepower and 500 lbs.-ft. of torque, the Chevelle's top powerplant featured high compression (11.25:1) thanks to its cylinder head design, a high-lift solid-lifter camshaft, and a large Holley carburetor. A functional cowl induction hood was optional to further aid performance.

The buff magazines flipped for the new Chevelle, which had also undergone a flattering face-lift. *Hot Rod* correctly predicted, "The past is gone, the future may never see a car like this." With minor tweaks, it posted a 13.44 quarter-mile time at 108.17 mph (174kph). Sister publication *Car Craft* reported a 13.12, while *Super Stock & Drag Illustrated* did nearly as well, reporting a 13.2 at 106 mph (170.5kph).

An across-the-board drop in compression ratios at General Motors created an immediate drop in horsepower, and pressure from the insurance industry caused many performance models to either disappear or be watered down. The LS6 engine, downrated to 425 horsepower, was no longer available in the Chevelle. The LS5, now with 8.5:1 compression and 365 horsepower, was the lone 454. The standard engine in the SS Chevelle was the lowly 245-horsepower 350 small-block, with a 270-horsepower 350 optional. De-emphasized was the SS396/402. Now producing 300 horsepower, it was listed in sales literature, but most of the emphasis was on the more potent 454.

For '71, the Chevelle got a slight makeover. The quad headlamps were replaced by a single bulb on either side, and the grille was split horizontally by a chrome bar. In the rear, the one-year-only single taillamps were replaced by two round units per side, à la Corvette and Camaro.

A new model, the Heavy Chevy, was introduced. It was more bare-bones than the SS but came with some of the same features: a domed hood with pins, a blacked-out grille (sans SS emblem), 14×6-inch (35.5×15cm) wheels, and unique striping and decals that spelled out the model name. All of the SS engines except the LS5 were available; standard in the Heavy Chevy was the 307 V8.

By '72, it was just about over for high-performance Chevelles. If you lived in California, you were restricted to 350-cubic-inch small-blocks. Neither the 402 nor the 454 could be purchased in that state, though they were legal in the other forty-nine states. For the first time, you could get the anemic 307 in the SS. Thanks to a change in the rating system from gross horsepower to net horsepower, the numbers appeared lower than ever. The 454 was now advertised at just 270 ponies, the 402 at 240, and the 307 at an awful 130.

The SS name continued in the Chevelle until '73, but things had deteriorated so badly that, by then, you could order a Chevelle SS station wagon. The car was completely redesigned for that year as well, and the clean styling of years past was history.

Zora Arkus-Duntov

To some, the story of Zora Arkus-Duntov reads like a Hollywood movie script, but remarkably it is all true. Born in Belgium, he grew up in the Soviet Union and was educated there and in Germany. He smuggled gold out of France in the tube axle of his modified V8 Ford just before World War II. He flew fighter planes for France during the war.

Recognizing the need for better breathing for the flathead Ford V8, Duntov designed the Ardun overhead-valve conversion, a hemispherical design that was so good that he thought Chrysler copied it for its early-1950s Hemi engines.

Later, upon viewing the 1953 Corvette at the GM Motorama at New York's Waldorf-Astoria, he wrote a letter to Harley Earl calling it the most beautiful car he'd ever seen and suggested ways to improve it. Duntov, an accomplished racer with victories at Le Mans and world speed records to his credit, went to work at Chevrolet, and in 1955 wrote a confidential memo to Earl that is credited with saving the Corvette.

The Vette was an abysmal sales failure, and GM was about to pull the plug on it. Duntov convinced management that to do so would publicly tarnish the image of Chevrolet and GM, especially considering the success of the new two-seat Ford Thunderbird.

In his early years at Chevrolet, Duntov was credited with helping develop the Ramjet fuel-injection system for the '57 models, revising the suspension on the Corvette to make it handle better, and designing the 348/409 W engine, as well as making the Corvette a successful road racer.

Later he was promoted to chief engineer of the Corvette, a position he held until he was forced out by the GM mandatory retirement age of sixty-five. Along the way, he helped pioneer the Corvette's independent rear suspension and upgrades for the big-block engine. He helped the car make the smooth transition from barely civilized street car in the '50s and '60s to a more proper boulevardier in the '70s, when tightening emissions laws squeezed much of the horsepower out of it.

Duntov wrote in *Vette* magazine that his biggest disappointment was not being able to develop a mid-engined Corvette (where the engine is mounted toward the middle of the car rather than in front of the driver or in the rear where the trunk would normally be) with all-wheel drive and all-wheel steering before retiring. After he retired, Duntov worked on numerous aftermarket projects, becoming a regular on the Corvette show circuit and a semiregular contributor to *Vette*.

When he passed away at eighty-plus years of age, he was building a high-performance airplane with the intention of setting a speed record. So devoted was he to his favorite sports car that when he died in 1996, he left instructions for his ashes to be put on display at the National Corvette Museum in Bowling Green, Kentucky.

Opposite: The SS396 badge sat in a blacked-out panel below the trunk on the '69 model.

Left: Here's the decklid badge of a 1971 Chevelle.

Perhaps the ultimate "sleeper" was this 1966 Chevy II with the optional 327/350-horse Corvette engine. Only six were built in 1967 before the option was discontinued.

Chevy II/Nova

When this compact Chevrolet was introduced in 1962, no one probably ever thought it would be anything more than a cheap economy car. But in the muscle car '60s, anything was possible.

The Chevy II/Nova started life as Chevrolet's conventional answer to the successful Ford Falcon. Chevrolet already had the Corvair in the lineup, but its unusual styling and air-cooled, rear-mounted engine was too unconventional for some buyers. By 1963, a Nova SS appeared, but its only engine was a 6-cylinder. In 1964, a V8 became available, but it was a 283 with only 195 horsepower, hardly the stuff of muscle car dreams.

Then, in 1965, two versions of the 327 V8 were offered, one with 250 horsepower and the other with 300. Neither sold in great numbers, but the latter offered an excellent power-to-weight ratio and was a decent performer. It wasn't until 1966, however, that Chevrolet introduced its first compact muscle car.

The Chevy II wore new sheet metal for '66, and the prettiest was the two-door hardtop. Its styling bore a strong resemblance to the '55 Chevrolet, which was entirely intentional. And like that classic from eleven years earlier, the Chevy II packed plenty of punch under the hood. A 275-horsepower 327 superceded the 250- and 300-horse motors from '65, but there was one more mill available. The top engine option was now the Corvette's 350-horsepower 327 (RPO L79). It came standard with a 3-speed manual gearbox, and a 4-speed could be yours for a few extra dollars.

In a car that weighed barely 3,000 pounds (1,362kg) with a driver, it was one of the quickest muscle cars available that year. *Car Life* evaluated one in its May '66 issue and achieved a 15.1-second quarter mile at 93 mph (149.5kph). *Car Life* reported a weight of 3,530 pounds (1,602.5kg), which indicates the car may have been tested with a driver and a passenger. (*Car Life* often did this.) Judging by the speed, the Nova SS had 14-second potential.

The following year the SS was back, but the 350-horsepower engine made it into only a half-dozen cars before it was discontinued, leaving the 327/275 as the top motor choice.

Chevrolet completely revamped the Nova for '68 and this time did what might have been unthinkable just a few years earlier—it offered the L78 396 engine as an option late in the model year. Previously, the best-performing Nova for sale was the SS with the Camaro's 295-horsepower 350 with a 4-barrel carb. The advent of Rat power in the compact (if slightly larger than before) Nova was big news in the performance community. Dodge had offered a 383 Dart in 1967, but the car had

1966
California
RPO L79
NOVA
CHEVY II
BFGoodrich

only 280 horsepower and was produced in limited quantities. The 383 Dart returned for '68, but it still had only 300 horsepower.

The 396 engine with solid lifters and 375 horsepower made the Nova SS the king of compacts. *Car and Driver* wrung one out and hit 60 mph (96.5kph) in 5.9 seconds and finished the quarter mile in 14.3 at 101.1 mph (162.5kph). *Hot Rod*, testing a '69 version with a Turbo 400 automatic, claimed 13.87 at 105.1 mph (169kph), though that speed seems a little high.

Given the fact that the Camaro and the Nova shared the same basic architecture, perhaps it should not be surprising that the 396 made it into the Nova. Chevy did little to promote such a beast, as the company was in the odd position of trying to be competitive in the muscle car wars while trying not to seem reckless to the burgeoning safety gestapo in Washington. The L78 option cost an extra $500.30 on the Nova SS, and only 667 were produced that first year. The 350-horsepower 396 with hydraulic lifters was also listed as an engine option.

The '69 Chevy Nova (gone was the "II" designation) was a virtual carryover vehicle, and the hot 396 was back once more. Little-known then or now was the availability of the L89 aluminum cylinder head option which, though expensive, helped alleviate the car's nose-heavy weight distribution. The 350-horsepower 396 was back as well. If you preferred small-blocks, the L48 350 was now rated at 300 horsepower. Not only was this 5 more than the year before, but a stronger block with 4-bolt main caps was employed.

Minor trim changes identified the '70 Nova SS. This was the last year the SS396 was offered, and as with the Chevelle and Camaro, it actually displaced 402 cubic inches due to a slight overbore. This was the swan song for muscular Novas. The hottest Nova for '71 was the 270-horse 350 4-barrel. *Road & Track* actually tested a 350-horse SS396 in '70. This West Coast–based magazine, which did not powershift when testing, still reported a respectable 15.3-second ET at 92.7 mph (149kph).

If you wanted the absolute craziest Nova possible, you had to search out a special dealer like Baldwin Chevrolet in New York or Yenko Chevrolet in Pennsylvania; they would sell you a 427- or 454-powered Nova. By 1970, COPO Novas with the Z/28's 360-horsepower 350 were filtering out to the general public. But these cars were rare and could be quite expensive, though they offered explosive performance. *Car Craft* got hold of a Harrell-prepped 454 Nova with 450 horsepower and tested it to the tune of a 12.11 at 114.91 mph (185kph) at the strip.

Comet/Cyclone

The Mercury Comet hit the streets in 1960 as the slightly more upscale cousin to the plebian (but ultra-successful) Ford Falcon. The Comet had a longer wheelbase, better trim, and quad headlights, but those were about the only differences. With its 114-inch (289.5cm) wheelbase, the Comet fit somewhere between the Falcon (109-inch [277cm] wheelbase) and the Ford Fairlane (115.5-inch [293.5cm] wheelbase).

There was not much to recommend the Comet as a performance car until 1964, when Mercury built fifty or so 427 Comets for the NHRA's Factory Experimental class, the forerunner of today's Funny Cars. They ran on 10-inch (25.5cm) slicks and were the scourge of the class. A 427 Comet won Top Stock Eliminator in A/FX at the NHRA's

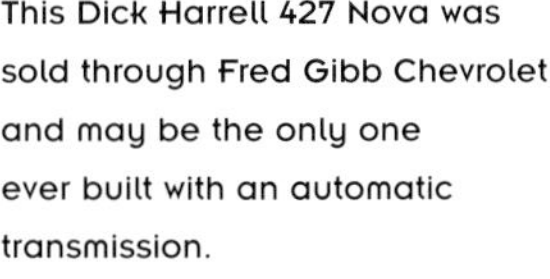

This Dick Harrell 427 Nova was sold through Fred Gibb Chevrolet and may be the only one ever built with an automatic transmission.

'64 Winternationals, and some were capable of 10.9-second ETs. This was flat-out getting with the program in 1964.

At the same time, Mercury introduced the Cyclone option package, which delivered a tachometer mounted atop the padded dashboard, front bucket seats with a console, a 3-spoke steering wheel, and less exterior brightwork (with the exception of chrome hubcaps that looked like the chrome-reversed aftermarket wheels popular during that era).

Under the hood, a 210-horsepower version of the Fairlane V8 with a 4-barrel carb was standard. Optional was the hot 271-horsepower, solid-lifter, high-performance 289. This high-winding mill made the Cyclone a decent performer, but still not in the same league as the Pontiac GTO.

For 1965, Ford assembled one of the greatest drag teams ever. It was composed of "Dyno" Don Nicholson (who was best-known for his success with Chevrolet's 409 when it was new), Arnie "the Farmer" Beswick, and Hayden Profitt. This trio competed in Comets fitted with the new 427 single overhead cam (SOHC) V8, an all-out racing engine.

It wasn't until 1966, when the Comet became a true intermediate, that a big-block was offered in an assembly-line vehicle. That year, the Comet was all-new with a stretched wheelbase of 116 inches (294.5cm). Standard equipment in the Cyclone GT was, in the beginning, a 315-horsepower 390 V8. Shortly after the model year began, the engine was upgraded with a Holley carb and a different hydraulic-lifter camshaft, giving it 335 horsepower at 4800 rpm and 427 lbs.-ft. of torque at 3200.

Also standard on this model was a heavy-duty suspension, stripes, a nonfunctional twin-scooped hood, and chrome wheel covers. A functional fiberglass hood with twin scoops at the leading edge of the hood could be specially ordered for additional horsepower. This was a decently performing automobile with 3.90:1 gears and the 335-horse engine. *Cars* magazine was impressed by its 14.95 ET at 98 mph (157.5kph). "We were able to walk away from most of the average stop light drag racers," wrote Martyn L. Schorr.

Dealer literature stated that the 427 engine, in 410- or 425-horse tune, would be available after January 1, 1966, but it wasn't until 1967 that Mercury openly marketed said vehicles. In 1967, the 427s were available in any closed body style, including the lightweight coupe. The difference between the two engines was carburetion; the 410-horsepower variant had a single 4-barrel while the 425-horsepower version had dual quads. (It should be noted, however, that you could actually

Above: Aftermarket gauges were part of the Harrell package, as was the console badge.

Left: This print ad shows off Chevrolet's four car lines for 1963: Corvette, Chevy II, Corvair, and full-size (from top to bottom).

Nearly forgotten in the annals of muscle cars is the 1966 Mercury Cyclone GT. Here is a vintage Rotunda tachometer, which was sold by Ford Motor Company through its aftermarket parts and accessories program.

buy a Cyclone hardtop coupe, though they were extremely rare; only 1,368 were produced. The vast majority of Cyclones were fastbacks.)

Short of Chrysler's Street Hemi, the 427s were as close as you could get to an all-out race engine on the street. Both had 11.1:1 compression, 6-quart (5.5L) oil pans, solid-lifter camshafts, and heavy-duty internal parts such as rods and pistons. Either the 410- or 425-horsepower 427 added a robust $1,129 to the cost of your Comet, but a functional hood scoop and 4-speed transmission were standard fare. Once again, drag racing was an integral part of Mercury's marketing plan. Comet Funny Cars with flip-up bodies were piloted by Nicholson, "Fast" Eddie Schartman, and Jack Chrisman.

When Mercury's completely revamped line of intermediate cars arrived in 1968, the Comet moniker was predominantly replaced by the name Montego and was completely lost by 1969. Cyclone was still the name attached to the hottest Mercury. With the introduction of a sweeping fastback roofline in '68, it was a fairly aerodynamic car for the time, and to prove it, Mercury dived into NASCAR racing. Mercury hired Cale Yarborough to be the main shoe, and he did not disappoint them. In fact, he won the Daytona 500 from the pole in February and the Firecracker 500 at Daytona on July 4, as well as four other races in '68. Yarborough's average speed of 167.242 mph (269kph) was by far the fastest in 1968. Lee Roy Yarbrough had the other Mercury victory that year, and together the pair won more races than Dodge. Only Ford and Plymouth won more often in '68.

Ordering a Cyclone didn't guarantee you a strong performer, as the standard engine was a 302 with a 2-barrel carb. The two hot ones for the street were again the Cyclone and Cyclone GT. The 425-horsepower 427 was no longer available, and for a while the meanest Cyclone sold had the 390 with 335 horsepower (this engine was standard in the GT). Midyear, the soon-to-be legendary 428 Cobra Jet became standard in the new Cyclone CJ and it was an option on the rest of the models.

The Cobra Jet combined many of the best features of the 427 from the year before with the drivability of the more civilized 428. The CJ featured the 428 block and internals, but the 427 heads and exhaust manifolds guaranteed good airflow. A single 4-barrel carb on a Police Interceptor manifold and more street-friendly camshaft assured good manners in traffic, something that was never a hallmark of the race-bred 427s.

The CJ had 3.90:1 gears and an automatic transmission. *Car Life* ran a 14.4 in the quarter mile at 99.44 mph (160kph), very impressive given that the car weighed more than 4,000 pounds (1,816kg) with two testers aboard. *Motor Trend* fared even better, recording a 13.86 at 101.69 mph (163.5kph) (again with two on board), but the *Motor Trend* test drivers benefited from 4.11:1 gears. Not bad for just $3,703 as tested.

Being the second in a two-year model run, there was little change for the 1969 model, with a few significant exceptions. An optional functional ram air hood with a forward-facing scoop worked with a flapper atop the air cleaner to boost performance on the 428 Cobra Jet. A Drag Pack option was released, which gave you either a 3.90:1 limited slip differential or 4.30:1 gears with a Detroit Locker differential, LeMans-style connecting rods, and an oil cooler.

Two new models, the Cyclone Spoiler and Spoiler II, appeared to homologate aerodynamic enhancements for NASCAR. The Spoiler had the standard front end styling treatment but added a decklid-mounted wing to increase downforce. The Spoiler II had the rear wing but added the Torino Talladega's sloping aerodynamic nose.

A pair of limited editions were released as well, the Dan Gurney Special and the Cale Yarborough Special. Both men were driving for Mercury in NASCAR. The Spoiler II versions were all built with 290-horsepower 351-cubic-inch engines. (See also *Cyclones/Spoilers, Cale Yarborough/Dan Gurney Special Editions.*)

For 1970, the Montego/Cyclone body was all-new. Gone was the wind-cheating fastback, called the SportsRoof in Ford-speak, which was now a Ford Torino exclusive. This hardly mattered, for as it turned out, the new fastback was not very aerodynamic and the standard coupe body actually worked better on the superspeedways.

The Cyclone and Cyclone GT were handsome if unconventional-looking cars. Up front was a trident-style grille with a gun sight in the center, flanked by a pair of low-intensity driving lights. The Cyclone had exposed headlights with two taillights per side, while the GT got stylish hideaway headlamps and three taillights per side.

The interiors were redesigned; gone were the four round instrument displays located directly in front of the driver, replaced by a rather ordinary-looking horizontal speedometer. An optional gauge cluster (standard on the Spoiler and GT) put a driver-turned tachometer and oil pressure, water temperature, and amps gauges in individual pods across the dash, spilling onto the passenger side of the interior. They looked cool, but their placement was less than ideal.

Returning was the Cyclone Spoiler, and Mercury listed the actual aerodynamic improvements in its advertising: "Here's the muscle machine that puts the wind to work for you. Tested out at 100 mph [161kph], front spoiler drops lift from 186 to 120.5 pounds [84.5 to 54.5kg]. Rear spoiler cuts it down from 67.5 to 5.8. This Cyclone comes equipped with all the basic competition hardware." According to the ad, the new-for-1970 429 Cobra Jet with ram air was standard on this model, as was a 4-speed with a Hurst shifter; this wasn't entirely true, as the 429 4-barrel with 360 horsepower was standard on the base Cyclone, while the CJ was standard on the Spoiler.

The Cyclone and Spoiler got the passenger-car 429 as standard equipment, while the GT was powered in base form by the 351-Windsor with a 2-barrel carb. A 4-barrel was available for the 351, which gave you the Cleveland V8 with canted valves. Further up the options list was the 429 Cobra Jet making 370 horsepower, or 375 with

Border Bandits

The Canadian drag racing team owned by Sandy Elliot, his son (John), and Barry Poole was famous for its Super Stock and Stock exploits both north and south of the border—hence the nickname Border Bandits. Elliot owned Sandy Elliot Ltd., Canada's oldest Ford-Mercury dealer, and Poole was its performance advisor.

Poole met a ton of success as early as 1966 while driving a Stock Eliminator 390 Comet, but in '68, the team's focus shifted to Super Stock Cobra Jet Mustangs. Poole twice set the Super Stock/E automatic record that year, the second time with a finish of 11.32 seconds in the quarter mile.

Things only improved for Poole in '69, when he set the Super Stock/I mark in Sandy Elliot's Cobra Jet Mustang with an 11.26 ET in the quarter mile. Poole was the Division III champion that year, edging out John Elliot in the points. In 1970, he won that crown again, and he took two Canadian national Eliminator titles. He earned the nickname Pomona Poole when he won the Super Stock class at the NHRA Winternationals in Pomona, California, in 1970 and 1971.

John Elliot, at seventeen years of age, was the youngest Canadian ever to win an NHRA national event, taking the title at the Winternationals and the U.S. Nationals in 1968 in a 427 A/Stock automatic Comet. In 1970, he drove his Cobra Jet Mustang to the Super Stock/F-class title at the Springnationals and went on to take the Super Stock Eliminator crown at the same race.

In all, the Border Bandits set nine Super Stock records, and in one period made it to the finals in sixteen of seventeen races. Poole also drove Sandy's Pro Stock Comet starting in 1971.

the Super Cobra Jet package. In addition to drag racing–style gear ratios and an oil cooler, the SCJ had a 4-bolt bottom end and forged aluminum pistons, a mechanical-lifter camshaft, and a 780-cfm Holley carburetor (a Rochester carburetor was standard on the Cobra Jet). Both used the same iron high-rise intake manifold.

No longer available in the Cyclone were the 428 Cobra Jet or Super Cobra Jet. They were being phased out and in 1970, their last year, they were available only in the Ford Mustang and Mercury Cougar.

The 429 itself was based on Ford's new 385-series engine family. The engine had enough meat in the block to allow displacement of more than 500 cubic inches. While this seems outlandish today, when the 385 series was designed, cars were getting larger and heavier, and such displacement was deemed necessary to propel them. Today, Ford sells a high-output 514-cubic-inch version through its Racing Parts program.

Cobra Jet Cyclones were good for low- to mid-14s at the drags, with Super Cobra Jet versions capable of high 13s. *Hot Rod* reported a 14.23 at 101.12 mph (162.5kph) with a plain Cyclone fitted with the 370-horse CJ, automatic transmission, and 3.50:1 gears. Its best time was achieved with the air flapper door/air filter lid removed, which resulted in an improvement of two-tenths of a second. *Super Stock & Drag Illustrated* achieved a sub-14-second ET, 13.97 at 100 mph (161kph), in a CJ automatic Spoiler.

The year 1971 was the last for the Cyclone. The engines and models were carried over, though for some reason the hole in the gun sight was slightly larger. Mercury and Ford intermediates were redesigned the following year, and the emphasis was more on luxury than performance. All the Cobra Jets were gone. In 1972, there was a very rare Cyclone option on the Montego. A total of twenty-nine GTs and one MX were ordered with the Cyclone option and it included a functional ram air hood scoop, striping on the rocker panels, dual racing mirrors, rim blow steering wheel, and larger tires (F70×14-inch [35.5cm] with the 351 CJ engine and G70×14-inch [35.5cm] with the 429). There was a Montego GT added in '72, which resurrected the fastback roofline, but the only big-block was a 429 4-barrel with 205 net horsepower. It was a good-looking car and, in addition to the fastback, gave you twin faux scoops on the hood and hash marks on the rear quarters. The basic body style was fairly successful in NASCAR for years to come, especially in the hands of David Pearson, the "Silver Fox," who retired as the second-place holder for the most wins in stock car racing history.

COPO

Central Office Production Order: the phrase suggests nothing too fancy, but behind the abbreviation were some of the most remarkable, quickest, and most unusual cars of the muscle car (or any) era.

Thanks to General Motors' various edicts, there were certain cars that customers wanted but just couldn't readily order, such as 427 Chevelles and Camaros and LT-1 350 Novas. With Ford building 428 Mustangs and Chrysler spitting out 440 'Cudas and Darts, dealers needed some way of getting around the GM corporate red tape.

A Central Office Production Order was the way. COPO was nothing new; it was Chevrolet's way of filling unusual orders, through the Fleet and Special Order Department. For instance, if

A good power-to-weight ratio and low cost were what the 1970 LT-1 COPO Nova was all about. This is a rare car in that it was originally sold in Canada.

you wanted to order municipal vehicles or one hundred taxis in a nonfactory color, you did it through your dealer via a COPO form. It could have been something as simple as ordering a Chevy in a color offered only by a different GM division.

Then some of the more enterprising dealers realized they could get factory hot rods the same way. There are reports of some '64 Chevelles being built with the 365-horsepower 327 from the Corvette through the COPO program, not to mention 427 Chevelles in 1966, though there are no documented examples. Don Yenko ordered a number of specially outfitted Corvairs in 1965 (he called them Yenko Stingers) for his Canonsburg, Pennsylvania, dealership.

One of the first high-profile examples was Fred Gibb Chevrolet, which wanted to drag race automatic transmission–equipped L78 396 Novas in 1968. Although the factory did not produce this transmission setup, Chevy's Vince Piggins blessed a COPO order and fifty 375-horse Novas were built with the Turbo Hydro-Matic 400 gearbox. Voila—NHRA stock class production requirements were met.

There were also COPO Camaros built for Yenko Chevrolet as early as 1968 with the 425-horsepower 427 engine that was technically only available in the full-size Chevys and the '66 Corvette. A number of Chevrolet dealers had been swapping these engines into the ponycar since 1967, but this was the first instance of it happening on an actual assembly line.

Jim Mattison was in charge of processing the COPO orders from 1967 until 1972. In a 1998 interview in *Musclecar Review* magazine, he said that seventy-one 427 engines were shipped to the Camaro's Norwood, Ohio, assembly plant in 1968 under COPO 9737, a package that included Pontiac Rally wheels, a special suspension, and a heavy-duty rear. Unfortunately, no paperwork has been found to substantiate his claim and only one car is known to exist.

The COPO rules were simple: you couldn't order just one car (ten was the minimum), the parts had to be readily available, and the cars and parts

A bench seat and a 4-speed were part of the no-frills approach taken by the LT-1 COPO Nova.

had to be compatible. For instance, you couldn't put a 427 in a 6-cylinder Camaro.

Off the success of the Yenko program, more 427 cars were built in '69, including both Camaros and Chevelles. Yenko ordered some five hundred Camaros alone, and other dealers like Berger Chevrolet, Nickey Chevrolet, and Dana Chevrolet combined to order at least that many. It is not known how many were built of either the COPO Camaro or the COPO Chevelle in 1969.

The Chevelles were especially interesting because they bore no external SS markings and had no 427 nomenclature on them. They were built as everything from bare-bones basic to fully optioned screamers.

There is no record of any 427 Novas being produced, nor is there any information indicating that any 454 Camaros were made in 1970. There were COPO cars that year, however, and they were Novas. But instead of the hairy big-blocks, they came with the new 360-horsepower 350 from the Camaro Z/28. As usual, Yenko was behind this. He ordered 350/250-horse Novas and, through COPO 9737, got LT-1 powered compacts. Yenko added stripes, a hood tach, and other goodies as part of his Yenko Super Car program. These were easy 13-second street cars as delivered. Simple modifications could help you achieve 12-second quarter-mile times.

The LT-1 Novas were nothing, however, compared to the ZL-1 COPO Camaros. A total of sixty-nine Camaros were built with the all-aluminum 427 ZL-1 engine in 1969, and they were intended solely for sanctioned drag strip competition in the Super Stock classes. This engine, which had unique aluminum cylinder heads, an alloy cylinder block, and about 580 horsepower, weighed about as much as a small-block Camaro. In showroom trim, these Camaros could turn 110.21 mph (177.5kph) in the quarter mile at 13.16 seconds, according to a *Cars* magazine test. With headers, slicks, and blueprinted engines, they were capable of low 10s at 130 mph (209kph). The option cost $4,180—more than the car itself—making the overall cost of a COPO ZL-1 more than $7,800.

Before pricing was announced, Fred Gibb Chevrolet ordered fifty cars. Once the more-than-$7,000 price was released, he sent many of them back and they were distributed to other high-performance dealers, such as Berger Chevrolet in Grand Rapids, Michigan.

GM lifted its ban of engines larger than 400 cubic inches in its intermediates for the 1970 model year. This, combined with the dwindling demand for all-out supercars, eliminated the need for COPO muscle machines. They remain among the most desirable and valuable of all cars from this time period.

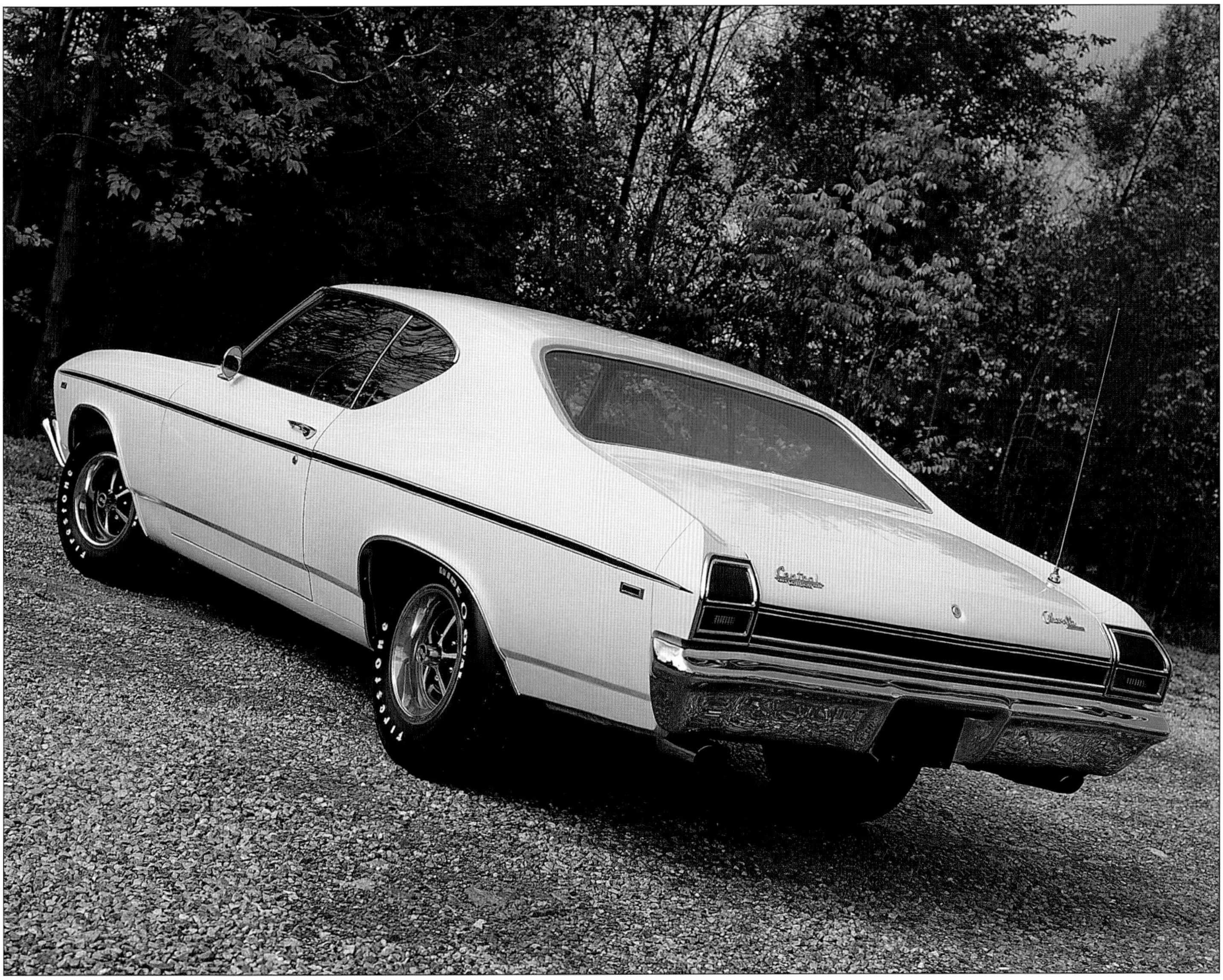

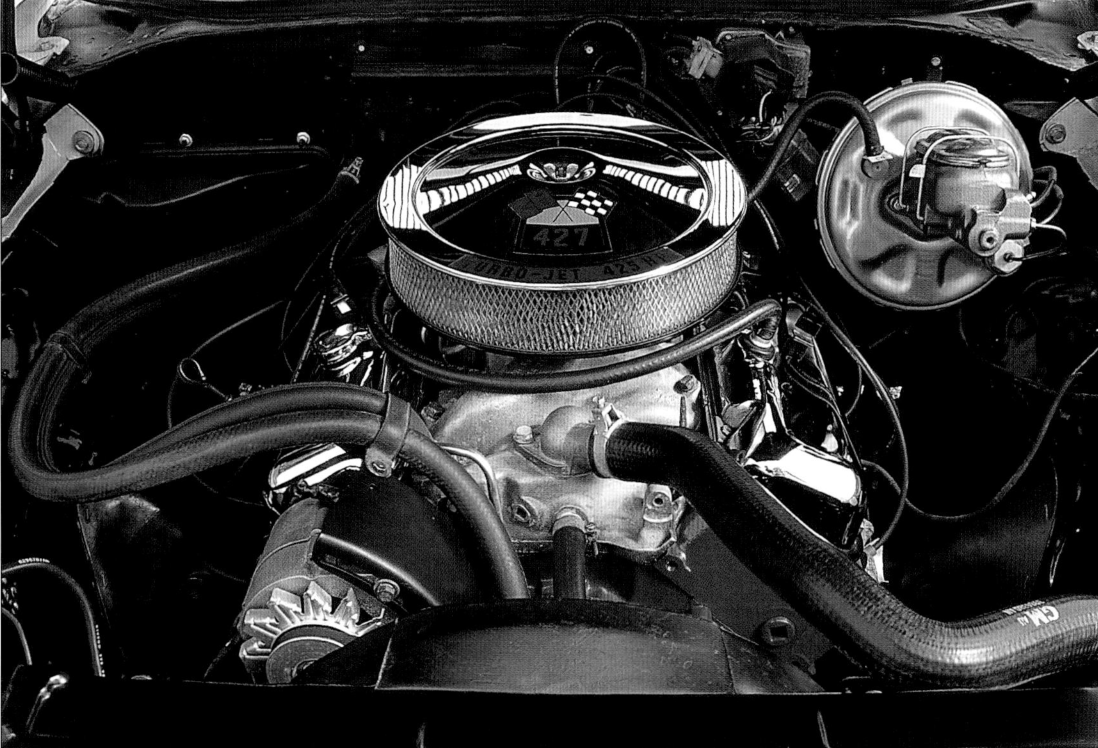

Above: The 1969 427 COPO Chevelles had no external badges to tip off the unsuspecting. Not a single SS or 427 designation was to be found.

Left: Here is the 425-horse engine under the hood of a 1969 COPO Chevelle. The engine had a solid-lifter camshaft and was only available with a 4-speed manual transmission.

Coronet

In 1965, Dodge reached into its past and plucked the Coronet name for its line of intermediates (it was last used in 1959). The stylish 1965 Coronet rode on a 117-inch (297cm) wheelbase and was available as a pillared coupe, a hardtop, or a convertible. The lowest line was simply the Coronet, the midline added 440 badging, and the top level was the 500, which featured acres of stainless steel, aluminum, and chrome trim—on both the exterior and interior. The 500 also featured a bucket seat interior with a console.

Dodge called the Coronet "the animal tamer" in its print ads, noting how it could subdue Impalas, Mustangs, and Wildcats. On the street, the top engines were the 330-horse 383 and the 365-horse 426-S. The former was competitive with a 389 4-barrel GTO, which was a step or so behind a Tri-Power Goat. For real performance, you could step up and order a Coronet with Chrysler's new Race Hemi engine. How wild was the muscle car era? Dodge went so far as to advertise this beast in magazines. "Our new 426 Coronet should have its head examined. You know what the Hemi is...It's got valves as big as stove lids. A plug jammed right in the middle of the combustion chamber. 426 cubes. Why not drop a Hemi in the new Coronet 500?" So read the ad copy.

For the strip, Dodge built enough Hemi Coronets to shake up the competition (see *Altered Wheelbase Mopars*). In NASCAR's Grand National division, the Hemi Coronets were outlawed.

Two versions of the Race Hemi were offered, a single 4-barrel-equipped model for NASCAR and one with dual quads for drag racing. The former was rated at 415 horsepower and had 11:1 compression, while the latter was said to produce 425 with 12:1 compression. Both ratings were significantly lower than actual output.

For 1966, Dodge significantly updated the Coronet with changes to the sheet metal to the chassis as well. More importantly, the mighty new Street Hemi, a detuned version of the fabulous race engine, was optional equipment. Street Hemis weren't the prettiest or sportiest muscle cars, but many cars from the factory could run with them, especially if you ordered this 425-horsepower engine in a lightweight two-door post body. Even a 3,900-pound (1,770.5kg) convertible Coronet Street Hemi could run 14.17 at 98.3 mph (158kph), according to a *Car Craft* test.

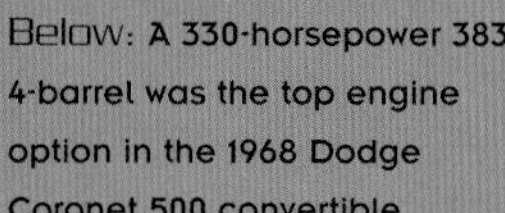

Below: A 330-horsepower 383 4-barrel was the top engine option in the 1968 Dodge Coronet 500 convertible.

The 383 was still available in the Coronet, but at 325 horsepower it did not compare to the Hemi. This was all Dodge performance fans could get short of the Hemi in '66, but that changed the following year with the introduction of the R/T.

Available only as a Coronet model in 1967, the R/T (for road and track) came standard with a 375-horsepower version of the 440 RB engine. Called the Magnum, it had superior cylinder heads and improved intake and exhaust manifolds, and was derived from the mighty 413 and 426 engine family. The R/T's 440 was the largest engine you could get in any muscle car up to that point, and it made 480 lbs.-ft. of torque. It could very nearly run with a Street Hemi, but at a more affordable price.

Also standard with the R/T package were heavy-duty brakes and suspension, red streak tires, dual exhausts, bucket seats, and fake mag wheel covers.

Road & Track magazine, for which the R/T was not named, complimented the car's handling: "I am happy to say that the Dodge was a revelation in its flat ride, controllability and consistent brakes in spite of obviously being more than a little nose heavy." Low- to mid-14-second ETs in the quarter mile were easily achieved.

The ultimate racing option in '67 was RPO WO23, which delivered to your door the Super Stock Hemi Coronet. Totally stripped down for drag racing, these cars came with Street Hemi engines that were slightly modified from their roadgoing counterparts. All were built on the Coronet 440 body, which was the lightest hardtop in the lineup. An enormous functional ram air hood was standard, and engine modifications included a transistorized ignition and solid-core spark plug wires. Radios and heaters were not part of the package, nor were body insulation and sound deadeners. A rubber floor mat replaced the carpeting; and power steering, a radio and heater were not available. Only fifty-five were built.

Because the cars were meant for racing, Hooker exhaust headers and a pan to seal the carburetors to the functional hood were delivered in the trunk. The short-block and cylinder heads were standard Street Hemi, but the intake and carburetors were modified by racer Arlan Vanke. Compression was the same 10.25:1 as any other Street Hemi.

Transmission choices were a Hemi 4-speed with a coarse-spline, heavy-duty input shaft and a specially prepared automatic, last seen in the '65 Race Hemi cars. The 727 TorqueFlite utilized a 5-clutch drum rather than the standard 4-clutch unit, the bands were thicker, and most importantly, the TorqueFlite transmission had a reverse-pattern-manual-valve body, meaning the driver had to shift it himself. If you had the A-833 4-speed, you got a Dana rear with 4.88:1 gears; the automatic gave you the 8.75-inch (22cm) rear with a 4.89:1 cog.

In the back, Super Stock leaf springs helped plant all the power. Special spring rate torsion bars

Left: In the swinging '60s, Chrysler used advertising to recruit people to join the "Dodge Rebellion."

These Pages: A heavy-duty 4-speed transmission (shifter pictured above) was standard with the Hemi option in the '67 Dodge Coronet R/T pictured here. A pair of inline Carter 4-barrel carburetors (inset) were standard on the Street Hemi from 1966 until its demise in 1971.

that were lighter than those used in the Street Hemi were installed for improved weight transfer.

The Coronet R/T emerged from its 1968 redesign better than ever. Styling was still uncomplicated and strong. It was obviously related to the new-for-'68 Charger but was more subdued. The 440 was still standard; the Hemi was optional if you needed more beef. To illustrate the point, *Super Stock & Drag Illustrated* reported a 14.01 ET at 102.98 mph (165.5kph) with its TorqueFlite-equipped 440 Magnum tester, while *Popular Hot Rodding* claimed 13.9 at 104.96 mph (169kph) for a 4-speed Hemi model.

If anything, the '69 R/T was even nicer to look at than the '68. The grille was pinched around the headlights, and the car now had three taillights, which looked a lot better than it sounds. A functional ram air hood was optional, and the 440 and 426 were back in the same state of tune. Dodge wasn't making many mechanical changes—it didn't need to.

The Coronet received a controversial face-lift for 1970. A pair of chrome loop bumpers that greatly resembled horse collars adorned the front end. Fake side scoops appeared aft of the doors, and the taillights were reconfigured. This was the last year for the convertible, not to mention the last year for a Coronet-based muscle car. For '71, all two-door Dodge intermediates were Chargers.

But the news wasn't all bad. The 440 Six-Pack, making 390 horsepower and introduced the previous year in the Dodge Super Bee, was now optional in the R/T. Its aluminum intake manifold was replaced by a cast-iron unit that hardly slowed the car down. R/T sales plunged to 3,118, with only 13 getting the Hemi and 210 opting for the Six-Pack.

The R/T enjoyed a short but exciting life.

426
HEMI
426

Cougar was the upscale ponycar in 1969 and the Eliminator above is a shining example. Its interior was far more luxurious than that of its mechanical cousin, the Mustang.

Cougar

What Ford had, Mercury dealers wanted also, especially when the Mustang became the runaway sales success of the '60s. Thus was born the Cougar, an upscale ponycar with a longer wheelbase, better trim, and arguably improved styling.

Upon introduction, the Cougar was available in only one configuration, a two-door hardtop with a formal roofline. Unlike with the Mustang, there was no fastback (2+2) or convertible. The Cougar had a 111-inch (282cm) wheelbase as opposed to the Mustang's 108 inches (274.5cm), but like the Ford it could accommodate the FE-series big-block engines. The standard engine was a 200-horsepower 289 with a 2-barrel carburetor; a 4-barrel version with 225 horsepower was optional, as was a 390 with 320 horsepower.

What made the Cougar stand out from the start was its styling. It had flip-up headlights packaged in what enthusiasts pegged an "electric shaver" grille. The taillights, which mirrored the theme set by the grille, blinked sequentially, an attention-getting gimmick that proved to enhance safety (when it actually worked).

The ride was softer than the Mustang's but the Cougar handled better, according to *Car and Driver*. The bucket seats featured adjustable seat backs for improved comfort, and GT models featured simulated wood grain on the dash.

For performance lovers, the GT was the only way to go. Standard were the 390, Firestone Wide-Oval tires, and power front disc brakes. A special handling suspension came with the GT and included a stiffer front sway bar, larger shocks, higher rate front and rear springs, and 6-inch-(15cm) wide wheels. It was far from the fastest ponycar—*Car and Driver* went 14.9 at 94 mph (151.5kph) in an automatic GT—but its combination of style and spirited performance helped it find its way into 123,684 homes.

Mercury added more models and engines for 1968. The GTE was the strongest performance model. Early in the year, the fabled 427 with 390 horsepower was available; it ended up being the last application for this race-bred powerplant, replaced midyear by the 428 Cobra Jet, rated at 335 horsepower. Neither was produced in large quantities, but the 427 was far more common. Total production was less than four hundred for the two combined. The GTE came with two-tone paint, fake hood scoops, a horizontal divider that ran across the middle of the grille, and styled steel wheels, among other features.

A 325-horsepower 390 was standard in the regular GT, with a 335-horse variation available for a few extra dollars. Naturally, the Cobra Jet was available in the GT when it arrived.

Another special edition was the XR-7 "G," which stood for Dan Gurney Specials. Gurney, the famous American road racer, campaigned a Cougar in the SCCA's Trans-Am series. A limited-edition model was a natural. The "G" option gave you a vinyl roof, fake scoops on the hood, special wheels and tires, and a sunroof.

Entirely new sheet metal arrived for 1969. The second-generation Cougar was 3.5 inches (89mm) longer and nearly 3 inches (76mm) wider, and a new body style, a convertible, was offered. The grille still featured hideaway headlights, but in a more horizontal motif. The taillights were still sequential, but their lenses were concave, à la the 1967–1968 Mustang. Overall, it was a fairly clean redesign except for a sweeping body line that looked like it came off a Buick. The interior was redesigned as well, with four round gauge pods directly in front of the driver, a 3-spoke steering wheel, and toggle switches to operate some of the features.

Under the hood, the big change was the standard engine, which was the new 351, a variation of the earlier small-block that featured a taller deck height, longer stroke, and improved oiling. Torque was noticeably improved over the previous year's 302, even in 2-barrel form.

The performance engines were basically carryovers at the beginning of the year, although a functional hood scoop with ram induction was offered for the 428 Cobra Jet. *Motorcade* magazine put one such XR-7 through its paces (automatic transmission) and got a 14.1 at 102.2 mph (164.5kph).

Later, the Cougar Eliminator was born. With a graphics and spoiler package by noted designer Larry Shinoda, it could be ordered with any of the high-performance Ford engines, including the new Trans-Am-bred Boss 302.

The Boss 302 could rev forever, thanks to its canted valve cylinder heads (which were actually supposed to appear on a different version of the 351 in 1970) and to its enormous 2.23-inch (56mm) intake valves, which it needed to make its 290 advertised horsepower. The Boss 302 actually had larger intake valves than the 428 Cobra Jet, which did little for torque production at low revs. With 3.91:1 gears, high 14s at 96–97 mph (154.5–156kph) were possible.

If you ordered your Eliminator with the 428 CJ, your forward-facing hood scoop was made functional. Standard on all Eliminators was an upgraded suspension package to improve handling. Heavy-duty shocks were used all around, the rears staggered to control wheel hop during hard acceleration. Higher rate front and rear springs and wider-than-standard tires (F70×14-inch [35.5cm]) were also part of the package.

Cougar styling took another odd turn in 1970, when a center section sprung up in the grille. (This was a portent of what would come in 1971, when the once-small ponycar would grow into a larger, more luxurious vehicle.) The engine choices were the same, except that the 351-Windsor was replaced with the 351-Cleveland, and the 390 was finally laid to rest. The 351-C was the standard mill in the Eliminator.

By '71 the Cougar was well on its way to becoming a midsize version of the Thunderbird. Another revamping saw the Cougar's wheelbase grow to 112.1 inches (284.5cm) and overall length stretch to 196.7 inches (499.5cm). This was 7 inches

The top option in the Cougar Eliminator for 1969 was the 428 Cobra Jet, which came standard with a functional hood scoop. Note the flapper door on the air cleaner assembly.

Optional in the Cyclone Spoiler were the Q- and R-code 428 Cobra Jets. Spoiler II models (not shown) only came with the 351 4-barrel. Shown is the 1969 Cale Yarborough Special.

(18cm) longer than the '67. Gone were the hideaway headlamps, replaced by exposed units that flanked a Lincoln Mark III–inspired grille.

Strong engines were still available. The 428 Cobra Jet was retired and replaced by the 429 Cobra Jet and Super Cobra Jet. The 429 CJ was good for low- to mid-14-second ETs in the newer, heavier body.

The following year saw the big-blocks vanish, with the top powerplant being a low-compression 351-Cleveland producing 266 horsepower. Naturally, it was called the 351 Cobra Jet. The last convertible was built in 1973, and not too long after that, a Cougar station wagon was offered.

Cyclones/Spoilers, Cale Yarborough/Dan Gurney Special Editions

The Cale Yarborough Special-edition and Dan Gurney Special-edition Cyclone Spoiler and Spoiler II models were Mercury's answer to the Ford Torino Talladega. There was no sloping nose on the Spoiler models. There was a rear wing, which the Talladegas did not get.

The Spoilers also came with unusual paint and stripe packages. The Yarborough model had a red roof and decklid, a twin-black-stripe hood treatment and twin red body stripes, which ran up from the leading edge of the front fenders and down the tops of the front fenders, doors, and rear fenders. The tail panel was blacked out between the lights. The Gurney cars were essentially the same, except they were white with a blue roof and stripes.

Under the hood was nothing special, just a garden-variety 351 4-barrel; all had the FMX 3-speed automatic and 3.25:1 gears.

The Spoiler IIs, however, did have the reconfigured beak of the Torino Talladega with the flush grille.

Dana Chevrolet

One of the famous high-performance Chevy car dealerships that sold 427 Camaros was Dana located in South Gate, California. In 1967, a co-owner was Peyton Kramer, who had worked at Shelby American on the GT350 project. It was a given that Dana would start turning out 427 Camaros.

For three years, 1967 to 1969, the dealership did. An early '67 model was tested by *Car Life* at Carlsbad Raceway. Equipped with a 4-speed transmission, Hurst shifter, and a 425-horse, 460-lbs.-ft. 427 engine, the Camaro turned a 14.2-second ET at 102 mph (164kph) in the quarter mile, but this only hinted at the potential. With the correct gearing, open headers, and slicks, 11-second ETs were possible.

Little is known about Dana Chevrolet cars today. Some had special fiberglass hoods, though the *Car Life* test machine had a stock SS hood. Doug Thorley headers were standard equipment; optional was a three 2-barrel carb setup and/or aluminum cylinder heads. The L88 race engine was also available.

Dart

The Dart was one of the most successful compacts of the 1960s and 1970s, but at the beginning of the '60s it was the name attached to a full-size Dodge. In 1962, these cars were downsized somewhat, but the Dart name was still not associated with a small car. (The compact Dodge at the time was the Lancer.) Wheelbase had shrunk from the year before by 2 inches (5cm), to 116 inches (294.5cm), and the sheet metal was smaller, too. The Dart was the least expensive of the B-body Dodges; it was also the lightest, which made it perfect for drag racing. It was also about 200 pounds (91kg) lighter than a 409 Chevy.

This was also the year Dodge introduced the 413 Ram Charger V8s, perhaps the most potent engines offered by an automaker to that point in

Dodge created the 340 Dart GT Sport (or GTS) in 1968 and it was one of the best-balanced muscle cars. The 340 engine was one of the most powerful small-blocks around, and the Dart didn't weigh very much. This is a 1969, the last year a convertible was offered on this model.

The 1969 Dart Swinger was created in the same spirit as the Dodge Super Bee. The Dart GTS was better equipped, while the Swinger had a bench seat and rubber floor mats instead of carpeting. Note the column-shifted automatic.

history. Based on the RB engine family, the street-going variant offered a full 410 horsepower, 11.0:1 compression, and dual 4-barrels on a short ram intake manifold, while the 420-horse race version had 13.5:1 compression. Both had radical solid-lifter camshafts, TRW forged aluminum pistons, and excellent cylinder heads with large intake and exhaust valves.

A set of 3.91:1 gears with a Sure-Grip differential was standard, and other ratios were available as a dealer-installed option. Transmission choices were limited to a T-85 Warner 3-speed manual or a fortified 3-speed TorqueFlite automatic. The latter was the first automatic that could shift more quickly than a stick.

The street versions came with flat steel hoods and steel noses, and the battery was mounted under the hood, while the higher-output Max Wedge engines came in cars with aluminum front ends and scooped hoods, with the battery relocated to the trunk.

Two other trim levels appeared in 1962, the Dart 330 and 440. The 330 was the midlevel package; standard were a cigarette lighter, rear armrests, and a foam seat cushion on two- and four-door nonwagons. The 440 was the top-of-the-line package. It had all the Dart and 330 goodies plus backup lights, custom upholstery and trim, and unique exterior moldings.

When the 1963 model year arrived, Dodge took the Dart name from its B-body-based automobile and applied it to its compact line (the 330 and 440 became unique models). These were economical, reliable cars, but big-blocks and high horsepower were not available until 1967. It was in 1967 that the Dart joined the muscle car fray, when it was offered with a 280-horsepower (at 4200 rpm) 383 engine. Horsepower was severely limited by the exhaust manifolds, which had to be contoured to fit the steering box (no power assist could be ordered because it didn't fit in the confined engine bay). The entire exhaust system was smaller than that of a similarly equipped intermediate. Only 457 383 Darts were built.

In 1968, horsepower increased to 300 because of the addition of new cylinder heads from the Road Runner/Super Bee 383 and GTX/R/T 440. A new intake manifold and larger Carter AVS carb were added as well.

Though the big-block was available in ever-increasing quantities, the hot ticket for a street Dart customer was the all-new 340 GT Sport or GTS, as it was badged. This engine was smaller and lighter than the 383, made similar power, and was a better match for the chassis. Underrated at 275 horsepower, it became a favorite of gearheads everywhere. *Car and Driver* reported a 14.4-second ET at 99 mph (159.5kph) after it tested a 340/4-speed Dart in its September '68 issue, while *Hot Rod* claimed a 14.38 at 97 mph (156kph) for an automatic GTS in its April '68 issue.

As a side note, 4-speed 340 Darts came with a more aggressive camshaft than the automatic cars, which was designed to give the latter better idle qualities. The 340, based on Chrysler's LA engine family (273, 318), was a high-performance engine all the way. Standard was an oil pan windage tray, 10.5:1 compression, a forged crankshaft, a double roller timing chain, stronger connecting rods, and excellent cylinder heads. Chrysler engineers have since said that the 340's heads were a good copy of those on the small-block Chevrolet V8.

Not only could the Dart accelerate, but its handling was lauded as well. *Car Life* praised it for its excellent steering response and near-neutral cornering: "Driven properly, using brakes and power to set up four-wheel drifts, the Dart displayed near-perfect controllability."

The most potent Dart ever came from Chrysler courtesy of the Hurst Corporation that same year. See *Hurst Hemi Darts*, but suffice to say that, more than thirty years later, they still dominate Super Stock drag racing with their cousins, the Hurst Hemi Barracudas of the same vintage.

Advertised horsepower increased again for the 383 Dart in 1969, reaching 330 at 5200 rpm, while the 340 stayed at 275. The Dart Swinger model was introduced, basically as a stripped-down model. A rubber floor mat was standard, and with the 340, the car became a compact, small-block version of the Super Bee. But that wasn't the big news. Incredibly, this was the year Dodge decided

This is the 1968 Grand Spaulding Dodge Dart GSS. Grand Spaulding swapped 440-cubic-inch RB engines into the Dart, something the factory would not do for another year.

to install the 440 RB engine in the tiny (for its time) economy car. With 375 horsepower, it was almost more horsepower than the car could handle. It was a nose-heavy beast—not a great handler, but outstanding when set up for racing.

A sleeker, less boxy Dart was introduced in 1970. The Swinger 340 was still quite popular and could be ordered with hood scoops, hood pins, and a 4-speed transmission. It remained a giant killer. Gone were both optional big-blocks, the 383 and 440, which were now being pushed hard in the brand-new Challenger ponycar.

For '71, the Dart returned to its roots as an economy car. The 340 engine was available solely in the new Dodge Demon 340 and the Challenger. The next performance model was the Dart Sport, which replaced the Demon in 1973. The 340, now rated at 240 net horsepower, could still smoke the tires and ranked as one of the quickest cars, foreign or domestic, of that year.

The Dart Sport, which inherited the Demon's body, was still quite inexpensive at $2,793, with optional sunroof and a fold-down rear seat. (There was still a Dart two-door coupe, but the high-performance engine was not available in it.) The 340, now in its last year of production, had 8.5:1 compression and a host of smog goodies to sap power. That's not to say the Dart Sport 340 wasn't fast—it could still turn a mid-15-second quarter mile, about average for the era.

The 340 grew to 360 cubic inches in '74 via an increase in stroke and a slight decrease in bore, which greatly improved torque, from 295 to 320 lbs.-ft., with a moderate gain in horsepower, to 245. This model, the Dart Sport 360, stayed alive though the end of the bicentennial year of 1976. In fact, in a *Car and Driver* test called "America's Fastest Cars," it ranked second only to the L82 Corvette in top speed (124.5 versus 121.8 mph [200.5 versus 196kph]) and was a full 4.2 mph (7kph) faster than the 455 Pontiac Trans Am. It placed third in quarter-mile acceleration behind the Corvette and the Firebird with a 15.7 at 88.3 mph (142kph)—not too shabby for a car now rated at 220 net horsepower. Thanks to Chrysler's Lean Burn engine-management system, the Dart Sport 360 was the only car in the test unencumbered by a catalytic converter.

Somehow the car whose name helped usher in the muscle car era—a name that became synonymous with fuel economy and bare-bones transportation for much of its life—was one of the last holdouts of the muscle car era. The Dart outlasted such notables as the Camaro Z/28, the Chevelle SS, and the GTO.

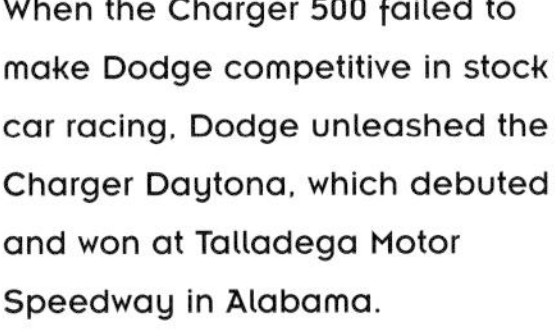

When the Charger 500 failed to make Dodge competitive in stock car racing, Dodge unleashed the Charger Daytona, which debuted and won at Talladega Motor Speedway in Alabama.

Daytona

See *Charger*.

Demon

Its controversial name and emblem threw many church groups into an uproar, but this Dodge, which was introduced in 1971, got the enthusiasts in a frenzy as well when equipped with the high-winding 340 engine.

The Demon debuted as a sister car to Plymouth's Duster, which had arrived a year earlier. It shared the basic body shell of the Duster, but its grille more resembled the Dart Swinger. It rode on the Duster's 108-inch (274.5cm) wheelbase, which was 3 inches (7.5cm) shorter than that of the Dart. Like the Duster, it was designed to be base, 6-cylinder transportation, but there was to be a high-performance version of virtually every car in the Dodge lineup in those days; thus the 340 Demon was born.

Weighing about 100 pounds (45.5kg) less than a similarly equipped Dart, the Demon was roughly one-tenth of a second quicker and 1 mph (1.5kph) faster in the quarter mile. While other supercars were struggling with drops in compression and declining horsepower, the 275-horsepower Demon was still capable of 14.4 quarter-mile times, according to *Motor Trend*.

On the Demon 340, a 3-speed manual transmission and E70×14-inch (35.5cm) Goodyear Polyglas tires were standard, as was the Rallye suspension, chrome exhaust tips, larger-than-standard wheels, and tape stripes for the body, hood, and rear deck panel. A 4-speed manual and 3-speed TorqueFlite automatic were available at extra cost. So was a hood with two fake scoops, hood pins, and Rally rims.

The Demon 340 started at a mere $2,721 and attracted 10,089 buyers in its rookie year. Overall, just less than eighty thousand Demons were built, which was quite good for Dodge.

Following up this success proved difficult, and sales slipped below the fifty thousand mark, though the Demon 340 still found nearly nine thousand customers. In an effort to increase performance, Grand Spaulding Dodge built the Demon GSS, which had a Paxton supercharger.

The Demon name gave way to Dart Sport in 1973. Certain groups had never gotten used to its devilish name or, especially, its emblem—a red, horned devil holding a pitchfork, the prongs of which were used to form the "M."

Diamante

This 1970 Dodge concept car started off as a Challenger R/T ragtop with a 426 Hemi engine. The Diamante, which had a 4-speed transmission

John Z. DeLorean

The trials and tribulations of John Zachary DeLorean and his failed car company, DeLorean Motor Cars, are well documented. What is often overlooked by the mainstream media is that in his time, he was one of the brightest young executives at General Motors, a man who walked away when he was one step from heading the entire company.

After a stint at Studebaker-Packard (which had gone belly-up), DeLorean was hired by Bunkie Knudsen at Pontiac. Working under Knudsen and E.M. "Pete" Estes, DeLorean was assistant chief engineer. Later, he became the chief engineer at the Wide-Track division when Knudsen became general manager of Chevrolet and Estes got the G.M. title at Pontiac.

As chief engineer, DeLorean, along with staff engineers Bill Collins and Russ Gee, came up with the GTO concept as an option package on the Tempest. This was a car with which DeLorean took a real risk in the face of the 1963 GM racing ban, not to mention the fact that engines larger than 330 cubic inches were barred from GM intermediates and the GTO blatantly offered a 389-cid engine.

The GTO, of course, is one of the great success stories of the 1960s, and DeLorean was eventually promoted to head up Pontiac when Estes got moved up to the general manager position at Chevrolet. Not only was DeLorean a talented engineer, but he was a brilliant marketer as well. The original GTO is proof of that, but further testimony was provided when he came up with the name "the Judge" for Pontiac's wild new GTO in '69.

***Laugh-In* was the top-rated TV show in the country and comedian Flip Wilson had a skit in which he yelled, "Here come the Judge!" It became a catchphrase around the country. The original name for the new model was the GTO E/T (for elapsed time). DeLorean recognized that the acronym was a terrible idea and recommended the Judge. It was a natural.**

The one dream he couldn't make happen at Pontiac was an economical two-seat sports car—not a Corvette challenger, just a low-priced, fun machine with style and flair. General Motors wanted none of this, and when the four-seat Camaro was conceived, the corporation wanted Pontiac to have a version of it. DeLorean fought the move for so long that when the company told him to take the F-body and like it, Pontiac engineers had only six months to develop the car.

In 1970, DeLorean's star was still rising. He was made general manager of Chevrolet, and by 1973 the division had moved three million cars and trucks—a first. He was made vice president of North American Cars and Trucks later that year, a position that paid $650,000. He soon got tired of the corporate politics and quit GM in order to start his "ethical sports car company."

In 1979, against his wishes, his memoirs were published. Titled *On a Clear Day, You Can See General Motors*, it was a stinging indictment of his former employer. The first DeLorean sports car, the DMC-12, was built in 1981, and the company lasted until 1983, when it folded.

Mark Donohue

Born and raised in Summit, New Jersey, Mark Donohue was perhaps America's greatest road racer. The Ivy League–educated (Brown) engineer won the first competitive event he entered—a hill climb in Belknap, New Hampshire—in his Corvette. He later won three Trans-Am series championships—two with Camaro in '68 and '69 and one with AMC's Javelin in '71.

American Motors actually introduced a Mark Donohue Javelin in 1970, with a rear spoiler designed by the famous race driver. Based on his experience with the '70 Trans-Am, Donohue added to

his legacy by designing another rear spoiler, for the all-new '71 Javelin AMX, as well as an optional fiberglass cowl induction hood.

But Donohue was at his best on the race track. His list of achievements is mind-boggling. He won the Sports Car Club Association (SCCA) E-production national championship in '65 and the B-production title that same year. Donohue captured back-to-back SCCA U.S. Road Racing championships in '67 and '68 and was named the Rookie of the Year at the Indianapolis 500 in 1969, when he finished seventh.

His record in Trans-Am competition is unparalleled. In fifty-five races, he was victorious twenty-nine times and landed in the top three forty-three times. In the five years he competed in the series, he won three championships and finished second in points the other two years.

Donohue won the 24 Hours of Daytona in 1969 and the Indianapolis 500 in '72 and was the Can-Am champion in '73. He even dabbled in stock car racing. At a select few NASCAR events, he drove a Roger Penske–prepared AMC Matador, one of the first cars to use disc brakes in NASCAR. He won the Schaefer 500 in Pocono in '71 and the Western 500 in '73.

The year 1974 saw him win the International Race of Champions series title. He retired from racing that year, but decided to return that September for the Canadian Grand Prix. He established a closed-course world speed record in 1975, but died later that year after he crashed while practicing for the Austrian Grand Prix. It is believed that a tire deflated and pitched his car into the catch fencing and over a barrier, killing a marshal and injuring another. His helmet struck one of the fence posts, and he was momentarily knocked unconscious but otherwise apparently unharmed. He continued to complain of headaches and lapsed into unconsciousness, dying two days later in a Graz hospital, despite brain surgery.

Donohue's autobiography, *The Unfair Advantage* (cowritten with Paul Van Valkenburg), was recently reissued with extra photos and a foreword by his sons.

and 4.10:1 gears, sported a new front fascia with hideaway headlamps and Honey Gold Pearlescent paint over a yellow base. It had a pair of functional scoops at the leading edge of the hood to duct cold air to the carburetors, sidepipes similar to those used on the '69 Corvette, and scoops in the top of the rear fenders, à la the '69 Mustang SportsRoof. A targa top let the sunshine in, and a pair of high-back bucket seats surrounded by a headrest fairing were among the interior highlights. The rear deck had a short spoiler, and the taillights were a preview of what would appear on the production 1972 Dodge Challenger.

Dodge 330/440

When Dodge moved the Dart name from its large car to its compact in 1963, the 330 and 440 (which had been trim upgrades) became separate models on what was now considered an intermediate lineup. Wheelbase increased to 119 inches (302.5cm), but the controversial styling of 1962 was toned down quite a bit. The 330 was the base car, while the 440 was the intermediate (the Polara was the plushest intermediate Dodge offered).

The 330 was now the most likely recipient of the Max Wedge engine, which received an increase in bore from 4.18 to 4.25 inches (10.5 to 11cm) pushing displacement of 426 cubic inches. The 440 was the next model up, giving you a foam seat cushion and carpeting.

Except for the bore and stroke and an improved oiling system, the 426 was basically a carryover engine. The carbs, heads, intake, and so on were the same as the 413. Now, however, the street version pumped out 415 horsepower at 5600 rpm and 470 lbs.-ft. of torque at 4400 rpm.

Racers got the same goodies, plus 13.5:1 compression for a total of 425 horsepower at 5600 rpm and 480 lbs.-ft. of torque at 4400. Racers also got the benefit of the aluminum front end package. The fenders, splash shields, cold-air hood, bumper brackets, and other minor pieces were all made of the lightweight material. This dropped the weight by about 200 pounds (91kg). Naturally, there was no radio or heater. The battery was trunk-mounted in the race cars; lower-compression Max Wedge cars got batteries mounted under the hood.

Later in the year the Stage II Max Wedge was born, which gave more power although the ratings stayed the same. The following year, Chrysler introduced the Stage III version. Packed into the 330, this might have been the dominant drag car in 1964, but Chrysler reintroduced the Hemi shortly thereafter. This was the company's first hemispherical headed engine since the 1950s and was available in either a lightweight or all-steel drag car or in a

steel body for NASCAR racing. (A street version would not be available until 1966.) A grand total of fifty-five Race Hemis were built for both Dodge and Plymouth in '64.

All intermediate Dodges underwent another significant face-lift in 1964. The result was far better than the previous two years, especially if you ordered the two-door 440 hardtop or Polara hardtop. The headlights were encased in a revised, very pleasing, simple grille. The roofline on the sedans was similar to the year before, but the hardtops gave the car a very modern, upscale appearance.

Dodge played the name game again in 1965. All intermediate Dodges were named Coronet. The 330 went away for good, while the 440 became a midlevel trim package on the Coronet.

E-body

This was the modified B-body intermediate platform used for the 1970–1974 Dodge Challenger and Plymouth Barracuda.

El Camino

The El Camino was a combination car/pickup truck that was Chevrolet's answer in 1959 to Ford's Ranchero (which had been introduced two years earlier). It is redundant to say that it was built on the full-size Chevrolet frame, because except for the Corvette, Chevys that year came in only one size. The first two years of the El Camino could hardly be called muscle cars, though a three 2-barrel version of the 348-W motor was theoretically available in 1960 making 335 horsepower.

Chevrolet canceled the El Camino in 1961 and it did not reappear until 1964, when it returned on the new intermediate Chevelle chassis. That car trumped the Ford Ranchero, which was now based on the much smaller Falcon platform.

The top powerplant for '64 was a 300-horse 327. There was not a true El Camino muscle car until 1966, when the 396 big-block became an option. All three versions of the 396 (325, 350, and 375 horsepower) that were available in the Chevelle could be ordered in the quasi-pickup. These engines carried over to 1967 and *Motor Trend* got hold of a 325/396 for testing in its July 1967 issue. The car covered the quarter mile in

Opposite: Mark Donohue poses in the number 66 car on May 21, 1971 in Indianapolis.

Top: Chevrolet made both the LS5 and LS6 454 available in the El Camino SS in 1970.

Above: The LS5 454 engine produced 360 horsepower in 1970. It had a hydraulic-lifter camshaft and was available in the Chevelle, Monte Carlo, and El Camino at this output. Installed in the full-size Chevrolet or Corvette engine, the LS5 454 was rated at 390 horsepower.

E.M. "Pete" Estes

Not as well known as some of the more high-profile figures from the super car era, Elliot "Pete" Estes played a major role in post–World War II automotive history by working on the development of the Oldsmobile Rocket V8 engine.

Born in Mendon, Michigan, Estes built his first car at age twelve, a 1-cylinder engine on a coaster wagon. He joined the GM Institute in 1934 at age eighteen, and in 1940 he graduated from the University of Cincinnati with a degree in mechanical engineering.

Upon Estes, return to GM, he began working for Charles Kettering in the Research Labs. He moved to Oldsmobile and worked his way up to assistant chief engineer. When Semon E. "Bunkie" Knudsen was named general manager of Pontiac, one of his first moves was to bring in Estes as his chief engineer. After Knudsen was tapped as general manager of Chevrolet in 1961, Estes was promoted into Knudsen's former job. As a result of this promotion, Estes became the youngest auto division chief in the history of General Motors. One of Estes' boldest moves was moving John Z. DeLorean into his old role as chief engineer at Pontiac. On an upward swing since 1956, when Knudsen took over, Pontiac experienced even further growth under Estes, who later succeeded Knudsen at Chevrolet.

Estes was known as a great motivator who loved cars and had incredible instincts about the internal workings of automobiles. He climbed to the top of the GM corporate ladder, eventually becoming president. He died in 1988.

15.7 seconds at a very respectable 90 mph (145kph), hitting 60 mph (96.5kph) in 7.4 seconds.

Although the 396 had been available for two years, the first El Camino SS was built in 1968. This was the only year during the muscle car era that the El Camino was a separate model, which could be verified by a specific digit in its Vehicle Identification Number (VIN). It had achieved true supercar status, according to *Car Life*, for its ability to record sub-15-second quarter-mile times. With a test weight of more than 4,000 (1,816kg) pounds, highway-minded 3.31:1 gears, and a Turbo 400 automatic transmission, the 350-horse El Camino ran a best of 14.8 at 94.93 mph (152.5kph) at the drags. It ran from 0 to 60 (96.5kph) in 6.8 seconds.

"The El Camino was a supercar. Or even a supertruck, if such exists. Quarter-mile times were in the high 14s, run after run. No drag, no quick starts, no between-run trips to the garden hose for emergency cooling, just instant performance," according to *Car Life*. With a similarly equipped test El Camino, *Hot Rod* reported an even better elapsed time, 14.49 at 98.79 mph (159kph).

The El Camino SS came with the same standard features as the Chevelle SS but rode on the station wagon and sedan's 116-inch (294.5cm) wheelbase. The Chevelle's F41 heavy-duty suspension (and rear sway bar) was not available. On the other hand, it did have air-adjustable shocks in the rear, which gave the owner the ability to keep the rear level when the bed was loaded.

Along with the Chevelle's supercar performance, the El Camino enjoyed the '68 model's exceptional styling. The front end retained the Chevelle's traditional quad-headlamp arrangement, but it was far more aggressive than that of the previous year.

The '69 El Camino SS was more or less a carry-over vehicle, as it was the second in a two-year styling cycle. The most important news was that, for the first time, the L89 aluminum cylinder head option was listed. Like the Chevelle, the El Camino SS received a major face-lift for 1970, and like its passenger-car brethren, it received the same thundering 454 big-blocks. Two versions of the 454, the 360-horsepower LS5 and the 450-horspower LS6 with its full-on solid-lifter camshaft, were offered. The LS5 made peak power at 5400 rpm and peak torque (500 lbs.-ft.) at 3200. Compression was 10.25:1. As for the LS6, peak power was rated at 5600 rpm, while its 500-lbs.-ft. torque rating was measured at 3600. Compression on the LS6 was 11.0:1.

Two SS396s were also available, though a running change during the model year saw the engine grow to 402 cubic inches. The more powerful of the two was still the solid-lifter L78, which continued to be rated at 375 horsepower at 5600 rpm and 415 lbs.-ft. at 3600. The more subdued 350-horsepower L34 with its hydraulic-lifter cam and 10.25:1 compression ratio had the same torque rating, but at 3200 rpm.

Chevrolet kept the bold 1970 front end treatment for only one year; it was revised the following fall with one headlight per side (a Chevelle/El Camino first) and a less menacing grille. Regardless, the 1971–1972 El Camino was a very handsome car, and as its performance versions went away, so did its looks. By 1973, all the good engines were history, and its once-handsome design gave way to one that was at best bland and at worst truly ugly. The top gun in '71 was the LS5, now rated at 365 horsepower, while the LS3 402 (396) was detuned to 300 ponies. This was the year Chevrolet (and the rest of General Motors) dropped compression ratios across the board, and performance suffered accordingly. The last true high-performance El Camino was the '72 LS5 454 with 270 net horsepower.

Fairlane/Torino

As cars continued to get larger in the late 1950s, Ford executives saw a market for a car that would be larger than Ford's upcoming Falcon yet smaller than its full-size offerings. Ford decided to create a car for this niche, and the result was not only a car that would play a pivotal role in the muscle car era, but an engine as well.

The car was the Fairlane, and the engine developed for it was the small-block Ford V8, a powerplant that, from humble roots, became known the world over for its racing exploits.

At its conception, the Fairlane was considered an extremely important project for which the small-block Ford V8 was specifically developed. Traditionally, it was important for a Ford to be available with a V8 engine—this had been true since 1932, when Ford became the first of the so-called low-priced three (Chevrolet and Plymouth were the other two) to offer a V8 engine in its cars. The problem was that neither of the two V8-engine families that Ford offered was suitable for the Fairlane. The big-block FE series was too large for an intermediate (or so went the thinking at the time), while

Rare is the 427 Fairlane coupe from 1967 with the functional fiberglass hood. Note the bench seat and 4-speed (inset).

This is the original telegram that the factory sent to Dobbs Ferry Ford in New York to confirm the dealership's order for a new 1964 Thunderbolt drag car.

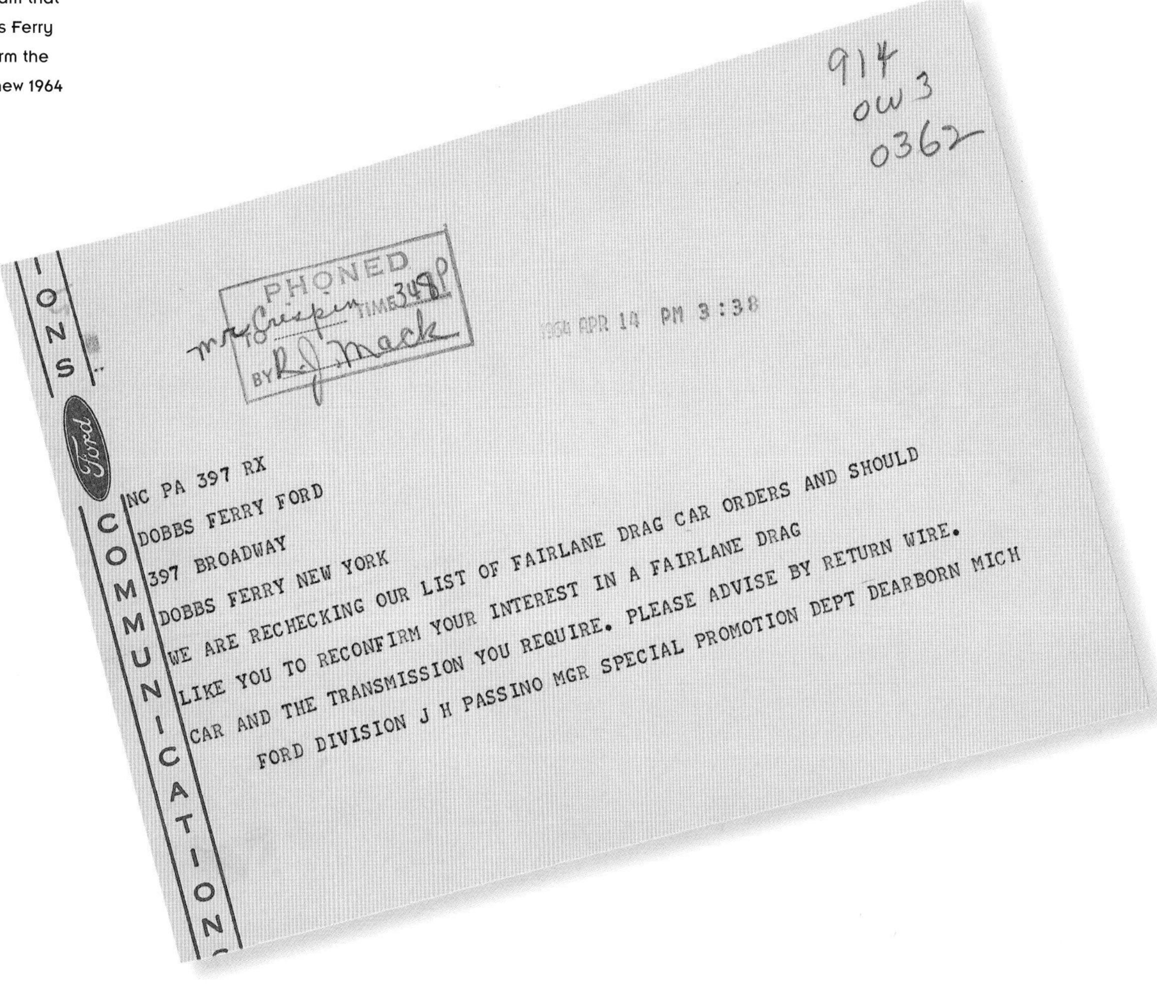

914
OW3
0362

PHONED
TO Mr Crispin TIME 3:49P
BY R J Mack

1964 APR 14 PM 3:38

NC PA 397 RX
DOBBS FERRY FORD
397 BROADWAY
DOBBS FERRY NEW YORK
WE ARE RECHECKING OUR LIST OF FAIRLANE DRAG CAR ORDERS AND SHOULD
LIKE YOU TO RECONFIRM YOUR INTEREST IN A FAIRLANE DRAG
CAR AND THE TRANSMISSION YOU REQUIRE. PLEASE ADVISE BY RETURN WIRE.
FORD DIVISION J H PASSINO MGR SPECIAL PROMOTION DEPT DEARBORN MICH

COMMUNICATIONS

the Y-block, introduced in the fall of 1953, was a poor design, outdated, unreliable, and prone to oil problems. Thus, the work began to create a lightweight, modern, efficient small V8. When it arrived with the Fairlane in 1962, this engine displaced 221 cubic inches, not coincidentally the same size as Ford's original flathead V8 in 1932.

Like many small cars of the 1960s, the Fairlane bore a strong family resemblance to its full-size counterpart in the Ford line, the Galaxie. Reasonably compact on the outside, with a commodious interior and large trunk, the Fairlane was a smash hit (unlike the Mercury twin, dubbed the Meteor, which was never as successful and discontinued after 1963). At this point, there was nothing resembling a muscle car in the Ford lineup.

This continued into 1963. But one Ford dealership involved in drag racing saw an opportunity to infuse the Fairlane with some much-needed horsepower and at the same time create a powerful drag racer. Bob Tasca Sr. at Tasca Ford in East Providence, Rhode Island, came up with the idea of transplanting Ford's mighty 427 wedge engine into the lightweight Fairlane in 1963. Driven by Bill Lawton, it was a successful strip warrior (Lawton made it to the finals of the U.S. Nationals that year, losing to a Z-11 Chevy), and the Tasca car basically became the prototype for a full-on factory effort in 1964.

Ford decided to build these so-called Fairlane Thunderbolts in 1964 to compete in NHRA Super Stock competition. Obviously they were lighter than the full-size Galaxies and could more easily meet the 3,200-pound (1,453kg) weight requirement of the class. The shorter wheelbase also improved weight transfer, thus aiding traction. With the help of Dearborn Steel Tubing (an outside vendor that provided much of the fabrication), Ford stuffed race-prepped 427s into Fairlane 500 two-door sedans.

Power came from modified 427 high-rise, center-oiler engines (these were not side-oiler engines, which is a common misconception about Thunderbolts). These motors had Ford's high-rise cylinder heads and high-rise intake manifolds with dual 4-barrel carburetion. Engineers raised the ports on the cylinder heads 0.5 inch (12.5mm) to get more flow area and the new high-rise manifold positioned the carburetors a full 3 inches (76mm) higher than other 427s. Equal-length tube headers snaked their way through suspension components. The carbs—which relied on a large, teardrop-shaped scoop for hood clearance—breathed fresh air through long, flexible tubing that ran from 6-inch-(15cm) diameter holes in the grille, one each attached to a hole where the inboard headlights would normally have been mounted.

To get weight down to the 3,200-pound (1,453kg) range required by the class, a fiberglass hood and front fenders were substituted for steel. Early versions had a fiberglass front bumper, but later on this part was made of aluminum (to enhance traction, the rear bumper was factory steel). Plexiglas side windows replaced the heavier glass, and some cars had Plexiglas for the rear window as well. Lightweight van seats supplanted the heavier stock units, and a rubber floor mat was used in lieu of carpeting. Another tactic to improve weight transfer and traction was to relocate the battery to the trunk. To put more weight on the right rear tire, a heavy diesel truck battery was used.

Race-only features found on the Thunderbolts were tow hooks in front (not found on all cars) and traction bars, which were welded to the axle housing. As delivered, the cars came with 7-inch (18cm) Firestone tires. With slicks and nothing else, they could run in the high-11- to 12.0-second range in the quarter mile. Driven by such luminaries as Hubert Platt, Butch Leal, Gas Ronda, and Dick Brannan, the Thunderbolts made history. Ronda won the Super Stock category at the '64 NHRA Winternationals, while Leal did the honors at the U.S. Nationals, the most prestigious event of the year. Ronda, who was the Super Stock champion that year, also set the ET record in his T-bolt, 11.52 seconds.

It is important to note that Mercury built 427-propelled lightweight Comets in 1964 to compete in the NHRA's A/FX category. As A/FXers, they would generally not race against Thunderbolts, though some T-bolts were converted to A/FX specifications. The Comet was based on the compact Ford Falcon chassis, except the Comet had a longer wheelbase and was considered a senior compact. "Dyno" Don Nicholson held the A/FX ET record with an 11.05 that year—in a four-door Comet wagon, no less. Ronnie Sox, driving a two-door 427 Comet, beat Nicholson in the A/FX final at

Here's the Dobbs Ferry Ford Thunderbolt in action at Flemington Dragway (in New Jersey) in May 1964 with Chuck Graap behind the wheel. On the 7-inch (17.8 cm) factory cheater slicks, the car ran 12.0 ETs at 119 mph (191kph). With the recommended Ford tuning procedures and 9-inch (22.9cm) drag slicks, the Thunderbolt ran a best of 11.23 at 122.88 (198kph) later that year at the Cars Magazine Invitational at Cecil County Dragway in Rising Sun, Maryland.

The 1968 Fairlane Cobra was available as a fastback or a standard coupe. Coupes are far more uncommon.

the Winternationals in '64. A total of fifty of these cars are believed to have been built, and with 10-inch (25.5cm) slicks, they were the scourges of the class that season.

The price was $3,780 for a 4-speed Thunderbolt; add $100 more for an automatic. The 4-speed versions used Ford's sturdy new Toploader and their differentials carried 4.44:1 gears. The automatics were fortified versions of the Lincoln transmission, enhanced with higher line pressure for firmer shifts and special torque converters. They also had no kickdown linkage. These cars came with 4.58:1 gears.

Those looking for a high-performance street Fairlane had their wish granted when Ford produced a handful of them with the solid-lifter, high-performance 289 from 1963 to 1965. Introduced midyear in 1963, this engine churned out 271 horsepower at 6000 rpm and 312 lbs.-ft. of torque at 3400. This 10.5:1 compression mill made for a decent performer in the Fairlane, capable of mid- to high-15-second ETs, and Ford sold about five hundred of them that year.

This Fairlane was completely overshadowed in 1964 by the Mustang, which turned the auto industry upside down after its April 17 introduction. The Fairlane was also completely lacking in image at that time. Fewer than twelve hundred hi-po (K-code) 289 Fairlanes were produced from 1963 to 1965, and vintage road tests of them were unavailable. They were so downplayed by the factory that many interviewed for this book could not remember such a car even being built.

In 1966, the Fairlane received a complete face-lift, and both the front and rear suspensions were overhauled. They were longer, lower, and wider than before, and with stacked headlights and semi-fastback rooflines, they greatly resembled the full-size Fords. The wider front track helped Ford use the 390 big-block in the Fairlane for the first time. Available as standard fare in the GT model, the 390 made 335 horsepower and 427 lbs.-ft. of torque, but it was never the great performer the numbers would lead you to believe.

To counter this, Ford built a very limited run of 427 Fairlanes. As was the case with the full-size models, you could only get a 425-horse with a single 4-barrel. With this, you got 11.0:1 compression in a side-oiler package. These Fairlanes came with lift-off fiberglass hoods that carried a built-in functional air scoop, and the 427 could be ordered in a two-door hardtop or sedan. On the tires of the day, they were capable of mid-14-second quarter-mile times at 100 mph (161kph), according to Ford, the latter figure giving an indication of their true potential. With slicks, a 100-mph (161kph) car should be capable of high 13s. These engines required heavier springs and relocated shock towers, but they were worth the effort. Only fifty-seven Fairlane 500s are thought to have been built.

For '67, the 427 returned and this time a steel hood was standard (fiberglass was now an option). In addition to the 425 dual quad setup, you could order a 427 with 410 horsepower with a single 4-barrel. Again, only Fairlane 500 and 500XL models could get the ultrarare 427s; the GT (and GTA, as it was called if you opted for automatic transmission) got only the 390, the 4-barrel version of which was now downrated 15 horsepower, to 320. These were no match for the other muscle cars of the day. *Road & Track* tested a GTA and could muster only a 15.94 ET at 91.46 mph (147kph).

Things got serious again in '68 with the introduction of a new body and a new engine. The Fairlane got a handsome restyling, and the performance versions were available as a two-door hardtop, a sleek two-door fastback, or a ragtop. The chassis was basically a carryover, but the styling was fresh; the long, sloping roofline of the fastback—and it was a true fastback—gave the Fairlane (and its two new top-of-the-line variations, the more upscale Torino and Torino GT) a real edge in NASCAR competition.

Under the hood, the hottest engine supposedly available at the start was the 427, now equipped with a hydraulic-lifter camshaft and single 4-barrel carb. Its output fell to 390 horsepower at 5600 rpm and 460 lbs.-ft. of torque at 3600. The big debate is whether or not this engine was ever actually installed in a Fairlane or Torino (or non-Shelby Mustang, for that matter). There are some who believe it was used that year only in the Mercury Cougar. Regardless, it is known that some Fairlane drag cars, like the one belonging to the "Georgia Shaker," Hubert Platt, had this engine.

Midway through the year, the new 428 Cobra Jet was released, and this one was definitely installed in the Fairlane and Torino. With 335 horsepower and 445 lbs.-ft. of torque on tap, it was the equal of most street brawlers. *Popular Hot Rodding* tested an automatic-equipped one for its April 1968 issue and recorded a 14.34-second ET at 100.33 mph (161.5kph).

Equally important to Ford at the time was how well the sleek new body did in NASCAR Grand National racing. Its sleek fastback made it a natural race car, giving it an aerodynamic edge over the Dodges and Plymouths it competed against. The Torino won twenty races in 1968, its Mercury Cyclone cousin another seven. Ford knew the Torino wasn't perfect and developed a nose with a dropped leading edge and a flush grille and headlights. The rear bumper of the standard Fairlane was used up front because it was more slippery through the air than the standard front bumper. It was called the Torino Talladega (after

An 8000-rpm Rotunda tachometer from Ford's aftermarket parts program sits atop the dash of a 1964 high-performance 289 Fairlane.

Bill France's new 2.66-mile [4.5km] superspeedway in Alabama), and it won its maiden outing, the 1969 Daytona 500.

Naturally, in order to compete in NASCAR, Ford had to build a suitable number of Talladegas for the street. They were available only with the 428 Cobra Jet engine, with either the Toploader 4-speed or C-6 3-speed automatic transmission. More than seven hundred were made, and they were available in three colors: Royal Maroon, Presidential Blue, and Wimbledon White. All three hues came with a flat-black hood.

In a weird development that was typical of Ford in the era, the actual NASCAR stockers used the new semi-Hemi Boss 429 "shotgun" engine. This one had all the making of a very successful race engine, and on the track it was quite formidable. Ford, however, never installed it in any street car other than the 1969–1970 Mustang, which required a lot of work, an off-site installation, and a revamping of the front suspension.

The year 1969 was also when Ford introduced its Fairlane as the new Cobra model in its intermediate line. Designed to compete with the successful Plymouth Road Runner and Dodge Super Bee, the Cobra was a stripped-down intermediate. It was available as a two-door coupe or two-door fastback, the former being a real sleeper. The standard engine was the 428 Cobra Jet; the coupe cost $3,164, the fastback $25 more. The 383 Road Runner was no match for this car.

As Ford was on a two-year styling cycle for its intermediates, 1970 meant a new body. *Sleek* is the best word to describe the 1970 Fairlane and Torino line. The styling was completely new, and the SportsRoof model sitting on the showroom floor looked like it was ready for the Daytona 500. Wheelbase was up 1 inch (2.5cm), overall length 5.2 inches (13cm). Hidden headlights were an option on the Torino GT, but not the Torino Cobra. A new engine, the 429, was standard in the Cobra and made 360 horsepower at 4600 rpm. A Toploader 4-speed was standard, as was a Hurst shifter, a heavy-duty suspension, and 7-inch (18cm) -wide wheels.

The next optional powerplant was the 429 Cobra Jet, rated at 370 horsepower at 5400 rpm and 450 lbs.-ft. at 3400. It used 11.3:1 compression, a 700-cfm Rochester carburetor, and a hydraulic-lifter cam. A ram air Shaker hood was optional. At the top of the performance ladder was the Super Cobra Jet. This 429, available only with the Drag Pack option, gave you a Holley carburetor, a solid-lifter cam, an oil cooler, 3.91 or 4.30 gears (the latter with a Detroit Locker differential), and a much stronger 4-bolt-main cylinder block. It was rated at 375 horsepower but was probably a bit underrated.

In reality, there was probably a lot more of a difference between the 429 Cobra Jet and the standard 429 performance-wise. The cylinder heads were much improved on the 429 Cobra Jet with larger ports.

The 429 engine was part of a new big-block engine family from Ford, the 385 series. With the way things were headed when it was designed, Ford fully expected its large passenger and luxury cars to weigh more than 5,000 pounds (2,270kg). For this, Ford needed a powerplant that could easily displace more than 500 cubic inches. The 385 series (though never developed to its full potential because the supercar era ended shortly after it was introduced) would, in later years, see well in excess of 600 cubic inches in race applications. Its cylinder head design, with staggered valves similar to the 351-Cleveland V8, also had incredible potential that wasn't realized until decades later, when Ford began developing serious race parts for it.

All three 429s that were available in the Cobra could be had in the regular Torino and Torino GT. These models, especially the GT with hideaway headlights, were boldly beautiful in SportsRoof form. Ford said they were "shaped by the wind," but in reality they were far less aerodynamic than the 1968–1969 cars, and after a poor start in NASCAR, many drivers reverted to their '69 Talladegas. But on the street, aerodynamics are far less important, and it is here where the Torino left a mark. Sales were incredibly strong although the market for the big-block muscle machines was beginning to wane.

The final Torino supercars were the '71 429 CJ and SCJs, and they were strong runners. *Motor Trend* tested a 4-speed CJ car in its February 1970 issue and it clicked off a 13.99 ET at 101 mph (162.5kph). *Super Stock & Drag Illustrated* ran an even better 13.82 at 102.15 mph (164.5kph) in its November '69 edition in spite of a 4,300-pound (1,952kg) curb weight. Super Cobra Jet versions were good for 13.7s. As was the case with most muscle cars, they were hamstrung by the tires of the day, especially since they were outfitted with 3.91 gears as standard equipment.

The 351-Cleveland was also available in Torinos, GTs, and the Cobra, and its 300 horsepower gave it respectable if not earth-shattering performance. One of the oddest things on the new Torino line was the optional tachometer, which was horizontal and mounted low and to the left of the speedometer. For a high-performance automobile, it was pretty much useless.

Ford briefly discontinued the Falcon name at the beginning of 1970, then brought it back midway through the year. Instead of being used on a compact, the new Falcon was the bare-bones, two-door sedan in the Torino lineup. It was available with up to 375 horsepower.

Another redesign came along in '72 and this one came with a new chassis as well. It was a decent-looking car, but no longer a hot one. Ford dropped compression ratios across the board in 1972 and shelved most of its dynamic powerplants. The Gran Torino Sport carried on with a fastback roof and enjoyed some success on the high banks. Unfortunately, street enthusiasts could opt only for a rather weak 429 with a 4-barrel carb that made 212 net horsepower.

Falcon

While Ford used the Falcon name for many Australian-built and -sold muscle cars up through the new millennium, in the United States the Falcon was strictly a low-performance economy car. It was born a compact for the 1960 model year, introduced in the waning days of 1959. Only one Falcon ever made serious power, and it was a rare bird.

In 1970 the compact Falcon was discontinued, but midway through the year, the name was briefly resurrected on the bottom-of-the-barrel Torino two-door sedan. Much like the Chevy Biscayne or the Ford 300 or Custom in the early to mid-1960s, the midsize Torino-based Falcon was as sparsely appointed as you could get. But as was the case with the Torino Cobra and GT models, you could order the 429 Cobra Jet or Super Cobra Jet engine in the Falcon.

Only a handful of customers did, but those with the gumption could get the lightest possible Ford midsize with up to 375 horsepower. These cars were capable of mid- to high-13-second elapsed times at about 103 mph (165.5kph) as delivered, putting them right in the thick of the muscle car pack. The name disappeared for good in the United States after 1970, but for a short time this rare bird could ruffle some feathers.

F-body

This was General Motors code for cars built on the Camaro/Firebird platform.

Firebird

For years, Pontiac general manager John Z. DeLorean wanted a two-seat sports car to complement the division's bigger, more muscular efforts. Pontiac in the early '60s was third in sales behind Chevrolet and Ford. The company's racing efforts—as represented by the high-powered Catalinas and Grand Prixs and the smash-hit intermediate GTO—made its cars wildly successful with the young and young at heart. More than anything else, DeLorean wanted a small sports car.

A couple of beautiful concept cars wearing the Banshee name toured the show circuit, but General Motors already had one sports car, the Corvette, and GM didn't want any internal competition. When the Ford Mustang exploded onto the scene in April '64, it caught GM completely off guard, and the company scrambled to ready a competitor.

Work on the Chevy Panther (as the Camaro was known internally) began, and while DeLorean continued lobbying for the Banshee, upper management told him to ready a Pontiac version of the Camaro—take it or leave it.

The Camaro was already far along in its development, so there wasn't much Pontiac could do to differentiate it from its interdivisional rival. The delay caused the Firebird to be released a few months after the Camaro. But the engineers used this time wisely and the resultant automobile was more refined. A Pontiac-style nose with a traditional split bumper, quad headlights, a large spear down the center of the hood, and unique "hidden" taillights were the biggest departures, from a styling standpoint.

Under the skin, DeLorean's team set out to separate the two cars. What emerged was a vehicle with significantly better cornering and traction. It sat 1 inch (25mm) lower than the Camaro, and all Firebirds wore 70-series Firestone Wide-Oval tires. The Firebird looked fast, and its potent 400 engine with Ram Air induction was available from day one (unlike the Camaro, which didn't get the 396 until three months into the model year).

The Ram Air 400 was essentially the same engine that was rated at 360 horsepower in the GTO, but because of a corporate edict that forbade a car from having more than 1 horsepower for every 10 pounds (4.5kg) of vehicle weight, it was rated at 325 horsepower in the Firebird. A more restrictive exhaust system sapped some power, but Pontiac got around this mostly by using a kink in the throttle linkage that didn't allow the carb to fully open. Straighten the linkage, and like magic the car picked up nearly 35 horsepower. Peak power came at 5000 rpm, peak torque (410 lbs.-ft.) at 3600.

This wasn't the only high-performance Firebird you could order in 1967. The 326 HO with 280 horses and 359 lbs.-ft. of torque was available, too.

Advertisements hailed the arrival of the Magnificent Five. There was the base 6-cylinder model for those looking for an economical sporty machine. Next up was the Sprint, which had a specially prepared overhead-cam 6-cylinder engine complete with a 4-barrel carburetor. There was the Firebird 326 ("a sports car for you, a family car for your wife," as the ads proclaimed) and Firebird 326 HO, which had the hotted-up version of that engine and a heavy-duty suspension. Reigning supreme was the Firebird 400, the heavyweight of the group, which could be ordered with Ram Air for extra power. This car also came with heavy-duty suspension, redline tires, and 3-speed manual transmission as standard equipment.

If the Ram Air option was ordered, the horsepower rating remained identical but the engine did not. It came with a recalibrated Quadrajet carburetor, a different camshaft, heavy-duty valve springs, and better exhaust manifolds. The carb was sealed to the hood and used a 14-inch (35.5cm) open-element air filter. A 4-speed manual transmission or 4-speed automatic was a mandatory option choice, and 3.90 gears came standard. Traction bars were standard to eliminate wheel hop.

Firebird was rushed into production in February 1967 after Pontiac general manager John Z. DeLorean lost his battle for a Pontiac two-seat sports car.

Car and Driver was excited: "Pontiac decided to take the Camaro's F-body and in the Pontiac tradition, raise a little hell in the new sport car market. We were immediately impressed by the solidity of the Firebird's suspension and the tight, integrated feel of the car at speeds approaching 100 mph [161kph]." At the track, *Car and Driver* got the Ram Air Firebird to run 14.4 at 100 mph (161kph), putting it at or near the top of the ponycar heap in '67.

For '68, the word was *improvement*: better legibility for the gauges, improved climate thanks to Astro Ventilation (which allowed stylists to delete the side vent windows), and, naturally, more power—a lot more. The 326 HO grew into the 350 HO, adding 40 horsepower to the mix (thanks in large part to redesigned cylinder heads with larger intake and exhaust valves).

The standard 400 was now up to 330 horsepower, and there was a 400 HO that made 335 because of its exhaust manifolds. There were two Ram Air options in '68: Ram Air I, which was now rated at 335 horsepower, and Ram Air II, which was introduced on May 20, came underrated at 340 horses, and replaced the RA I.

The first of the round-port Ponchos, Ram Air II had completely new cylinder heads with large, round exhaust ports and swirl-polished tuliped valves. It used a new intake manifold with an improved Quadrajet 4-barrel and free-flowing exhaust manifolds. The cam was hotter, and forged pistons swung on a beefier crankshaft. This package was as good as it was rare; a mere 110 such Birds flew the coop in '68.

As good as it was, the RA II was replaced the following year by the Ram Air IV, perhaps the ultimate Pontiac engine of the muscle car era. It carried an aluminum intake manifold, round port heads with larger valves (the RA II's 2.11-inch [5.5cm] intake, 1.77 [4.5cm] exhaust), 1.65:1 rocker arms, and a very hot 0.520-inch (13mm) lift cam, among other bonuses. It came rated at 340 horsepower and 430 lbs.-ft. of torque. This was a legitimate 13-second ponycar, capable of 102-mph (164kph) trap speeds.

Of course, 1969 was also the year Pontiac unveiled its most revered Firebird, the Trans Am (T/A). Grabbing its name from the SCCA road race series (for a fee of $5 per car), it came one way, white with two blue stripes running the length of the body. A unique hood with functional scoops at the leading edge was a Trans Am exclusive, as were the wings on the decklid and the functional air extractors on the front fenders behind the wheels.

Standard in the T/A was the 400 HO, which when ordered with a fresh air hood was called the Ram Air III, but the RA IV was available, making it the ultimate Firebird. To improve handling, quicker variable ratio power steering was standard, as were heavy-duty springs, staggered shocks, a 1-inch (2.5cm) front sway bar, and 14-inch (35.5cm) wheels. Just 697 Trans Ams were built in its first year, 8 of them convertibles. They were the last convertible T/As produced until the 1980s.

Styling on the '69 Firebird evolved. Like the Camaro, it got a brawnier appearance, with bold body lines running down the fenders and a tougher-looking grille that had the headlights in their own surround—a preview of the 1970 GTO.

Due to an extended 1969 model year, the all-new rebodied 1970 Firebirds didn't appear until midway through the model year (February 26). When they did, the public and press alike went wild. "Every detail right down to the tach needle has been fine tuned," raved *Car and Driver*. "The result is an 'expert' driver's car, a car that, even at the limit of adhesion, responds eagerly to minute movements of the throttle and steering wheel."

Only one body style was available, the two-door coupe, relegating the convertible to history.

While the Firebird shared the basic shell with the Camaro, it was uniquely Pontiac. The split Endura bumper with one headlight per side integrated beautifully with the Euro-influenced body. The semifastback roofline eliminated the rear quarter glass, though the longer doors needed to accomplish this were uncommonly heavy. The only brightwork on the car was around the windows and rear bumper. This was a car that was years ahead of its time.

The interior bore no resemblance to the previous generation, either. The gauges were directly in front of the driver, white numerals on a black background, set in a woodgrain panel on Firebird and Formula models, and in an engine-turned dash appliqué on the Trans Am. On models with a tach, the redline was straight up at the 12 o'clock position, a nod to how seriously its designers took the car.

There were still basically five Firebird models, including two base versions (the first with an inline 6-cylinder engine, the second with a 350 2-barrel V8). Next up was the more luxurious Espirit, which came with the aforementioned 350, though a 400 4-barrel was available.

This 330-horse engine was standard in the new Firebird Formula 400. The Formula had two sinewy-appearing forward-facing scoops at the front of the hood as standard equipment, although they were nonfunctional. If you wanted them to work, you got the optional Ram Air III with 345 horsepower. RA III was the base engine in the Trans Am, capable of propelling the '70 Trans Am to a 14.1-second ET at 103.2 mph (166kph) in the *Car and Driver* test. (*Hot Rod* claimed 13.9 at 102 mph [164kph] with an automatic transmission.)

At the top of the heap was the Ram Air IV, now rated at 370 kicking ponies. Except for this engine, the Trans Am had all the great enthusiast equipment standard. Extremely quick variable rate

The 1971 Trans Am had the superb 455 HO on its list of options.

PONTIAC
Firebird
YFB 170

The last year for a Firebird convertible during the muscle car era was 1969. This one was equipped with a Ram Air 400 engine, a hood tach, and a customized two-tone interior.

In its maiden season (1969), the Pontiac Firebird Trans Am was available solely in traditional American racing colors: white with blue stripes. Pontiac continued this scheme in 1970, but added Lucerne Blue with a white stripe as the only other alteration. The spoilers, air vents, and fender spats weren't just for looks. They were tested by Pontiac and at high speeds were found to collectively reduce lift and turbulence, plus the decklid spoiler provided downforce.

power steering, stiffer rear springs, revalved shocks and harder bushings, and thick sway bars front and rear gave the car handling that was better than any American car except for possibly the Corvette, according to *Car and Driver*.

As with all GM divisions, compression ratios were cut at Pontiac for 1971. This, along with other factors, sapped plenty of horsepower from the Firebird. Unlike GM's other divisions, though, Pontiac would not let the muscle Firebird go away that easily. But the Ram Air III and IV engines were lost forever. Despite 2-point drops in compression on the 400 and 455, Pontiac managed to introduce another strong engine in '71, the 455 HO. It had good round port heads, an aluminum intake manifold, and Ram Air. Standard in the Trans Am and an extra-cost option in the Formula, it was rated at 335 horsepower at 4800 rpm and 480 robust lbs.-ft. of torque at 3600. While not as strong as the RA IV, the 455 HO could still turn a low-14-second quarter-mile time at about 97 mph (156kph). A less potent 455 with 325 horsepower was also available in the Formula, as was the HO, and the 400s were now putting out 300 ponies.

Muscle car sales in general were going down the tubes by 1971, and a sixty-seven-day labor strike that started in September 1970 didn't help Firebird sales. Production slipped from more than 80,000 in 1970 to 53,125 in '71. Things got worse in '72 when another strike kept the Firebird (and Camaro) plant in Ohio closed for nearly five months. Sales dropped to only 29,951, of which there were 5,249 Formulas and 1,286 Trans Ams.

Horsepower was down again in '72. Now rated with all the accessories hooked up (net), the 455 HO made just 300 horsepower, the good 400s just 250.

Just when it seemed things couldn't get any worse (there were rumors of the F-bodies going out of production, and the 455 HO got the axe), Pontiac released the last great supercars of the 1970s, the 1973 (and '74) Super Duty 455 Trans Am and Formula. Though they were supposed to use the Ram Air IV cam, they didn't because of emissions rules. Still, a fairly stout cam was employed, as were round port, 111cc heads with oversize exhaust valves, a Super Duty–specific cast-iron intake manifold, and an 800-cfm Rochester carburetor.

Iron exhaust "headers," 2.5-inch (64mm) head pipes, dual resonators, and 2.25-inch (57mm) tailpipes comprised the exhaust. The Shaker hood was standard on both the Formula and the Trans Am with the Super Duty, but was now nonfunctional. (Supposedly, there is paperwork to prove that 533 non-SD Formulas did get functional Ram Air hoods.)

For durability, the cylinder block was reinforced and 4-bolt mains were used. The pistons and rods were forged, and the cast-iron crank was nitrided. *Car and Driver* tested a preproduction automatic model, which had the never-certified Ram Air IV cam, and ran a 13.75-second ET at 103.56 mph (166.5kph) in the quarter mile. All

this and it topped out at 132 mph (212.5kph). Actual production versions were a couple of ticks slower because of the milder cam, but by 1973 standards it was unequivocally the quickest production car on the road. Output was 310 net horsepower at 4000 rpm and 390 lbs.-ft. at 3600. Few were built. Forty-three Formulas were sold and 252 Trans Ams made it off the assembly line in '73. This total was no doubt held back by the Arab oil embargo and crippling insurance rates.

The second-generation Firebird got its first major restyling in 1974. The taillights were larger, filling the tail panel and separated only by the license plate. In the front, the beak was gone; now the grille was laid back for better aerodynamics. Also, 5-mph (8kph) bumpers were standard in the front and the rear. In an era when most cars wore the equivalent of chrome railroad ties for bumpers, those of the Firebird were remarkably well integrated. As they had been for years, they were covered by resilient rubber.

Under the hood, the Super Duty was again the top option, one with 58 takers in the Formula and 943 in the Trans Am. A 350 with a 2-barrel carburetor was now standard in the Formula, though a 400, a 455, and the SD 455 could be ordered. The 400 4-barrel was the base engine in the Trans Am.

The 455 engine soldiered on in the Trans Am for two more years, but it wasn't much of a performer after '74. Remarkably, as the Trans Am got slower, its popularity exploded. More than 27,000 were built in '75, and 46,704 were built in '76. Production peaked at 117,108 in 1979, when the most powerful V8 was a 220-horsepower 400.

Fred Gibb Chevrolet

Heavily involved in racing, this dealership took advantage of the COPO system to further its image and bank account. One of the best examples came in 1968, when Gibb wanted automatic transmission–equipped L78 396 Novas for drag racing. This was not available from the factory because Chevy didn't offer automatic transmissions with engines using solid-lifter camshafts. The NHRA said that fifty needed to be built to legalize the combination for the stock classes. Through a COPO order blessed by Chevy's Vince Piggins, fifty 375-horse Novas were built in '68 with the Turbo Hydro-Matic 400 gearbox.

This dealership's biggest (and costliest) claim to fame was that it ordered fifty ZL-1 aluminum-engined Camaros in 1969. Little did it know that the cars would have a sticker price of more than $7,000. The engine option itself cost more than the base price of the car. *Cars* magazine tested one and it stickered at $7,800. The solution was to accept some of the cars and divert them to other high-performance dealerships.

Aside from the COPO cars, Gibb built 427-engine equipped Novas and Camaros.

Fury

If there were muscle cars in the 1950s, the Plymouth Fury would have been one. It was a special model introduced within the 1956 model year. It was available in only one color, white, with gold anodized trim and a high-output (for the time) engine, the 240-horsepower 303. Plymouth played off its success over the next couple of years, delivering larger, more powerful engines and styling that was completely over the top, even by 1950s standards.

In 1962, Plymouth downsized its full-size cars and treated them to styling that was controversial to say the least. While not as unusual as their Dodge counterparts, the '62 Plymouths were definitely different, although not as odd as they could have been. There was a time when these Plymouths were slated to have asymmetric styling, meaning one side of the car would look completely different than the other—mismatched headlight treatments, different taillights on either side, separate trim, and so on. Even the interiors were to carry this theme. This plan was eventually abandoned and the only remnant that actually made it to production was the interior, where the instrument panel was trapezoidal.

In 1962, the Fury name was attached to the most opulent cars in the Belvedere lineup. All were either hardtops or convertibles. Later in the model year, the Sport Fury was introduced with bucket seats, a console, full wheel covers, all-vinyl interior trim, and a slightly different grille, plus other goodies. The performance engines available in the lower-line Belvederes were all common to the Sport Fury, including the powerful Max Wedge 413s.

It wasn't long after the introduction of these controversial cars that the designers were ordered to rework the styling of the Furys and Belvederes. These cars flopped in the marketplace, as did the Dodges. Remarkably, the '63 came out of this a much improved automobile. The sheet metal was new from the front fenders and grille to the taillights. Even the roofline was dramatically altered. The Fury and Sport Fury retained their status as the plushest Plymouths, but with the new 426 Stage II engine, they were nothing short of pure racing engines. Streetgoing versions got the lower-compression version of the 426.

The big news for '64 (besides another face-lift) was the Stage III Max Wedge engine, which was supplanted later in the model year by the all-out 426 Race Hemi.

Those looking for a street cruiser could order the 426-S, a 426 RB engine that used the 383's heads, cam, intake, carburetor, and exhaust manifolds. It was rated at 365 horsepower.

For 1965, the Fury name was moved to a new line of larger Plymouths, which were true full-size automobiles. A Sport Fury convertible paced the Indianapolis 500 that year, but it was not considered a muscle car. There wasn't a true high-output Fury again until 1970, when the Sport Fury GT became the largest member of Plymouth's Rapid Transit System. (Rapid Transit System was what Plymouth called its lineup of muscle cars in its ad campaign for the 1970 model year.) This car came standard with a 350-horsepower engine; optional was the 440 Six-Barrel with three 2-barrel carburetors and 390 horsepower. In 1971 you could order the 440 Magnum with 4-barrel carb putting out 375 horsepower. Unfortunately, these cars weighed more than 2 tons (1.8t) and were not terribly quick. Few of these performers were built, and they went away after the '71 model year.

Galaxie

Ford produced one of the first muscle cars in 1960, the Galaxie equipped with the 352 Interceptor V8 (or Special, as it was also known). The 352 was a member of the big-block FE engine family. It was designed with a rugged bottom end, which included stronger-than-standard connecting rods, tougher bearings, and a 60-psi oil pump.

Ford's engineers enhanced its breathing with a camshaft that was pretty wild for its day, an aluminum intake manifold topped with a Holley 4-barrel and special high-flow exhaust manifolds plus dual exhausts. The combustion chamber on the heads was reduced in size to bring the compression ratio up to 10.6:1, but the ports were larger for improved airflow. The resulting engine package was rated at 360 horsepower at 6000 rpm and 380 lbs.-ft. of torque at 3400.

At first, the 352 Special was plagued by weak valve springs, which would cause the valves to float over 5000 rpm. Soon thereafter, Ford replaced them with stiffer springs, which allowed the 352 to comfortably turn about 5800 rpm. The late Roger Huntington, one of the deans of automotive journalism, once reported testing a 3-speed, two-door Galaxie with absurd 5.14:1 gears and achieving a 15.9 at 89 mph (143kph). This was respectable performance for the era, but no doubt the race-only gears helped a great deal.

Left: Ford used this taillight—seen here on a Galaxie—only in 1965.

Below: Although the 1965 Galaxie was redesigned following formal styling cues, the 427 engine did not restrict performance-minded drivers.

The 352 was available in all full-size Fords that year, including the Custom, Fairlane, Fairlane 500, and Galaxie Skyliner, which had a sloping roofline that improved its performance on the NASCAR circuit, where Ford collected a season-high fifteen victories. The only transmissions offered were a 3-speed on the column or a manual with overdrive.

For '61, the Galaxie got another complete facelift, its third in three years. The new car was shorter, narrower, and far better-looking than the '60. Short fins and large, round taillights gave it a distinctive appearance. The grille was also reworked and was not only a major improvement but set the tone for full-size Ford styling through 1964.

An increase in both bore and stroke saw the 352 grow to 390 cubic inches in '61, and horsepower rose accordingly. You could get 300 or 375 horsepower with a single 4-barrel carb or 401

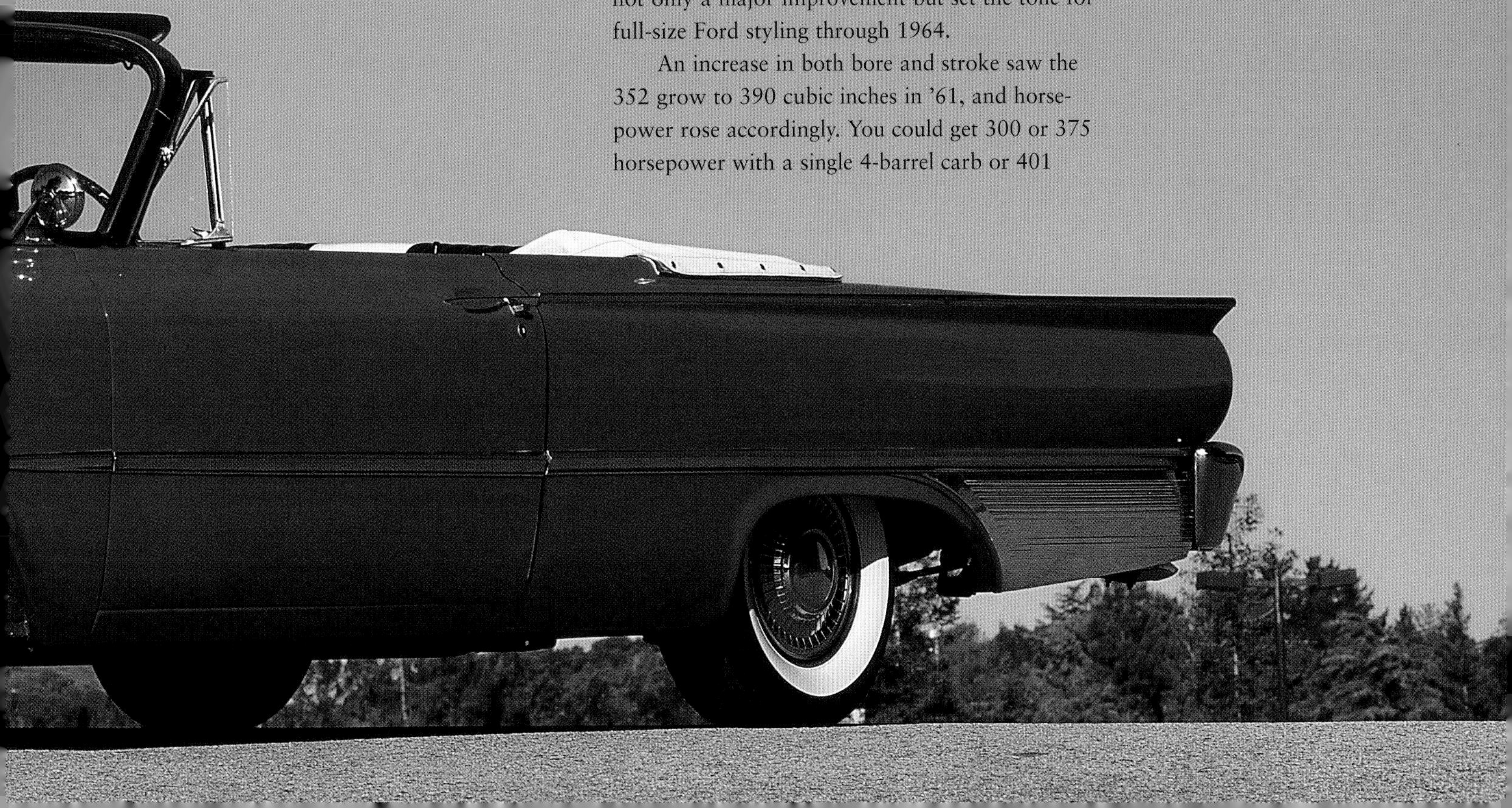

Right: The gun sight in the center of the grille is a tip-off that this is a 1962 Ford.

Below: You could still get a full-size Ford muscle car with a 4-speed in 1965. This is an R-code 427 Galaxie.

ponies and 430 lbs.-ft. of torque with three deuces. In addition, this was the year Ford began backing the FE with the Borg-Warner T-10 4-speed gearbox. It offered a huge performance increase over the 3-speed of the year before, though it was fragile.

For '62, Ford enlarged the FE once again, now to 406 cubic inches thanks to a bore job. In order to be more competitive at the drag strip, Ford built a miniscule number of lightweight Galaxies in '62. Through the use of aluminum, fiberglass, and thin-gauge steel, Ford was able to cut about 500 pounds (227kg), bringing the Galaxie's weight down to around 3,220 pounds (1,462kg). It was not an inexpensive program, however.

Ford's annual restyling did away with the sloping roofline that had been so helpful on the NASCAR circuit. When it became apparent that the squared-off roof was problematic at high speed, Ford attempted to slip one by the rulemakers. It fabricated a bolt-on hardtop for the convertibles and tried to pass it off as a factory option. NASCAR allowed the Starlift top for one race and then banned it.

The year 1963 may have been the last truly great one for the Galaxie as a muscle car. The following year saw the midsize Fairlane Thunderbolt supplant it as the most important race car and the Mustang zoomed past it in importance as a street machine. But '63 was magical. This was the year Ford coined the phrase "Total Performance" in its advertising.

First, Ford introduced the ultimate production-line FE, the 427. This was an all-out race engine, bred to battle it out with the Chevys and Mopars on the drag strips and stock car ovals. Not only did the FE get larger exhaust valves and more cubic inches, but it also came with a single 4-barrel (410 horsepower) or dual Holleys (425 horsepower) on a free-flowing aluminum intake. It even had cross-bolted main caps for durability. This engine could run with anything the competition had. Torque was 476 lb.-ft. at 3400 rpm with one 4-barrel or 480 at 3700 with two.

In addition, for 1963½, Ford unleashed a fastback roofline for the Galaxie. This mid-year release proved its value immediately, helping Tiny Lund win the Daytona 500. Overall, this model may have been the prettiest of all of Detroit's 1963 offerings.

Another batch of lightweight drag Galaxies was produced for '63 that used fiberglass doors, hoods, and decklids and aluminum bumpers. Naturally, these cars were stripped of nonessential items like radios and heaters. But these were still fairly heavy cars, and they didn't fare as well at the strip as the Z-11 lightweight Impalas and aluminum front end Mopars.

On the street, however, the 427 Fords were tough to beat. And with nearly five thousand units sold that year, they weren't uncommon.

The year 1964 saw Ford's full-size offerings restyled yet again. Things were status quo under the hood on the street cars, but if you were racing you could get your Galaxie with the new 427 high-rise engine. It had raised intake ports on the

heads and a new intake manifold, which raised the carburetors 3 inches (76m). They required a teardrop-shaped bubble hood for clearance. This was also the year Ford introduced its new heavy-duty Toploader 4-speed.

Ford claimed that its full-size '65s were the "newest since 1949." They were reengineered from the ground up and looked completely different. Coil springs were employed in the rear for the first time on a full-size Ford, and the styling was a more formal version of what Pontiac started in 1963 with stacked headlights. Although the 427s were still offered, as was the 4-speed, this Galaxie looked less like a performance car.

But the Galaxie still got with the program. The 427's heads were revised for better breathing, getting reshaped ports (among other things). Also, the crank was now forged steel. On a set of cheater slicks, *Hot Rod* ran 101.69 mph (163.5kph) at 14.93 seconds. By unbolting the exhaust system from the factory headers and removing the fan, *Hot Rod* improved this time to 14.43 at 108.04 mph (174kph)—this with only 3.50:1 gears. At $4,725, this was a terribly expensive machine, out of the price range of most supercar enthusiasts.

The 427 soldiered on in the Galaxie until '67, a handsome but tremendously large and heavy car. Ford tried its hand at a more "European" high-performance Galaxie in '66 with the 7-Liter, which was powered by the new 345-horse 428 and came standard with bucket seats, a simulated wood-grain steering wheel, floor shift, low-restriction exhaust, and air cleaner assembly. Power disc brakes were also standard, and the 4-speed was a no-cost option. Its main competitors were the Pontiac 2+2 and the Impala SS, but the 7-Liter Galaxie lasted only one year.

More telling was the wild success of the Galaxie LTD, which came to market as the top trim level on the Galaxie in '65 and really took off in '66. The market for full-size Fords (and Chevys and Mopars) was heading toward inexpensive luxury. Many features formerly found only on Lincolns and Cadillacs were showing up in their cheaper cousins. That spelled the end of hot Galaxies, although the sporty XL model continued until the end of 1970.

Grand Spaulding Dodge (including Mr. Norm)

Opened in the fall of 1962, Grand Spaulding Dodge in Chicago was known from the very beginning as a high-performance car specialist. Located on the corner of West Grand and Spaulding Avenues, it was owned by Norm Kraus, who simply became known as Mr. Norm.

Ford sold more than 900,000 full-size cars in 1960. Was it because of advertising like this or in spite of it? The 352 with 360 horsepower was a rare option, but it helped start the muscle car era.

Soon after the dealership opened, Kraus formed Mr. Norm's Sport Club to further the franchise's relationship with people interested in high-performance cars. Soon thereafter, in 1963, a Clayton chassis dynamometer was installed to measure horsepower and facilitate tuning of these fire-breathing beasts.

Grand Spaulding Dodge began racing in earnest in 1964, when it fielded a Max Wedge and a Hemi car. A year later, Mr. Norm and driver Gary Dyer paired up to campaign an Altered Wheelbase Coronet on the match race circuit. All the while, sales of new cars were exploding and the dealership continued to expand.

Its burgeoning parts, sales, and service departments helped the dealership's reputation grow by leaps and bounds. While Chrysler wasn't generally bashful about installing large engines in its cars—the 440 was standard in the Dodge R/T and Plymouth GTX—it didn't have much displacement available for its smaller cars. In '67, Mr. Norm stepped in, and he is credited with building the first 383 Dart, a car that Dodge eventually sold from the factory. Grand Spaulding went a step further the following year by introducing the 440 Dart GSS. Neither was an easy swap, but the performance was sublime.

Like some, Mr. Norm saw the handwriting on the dealership wall and tried to build an insurance-beater supercar. In 1971, he introduced the 340 Six-Pack Demon. While the 340 could be had in the compact Demon, Grand Spaulding added the induction setup from the prior year's Challenger T/A.

For '72, most of the market was reeling from sluggish sales of performance cars, but Kraus saw it as a good time to introduce the 340 Demon GSS, a Paxton-supercharged special edition. With a single 4-barrel carb and 6 psi of boost, the car was rated at 350 horsepower. *High Performance Cars* tested one in its July '72 edition and cranked off a 13.92-second ET at 106 mph (170.5kph). This was staggering performance in 1972.

While Grand Spaulding moved nearly two hundred of these cars, they were sold only one year. After this, Mr. Norm made a name for himself selling conversion vans. His dealership eventually became the number one–volume Dodge outlet in the country.

Gran Sport

When Buick decided to respond to the Pontiac GTO challenge in 1965, it did so with a modified Skylark called the Gran Sport. Contrary to General Motors' edict that intermediates couldn't have more than 400-cubic-inch engines, the GS displaced 401 from its Wildcat 445 V8. The engine took its name from its torque rating, 445 lbs.-ft. It was the latest version of the antediluvian nailhead (or nail valve) engine that had powered Buicks for what seemed like forever.

All Skylark Gran Sports were built on the convertible model's heavier, more rigid frame. Other standard features included the 325-horsepower engine, 7.75x14-inch (19.5x35.5cm) tires, dual exhausts, a heavy-duty suspension, and a 3-speed manual transmission. Drive one of these, Buick promised in its ads, and you could start billing yourself as the human cannonball.

Naturally, most came with a 2-speed Super Turbine automatic gearbox—it was a Buick, after all—and this proved to hinder performance. *Car Life* reported a 15.3 ET at 88 mph (141.5kph).

Perhaps the GS Skylark's most distinctive feature (aside from its robust torque) was its full-width taillight treatment (common to all Buick intermediates in 1965 only). Combined with the bright, shiny chrome common to almost all cars of the era, it made quite a visceral statement at night when viewed from behind.

There was also the Riviera Gran Sport in '65, which came with a 425-cubic-inch version of the same engine, but with available dual 4-barrel carburetors. In fact, the GS label stuck on the Riviera straight through the mid-1970s, but it was actually just a high-powered luxury car; to call it a muscle car would be a stretch.

Certainly, all Rivieras were exciting vehicles with flashy styling, especially from 1965 to 1969, when they had concealed headlamps and wide, low-slung bodies. There were also trick interiors, with barrel-roll speedometers and inverted-U shift handles, but for this book, only the intermediate GS will be addressed.

In 1966, the GS Skylark went under the stylists' knife and emerged fairly unharmed. Gone were the fender-to-fender taillights, replaced by more conventional units separated by a matte-black panel, but the front end was slightly improved and the codgeresque hood ornament was relegated to the scrap heap on this model. The standard 401 (advertised as a 400, same as in '65) was unchanged, and there was a 340-horsepower version advertised as an option. While it was a nice car, the GS was a nonplayer on the street. With a few tricks, however, it could surprise people.

Buick's stature picked up a bit in 1967, when the all-new 400-cubic-inch V8 was introduced. It shared nothing with the old nail valve V8 (introduced in 1953) and was lightweight, with a modern

valvetrain that could rev and breathe far better than its predecessor. The new 400 made 340 horsepower at 5000 rpm and 440 lbs.-ft. at 3200 thanks in part to 10.25:1 compression, a single Rochester 4-barrel carburetor, and dual exhausts. The other good news for the GS in '67 was the introduction of the Turbo Hydro-Matic 3-speed automatic transmission. The GS could be identified by the numerous external GS badges or by its two faux hood scoops.

Car Life, which had tested the '65 GS, got a hold of a '67 hardtop equipped with the new 3-speed automatic. Even with a test weight of 4,175 pounds (1,895.5kg), it turned a 14.7 at 97 mph (156kph). That's six-tenths of a second and 9 mph (14.5kph) better than the original, despite an extra 145 pounds (66kg). For those who couldn't afford a GS400 (as it was now called), Buick introduced the first "junior supercar," the GS340. Based on a smaller-displacement version of the 400, it made a respectable 260 horsepower.

Like every intermediate in Detroit in 1968, the GS was totally redesigned. The wheelbase was shortened from 115 to 112 inches (292 to 284.5cm) and overall length was reduced nearly 5 inches (12.5cm), to 200.7 inches (510cm). Gone was the old car's boxy shape, replaced by a modern, sculpted look. Under the hood, the GS340 became the GS350, but the GS400 was the real muscle machine. The engine was basically a carryover from the previous year, but *Hot Rod* squeezed a 14.78 ET out of it at 94 mph (151.5kph).

That same year, Buick engineers released the first of its Stage engine and option packages for the new engine. Unadvertised and known only to racers and those who developed it, the misnamed Stage 2 (which preceded the Stage 1) was rated at

An iron fist in a velvet glove is the best way to describe the GS455 Buick convertible for 1970. Performance was eye-opening, but the creature comforts lacking in many muscle cars were supplied in abundance.

350 horsepower. It had 11.0:1-compression pistons, a unique camshaft and valvetrain, and heavy-duty internal components. Its specifications were filed by Buick with the NHRA that year as the "Heavy Duty Stage 2 option on Skylarks." This legalized the hardware for competition.

In '69, the Stage 1 appeared as an assembly-line upgrade for the GS400. It was advertised at 345 horsepower at 4800 rpm. It used a special Quadrajet carb set up to open the secondaries quicker. A functional cold-air hood was sealed to the air cleaner, and there was a high-lift cam. A 2.25-inch (57mm) exhaust system released the combusted mixture, and a 3.64:1 gear was standard in the rear (3.42:1 if you ordered air conditioning).

Buick, always the conservative division, did little to market the Stage 1 option, and only 1,256 were built. This author had the opportunity to drag test an original non-A/C example in 1991 (it had less than 33,000 miles [53,097km]). The car ran a 14.74 at 92.96 mph (149.5kph) that day, the only deviation from stock parts were the mufflers. On the stock tires and with a full tank of fuel, this is indicative of what the car ran in the '60s. The owner had timeslips for the car back in the day, and its best elapsed time was 14.75 seconds.

The Stage 2 package, rated at just 350 horsepower, had aftermarket pistons and intake manifold, a different carburetor, exhaust headers, and 4.78:1 gears.

When GM took off the handcuffs in 1970 and allowed its divisions to use engines larger than 400 cubic inches in its intermediates, few would have suspected that Buick would turn out perhaps the ultimate muscle car from the corporation. Unlike Chevrolet and Pontiac, which used the 396 and 400 as standard in the Chevelle and GTO, respectively, Buick did away with the GS400 entirely. The base muscle Buick was now the GS455 (although the GS350 with 315 horsepower was still available). It was a stout automobile, with 350 horsepower and 510 lbs.-ft. of torque, but the car that became a legend was the Stage 1 455—360 horsepower and 510 lbs.-ft. of torque. Although the basic shell was similar, the styling was exceptionally clean, with the sweeping strakes of the 1968–1969 models gone for good. The front end was revised, as was the tail.

On paper, these ratings don't seem that outrageous, other than the fact that the advertised torque figure was the highest for any performance car of the era. As with the original Stage package, these cars were significantly underrated from the factory. The reality was that the Stage 1 cars were the equal of just about anything else available that year.

The Stage 1 had larger intake and exhaust valves than the GS400, a cam with more duration and higher lift, and compression of up to 10.5:1 (versus 10.0:1 in the GS455). A 3.64:1 gear was standard, as was a low-restriction dual exhaust, functional hood scoops, special head gaskets, a revised oil pump, and a higher shift-point transmission if you ordered the automatic. *Hot Rod* called it "Mister Muscle of 1970" because of its performance at the new car intro that year. Tested with two people on board in 100°F (38°C) Arizona heat, it still ran 14.4 at 96 mph (154.5kph). In actuality, in cooler weather and with only the driver aboard, a Stage I Buick was capable of mid- to high-13-second quarter-mile times at speeds faster than 100 mph (161kph).

Buick never advertised its Stage 2 in 1970, but a few definitely made it out the door to racers. They ran with 12.1:1 compression, and the heads had D-shaped ports. According to automotive journalist and former Buick spokesman Martyn L. Schorr, few D-port heads made it into racers' hands because of casting problems. Even rarer were Tunnel Port heads.

When GM slashed compression ratios in '71, the GS and GSX suffered accordingly. The regular GS455 was down to 315 horsepower and 450 lbs.-ft. of torque, while the Stage 1 was at 345 horsepower and 460 lbs.-ft. Combined with leaned-out carburetors, milder spark timing, and rudimentary emissions controls,

Ford built seven road-legal GT40 sports cars in 1967. One sold for more than $400,000 at auction in 2002.

performance was way off, adding about a second to elapsed times.

With net horsepower ratings cutting the power of the 455s to 260 and 270 (Stage 1) in '72, the good times were all but gone in Flint, Michigan. Neutered versions of these engines soldiered on in '73 in the oddly shaped intermediates, which still wore the GS badges (the Buick intermediate was now called the Century). The last GS intermediate was the '74 Century, though the Riviera GS survived a year after that and Buick revived the GS badging in the '80s and again in the '90s.

Grand Sport

This was the purpose-built, lightweight Corvette race car designed to compete against the Shelby Cobra in 1963. Chevrolet built five of them before GM's corporate ban on racing that year.

GSX

In spirit, the GSX was Buick's response in 1970 to the 1969 GTO Judge and came as quite a shock to those used to normally conservative Buicks. Available in two colors, Saturn Yellow and Apollo White, the GSX came with an interesting decklid spoiler, plus a bold black stripe (outlined in red) that ran down the body from the front fenders to the rear and then over the top of the spoiler. The same theme carried over to the hood, which featured wide black stripes outlined in red. To top it off, there was also a front spoiler.

Also included were a hood-mounted tach, a Rallye steering wheel, power front disc brakes, 4-speed manual transmission, 3.42 rear with Positraction, special suspension, black bucket seats, heavy-duty cooling package, a consolette, G60 tires on 15×7-inch (38×18cm) wheels, Rallye instrumentation, GSX ornamentation, and a custom interior package.

The 455 was standard, the Stage 1 optional. Other extras available included a full-length console and Turbo Hydro-Matic automatic transmission.

GT-37 and T-37

Like the original GTO in '64, the GT-37 was an optional package on the 1970–1971 Tempest. In an effort to sell a less expensive intermediate muscle car (à la Plymouth Road Runner and Ford's Fairlane-based Cobra), Pontiac introduced the GT-37. Introduced midyear in 1970, it actually fulfilled the promise of the original GTO Judge, which was to be a bare-bones, stripped-down muscle car—an idea then–division general manager John Z. DeLorean flat-out rejected.

The T-37 was a marketing promotion to replace the Tempest series. In base form, it was a complete stripper. Although not a performance car, you could order it with performance engines. Pontiac's new boss, F. James McDonald, liked the idea of a lower-priced muscle car. Both the T-37 and GT-37 were low-line pillared hardtops, making them lighter than the GTO, which was getting heavier every year. They were available with the 330-horsepower 400 with an automatic transmission and the 366-horsepower Ram Air III engine, without the cold-air induction hardware if you took the 4-speed, effectively making it a 400 HO.

For 1971, the T-37 and GT-37 were even more interesting. The exceptional new 455 HO was now an option (with manual or automatic transmission) and produced 335 horsepower. These were very much supercars in the truest sense—lots of power, few frills. But the Pontiac customer, especially one weaned on the GTO, was accustomed to more luxury and style with his performance. The budget supercars never caught on (they were never marketed very heavily either) and disappeared after '71.

GT40

When Ford embarked on its "Total Performance" program to dominate all forms of motorsports in the 1960s, the GT40 was the sports car it built to compete in European GT-class racing. The goal was to beat Ferrari at its own game, a goal conceived after Henry Ford II's plan to buy the Italian automaker was rebuffed.

Pontiac aficionados will tell you this is the car that started the muscle car craze—the 1964 GTO.

The cars were hand-assembled in England and debuted in March 1964. By the end of the '60s, the GT40 had won Le Mans four times between 1966 and 1969 and had established itself as perhaps the finest, most successful race car ever. That the GT40s were powered by conventional pushrod V8 engines designed to propel station wagons and Galaxies made them even more astounding. The 289s, 302s, and ultimately 427s were all supplied by Carroll Shelby.

What's more interesting is that there were actually street versions of the GT40 Mk III—seven in 1967, the only year Ford produced a roadgoing version. These mid-engine supercars were powered by Shelby-built 289s producing 306 horsepower and 329 lbs.-ft. of torque, which was transmitted through a 5-speed German ZF gearbox to a 2.50:1 differential. Despite gearing designed to go more than 200 mph (322kph) on the Mulsanne Straight in France, the Mk III could turn a high-13-second quarter mile at about 104 mph (167.5kph).

GTA

This was the designation given to both the Fairlane and Mustang GT when equipped with the 390 engine and automatic transmission.

GTO

Gran Turismo Omologato—that's what the three most famous letters of the muscle car era stand for. The GTO was a grand touring car homologated for competition. When Pontiac stole this name from Ferrari in 1964, lovers of Europe's finest practically lapsed into spasms. That an American car based on the lowly Tempest would dare swipe a name reserved for one of the greatest road cars of the era was considered heresy.

At the same time, General Motors' sister divisions Chevrolet and Oldsmobile were crying foul, too. Pontiac was not supposed to put an engine with so much displacement into an intermediate. But it was too late. You can't put you-know-what back into a goose, and once the public got a taste for the Pontiac GTO, the orders flooded in and GM brass looked the other way.

The circumstances that led to the creation of the GTO were many. First, the original Tempest's weak and unreliable transaxle needed to be replaced by a more conventional setup, one that could handle a lot more horsepower. The GTO was also borne out of the 1963 GM racing ban, which hit Pontiac especially hard. Pontiac had promoted its success on the drag strips and in stock car competition quite effectively, enough so that it had as strong a performance reputation as Chevrolet—perhaps even more so. Without racing, it needed a new selling tool, and street performance was in.

GTO
CALIFORNIA
MHS 619
BALESTRA
XP 2000

Above: A mere 108 1969 GTO Judge convertibles were produced in the model's inaugural season.

Below: The Judge returned for 1970; this one is painted Orbit Orange.

Millions of postwar baby boomers were coming of driving age at this time, an era when the automobile—especially the high-horsepower image automobile—was king. Finally, according to former Pontiac advertising executive Jim Wangers in his autobiography, *Glory Days*, Pontiac staff engineer Bill Collins casually mentioned to general manager John Z. DeLorean that it would be quite easy to put a 389 into the Tempest since the engine mounts were the same. A week later, such a car was delivered to the next staff meeting and everyone was overwhelmed by it.

The original GTO was an option package on the Tempest LeMans series. It came standard with high compression (10.75:1), a 389-cubic-inch engine, and a 4-barrel carburetor with 325 horsepower and 428 lbs.-ft. of torque. Optional was the same engine fitted with three 2-barrel carburetors making 348 horsepower.

Now, it wasn't like Detroit hadn't offered cars with lots of power in the past. But the GTO had it all in a smaller package than most, plus bucket seats were standard. Six emblems adorned the exterior, making sure everyone knew what you were driving,

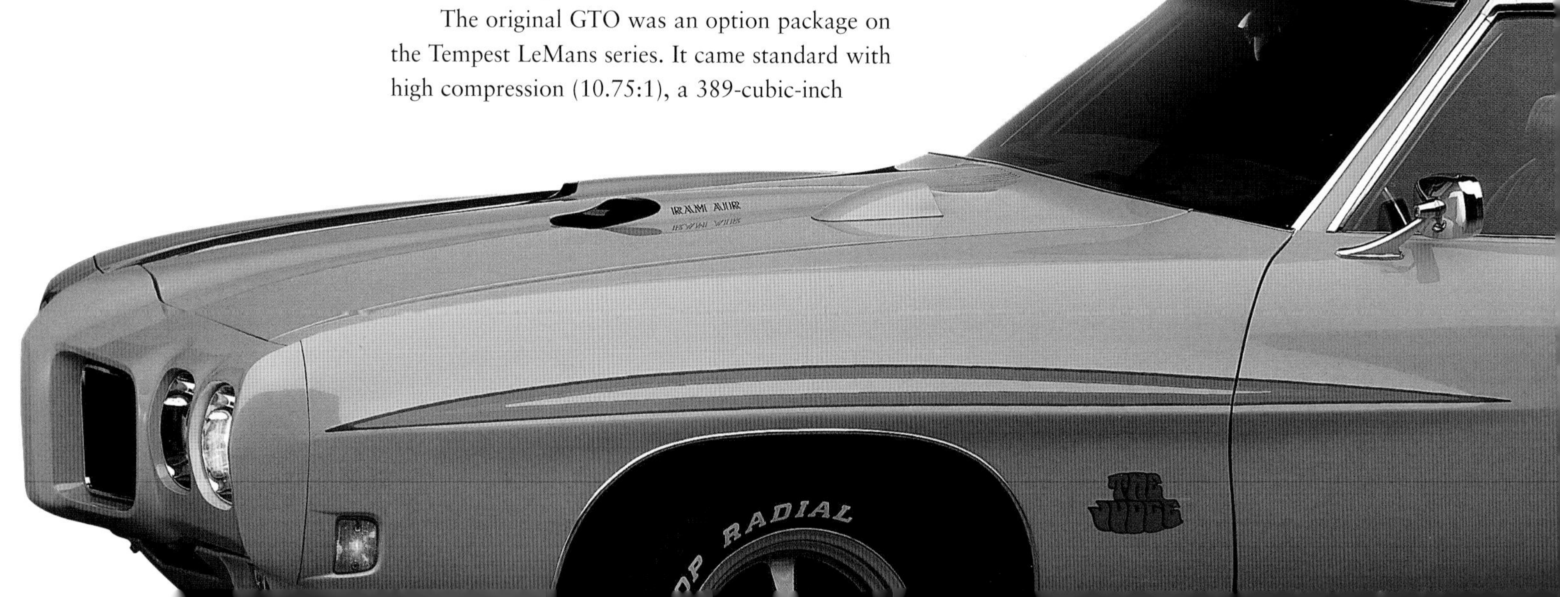

with a bunch more on the interior to remind you. The suspension was upgraded to match, with higher-rate springs, revalved shocks, a larger diameter, a stronger sway bar up front (there was no rear bar), and larger-than-Tempest wheels (14×6 inches [35.5×15cm]) and tires (7.50×14 inches [19×35.5cm]).

The tires themselves were part of the GTO mystique. Uniroyals with thin red stripes were standard. Later known as Tiger Paws, they actually offered fairly poor adhesion. Any heavy throttle application would send them spinning, screaming, and smoking, creating the illusion that the GTO's engine was a lot more powerful than it actually was.

As for the engine, Pontiac used the 389 short-block from its larger passenger cars and added 421 HO cylinder heads and lifters, a hotter hydraulic cam, a Carter 4-barrel intake manifold, and dual exhausts. Compression was a premium fuel–only 10.75:1 producing 325 horsepower. Optional was a Tri-Power version bringing the tally to 348 horsepower.

In a coup for Pontiac, all GTOs equipped with manual transmissions were delivered with the popular Hurst shifter. A 3-speed was standard, and a 4-speed cost an extra $188.30. The only available automatic was a 2-speed that cost $199.06.

Car Life tested a two-door hardtop in its June '64 issue that was equipped with the 348-horse engine and a 4-speed tranny. It recorded a 14.8-second ET quarter mile at 99 mph (159kph). In a 325-horsepower, 4-speed convertible, *Motor Trend* clocked a 15.8 at 93 mph (149.5kph). These were decent performances, but hardly earth-shattering. There were plenty of early-1960s cars that ran as well or better, but the GTO was a smash hit. Why?

Certainly, the Pontiac CTO had a lot going for it. Its size, styling, and handling were all best in its class. The price was extremely reasonable, the hype was unbelievable, and the timing of its intro was perfect. Also, the GTO was (and remains) an extremely exciting car to drive. Combine all of these factors and you have the makings of not just a sales success but a potential classic. However, it should not be overlooked that while there were cars that could run faster on the highway and quicker in the quarter mile, they were usually high-maintenance machines that were barely drivable on the street. The GTO delivered outstanding performance, reliability, and drivability.

While DeLorean sold the brass on the idea that it could sell five thousand of them, in actuality more than thirty-two thousand moved in '64, a number that peaked in 1966 with 96,946 Goats sold. It remained America's best-selling muscle car for most of the decade.

Left: A 1969 GTO Judge with the factory-fitted Hurst T-Handle shifter.

With Tri-Power, the 389 was rated at 360 horsepower in 1965. This was the first year you could purchase an over-the-counter kit to convert the factory hood scoop into a functional Ram Air setup. The GTO emblem could be found on the dash and on both door panels in '65. This was also the year Pontiac switched to a 3-spoke steering wheel (inset).

For '65, the GTO's body was extensively updated. The headlights were stacked and the grille was split and recessed. A single nonfunctional hood scoop replaced the similarly decorative twin scoops of '64. The rear was as distinctive as the nose, with wrap-around taillamps integrated into a decklid trim panel.

The GTO was still an option package on the Tempest in '65, and the 389 returned as the sole powerplant. The base 4-barrel version picked up 10 horsepower thanks to a new cam, and the optional Tri-Power version was now rated at 360 gross thanks to an improved intake manifold and a different camshaft. If you ordered your GTO with three deuces and an automatic, your carb linkage was vacuum-controlled, whereas stick shift models used mechanical linkage, which offered improved drivability and throttle response.

Late in the model year, a dealer- or owner-installed Ram Air system became available. For $50 you got a sheet metal tub that fit around the carburetors (under the air cleaners) with a thick foam gasket that sealed the carbs to the hood. Once installed, all you had to do was remove the metal plugs from the hood scoop and the setup was functional. It added approximately 5 to 10 horsepower to the engine, an exceptional value considering its price. Customers responded positively, to say the least. GTO sales more than doubled, to 75,352—20,547 being of the Tri-Power variety. Manual transmissions outsold automatics by almost three to one.

As well as the '65 GTO sold, '66 saw a nearly all-new model. The wheelbase remained at 115 inches (292cm), but the car was longer and wider. The front retained its stacked headlights and recessed grille, but the parking lights were moved into the grille. The taillights were six bars that again appeared almost hidden. This was the first year for the GTO's so-called Coke-bottle styling theme on the sides.

The instrument panel retained its four-gauge theme, set in a wood veneer. The interior remained one of the best parts of the GTO, with comfortable bucket seats standard (a bench was optional). This was the last year for tri-carburetion on the GTO, not to mention the swan song for the mighty 389. The standard 4-barrel model continued with 335 ponies and the three 2-barrel option still had 360, although the center carb was now slightly larger.

Most importantly, the XS Ram Air option debuted. The dealer-installed package was now a factory piece, but it included a better camshaft. It retained the same 360-horse rating as the normal 389 but was quite a bit quicker. *Car and Driver* reported a 0-to-60-mph (96.5kph) time of 6.5 seconds and a quarter mile of 14.05 at 105 mph (169kph), though this car was probably tweaked—most Pontiac test cars were.

Sales hit 96,946 in '66 and this was the high watermark for any performance car during the muscle car era. Only the Plymouth Road Runner came close, selling 84,420 in '69.

A General Motors corporate edict banning multiple carburetion in passenger cars in '67 spelled doom for the Tri-Power setup in the GTO, but an increase in displacement to 400 cubic inches helped offset the disappearance. The bore of the 389 was increased from 4.06 to 4.12 inches (103 to 104.5mm) to achieve this. The base 400 still made 335 horsepower; optional was the new 400 HO, which was rated at 360 ponies thanks to a long-duration cam, revised exhaust manifolds, and an open-element air cleaner. The Ram Air option returned, at a cost of $263.30, and 751 were produced. It, too, was rated at 360 horsepower.

A lesser-known option was the 400 2-barrel V8, a no-cost package that had lower compression (8.6:1 versus 10.75:1). It produced 255 horsepower and was not at all popular.

Optional red plastic inner fender liners, introduced in '66, were back in '67. Pontiac's now-famous Rally II 5-spoke rims debuted this year, as did the GTO's hood-mounted tach. On the interior, the most interesting news was the introduction of the Hurst His/Hers shifter for the new 3-speed Turbo 400 automatic transmission. A federally mandated dual master cylinder arrived, as did optional 11.5-inch (29cm) front disc brakes. California cars felt the most intrusive wave yet of emissions controls. Cars headed for the Golden State received an Air Injection Reactor system, which contained a large air pump. These would be federally mandated soon in all fifty states.

Externally, the '67 GTO was very similar to the '66, but there were differences. The newer car had a wire-mesh grille, and the taillights were now

A wire-mesh grille is a styling tip-off that this is a '67 GTO, not a '66. Nineteen sixty-seven was also the last year for stacked headlights on the GTO.

composed of four slits per side. A two-door coupe, hardtop, and convertible remained the three body styles available. It was another classic, but for the first time sales failed to exceed those of the previous year. Thanks to the proliferation of strong competitors—such as the SS396 Chevelle, the Dodge R/T, and the Plymouth GTX, which sported 396-cubic-inch powerplants and 375 horsepower as standard equipment—sales dipped to just less than eighty-two thousand units. On the plus side, it was still the number one seller in its class.

For the fourth time in five years, the GTO received a major overhaul for 1968, and this time it was more than just cosmetics. The A-body platform had its wheelbase shrunk to 112 inches (284.5cm) and a dynamic new shape draped over it. The GTO was totally redesigned and had such unusual features as the Endura front bumper, which was made of a rubberlike material that was resistant to dents and dings, and a painted body color, an industry first. Also, the taillights were integrated into the bumper, and concealed headlights were optional for the first time. The parking lights wrapped around the front valence and also served as side marker lights.

All-new, too, was the interior. A three-pod gauge cluster replaced the four-pod unit that had been a GTO staple since its introduction. Bucket seats were still standard, and an AM/FM stereo radio became available. (An 8-track tape player had been optional since '67.)

Only two body styles were offered, a two-door hardtop and a convertible. As life on the streets of America got meaner and auto theft and break-ins increased, the popularity of convertibles declined steadily. For the second year in a row, Pontiac sold fewer than 10,000 GTO ragtops, though overall GTO sales climbed to 87,684.

All kinds of interesting things were happening under the GTO's sleek new hood. The base 400 got its power bumped to 350 horses and 445 lbs.-ft. of torque, while the economy 400 2-barrel was now at 265 horsepower. The 360-horse 400 HO was the first high-output optional V8. If you ordered it with the stick shift, you got a different carburetor and a hotter camshaft. The similarly rated 400 Ram Air was available at the start of the year, but was replaced shortly thereafter by the excellent Ram Air II, which had forged pistons, round port heads, and a forged steel crankshaft. It was not offered with air conditioning and was rated at 366 horsepower and 445 lbs.-ft. of torque at 3600 rpm.

The RA II was available with only the M21 4-speed manual or TH 400 3-speed automatic, both of which used Hurst shifters. The only gear ratio available was 4.33:1. These were true stormers, perhaps the quickest GTOs yet, capable of high-13-second quarter-mile times at 102 mph (164kph).

Typical of the muscle car era, the RA II came and went in less than a year. By '69, it had been supplanted as the top dog by the Ram Air IV; and

An easy way to distinguish a 1971 GTO from a '72 is that the '72 has a side air extractor cut out of the front fender behind the wheelwell. This is a '71 with the uncommon Judge package.

another option, the Ram Air III appeared. There was also a special GTO model introduced, one totally in keeping with the spirit of the times. It was called the Judge.

The original Judge concept called for a low-buck, stripped-down, limited-option vehicle that could compete with the likes of the Plymouth Road Runner, Dodge Super Bee, and Ford Cobra. When John Z. DeLorean got word of it, however, he was totally against the idea of a decontented GTO. When the Judge emerged as a production car, it was a colorful bespoilered machine with wild graphics and the Ram Air III engine as the standard mill. In addition, the heavy-duty suspension and Rally II rims were thrown in, the latter without trim rings—one of the ideas from the original concept that survived.

The name itself came from a skit on a popular comedy show at the time, *Laugh-In*, as in "Here comes the Judge!" The Judge name appeared in cartoonish script on the leading edges of the front fenders and on the top right side of the oddly shaped decklid spoiler, which was a Judge exclusive.

Inside, a Judge decal was affixed to the glovebox door on later cars, though the first two thousand didn't get one. The 4-speed Hurst shifter got a T-handle. Most Judges were painted Carousel Red, which was actually orange, and multicolor stripes ran from the front fenders rearward to the end of the quarter windows. Originally, these stripes were yellow, blue, and red, but that later changed to yellow, black, and red. A total of 108 Judge convertibles were produced in its maiden season, making them among the rarest GTOs that year. Total Judge production was 6,833.

Many magazines (and customers) of the day didn't know what to make of this new GTO. Some called it loud and obnoxious; some had a hard time taking it seriously; others thought it was perfect. Performance, especially with the Ram Air IV, was nothing to scoff at, however. *Car and Driver* turned 0 to 60 mph (96.5kph) in 6.2 seconds and the quarter mile in 13.7 at 103.6 mph (166.5kph).

As for other '69s, the 350-horse 400 was still the base powerplant. The 265-horse "economy" 400 was hanging in there, but it was available with only an automatic tranny. The styling was pretty much unchanged, although the taillights were now separate from the bumper. The vent windows on the doors were eliminated, and a horizontal divider ran the width of the grille. Pontiac executives were smart to look over their shoulders at the Road Runner; it was 1969 when that particular car stole the supercar sales crown from the GTO.

Pontiac gave the GTO a new body for 1970, one that echoed the styling theme begun in 1968, but added a touch of the soon-to-be-released 1970½ Firebird as well. *Car and Driver* called the shape "voluptuous—yet tasteful." The grille was the part that would be likened to that of the new

The 455 HO engine debuted in the '71 GTO and Trans Am. Offering 335 horsepower, this engine supplanted the discontinued Ram Air IV 400 as the top engine option.

Bird, but it had four headlights rather than two. The taillights wrapped around the chrome rear bumper, and up front the Endura bumper soldiered on.

The biggest news for muscle car enthusiasts was that the new 455 Pontiac engine was available in the GTO. It produced 360 horsepower at 4600 rpm and 500 lbs.-ft. of torque at a mere 3100 rpm, but it was not truly a high-performance engine. It was introduced because Chevrolet, Oldsmobile, and Buick were getting engines bigger than 450 cubic inches, and that meant Pontiac needed one, too. It had only 10.25:1 compression and was actually rated at 10 horsepower less than the same engine installed in the Grand Prix, the Catalina, and other full-size Ponchos. But it did make for an extremely nice cruiser when you loaded up the power options and Ram Air. If you opted for the 455, you got a 12-bolt rear standard, while 400 GTOs got the weaker 10-bolt.

Those battling it out on Main Street still looked to the Ram Air III and, especially, the Ram Air IV—though the 350-horsepower 400 was plenty tough as the base engine. (Thankfully, the 400 2-barrel got the axe.)

It was also in 1970 that Pontiac finally used a rear sway bar on the GTO. Though GTOs were considered among the best handlers without one, the new rear bar (measuring 0.875 inches [22mm]) combined with a fatter front sway bar gave the GTO much improved road manners. Those who ordered power steering got a variable-rate box, which made things even better.

For collectors or lovers of the unusual, option code W-73 appeared briefly on the order sheet. If you spent the $63.19 for the Vacuum Operated Exhaust, you got a pair of specially baffled mufflers. If you pulled the Exhaust Mode knob on the dash, a pair of vacuum-controlled baffles on the mufflers would open, giving you reduced back pressure and more horsepower. This option was available from early November 1969 until January 1970. According to an article in *Musclecar Review*, a commercial was broadcast during the Super Bowl showing a VOE GTO cruising through a drive-in and then opening the baffles. GM brass grew angry and, according to the article, canceled the option. The article states that only 233 cars were ever so equipped.

The Judge returned, this time with a better-looking decklid wing and revised graphics. The new body had body creases over the wheel arches to give it a bolder look, and the new stripes accentuated these bulges. For the first time, the thick Formula wheel introduced on the '69 Firebird became a GTO option.

The '70 GTO was a great car, but the market was turning sour and the competition was tougher than ever. Only 40,149 Goats were produced, including 162 Judge convertibles. It never did so well again.

For '71, Pontiac gave the GTO a new front fascia and hood scoop setup. This was the year that GM lopped 2 points of compression from its engines, so the best you could get in the GTO was 8.2:1. Gone were the Ram Air III and IV. The base powerplant was a 300-horsepower 400; optional were a 325-horsepower 455 and the new 335-horse 455 HO.

The HO wore round-port heads with an aluminum intake and employed the 068 Pontiac cam, which helped breathing a great deal. Compression was a tepid 8.4:1. This was an excellent performer, available in the Firebird Formula and Trans Am as well. A set of 14×7-inch (35.5×18cm) aluminum "honeycomb" pattern wheels became available as an extra-cost option. They could also be ordered in 15×7-inch (38×18cm) size.

Pontiac discontinued the Judge partway through the model year, blaming poor sales. Only 357 hardtops and 17 convertibles were built; at least the 455 HO was standard.

For '72, the GTO reverted to an option package on the LeMans series, available only as a two-door hardtop or a coupe. The GTO's grille, flush the year before, was recessed again for '72 and wore a black eggcrate pattern. A quick way to differentiate a '72 GTO from a '71 is the cutout that appeared on the front fender behind the wheelwell for '72.

Horsepower was now rated as SAE net, and the GTO didn't fare well. A 250-horse 400 was standard equipment and a 230-horse 455 was optional. The top powerplant remained the 455 HO at 300 horsepower and 415 lbs.-ft. of torque. It was good for mid-15s at the drags at about 92 mph (148kph).

By 1973, muscle cars were totally out of fashion and the Arab oil embargo did nothing to help the GTO's cause. Nor did its controversial styling or weak engines. Although the GTO was supposed to be the recipient of the hot 455 Super Duty engine, production cars never got it. The most powerful 455 in the GTO made only 250 horsepower, just 20 more than the base 400.

Gone was the signature Endura nose, which for some reason ended up on a new, more luxury-oriented intermediate called the Grand Am. Technically, two body styles were available, both coupes. The Coupe had nonopening rear quarter windows, while the Sport Coupe had vertical louvers covering the glass. The only distinguishing GTO feature was the twin National Advisory Committee for Aeronautics (NACA) duct hood, made functional on fewer than ten cars at the factory. Production was at its nadir—4,806.

The following year, the GTO became an option on the Nova-esque Ventura, an unpleasant little compact. A 350 4-barrel was the only engine, and it wore the Trans Am's nonfunctional Shaker hood. In theory, the '74 was more in line with the car's original concept, that of a lighter car with a stronger-than-average powerplant. The 350 engine just wasn't very powerful (200 horsepower/295 lbs.-ft.), and the car was viewed as little more than a Nova with a Pontiac V8.

Ironically, sales rebounded to 7,058, but Pontiac killed the GTO name forever at the end of the model year. It has teased the public since with a handful of GTO concept cars and rumors, none of which was more disturbing than the ruminations in the late '80s and early '90s that said the name would be attached to a front-wheel-drive, 6-cylinder car.

GTS

This designation stood for GT Sport on the high-performance Dodge Darts of the late '60s beginning with the 1967 383 Dart GT. This included both the GTS 340 and the GTS 383. In '69, the 440 became available in the GTS.

See also *Dart.*

GTX

While most refer to the Chrysler 300 as the letter series cars (300B, 300C, and so on), this nomenclature was also used to describe the 1967 Plymouth GTX and Dodge R/T.

Both the GTX and R/T were borne out of Chrysler's need to compete with the GTO type of packaged muscle cars. The Satellite and Belvedere buyer had the 383, the 426 Street Wedge, and, later, the Street Hemi to pick from, but these robust engines were delivered in a package that was considered less than exciting by the general public. Outwardly, there was little difference between a Hemi Belvedere and one with a Slant Six engine. The letter cars changed that.

The GTX was based on the two-door Belvedere and used the 375-horse 440 Super Commando V8 as standard equipment. The idea was to one-up the GTO, and in base trim the X (as it was known) had 40 more cubes, 15 more horses, and 42 more lbs.-ft. of torque than the most powerful GTO. If that couldn't get the job done, the 425-horse Street Hemi with dual quads could.

"GTO owners had better look to their defenses" is how *Car and Driver* summed up the GTX in its first road test. With a 14.4-second ET at 98 mph (157.5kph) and exceptional handling, the GTX

Hood ornaments were not commonplace on muscle cars, but the '67 Hemi GTX had one.

Above: A console-mounted tachometer was soundly criticized on the '67 GTX. *Car and Driver* likened its placement to wearing a wristwatch on your ankle. The tach was moved to the instrument cluster for 1968 models.

Opposite Top: The last year for the GTX as its own model was 1971; the following year it became an option on the Road Runner. The Air Grabber hood was opened by pulling a lever in the cockpit.

Opposite Bottom: Grilles on the '70 Plymouth intermediates were revised with a kick up in the center, a portent of what was to come with the '71 remodeling.

impressed the magazine's staff. *Car and Driver* also praised the handling, stating, "This heavy duty set-up, plus excellent suspension geometry designed to keep the front wheels at right angles to the road surface, keeps the tires in firm contact with the ground at all times."

There was more to the GTX than sheer performance; the Belvedere had that for years. Standard equipment on the X included a pair of nonfunctional hood scoops, a pop-open chrome gas cap, wider-than-stock chrome wheels with red-stripe tires, and bucket seats. To further differentiate it from lesser Belvederes and Satellites, it had a unique grille and tail panel between the lights.

The new GTX sold fairly well, but it was introduced in the second year of a two-year styling cycle. For '68, the X wore stylish new duds. The B-body Plymouths were a smash hit, but the GTX got unexpected competition from its sister car, the Road Runner. The two cars were different enough that it shouldn't have mattered—the Road Runner was a stripped-down terror that lacked carpeting on the floor, used a bench seat, and had a 383 standard, while the GTX was more luxuriously appointed, with carpeting, bucket seats, and a 440-cube engine. But the Road Runner outsold the X by nearly two to one.

Still, the GTX was an awesome performer, so much so that *Car Life* reported that it had "never tested a standard passenger car with the accelerative performance of the Plymouth GTX."

This was a GTX convertible with 3.23:1 gears. It ran the quarter mile in 13.97 seconds at 103.5 mph (166.5kph) with a full tank of fuel and a driver (no passenger, which is how it was usually tested). After swapping in 4.56:1 gears and using 9×15-inch (23×38cm) slicks, the TorqueFlite automatic-equipped ragtop went a stunning 13.43 at 104.86 mph (168.5kph). At the same test session, *Car Life* tested a 440/automatic GTX hardtop. In base trim, it went 14.6 at 95.6 mph (154kph). The addition of slicks and 4.30:1 gears helped it break into the 13-second barrier—13.97 at 99.77 mph (160.5kph), to be precise.

The '68 GTX may not have been the sales success the Road Runner was, but it was a dynamic vehicle that over the next three years helped set the standard for muscle car performance. The '69 was a mildly face-lifted version of the '68, and the engines and transmissions were basically carryovers: you could have the 440 Super Commando or the 426 Hemi, both with either a 4-speed stick or 3-speed automatic. New was an optional cold-air hood, different taillamps, an updated grille, and striping, but it was the same basic automobile—a fault only if the product is deficient to start with and the GTX definitely was not.

There was plenty happening for 1970, both under the hood and out. The grille was revised, giving a sneak peek at the direction stylists were headed the following year, and the taillights were again changed. Performance enthusiasts were more concerned with the appearance of a new engine on the option list—the 440 Six-Barrel, introduced the year before as a Road Runner exclusive.

With a trio of Holley 2-barrels sitting atop a cast-iron intake (it had been aluminum the prior year), it made 390 horsepower and 490 lbs.-ft. of torque. A vacuum-operated, pop-up Air Grabber hood scoop could be ordered at extra cost. A dual-point distributor was part of the standard goodies, as was a long-duration, high-lift cam, and a high-rpm-upshift TorqueFlite automatic. Chrysler's durable A-833 4-speed with the infamous Pistol-Grip shift handle was an option. An uncommon option was the 440 6-barrel 4-speed with the Super Track Pack, which consisted of 4.10 gears in a Dana 60 rear. In an effort to make the Hemi maintenance-free, it now used a hydraulic camshaft. Still rated at

425 horsepower, emissions controls were creeping in and its days were numbered.

Despite these upgrades, sales of the GTX plummeted, to less than eight thousand units. For '71, the X got the same new body as all intermediate Plymouths. Dubbed "fuselage" styling, the body had much more pronounced fender arches and was clearly related to the Barracuda introduced one year earlier. It continued the four-headlight theme, and the grille was surrounded by a chrome grille that kicked up at the bottom. The nose was longer, the decklid shorter.

The interiors were also reminiscent of the 'Cuda's, although the materials used were a bit better. Engine-wise, the 440 4-barrel was the base mill, now rated at 370 horses thanks to a decrease in compression from 10.5:1 to 9.7, and the Six-Barrel was optional, now checking in with 385 ponies. The Hemi hung in there with 425 horsepower, but it, along with the two 440s, would go away forever after this year. It was an unappreciated vehicle, and sales didn't crack the three-thousand barrier and the GTX went away, though it did become an option package on the Road Runner from 1972 to 1974. So equipped, you got a 280-net-horsepower 440 with 8.5:1 compression and a 4-barrel carb (the Air Grabber was still an option, except in California). After '74, the letters GTX were retired for good.

Hornet SC360

In NASCAR's infancy, a car called the Hudson Hornet dominated the Grand National circuit. From 1951 to 1954, Hornets won consecutive championships with drivers like Marshall Teague and Tim Flock who racked up victory after victory.

Later, Hudson merged with Nash to form American Motors Corporation, which specialized in sedate, small economy cars. When the muscle car era forced the company into the performance arena, American Motors participated sparingly. For one of its last efforts, AMC built a performance package out of a compact named Hornet and stuffed a 360-cubic-inch V8 into it.

In base trim, the 1971 Hornet SC360 made 245 horsepower with a 2-barrel carburetor—hardly the stuff to make waves on Woodward Avenue (the street-racing mecca of the Detroit suburbs in the '60s and '70s.) But there was an optional 4-barrel engine complete with a functional ram air hood to wake things up. This SC360 produced 285 horsepower at 4800 rpm and 390 lbs.-ft. of torque at 3200. With 8.5:1 compression, it ran on regular fuel, but had a favorable power-to-weight ratio.

Available only as a two-door coupe, the SC360 came with a 3-speed manual as standard equipment. A Hurst-rowed 4-speed or 3-speed automatic was optional. In addition to the trick scooped hood, the SC360 was also differentiated by a stripe that ran back from the front fenders and over the decklid.

Priced at $2,663, the SC360 was inexpensive, even by the standards of the day. Most of the good hardware, like a tachometer, dual exhausts, and a handling package, were extra-cost options. *Hot Rod* managed to wring a 14.8 at 95 mph (153kph) out of an automatic-equipped model. Unfortunately for AMC fanciers, the Hornet was a rather plain-looking machine in '71, even fully decked out. A mere 667 were sold, and AMC pulled the plug on this budget specialty car after one year.

Hurst 300H

In an attempt to recapture some of the glory of the Chrysler 300 letter cars of the '50s and early '60s, Hurst injected some much-needed pizzazz into the 1970 Chrysler New Yorker. The cars were painted Spinnaker White with gold stripes on the side, hood, grille, trunk, and taillight area.

Standard equipment unique to the Hurst 300H were an integrated decklid spoiler, a bulging fresh air hood that ducted air to the passenger compartment, custom wheels and tires, and a vacuum-operated trunk lid—there was no keyhole.

The 440 engine was part of the price as well, as was a tan and brown leather bucket seat interior.

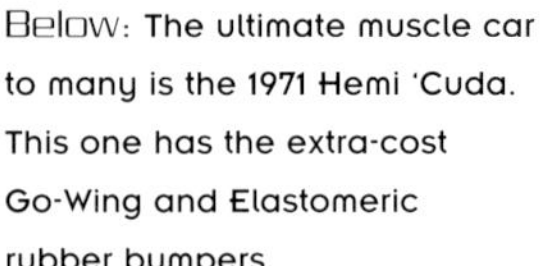

Below: The ultimate muscle car to many is the 1971 Hemi 'Cuda. This one has the extra-cost Go-Wing and Elastomeric rubber bumpers.

Opposite: The Hurst Olds came back for 1973 on GM's new colonnade body style. Horsepower was down, but the car came with such interesting features as the Hurst Performance Meter (located on the console) which allowed drivers to measure their own 0 to 60 quarter-mile times. This was the first year that Hurst offered more than one hue.

Hurst Grand Prix

Looking to inject a little magic into the Grand Prix in 1970, Hurst and Pontiac hooked up to produce the SSJ. This car was white with gold on the hood, roof, and decklid inside the body lines. A Hurst sunroof was available, as were American Racing wheels and a 455 engine. Not a muscle car in the truest sense, it was still an interesting period piece. A Hurst Dual Gate His/Hers shifter was installed in the console. Production picked up again in 1971 and a handful were built in '72.

Hurst Hemi Barracudas and Darts

During the muscle car era, the Hurst name ranked among the most recognizable of all the aftermarket companies. Founded by George Hurst and Bill Campbell, the company built its reputation on quality shifters, wheels, and other hot rod goodies. At the same time, George Hurst had the desire to build his own cars.

Hurst the company had already done some development work for Grand Spaulding Dodge in Chicago, building 383- and 440-powered Darts that essentially became the prototypes for cars the factory eventually built.

Thanks to the company's ability to act fast and deliver the goods, Hurst produced a number of superior muscle cars before the era ended, none more powerful than the Hurst Hemi Barracudas and Darts. These cars came about because Chrysler wanted to dominate Super Stock drag racing and decided that a take-no-prisoners, race-only brawler was the only solution. Chrysler contracted with Hurst to build Race Hemi–powered Darts and 'Cudas, which were based on the compact A-body platform. By the time the job was finished, Hurst delivered seventy-two Plymouths and eighty-three Dodges.

The cars were made lighter with the use of fiberglass front fenders and hoods (with built-in scoops) and acid-dipped doors. Front bumpers were made of thinner-gauge steel than production models, and Chemcor 0.080-inch- (2mm) thick side glass was used—thinner and lighter than stock. Rear seats, rearview mirrors, radios, and heaters were deleted as well.

The engines were similar to that of the production Street Hemi in that they used the same camshaft and cylinder heads. The major differences were

Jack "Doc" Watson

He was known as the Hurst Shifty Doctor and is one of the muscle car era's most successful promotional and advertising campaigners, but Jack "Doc" Watson was more than just a promotional figure. He was also involved in the early days of Pontiac's Super Duty parts program.

When he went to work at Hurst in the early 1960s, it was as an idea man, a promo man, and an engineer. By the time he was twenty-three years old, he was heading up Hurst Performance Research, which was the original equipment manufacturer (OEM) design and engineering arm of the company. It helped create and produce many of the most memorable supercars, including the Hurst Oldsmobile. According to Watson, four people were responsible for the original Hurst Olds—George Hurst and Watson on the aftermarket side and Olds engineers John Beltz and Ted Louckes.

On the race car side, Watson was instrumental in the creation of the Hurst Hairy Olds drag car, which had blown and injected powerplants front and rear, and the Hurst Hemi Under Glass.

Today, Watson lives in Michigan and makes appearances at high-profile car shows.

12.5:1-compression pistons and a cross-ram, dual quad intake manifold. For improved weight distribution, the battery (which was larger than stock) was relocated to the trunk. Instead of production Barracuda and Dart bucket seats, a pair of A-100 van seats on aluminum tracks were used.

Hurst installed the Hemi engines and the rest of the drivetrain, then bolted on the lightweight body parts and interiors. The rear wheelwells were slightly enlarged on the Darts. Once assembled, the cars were either picked up at Hurst by customers or shipped to dealers. Since they were slated to be race cars, they were shipped in primer. When new, they ran in the 10.3-second range in the quarter mile on the tires of the day; today they run in the high 8s.

Hurst Hemi Under Glass

This name was applied to a series of A-body Barracuda exhibition cars motored by powerful Chrysler Hemi engines. The product of Hurst Research, the engine was mounted behind the driver and passenger seats under the Barracuda's huge rear window, hence the name.

The first appeared in 1965 and was driven by Bill Schrewsbury. Power went to the rear wheels via a specially designed transaxle setup, while the radiator and fans were located in the rear. The fuel tank was placed under the hood and the wheelie bars were designed to support the entire weight of the vehicle; otherwise the front wheels would've lifted. These wheelie bars were quite necessary, as vintage photos show the car heading down the track with all four wheels off the ground.

Later, the Hemi Under Glass was driven by Bob Riggle. The cars made exhibition runs at events for years, and later incarnations were built on the second-generation Barracuda platform. The cars were all painted black and gold.

Hurst Oldsmobiles

Hurst's shifters had been standard equipment in every manual transmission–equipped Pontiac since the 1964 GTO, but the company's first of many ventures on an entire car with General Motors was the '68 Hurst Oldsmobile. The plan was to build an executive hot rod, one that would combine Oldsmobile's most powerful engine in a luxurious, Hurst-shifted supercar.

At the time, GM policy forbade installing an intermediate with an engine larger than 400 cubic inches, but if someone else did it, well, then that would be okay. Olds supplied Hurst with semi-finished Cutlasses (not 4-4-2s as some think), and Hurst installed modified 390-horsepower Toronado engines, among other things. The work was done at Demmer's Foundry in Lansing, Michigan, a once-abandoned factory building.

Opposite & Far Left Inset: A modified Toronado 455 engine producing 390 horsepower made the Hurst Oldsmobile one of the quickest muscle cars in 1968.

Right Inset: Naturally, the Hurst Dual Gate His/Hers shifter was standard in the Hurst Olds.

As a higher-priced "executive" hot rod, the Hurst Olds was far more plush inside than most muscle cars.

George Hurst

The name Hurst has become synonymous with great aftermarket shifters, and George Hurst's shifter was so good that it became standard equipment in the GTO in 1964 and eventually every other floor-shifted Pontiac. It was the first car part installed in a General Motors vehicle that had an outside vendor's name on it. Jim Wangers convinced Pontiac executives that it meant a great deal to potential customers to be associated with such a product.

There was more to Hurst's company in the '60s and '70s than just shifters. The company also made wheels and shocks, among other things, but amazingly, it also got into producing some of the most sought-after cars of the muscle car era.

The first was the 1968 Hurst Oldsmobile, which was fitted with a 455-cubic-inch engine, a Hurst shifter, and special paint and suspension, plus other goodies. Hurst produced a car for Oldsmobile every year through the end of the muscle car era (1974) except for 1970 and '71. Hurst eventually built cars for American Motors, Pontiac, Dodge, Plymouth, and Chrysler, too.

George Hurst invented something that would have an even greater impact on the motoring public than perhaps even he realized: the Jaws of Life, a device used for freeing trapped people from car wrecks.

An under-the-bumper ram air system fed a recalibrated carburetor. A high-lift, long-duration camshaft, free-flowing cylinder heads, and recurved distributor accounted for the engine modifications. Peak power was 390 at 5000 rpm and 500 lbs.-ft. of torque at 3600. Naturally, all the transmissions were fitted with a Hurst Dual Gate automatic shifter. A heavy-duty suspension, a rear end assembly with 3.91 gears and bigger brakes, a higher-capacity cooling system, and G70×14-inch (35.5cm) tires completed the mechanical end of things.

To make the cars distinctive, they were painted Peruvian Silver with black decklids and other accents. Unique Hurst/Olds badges and a specially trimmed instrument panel were also used. While a paper shuffle fooled the brass, the engines were installed on the Olds assembly line. The work done by Demmer Special Machinery included paint and installation of trim, like the wood for the dash.

The car was very well received by the media. Close to 2,000 were ordered, but only 515 were delivered to the general public. Supply just couldn't keep up with demand. (According to Watson, in addition to the 515, which were all automatics, four manual-transmission versions were built—one for him, one for John Demmer's son, and two others.) *Popular Hot Rodding* tested one and went 13.8 at speeds topping 102 mph (164kph); *Motor Trend* reported a 13.97, with a 0-to-60 (96.5kph) time of 6.65 seconds.

So successful was the program that it paved the way for a successor in 1969. This time each car was painted white with gold stripes, and in a departure for Oldsmobile, the fresh air was fed through a fiberglass hood with two scoops. Tire size was increased to F60×15 inches (38cm), and horsepower was downrated to 380.

Still, the folks at *Super Stock & Drag Illustrated* were impressed. They tested an air-conditioned model with 3.23 gears and a non-A/C-equipped car with 3.42s in their July 1969 issue. The former went a 13.87 at 97 mph (156kph), while the latter trucked to a 14.2 at 98.5 mph (158.5kph). The magazine raved about the car's ride, handling, comfort, and looks. Production improved to 906, plus 6 prototypes and 2 convertibles.

Hurst and Oldsmobile combined efforts a few times over the years after this, including three more during the muscle car era. The third Hurst Olds appeared in 1972, and this time it was picked to pace the Indianapolis 500. It was again painted Cameo White and Firefrost Gold. Power came from a 280-net-horsepower 455 with ram induction, and only an automatic transmission was available (Hurst-shifted, of course).

In '73, a Hurst/Oldsmobile was built using GM's controversial new "colonnade" body style. A total of 1,097 were produced; about 60 percent of the cars were painted white with gold accents, while the rest had black with gold. Swivel bucket seats were standard, as were a louvered hood and a padded landau top; options included a digital tachometer and air shocks. The engine was a nonrated 455, estimated to make in the 250-net-horsepower range.

Another Hurst/Olds made the scene the following year, again as the Indy pace car, but the 455 was gone. All that was left was a rather odd set of stripes and a landau top.

Hurst SC/Rambler

Few people paid much attention to American Motors Corporation during the muscle car era, and with good reason. Until the AMX and Javelin were introduced in 1968, AMC didn't offer a youth-oriented performance car. It needed an image enhancer, and in 1969 it turned to Hurst. The result was a powered pocket rocket dubbed the Hurst SC/Rambler.

By putting AMC's largest and most powerful engine, the 315-horsepower 390 V8, in the lightweight, compact Rambler, Hurst created a vehicle that could run with some of the best of the breed back in '69. The engine wasn't the most powerful, but the SC/Rambler barely weighed 3,000 pounds (1,362kg). *Road Test* magazine clocked one at 14.14 at 100.44 mph (161.5kph).

Naturally, the Borg-Warner 4-speed transmission had a Hurst shifter. A functional (and oddly shaped) ram air hood and 3.54:1 Twin-Grip rear were standard, as were gray vinyl bench seats (with red, white, and blue headrests) and a Sun tachometer on the steering column.

What made the SC/Rambler really stand out was its paint schemes. Initially, a run of five hundred cars was planned. All were white with bold red sides, plus blue stripes that ran up the fresh-air hood, across the roof and down the trunklid. The upward-tilting hood scoop had the word AIR written on top, and the engine's displacement was spelled out in big, bold numbers right in front of the scoop. The wheels were AMC's 5-spoke design, painted the same blue as the stripes. This became known as the "A" paint scheme.

Because the first five hundred copies sold so quickly, a second run was ordered (these had a toned-down paint scheme). After that, another run of cars with the first paint scheme were released and in the end 1,512 SC/Ramblers were produced. Like the 1971 Hornet SC360, the SC/Rambler was produced only one year.

Impala

If there were such a thing as a muscle car in the late 1950s, the '58 Chevrolet Impala would have fit the bill. It was introduced that year as a top-of-the-line automobile with a sporting flavor. Like all Chevys of the time, it was huge but came with a custom interior/exterior trim and insignia. Best of all, it could be ordered with the 283-horsepower fuel-injected small-block V8 or the new 348 W engine

The 335-horsepower, three-deuce 348 W engine and a 4-speed transmission combo made the 1960 Impala the quickest muscle car of that year.

These pages: The roofline of the '63 Impala was more formal than the '62 (right). Lower-output versions of the 409 (opposite bottom) in 1963 could be ordered with such convenient options as air conditioning (opposite top).

with three 2-barrel carburetors. The Impala rode 1.5 inches (38mm) lower than the Bel Air, was available only as a hardtop, and offered a lower seating position.

The Impala took a major evolutionary step as a muscle machine in 1960 when the Warner T-10 4-speed transmission appeared on the order sheets. Unlike previous models that came with either a 2-speed Turboglide automatic or 3-speed manual, this model was a definite step toward improved performance. The T-10 was sometimes brittle, but if it didn't break, it was a stormer behind the 335-horsepower 348.

The year 1961 will be remembered by enthusiasts as the year the immortal 409 engine debuted. To arrive at 409 cubic inches from 348, the bore was increased and stroke was lengthened. The block, while similar, was actually a different casting with a unique water jacket core to allow the overbore without making the cylinder walls thinner.

Forged aluminum pistons with solid skirts swung on rods that were one-eighth inch (3mm) shorter than those used in the 348. The Impala used the high-output 348's big-port cylinder heads, high-lift solid-lifter cam, aluminum bearings, and downswept exhaust manifolds. A dual-plane aluminum intake manifold sat on top, and it was fed by a new-model 650-cfm Carter AFB 4-barrel carburetor, the largest available at the time. Compression was rated at 11.25:1, although early models came with two head gaskets per side to lower the ratio slightly for use with pump gas.

Not many of these 348s were produced—just 142—and most (but not all) were in Impalas. The 409 didn't appear until about six months after the rest of the lineup, so tests were scarce. *Motor Trend* called the Impala "a family car that is really a racing machine" in its September 1961 issue. The magazine tested the car with the stock 3.36:1 gears and limited slip differential and ran 15.31 at 94.24 mph (151.5kph)—impressive but not close to its potential. It went back to the track at a later date with 4.56:1 gears installed and promptly ran 14.02 at 98.14 mph (158kph).

In the hands of drag racers like "Dyno" Don Nicholson, the 409s began cleaning up at the drags. In fact, Nicholson won the Stock Eliminator title and the inaugural NHRA Winternationals in Pomona, California, in 1961. The 409s also recorded twelve stock car racing victories that year, making the '62 409 a highly anticipated model.

But there was more to the Impala story in 1961 than just the 409 engine. This was also the first year for the fabled Super Sport, or SS, package. Available only on the Impala that year, the SS package gave you unique trim for the exterior and

Above: The 427 fender badge off a 1967 Impala SS.

Below: Despite the fact that Chevy backed out of racing completely in 1963, the street cars were still stout. A 425-horsepower 409 was optional in '64, even if the car—like this convertible Impala—looked more conservative than it had in years past.

Opposite Top: Full-size performance cars were falling out of favor by 1967, but the 427 Impala SS was still a heckuva ride. A hydraulic-lifter version of the 427 was available with 385 horsepower. With solid lifters, you got 425 horsepower.

interior. Heavy-duty springs and shocks and sintered metallic brake linings aided handling and braking, respectively. A 7000-rpm tachometer, dashpad, and passenger-side grab handle dolled up the interior, while spinner hubcaps and SS emblems dressed up the body.

Five engine/transmission combinations were available in the SS, all at extra cost, with the base powerplant being the 305-horse 348. A 4-speed or heavy-duty Powerglide automatic were your choices. After that it was the 340- or 350-horsepower 348 or the 409, a trio that could be mated only to the 4-speed.

Two body styles were available for the Impala if you wanted a two-door in '62, a convertible and the Sport Coupe, which somewhat resembled a ragtop. The bubbletop hardtop of '61 was available in only the lower-line Bel Air. The SS option was back, but now any engine was available, even the 6-cylinder. Many opted for the 327 small-block with either 250 or 300 horsepower. The 348 was gone, and if you were serious about performance, you went for one of the hot 409s—380 horsepower with a single 4-barrel or 409 horsepower with dual quads. The latter engine made peak power at 6000 rpm, not to mention 420 lbs.-ft. of torque at 4000. Inside, bucket seats and a console became standard equipment on the SS. Nearly 100,000 Impala Super Sports were produced for '62.

At the NHRA Winternationals in 1962, Nicholson piloted a 409 Impala SS to the Stock Eliminator crown, running 12.82 at 109.22 mph (175.5kph) in the final round and defeating Dave Strickler. (Strickler took the crown later that year at the U.S. Nationals in Indianapolis.) Partway through the year, Chevy built a very few Impalas for drag racing with aluminum body panels. These lighter vehicles were campaigned in the Factory Experimental classes (the parts were also available over-the-counter).

The '63 Impalas were the basis for Chevrolet's most potent and ill-fated drag racing project to date, the Z-11. Impala Sport Coupes were fitted with aluminum hoods, inner and outer fender panels, bumpers, and brackets—and that was just for starters. This brought the weight down to less than 3,500 pounds (1,589kg).

Under the lightweight bonnets was a specially prepared version of the W engine, displacing 427 cubic inches (to take advantage of the NHRA's and NASCAR's 7-liter displacement limit). The heads featured larger valves, reshaped ports, and an air-gap intake manifold. In theory, the high passages of the manifold made it possible to leave an open area between the manifold and block to allow air to circulate underneath, thus cooling the intake and providing a denser charge for more power. Whether the air gap provided any real benefit is questionable, but it sure looked good.

To take advantage of the better breathing, a special high-lift cam was ground, and the exhaust manifolds were more free-flowing than stock. The bottom end of the engine had stronger rods with larger bolts, enlarged oil passages, and a high-output oil pump. With 12.5:1 compression, the engines were rated at 430 horsepower.

These were true supercars, capable of running with anything out there. On slicks, they were capable of 13s at speeds faster than 111 mph (178.5kph) through the manifolds in stock trim.

Unfortunately, GM's withdrawal from all forms of motor racing in March 1963 aborted the program after only a few cars were produced. There weren't sufficient numbers made to qualify the cars for Stock or Super Stock, so they ended up in Factory Experimental, where they became legends.

Roadgoing Impalas with 409s were also tough to beat. In fact, they were probably *the* cars to beat on the street back then. The top dog was the 425-horsepower 409 with dual quads and

11.0:1 compression; a single 4-barrel model rated at 400 horsepower was nearly as quick. For the first time, a hydraulic-lifter 409 was produced, making 340 horsepower with a single 4-barrel Carter AFB.

As was the case the year before, the SS was available with any engine so it was less special than the '61 models, although the heavy-duty suspension was still standard, as were bucket seats. Aluminum trim and SS emblems gave the car away at a glance. More than 153,000 SS Impalas—31 percent of total production—were made in '63.

The all-new styling for 1964 was a very boxy affair with an upright grille. The SS again proved quite popular, although luxury was stressed more than in the past. Regardless, 185,325 Super Sports rolled out of showrooms that year, which undoubtedly made Chevy executives smile. The engine lineup was carried over from '63.

The '65 Chevrolets, new from the ground up, were larger and more comfortable than before. The Impala received a semifastback roofline on the two-door, and it was a striking automobile. This proved to be a changeover year for Chevy in more ways than one. The "real fine" 409 exited midway through the model year, replaced by the new big-block engine. The top-banana dual quad 409 was history after '64; only the 340- and 400-horsepower W motors could be ordered. As *Car and Driver* put it, "The beast of drag strip hollow has been transformed into a svelte beauty."

Then the 409s were gone.

Lee Iacocca

Lido Anthony Iacocca has had two distinct careers in the auto industry, first as an executive at Ford (eventually assuming the title of president) and later as the savior of the Chrysler Corporation. But beyond anything else, he will always be known as the father of the Ford Mustang, the rolling symbol of the swinging '60s.

Iacocca graduated from Lehigh University in Pennsylvania in 1945 and received a master's degree in engineering from Princeton in 1946. He was hired as an engineer by Ford and quickly proved that he might be more cut out for a sales position. His first big hit was the 56-56 program, which made it possible to purchase a 1956 for 20 percent down and $56 a month for three years.

It was in the early 1960s when Iacocca headed up the so-called Fairlane Committee (dubbed so because they met at the Fairlane Hotel) that he really made his mark at Ford. Iacocca knew that there had been a gaping hole in the Ford automotive lineup ever since the Thunderbird had sprouted a backseat in 1958. His plan was to offer a four-seat sports automobile that looked like a two-seater and offered all the goodies that the young people of the day were looking for in a new car—bucket seats, a floor-mounted transmission, nimble handling, good fuel economy, and an affordable price. The car that the Fairlane Committee came up with was the Mustang, which quickly set the industry on its ear.

Iaccoca would later run Ford after Henry Ford II canned Bunkie Knudsen. Iacocca ran Ford until 1978, when a personality conflict with Henry the Deuce ended in his dismissal.

Opposite Top: For those looking to get into the muscle car hobby with a modest investment, the 1968–74 AMC Javelin is an excellent choice. While the AMX option and 390- and 401-V8 engines can raise the price significantly, their value generally is far lower than a big-block Camaro or Mustang. This one has non-stock, oversized wheels and tires, plus the optional factory cowl-induction hood.

Opposite Bottom: The cockpit of the 1974 Javelin and AMX was very futuristic with its toggle switches and stamped sheet metal dash.

Chevrolet's engineers, operating on the idea that sanctioning bodies were going to limit cubic inches to 400, released the fresh powerplant at 396 cubes. The Impala could be had with either 325 horsepower with a single 4-barrel and mild hydraulic-lifter camshaft or 425 horsepower at 6400 rpm and 415 lbs.-ft. at 4000 with a solid-lifter cam.

The other change was in buyers' purchasing habits. Thanks to the success of the GTO, intermediate-size muscle cars were becoming more fashionable. It didn't help that the full-size supercars were getting portlier every year, thus slower. The Super Sports, regardless of which engine you chose, were decidedly less sporty. Sales peaked for the SS in '65, at 243,114, but slowed down drastically over the next few years.

The year 1966 offered basically a carryover model, with the styling cleaned up a tad. For the first time since 1959, full-size Chevrolets came without round taillights. The major change was the introduction of the 427, a bored-out version of the 396. The top engine in the Impala was the solid-lifter 427 with 425 horsepower. Next in line was a 390-horse version, which had 10.25:1 compression and hydraulic lifters.

Vinyl Strato-bucket seats remained standard, but the console was redesigned with an optional four-gauge cluster fit between the top of the console and the bottom of the dash. It was a fine car, but performance buyers were making the midsize SS396 Chevelle the number one–selling fastest "Bowtie," while those inclined to buy a luxurious full-size car opted for the new Caprice.

Chevrolet switched to a two-year styling cycle, so the '67 Impalas were updated quite a bit externally. The fenders were arched, and while the overall length was the same, the car looked larger. There was a non-functional louvered air scoop on the hood of the SS, and the roofline on the hardtop was more of a true fastback. The SS emblems were more pronounced for '67 after two years of being quite subtle.

The hydraulic-lifter 427 was now rated at 385 horsepower, and red-stripe tires were part of the SS package. The instrument panel was a vast improvement over the 1965–1966 models; in fact, the '67 was the best of any SS (up to that point) with large dials located directly in front of the driver.

For '68, the Impala was freshened up and appeared a lot sleeker than the previous models. Ultrarare was the hidden-headlight option, which was more common to the upscale Caprice. Very few U.S.-sold Impalas got hidden headlights. Also, a formal hardtop was added in 1968 for the SS.

The swan song for the Impala SS during the original muscle car era was in 1969. Styling for all Impalas was more formal, a near clone of the Caprice. The fastback roof was replaced by a squared-off one that would be equally at home on a Cadillac or an Oldsmobile. The interior was equally conservative, though bucket seats and a console were still part of the SS package. Sales of the SS plummeted some 90 percent from the peak year of 1965, to 2,455 units (out of some 770,000 Impalas total). The 427 was still available; the hydraulic-lifter version was again rated at 390 horsepower. The 425-horse stormer came back for one last fling; 546 full-size 427 Chevys (including the SS) were produced.

Javelin

American Motors was in a bad place in the mid-1960s. Millions of ponycars and muscle cars were being sold by its competition and it had nothing to counter with—not until 1968, that is. That's when the Javelin, a stretched version of the soon-to-be-released AMX two-seater, hit the showrooms. Designed to compete with the Mustang, Camaro, Firebird, and Barracuda, the Javelin was an instant hit that almost single-handedly reversed the fortunes of AMC.

Based on the AMX show car, the Javelin had the typical long-hood/short-deck ponycar look. A semifastback roofline, ventless side glass, and flush door handles gave it a smooth, uncluttered look. One headlight per side flanked a large open grille, and noted designer Richard "Dick" Teague is the man most often credited for its appearance.

Three V8s were optional in the Javelin, two of which appealed to the muscle car set. The first was a 343 with a 4-barrel carb that produced 280 horsepower. It was nothing to write home about, but it was a big deal to AMC fanciers. The good engine appeared at the same time as the AMX—the 315-horse 390 (unrelated to the Ford engine of the same displacement). The 390 was basically a bored and stroked 343 with big-valve heads and forged steel internals. Magazine ads prompted readers to "Test Drag A Javelin"—heady stuff for a company that once boasted that the only race it was interested in was the human race.

For cash-strapped American Motors, it would have been unthinkable to introduce a totally new car; thus the Javelin shared its parts with others in the AMC lineup. It rode on a 109-inch (277cm) wheelbase and utilized kingpin-style front suspension—antiquated stuff even in the late '60s, but the engineers made it work quite well.

The gauges were recessed into an ABS plastic instrument panel, and the Javelin was the first ponycar to have reclining front bucket seats as standard equipment (SST model).

If you wanted your Javelin to go, you ordered—what else?—the Go Package, which consisted of the 4-barrel 343, dual exhausts, power disc brakes, E70×14-inch (35.5cm) tires, the handling package, and Rally stripes for a mere $266. Dealer-installed gear ratios as low as 4.44:1 could also be purchased.

Then there was the Javelin SST, which gave you wood rim steering wheel and door trim, full wheel covers and moldings for the side windows, and rocker panels.

One way AMC attempted to get the Javelin some credibility was to enter it in the SCCA's Trans-Am series. Although no one could touch the team of owner Roger Penske and driver Mark Donohue and its Sunoco-sponsored Chevrolet Camaro, which

Second only to the Mod top and interior Mopars of the late '60s for their garishness was the Javelin with the Pierre Cardin–designed interior. To call it distinctive is an understatement.

won ten of thirteen races that season, the red, white, and blue Javelins managed a half-dozen second-place finishes. Where the Javelin was a true winner for AMC was in the showrooms. It outsold the well-established Plymouth Barracuda by more than 9,000 units, hitting a sales total of 55,124 in its first season.

AMC recognized a good thing and improved the Javelin for 1969. The nose now sported a "twin venturi" grille, which was basically just a center divider, and hood scoops were introduced. The side stripes were revised on the SST, and cars delivered after January 9 got a reverse "C" stripe along the side.

Then there were the Big Bad colors. Big Bad Green, Big Bad Blue, and Big Bad Orange paint was slathered all over the cars, including the front and rear bumpers, making them impossible to miss in traffic. The colors were nearly florescent, perfect for the late '60s. The ultimate Javelin was a Big Bad SST with the Go Package, which gave you either the 343 or 390 V8, dual exhausts, power disc brakes, E70×14-inch (35.5cm) redline tires, 6-inch-(15cm) wide wheels, the handling package, and black fiberglass hood scoops. Other desirable options include the Hurst-shifted 4-speed, roof spoiler, and Twin-Grip differential.

The optional V8 engines were essentially carried over from the previous model, and sales declined accordingly. From a marketing perspective, this was not the time to stand pat, not with Chevy unleashing 427 Camaros and Ford selling 428 Cobra Jets and Boss 429 Mustangs.

Two very special Javelins debuted in 1970, the Trans Am and the Mark Donohue models. The Trans Am had all the SST equipment except sill moldings, plus it was outfitted with front and rear deck spoilers, black vinyl interior, and the

390 Go Package. These cars were painted red, white, and blue to recreate the cars raced in the SCCA series by the Ronnie Kaplan Trans-Am Racing Team. Horsepower on the 390 was now up to 325, and only one hundred are believed to have been built.

The Mark Donohue car was built both to commemorate that driver's signing with American Motors for the 1970 race season and to homologate the car's rear spoiler for the series. All Mark Donohues were built on the Javelin SST. A special thick-wall 360 block was used in most of the twenty-five hundred replicas (it replaced the 343 that year) and was rated at 290 horsepower. The 390 V8 was optional. The spoiler itself rose from the decklid; designed by Donohue himself, the spoiler bore his signature on the right side.

Getting the Penske/Donohue combo away from Chevrolet was a real coup. Not only did it give AMC the smartest owner and perhaps the greatest American-born race driver in history, it skewered the Camaro's efforts. In '69, Chevy won eight of the series' twelve races. With Donohue and Penske gone, Chevy won two, while AMC recorded its first three victories in the T/A's history.

Feeding the V8 engines of the streetgoing Javelins was a new functional hood scoop if you opted for the Go Package. It was the same scoop that was standard on the restyled AMX. Interestingly, in a down sales year for performance cars, the SST outsold the base Javelin by more than two to one (the Trans Am and Donohue models are included in the SST total).

For 1971, the Javelin got a radical restyling and a new running mate, the Javelin AMX. Like the Mustang that debuted that year, the Javelin AMX was lower, wider, and heavier. The body had hints of the original Javelin in it, but with high arching fenders and broad shoulders, it somewhat resembled a four-place Corvette. A twin canopy roof had an integrated ducktail spoiler that rose at the top of the backlight. Full-width taillights were standard.

If you ordered a regular Javelin, the grille opening was recessed, while the AMX option gave you a flush-mounted, wire-mesh grille. A fiberglass raised cowl hood and a front spoiler were optional (a rear decklid spoiler was standard on the AMX; the design credit for the cowl hood, grille, and spoilers went to Mark Donohue).

"We made the Javelin the hairiest-looking sporty car in America, even at the risk of scaring some people off," bragged AMC in a *Life* magazine ad. "We may scare off a few librarians, but we think we'll gain a few purists."

The interior was as space-age as the exterior. The cockpit was driver-oriented, with a dash that curved to face the driver. Only one body style was available, the two-door hardtop, and the car came in base trim, SST, and AMX.

Power was a mixed bag. The largest and most powerful engine to ever grace a street AMC was introduced, the 330-horse 401. On the down side, the rest of the lineup saw compression drop to 8.5:1. Then, later in the model year, compression of the 401 fell from 10.2:1 to 9.5:1, sucking away a bunch of horses. Still, the 401 was a strong performer. With the higher compression ratio, peak power came at 5000 rpm, while torque topped out at 430 at 3400 rpm. *Super Stock & Drag Illustrated* put one through its paces and reported a 14.3-second ET at 97 mph (156kph).

For '72, compression was chopped again, to 8.5:1 across the board, and more conservative net ratings replaced gross horsepower numbers. The 401 was down to 255 horsepower and the 360 was down to 220.

All base Javelins were now labeled SSTs, and the AMX returned as the top image machine. There was an option on the SST, however, that made people take notice, even in the swinging '70s. American Motors teamed up with French fashion designer Pierre Cardin; the resulting Pierre Cardin Javelin had the freakiest interior since the floral-print Mod Mopars of 1969.

On a black background, Cardin added multicolored, pleated stripes in Chinese red, plum, white, and silver for the interiors. The stripes ran across the seats and the door panels. Five exterior colors were offered—Snow White, Stardust Silver, Diamond Blue, Trans Am Red, and Wild Plum—and there was a "PC" logo on the front fenders. Amazingly, 4,152 units were sold—that's more than the number of AMX produced that year.

If you were an AMC performance buff, the Go Packages were still floating around with the 360 and 401 engines. Javelin sales topped twenty-six thousand in '72, a year in which AMC reported a $30.2 million profit on sales of $1.4 billion.

Javelin and AMX received styling tweaks for '73, which included two taillights per side and a revised grille. There was a Trans Am Victory Javelin, which commemorated the car's second consecutive Trans-Am series crown the prior year. There was a decal proclaiming these titles on the front fender, and the model wore slotted mag wheels.

In a bit of good news for AMC, both Javelin and Javelin AMX sales were up, the latter to 5,707. According to *Road & Track*, the AMX with the 401 was still good for 15.4 in the quarter mile at 91 mph (146.5kph).

The 401 with 255 horsepower lived on until 1974, the Javelin's swan song, as did the Go Packages.

Marauder/Monterey S-55

Introduced midyear in 1962, the Monterey S-55 was Mercury's answer to the Impala SS and Galaxie 500XL. The S-55 was a full-size car with plenty of room and lots of curb weight. Bucket seats were standard, as was a full-length console with shifter. Under the hood, a 300-horsepower 390 V8 provided adequate acceleration, but those looking for improved passing and acceleration could choose a 330-horse 390 or the mighty 406 FE, with either a 4-barrel carburetor or three 2-barrels. The former gave you 385 horsepower, the latter 405.

About one year later, Mercury brought another "performance" model to the market, dubbed the Marauder. Available in base or S-55 trim, the '63½ Marauder had a more aerodynamic fastback roof, replacing the Monterey's rather formal roof. The 390/300 was the base powerplant in the regular Marauder, while the 330-horse Super Marauder V8 was standard in the S-55, as were bucket seats.

The most important news for 1963 was the introduction of Ford's 427 V8 in the Marauder series. With either 410 or 425 horsepower available, it made for a very interesting Mercury. *Car Life* reported a 15.1 at 87 mph (140kph) in the quarter mile for a 425-horsepower variant. Not bad considering the Marauder has a curb weight of more than 2 tons (1.8t). The arrival of the 427 spelled the end of the line for the 406.

The Monterey/Marauder lineup received a surprisingly tasteful face-lift for 1964, but the engine lineup remained basically the same. The 427s returned, but Mercury was concentrating more on the Comet for its muscle car sales.

The muscle car powerplants continued from 1965 to 1968, but the Monterey lineup was enormous and the styling mimicked that of the Lincoln Continental. The Marauder name disappeared in '66, and the S-55 soldiered on as the performance model. The FE-based 428 appeared in '66, making 345 horsepower. A 4-speed transmission was optional but extremely rare.

For two years beginning in 1969, Mercury resuscitated the Marauder name. The Marauder shared its basic profile with the Galaxie 500XL fastback and used the Marquis' grille with hideaway headlamps. Side trim behind the doors was unique to the Marauder, as was the taillight treatment. The standard engine was the 390 V8 making 265 horsepower. If you went for the top-of-the-line Marauder X-100, a blacked-out paint scheme that covered the rear decklid area, including the cove of the fastback roofline, and Ford's new 429 engine with 360 horsepower were standard. Also part of the X-100 package were a leather and vinyl interior, rim-blow steering wheel, electric clock, fender skirts, and glass-belted tires. There were no manual transmissions available.

Monkeemobile

This Dean Jeffries–built custom was based on a '66 GTO and was produced specifically for use on the hit television show *The Monkees*, about a fictional rock-and-roll band patterned after the Beatles. There were actually two Monkeemobiles built by Jeffries. Both started life as base-engine, automatic convertibles.

Jeffries added a wildly exaggerated split bumper nose with a tall split windshield. A third row of seating was added where the rear deck had been, and a street-rod T-bucket-style roof was added. The stock hood was removed; the engine was wildly modified and included a very large supercharger. The fenders were enlarged to accept wider tires, the taillights were heavily customized, and a parachute was added.

Both cars have survived the ravages of time and television.

Monte Carlo

When the Chevrolet Monte Carlo was introduced, it was intended to be a poor man's Cadillac Eldorado. The car arrived at the very end of the muscle car era, as a 1970 model, but the fabled SS package was available—with the 454 engine as standard equipment, no less. As the Monte Carlo was directed more toward the luxury end of the market, there was almost no external trim to identify the SS package. Small SS badges were affixed to the front fenders aft of the wheelwells in a blacked-out panel, but that was it for the 1970 model.

The SS454 Monte Carlo required a special suspension with heavy-duty shocks all around, the rear of which were of the self-leveling air-assisted variety. Power front disc brakes and G70×15-inch (38cm) tires were standard (Rally wheels became an option later in the year).

Under the 6-foot-(2m) long hood (a record for a Chevrolet at the time) was a 360-horsepower 454 4-barrel V8. Dual exhausts with chrome tips were a subtle tip-off for all SS454 Montes. Though a 4-speed was available, nearly or possibly every Monte Carlo SS for 1970 was automatic-equipped. *Motor Trend* claimed a 0-to-60 mph (96.5kph) time of 7 seconds flat and a quarter-mile performance of 14.9 at 92 mph (148kph) for one such machine.

Sales were fantastic for the Monte Carlo in general, but not so good for the SS. In 1970 just 3,823 were produced out of 145,975 total Montes.

Left & Below: Subtle, yet elegant performance was the hallmark of the 1970 SS454 Monte Carlo. The car was more suited for luxury cruising, but the 360-horsepower "Rat" Motor shown here could be ordered.

Opposite: This is a Boss 351, a one-year-only offering that ran like a big-block thanks to its free-flowing heads and hot solid-lifter cam.

The popularity of the regular production car exploded to nearly 300,000 in '71, but SS sales dropped to less than 2,000 units. The 454 was back as the only engine, now rated at 365 gross horsepower with 8.5:1 compression. Super Sport nomenclature was now found on the decklid in a blackout panel between the taillamps, and the 15x7-inch (38x18cm) Rally wheels with trim rings became standard fare. Again, the SS454 could be had with the special-order 4-speed, but the vast majority were automatic-equipped.

With production so low, it didn't make sense to continue the SS option when the second-generation Monte Carlo was unveiled in 1972, especially considering that Chevrolet was marketing it as a luxury car. Eventually the SS tag returned on the Monte Carlo, but not until 1983.

Motion Performance

See *Baldwin Chevrolet/Motion Performance*.

Mustang

When Ford added a backseat to its Thunderbird for 1958, sales skyrocketed. The Thunderbird was wildly successful, but it left the Dearborn, Michigan–based company without a sporty car in a time when millions of baby boomers were rapidly approaching driving age.

Ford president Lee Iacocca is credited with the idea for a stylish small car that would have the look of a two-seater but would really be designed with seating for four. This new car would have all the special touches young people looked for like bucket seats, spirited engines, and a floor shifter—plus it would be affordable.

Iacocca reportedly instituted a contest to design this car, but the proposals from styling left him unmoved. Joe Oros, a longtime Ford designer, supposedly heard this and sketched out a design on a cocktail napkin. Iacocca knew as soon as he saw Oros' rendering that it was what he was looking for.

The Mustang was introduced with great fanfare on April 17, 1964, as a 1965 model, and it was an instant smash. Available as a two-door coupe or convertible, it was reasonably priced but had one of the longest option sheets in the industry. This let customers spec out their Mustang just the way they wanted it and within their budgets.

The top engine that year was the solid-lifter, high-performance 289 with 271 horsepower. It was a decent performer, but slightly behind in the muscle car class. *Motor Trend*, *Road & Track*, and *Sports Car Graphic* all tried their hands with 4-speed versions, but none could do better than 15.7 at 89 mph (143kph).

This mattered very little as the 1965–1966 Mustangs were successful beyond anyone's expectations. They seemed to be the perfect compromise between the practical and the sporty—in short, the Mustang was the right car at the right time.

Excluding Shelby American–built GT350s (see *Shelby GT350 and GT500*), it wasn't until

Right: First-generation Mustangs were initially offered as coupes (shown) and convertibles. A sleek fastback was introduced later during the 1965 model year.

Below: It had controversial styling and it was bigger than before, but the 1971 Mustang was still one of the premier performance cars out there.

the second-generation Mustang arrived in 1967 that you could order more than 300 horsepower. Knowing that GM was going to put the big-block 396 into the '67 Camaro prompted Ford to make the '67 Mustang's engine bay commodious enough to house the 390 big-block. From the beginning of that model year, you could order a 335-horsepower FE in the Mustang GT (or GTA with the automatic transmission).

To accommodate the larger engine, Ford widened the Mustang by 2.7 inches (69mm) and increased the width of the track by 2 inches (50mm). For improved handling, the front roll center was raised by lowering the upper A-arm pivot. This reduced body roll and understeer. There was even a competition handling package that consisted of Koni shocks, stiffer springs, and a thicker sway bar up front.

Motor Trend found wheel hop to be a problem with its 4-speed-equipped 390 test car, but the quarter-mile times were still better than the 271-horse 289 of the previous years (despite more curb weight in the big-block car). *Motor Trend* reported 15.6 ET at 94 mph (151.5kph), while *Car Life* went 15.5 at 91 mph (146.5kph). *Hot Rod* claimed 15.31 at 93.45 mph (150.5kph). While the elapsed times weren't demonstrably improved over the hi-po 289s, more telling were the trap speeds, which are the true indicators of horsepower.

But statistics hardly tell the story of the '67 Mustang; the entire car was larger, heavier, and, in 2+2 trim, more aggressive-looking. There was plenty of competition from Chevrolet, Pontiac, and even sister division Mercury thanks to the Cougar, which naturally ate into sales, but the Mustang was still a runaway success and the class leader in volume.

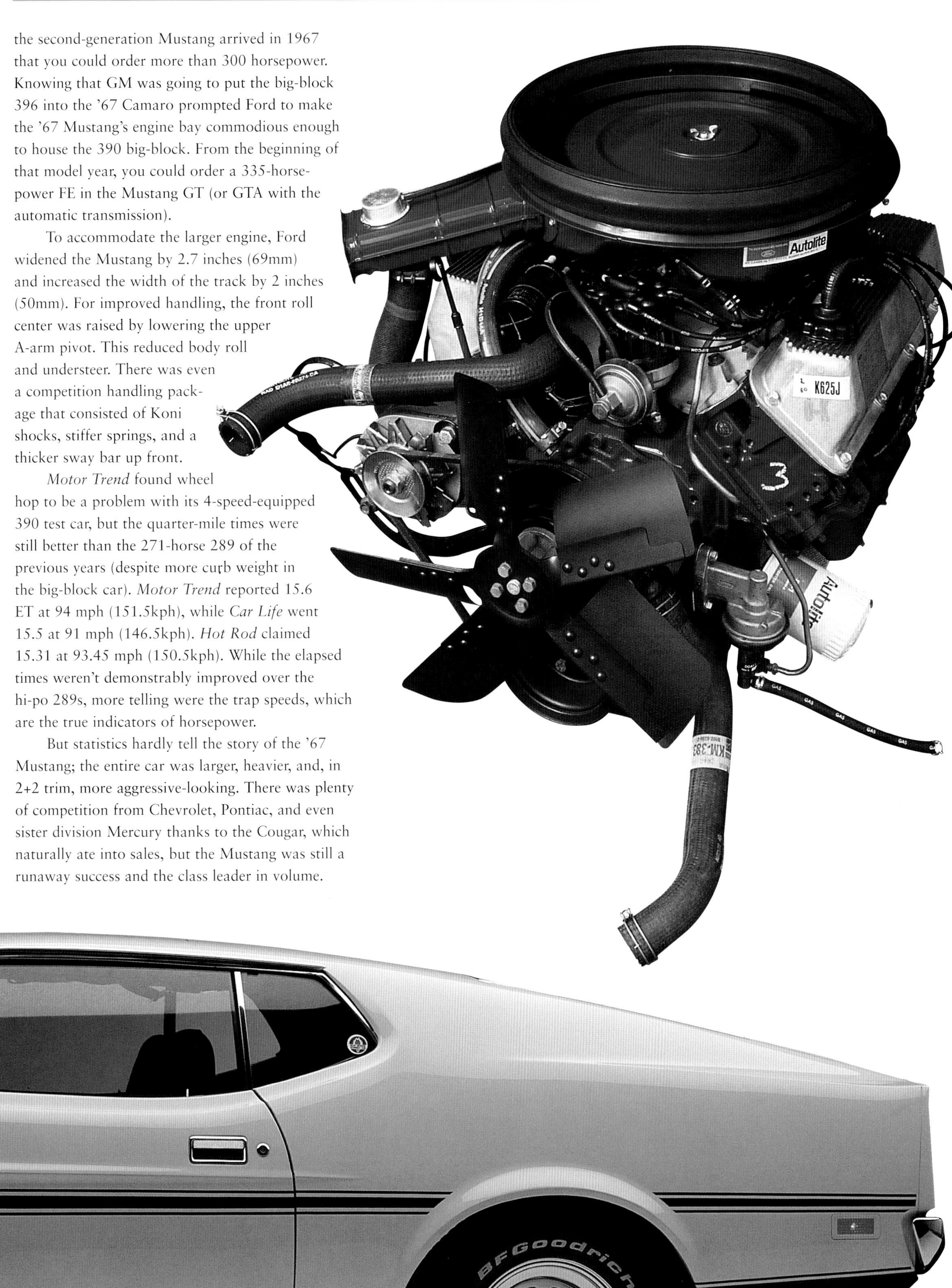

"Dyno" Don Nicholson won in his class at the Winternationals in the debut outing of the 428 Cobra Jet Mustang.

In 1968, the stakes in the horsepower game were being continually elevated. The 390 was never intended to be a high-performance engine. Its placement in the Mustang was a stopgap measure. By midyear 1968, Ford was ready with an engine that made no apologies to anyone. The 428 Cobra Jet was the perfect marriage of torque and horsepower to a lightweight ponycar. The result was not only a car that won in its class at the '68 NHRA Winternationals, but one that was called "the fastest running pure stock in the history of man" by no less of an influential publication than *Hot Rod*.

To get a favorable rating from both the insurance industry and the drag racing sanctioning bodies, the 428 Cobra Jet was rated at just 335 horsepower (5 less than the standard passenger-car 428) at 5600 rpm and 445 lbs.-ft. of torque at 3400.

"The CJ will be the utter delight of every Ford lover and the bane of all the rest because, quite frankly, it is probably the fastest regular production sedan ever built," said Eric Dahlquist in his road test for *Hot Rod*'s March 1968 issue.

Unlike some exotic big-block muscle cars, which suffered from limited availability, the 428 Cobra Jet could be had in any of the Mustang's three body styles, with either a Toploader 4-speed or a special C-6, modified to shift at a higher rpm and harder than stock.

The high-performance 289 engine was discontinued after the 1967 model year, and one would be foolish to say it wasn't missed. For 1968, the top small-block was the 302 4-barrel with a mere 230 horsepower. Ford felt the 271-horsepower 289 was superfluous thanks to the 390 and 428 engines, which were less expensive to build and sell—not to mention more powerful while requiring less maintenance.

For '69, Ford pulled out all the stops. Four new models were introduced: the luxury-oriented

Grande, the Mach 1, the Boss 302, and the Boss 429. The Mustang was successfully restyled and offered enough engines and variations of different engines to confuse anyone. It was great news for the performance buff who could figure it all out. There were two almost unrelated 302s, a new 351 available with either a 2-barrel or 4-barrel carb, the 390, the 428 Cobra Jet and Super Cobra Jet, and the wildest of them all, the Boss 429. The Mustang GT was still available, but there was a new model, the Mach 1, which was so exciting and popular that it caused the GT to be discontinued.

Many consider the '69 fastback to be the best-looking Mustang ever. For the first time, the front end housed four headlights, the low beams at the outer extremities, and the high beams in the grille (they almost looked more like driving lights than headlights). The nose came to a more pronounced point in the center, and the Mach 1 featured a blackout treatment on the hood with a standard nonfunctional scoop. The rear fenders kicked up aft of the rear doors, with fake air scoops trailing the doors, while a small ducktail spoiler kicked up at the rear. In addition to the flat-black hood, the Mach 1 added reflective tape stripes on the sides, styled 14-inch (35.5cm) wheels, dual racing mirrors, and a flip-open gas cap. The Competition suspension and 351 W 2-barrel engine were included, too.

Ford didn't forget about the interior, either. High-back bucket seats with built-in headrests and red inserts were standard, as was the Deluxe Interior Group, which offered woodgrain appliqués on the dash, console, and door panels plus a clock in front of the passenger seat. Matching red inserts were sewn into the carpeting as well.

The Mach 1 was a genuine sensation, accounting for nearly 25 percent of all Mustang sales in 1969—72,458 found owners.

New for 1969 on the restyled Mustang was the Mach 1 package. A 351 2-barrel was standard, but a 351 4-barrel, a 390 4-barrel, and two versions of the 428 CJ could be had.

BOSS
429

Perhaps the ultimate Mustang was the Boss 429. Its semi-hemi engine (inset) was installed in the ponycar solely to homologate it for NASCAR Grand National racing. It had a functional cold-air hood from the factory. The 15-inch (38cm) Magnum 500 wheels were used only on the Boss 302 and Boss 429 in 1969.

Starting in 1969, if you ordered 3.91 or 4.30 gears in your 428 Mustang, you automatically got what was called the Super Cobra Jet package. Among the race-proven hardware were the LeMans-style 427 connecting rods with cap screws that screw directly into the rod (as opposed to a nut-and-bolt setup). You also got an engine oil cooler with the SCJ option.

The enthusiastic press could not find enough superlatives to adequately describe the '69 Mach 1. *Car Life* asked, "Are you ready for the first great Mustang?" Said *Motor Trend*, "You will want [the 428 CJ] not so much because it turns the Mach 1 into one of the fastest cars in the world, but that the Ford suspension men have done such a lovely job of distributing the great weight of the engine... They created a machine that handles like a Trans-Am sedan."

But the Mach 1 was just the beginning. Two other special models were introduced, both inspired by the racetrack. The Boss 302 was a high-winding screamer needed to legalize the Cleveland-headed mill for the SCCA's Trans-Am series, while the Boss 429 filled the requirements necessary to get the newest big-block into NASCAR competition.

Ford had won the Trans-Am title in '66 and '67 only to see the Chevy Camaro of Mark Donohue and Roger Penske dominate in 1968. The engine being used in the Mustang, the Tunnel Port 302, just wasn't getting the job done, and Ford engineer Bill Barr got the idea to put the canted-valve cylinder heads slated to appear on a 1970 351 4-barrel engine on the 302. This required some work, but the result was an engine perfectly suited for the racetrack—if not a bit of overkill on the street.

The 1969 Boss 302 had the largest intake valves ever used on a production small-block Ford engine, and that pretty much killed any semblance of bottom-end torque on the street. But it had unlimited potential for racers. For the street, the motor was wrapped in a special car with a unique suspension and an appearance package penned by noted designer Larry Shinoda. For the Boss 302, Shinoda filled in the faux scoops in the tops of the rear fenders, added a reverse C-scoop, and blacked out the outside headlight buckets, most of the deck-lid, and the area around the taillights. He added a chin spoiler, an adjustable rear wing, and louvers for the rear window. Chrome 5-spoke 15-inch (38cm) wheels wrapped in F60 Polyglas rubber rounded out the exterior.

The engine was beefed up for racing with 4-bolt main bearing caps, forged steel connecting rods, and a stronger forged steel crank. A 10.5:1 compression ratio made premium fuel mandatory. A 300-degree-duration mechanical cam opened the

Louvers on the side on the '67–68 Mustang 2+2 were functional only in 1967. A sliding lever controlled the airflow.

monstrous 2.23-inch (57mm) intake and 1.71-inch (43.5mm) exhaust valves (the ports were insanely large as well for a 302-cubic-inch engine). A 780-cfm Holley 4-barrel atop an aluminum high-rise intake fed the fuel, which once burned was carried away by 2.5-inch (64mm) exhaust pipes. The Boss 302 was good for high-14-second quarter-mile times, but its real forte was its handling.

The Boss 429 was based on the new 385-series block but featured a semi-hemi valvetrain layout with big valves. The heads were dry-deck fit to the block (no head gaskets) and a 6-quart (5.5L) oil pan was used. The heads themselves had 2.3-inch (60mm) intake valves and 1.91-inch (50mm) exhausts, but Ford used a very conservative camshaft, and the carburetor, rated at 735 cfm, was tinier than the one in the Boss 302.

The mild stock cam and carburetor conspired to keep the Boss 429 from achieving its full potential in factory trim. In some road tests of the era, the Cobra Jet cars were as quick or quicker, but the potential for the Boss 429 was nearly limitless. *High Performance Cars* tripped the clocks in the quarter mile at 13.60 seconds going 106 mph (170.5kph) with the factory Polyglas tires and 13.34 at 107.5 mph (173kph) on 7-inch (18cm) M&H slicks. *Car Life* went 14.09 at 102.85 mph (165.5kph). To show the car's potential, *Car Craft* outfitted one with headers, slicks, and an aftermarket cam. The result was 12.32 at 113-plus mph (182kph).

Ford needed to homologate the engine for NASCAR, and even though it would have been a better fit for the Torino, the Mustang was the Dearborn image machine. To fit the massive Boss 429 in the Mustang, Ford had to revamp the front suspension. The entire front suspension was moved outward 1 inch (25mm) so that the A-arm pivot and spring tower would clear the huge aluminum valve covers. Ford also lowered the upper inside attachment point 1 inch (25mm), which gave the car improved camber (for better handling). Big-block Mach 1 springs and shocks were employed, and a rear sway bar was part of the package. The battery was even relocated to the trunk. The 429 Mustangs were assembled by Kar Kraft at its facility in Brighton, Michigan, and all this race-style hardware came at a price—fully optioned, the Boss 429 came in at just less than $4,900, a substantial sum of money in 1969.

Despite all the competition from Chevrolet, Pontiac, American Motors, and Plymouth, the Mustang remained the top-selling ponycar in 1969, with nearly 300,000 units sold. From the base

6-cylinder to the Grande and the Boss 429, there was a Mustang to suit any taste. Ford kept up this frenetic pace in 1970 and even added an engine, the 351-Cleveland. In total, there were nine engines available in ten different models.

As for the Boss 302, it now used smaller (2.19-inch [5.5cm]) intake valves. This gave it improved velocity and torque (although it was rated the same). This was the Boss 302's year, as it fulfilled its]promise by winning the SCCA Trans-Am championship.

As was the norm in a two-year production cycle, the styling was cleaned up for '70. Designer Larry Shinoda reduced the number of headlights by two; gone were the outboard headlamps while those in the grille cavity stayed, and simulated scoops replaced the outboard lights.

The faux air scoops on the rear fenders were filled in as well, and the taillights were now recessed into the rear panel. The Boss 302's rear window slats and decklid spoiler were now optional on all SportsRoof models. Those ordering the Competition suspension now got a rear sway bar, regardless of model.

Returning for an encore was the Boss 429, though it was still produced in very limited quantities. The Mach 1 now had a three-way stripe treatment on the hood. There was a fat stripe that ran down the center of the hood, flanked by two thinner stripes with callouts for engine displacement.

The Mustang was completely revamped for 1971. It was longer and heavier, and the styling was somewhat controversial. The 2+2 resembled one of Ford's LeMans race cars, with a huge, flat, fastback roof. It was nearly impossible to see out of, but the car was one of the most dramatic-looking on the road. The nose resembled that of the 1969–1970 Shelby Mustangs with an oval grille with a single headlight per side.

Inside, there was an improved driving position, thanks in part to a smaller-diameter steering wheel, though the basic dual-cockpit theme was carried over. The tach and speedometer were directly in front of the driver, and ancillary gauges were relocated to the center pod.

While General Motors reduced compression ratios in preparation for the changeover coming to unleaded fuels, Ford hung in there one more year. As was normal, Ford shook up the engine lineup pretty well. Gone were the 428 Cobra Jets, the Boss 302, and the mighty Boss 429. There was still plenty of horsepower for sale, however. The 429 Cobra Jet and Super Cobra Jet (rated at 370 and 375 horsepower, respectively), introduced the year prior in the Torino and Mercury Cyclone, were now available in the Mustang as the highest-output mills.

Replacing the Boss 302 was perhaps the ultimate Mustang, the Boss 351. Based on the 351-C, the Boss 351 was designed to meet the challenge thrown down by Chevy's new-for-'70 350/360 horsepower Z/28. Although Ford pulled the plug on its entire worldwide racing program after 1970, the Boss showed what it could have been capable of on the track. The free-revving small-block produced 330 horsepower at 5400 rpm and 370 lbs.-ft. of torque at 4000. Compression was a righteous 11.0:1.

Despite the Mustang's larger size and increased wheelbase (from 108 to 109 inches [274.5 to 277cm]), it wasn't as heavy as it looked. The Boss

This 1967 Mustang has the lower back panel grille, a $19.48 option.

351 was capable of running right with the larger-displacement 429s, a remarkable achievement. In magazine tests, 13.8s and 13.9s at more than 101 mph (162.5kph) were not uncommon for the Boss 351. *Super Stock & Drag Illustrated* went 13.97 at 100.22 mph (161.5kph) in a Super Cobra Jet Mach 1 with ram air. This is an indication of just how fortified the Boss 351 was—and it handled incredibly well, to boot.

By '72, the majority of Ford's good engines were put out to pasture. The Boss 351 didn't survive, replaced by the 351 HO, basically a low-compression version of the same mill. Rated at 275 net horsepower, it came standard with a 4-speed, 3.91 gears, dual exhausts, and the Competition suspension. Less than five hundred were built. There was also the 351 Cobra Jet, a pretty decent performer in its own right, which made 266 horsepower. Both the HO and the CJ were based on the 351-Cleveland. Both 429 Cobra

Jets bit the dust, falling victim to the devils known as the insurance lobby, the environmentalists, and declining interest.

In '73, Ford changed the Mustang very little. The parking lights were now vertical instead of horizontal, and the 351 Cobra Jet sang its swan song. It still had 266 horsepower and 301 lbs.-ft. of torque. Gone was the HO, another one-year-only option Ford was famous for. Even though sales increased, the Mustang took a sabbatical of sorts. The following year, Ford replaced it with the Mustang II, a Pinto-based sporty compact that was, in theory, a return to the car's roots. Sadly, muscle car enthusiasts got the short end of it with the Mustang II—a 4-cylinder engine was standard, a V6 was optional, and there was no V8 available when it was introduced.

Myrtle Motors

Based in Maspeth, New York, Myrtle Motors was a high-performance Pontiac car dealership, sort of the Royal Pontiac of the East Coast. Like Royal (and Baldwin Chevrolet, among others), Myrtle offered engine swaps into brand-new cars—428s into Firebirds and the like—as well as speed parts and tuning services.

Opposite Top: Many Mach 1 owners added parts from other Mustang models to personalize their cars. This one has the factory Boss 302 and 429 chin spoiler, which was not available on the Mach 1.

Opposite Bottom: Part of the Mach 1 package was a special interior with red inserts sewn into the carpeting and red piping in the high-back bucket seats. The Deluxe Interior Group was standard on this model.

Below: The last year for the Boss 429 Mustang was 1970.

Nickey Chevrolet

This was a Chicago-based high-performance Chevrolet car dealership noted for its 427-engine swaps in Camaros and Chevelles, not to mention its high-performance parts line.

Located at 4501 Irving Park Road, Nickey Chevrolet worked with Bill Thomas Race Cars in Anaheim, California, to develop and produce some of the most exciting cars of the muscle car era. Like its counterparts from Baldwin Chevrolet and Yenko Chevrolet, the Nickey cars (the *k* in *Nickey* was backward on the emblem) were overpowered beasts that could run in the 11-second zone as delivered. "As delivered" meant something different from stock because you could order them with traction bars, tube headers, oversize wheels and tires, and a variety of other hot rod goodies. You could get anything from a stock 425-horse 427 to 12.5:1 compression, radical cams, and dual quad intakes.

Nickey had a long reputation as a high-performance car dealer before it built its first 427 Camaro. It kept a massive inventory of factory racing hardware and for years sponsored numerous drag cars and road racers.

There is some confusion surrounding who did the development work on the Nickey Camaros. A February '67 article in *Car Craft* credits drag racer Dick Harrell, who worked at the dealership at the time, as having done the initial swap of the 427 into an SS350 Camaro. *Car and Driver*, in its September '67 issue, credits Bill Thomas Race Cars with doing the actual development work on the cars. It appears that Thomas came into the picture later, after Nickey started producing 427 Camaros. When it came time to sell the production cars, it was definitely Thomas who did the engine swaps and built the modified engines on the West Coast. Nickey and Thomas claimed to have one hundred dealers nationwide for their outrageous products.

In the *Car Craft* test, the 427 Camaro was pretty close to "stock," meaning it had one 4-barrel carb, a recurved distributor, different breaker points, and Nickey traction bars. With 4.56 gears and slicks, the car ran 11.9 seconds at 114 mph (183.5kph) in the quarter mile. A switch to the optional dual quad intake with a pair of Carter AFB carbs resulted in an 11.4 at 126 mph (202.5kph). Both *Car Craft* and *Car and Driver* marveled at how flat their respective 427 Camaros handled in spite of the extra weight on the nose.

Like most of its contemporaries, Nickey sold LT-1 and 427 Novas, 427 Chevelles, and the like throughout the duration of the muscle car era. As late as 1973 you could still get an LT-1 Nova for $4,035 or a 450-horse 454 in the same car for just $80 more. Traction bars, Hooker headers, a Stewart-Warner gauge cluster, and a Sun Super tach cost an additional $300.

Soon thereafter, the Environmental Protection Agency started going after dealerships that modified new cars, superstores like Nickey and Baldwin Chevrolet in New York. The fun was over.

Oldsmobile 4-4-2

It is interesting to note that the company credited with starting the postwar horsepower race was also known for having produced perhaps the best-handling supercars. When Oldsmobile introduced the 4-4-2 in 1964 to counter the GTO, the Olds was known more for its road-holding characteristics than its acceleration.

The 4-4-2 (for 4-barrel carb, 4-speed, and dual exhaust) was based on the F-85 and the Cutlass, and was the industry's first response to the successful launch of the GTO. To buy this car, one ordered

If you wanted the ultimate 4-4-2 in 1970, you got the W-30 455, which included a functional fiberglass hood, red plastic inner fender liners, and numerous other changes.

RPO BO9, the Police Apprehender package, which offered high-compression pistons, a high lift, long-duration cam, and a twin snorkel air cleaner bolted to the 330 Oldsmobile V8. Compression was 10.25:1, and the engine produced 310 horsepower at 5200 rpm and 355 lbs.-ft. of torque at 3600.

As for the suspension, you got a capable heavy-duty package, which included stiffer springs as well as front and rear stabilizer bars, which were fairly uncommon in '64. Most companies avoided using a rear bar because it took away understeer. A neutral-handling car is fine for enthusiasts, but manufacturers like to build in understeer for safety. Olds bucked this trend and the result was the best-handling early muscle car. The police brake setup was also standard.

Because the 4-4-2 was just an option based on the F-85 series intermediate, it was possible to purchase a four-door version. Ten of these cars were built in 1964. In fact, an ad in *Motor Trend* and *Hot Rod* showed a four-door 4-4-2 with two cops in the car. "Police needed it...Olds built it...Pursuit proved it! Put this one on your wanted list!" read the ad copy. Only the F-85 wagon was banned for the 4-4-2 package.

According to the ad, redline tires, a floor-mounted shifter, and heavy-duty chassis components were all part of the deal. The 4-4-2 hit showrooms approximately seven months after the GTO, so the '64 models are fairly uncommon today.

Both *Motor Trend* and *Car Life* tested 4-4-2 two-door hardtops; the former reported a 0-to-60 mph (96.5kph) time of 7.5 seconds and a quarter-mile time of 15.5 at 90 mph (145kph), while the latter printed 7.4 for 0 to 60 and 15.6 at 89 mph (143kph) in the quarter mile. This was respectable performance and the 4-4-2 was a good value, though it lacked the pizzazz and performance of the GTO.

Big changes were in store for '65. The Oldsmobile V8 block was new, the deck height was raised, and the bore and stroke were increased. Displacement was now up to 400 cubic inches and horsepower and torque had improved significantly, to 345 ponies at 4800 and 440 lbs.-ft. at 3200. Compression remained at 10.25:1, and a single 4-barrel carb was your only choice for induction. Thanks to the new engine, Olds said 4-4-2 now meant 400 cubic inches, 4-barrel carb, and dual exhausts. This dropped the quarter-mile times down to about 15.1 seconds.

With the introduction of the 400-cubic-inch engine in 1965, 4-4-2 now stood for 400 cubic inches, 4-barrel carb, and dual exhausts.

The most important changes came to the 4-4-2 in 1966. The F-85 series, upon which the muscle car was built, received a major face-lift and was a vast improvement over those of the previous two years. The grille featured a pair of headlights per side set into the design (a theme that continued for a long time). The taillights were set in a vertical pattern, and the roof on the two-door was concave. The slab-sided look of the previous two models was replaced by a much more sculpted design. It looked more massive than before, although overall length remained the same.

The 4-4-2 package was available on any F-85 Olds in 1964 except the station wagon. That meant you could get a good engine, the 330 Olds V8 (inset), and suspension on a four-door—it was the original sports sedan.

Compression was up a quarter of a point on the base engine, and horsepower increased to 350. But there were more exciting things happening in Lansing than this. First, Oldsmobile released a three 2-barrel induction option for the 4-4-2, which delivered an extra 10 horsepower at 5000 rpm. A total of 2,129 L69 4-4-2s were built for '66, but that model was still not the top of the performance ladder. If you wanted the most aggressive 4-4-2, you ordered the W-30.

During a two-week period in June 1966, Oldsmobile built 54 W-30 Force-Air Induction 6-barrel cars. This was done to legalize the cars for NHRA competition, whose rules required that at least fifty cars be produced. The cars went down a standard assembly line and each ram air cleaner was stamped with a number, though the numbers were not necessarily put on the cars in the order they were built.

The three deuces were fed fresh air by 5-inch (12.5cm) flexible fabric hoses that were reinforced with wire and ran from the chrome air cleaner to 7.75x3.5-inch (19.5x9cm) ducts located in the front bumper at the parking light location. This required changes to the bumper and meant relocating the parking lamps. A radical 308-degree, 0.474-inch (12mm) hydraulic-lifter cam offered a flatter power curve and 1.6:1 rocker arms, and improved valve springs were part of the package. Valve size was 2.06 inches (50mm) for the intake and 1.629 inches (40mm) for the exhaust. A different oil pump spring increased pressure. Higher-capacity axles were used in the rear and all fifty-four vehicles came with 4.11 gears. The final change for racing consisted of relocating the battery to the trunk for better weight distribution. Remarkably, the price for the W-30 option was a mere $279.

Almost half of the W-30 cars, twenty-five, were F-85 coupes; eight were Cutlass F-85 Sport Coupes, sixteen were Cutlass Holiday hardtops, and five were Cutlass Sport Coupes. Many of the cars were painted outlandish or mismatched colors so that they would stand out at the racetrack. If the colors didn't make you notice the cars, the performance should have. *Car Craft* tested one in its August '66 issue and delivered 13.8 at 105.2 mph (169.5kph).

In '67, GM banned multiple carburetion in its passenger cars (the Corvette, considered a sports car, adopted three 2-barrel carb induction that year as an option on its 427 models), meaning the best you could get in the 4-4-2 was a single 4-barrel. The base engine was again rated at 350 horsepower, and the W-30 option returned with the wild cam and Force-Air Induction, but without the trio of 2-barrels. *Hot Rod* tested two W-30s and ran 13.9 with a 4-speed and 14.5 with the optional automatic.

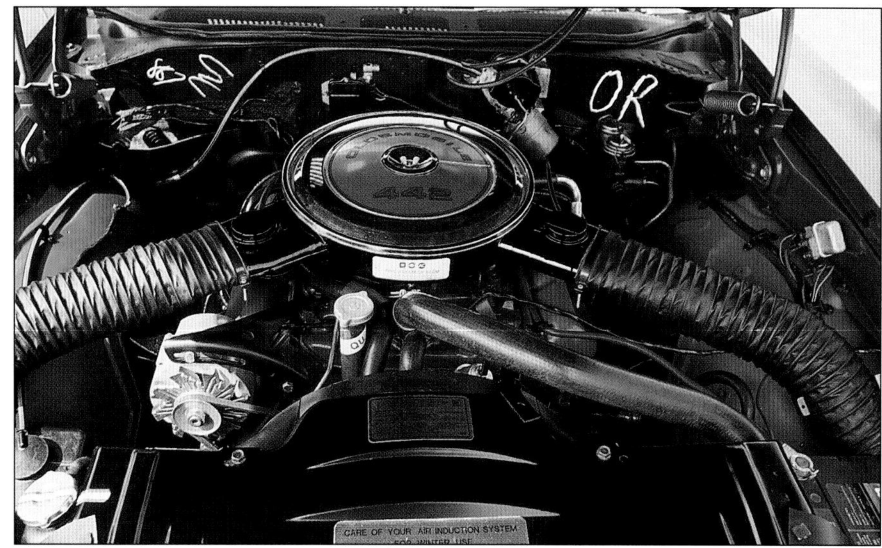

Above: With the Force-Air Induction package in 1968, your 400-powered 4-4-2 got cold air ducted to the carb via a pair of scoops mounted under the bumper.

Right: The ultimate factory drag cars from Oldsmobile were the 1966 W-30 machines (shown). The only engine available was the L69 tri-power 400, which got Force-Air Induction. A trunk-mounted battery, 4.11:1 gears, and heavy-duty axles were also included.

and F70x14-inch (35.5cm) tires. The Force-Air option was still around, with 13x2-inch (33x5cm) scoops under the bumper ducting air to the carburetor.

Under the hood, the 400-cubic-inch Rocket V8 was back, but the bore and stroke were altered. The bore decreased to 3.87 inches (10cm) while the stroke increased to 4.25 inches (11cm). The standard 4-4-2 mill was rated at 350 horsepower (325 if you ordered the automatic transmission, which necessitated a milder camshaft), while the W-30 made 360 at 5400 rpm and 440 lbs.-ft. of torque at 3600. Compression was 10.5:1 for both engines. The W-30 was still quite a runner. *Popular Hot Rodding* claimed a 14-flat ET at 99 mph (159.5kph), despite being hampered by an automatic transmission. The W-30 package was composed of plastic

Oldsmobile's tagline in 4-4-2 advertising was "Sedate It Ain't." The 4-4-2 option still retailed for less than $200, and functional hood louvers were standard. The grille was updated a bit, hinting at what was to come in '68 models. The quad headlights remained, but the parking lights were moved from the bumper and placed between the high and low beams. Also, the hood extended down slightly into the grille cavity between the high beams.

When the '68 Olds 4-4-2 arrived, it did so in grand style. The Big Three revised all their intermediates for '68, and few could match the style of the Oldsmobile. It had curves in all the right places, just the right amount of chrome, and a brawny stance that spoke volumes about the muscle under the hood.

The 4-4-2 became its own series that year rather than an option on the F-85. It included all the standard Cutlass features plus heavy-duty springs and shocks, front and rear stabilizer bars, special wheels, inner fenders, a blueprinted engine, a heavy-duty rear end, an upgraded cooling system, cold-air induction, and the high-performance cam.

The '69 Olds 4-4-2 had its nose reworked, the parking lights moved back to the bumper, and the headlights brought back together. The horizontal taillight motif of '68 was replaced with vertical-style units that curved up into the fenders. Things were basically unchanged under the hood, but base-motor cars were rated at 350 horsepower for the manual transmission and 325 for the automatic. The stout W-30 soldiered on as well, still with under-the-bumper cold air. Sales of the 4-4-2 slipped to less than twenty-seven thousand in spite of a colorful new advertising campaign featuring "Dr. Oldsmobile," kind of a cross between a mad scientist and a hippie.

In 1970, when GM lifted its ban on engines larger than 400 cubic inches in its intermediates, Oldsmobile jumped right in with a big stick. Unlike

You don't see many Oldsmobiles without a radio, but this '66 W-30 car's purpose was to win drag races, not tickle the eardrum. Note the bench seat and the 4-speed. The factory tach was mounted on the far left of the dash panel.

Pontiac and Chevrolet, which still offered a 400 and 396 (cum 402), respectively, the base engine in the 4-4-2 became the 455. The stroke remained at 3.87 inches (10cm), but the bore grew to 4.12 inches (10.5cm). With 10.5:1 compression and a single 4-barrel carb, the 455 made 365 horsepower at 5000 rpm and a whiplash-inducing 500 lbs.-ft. of torque at just 3200 rpm.

If you went for the W-30 cold-air package, you got an extra 5 rated horsepower, red fiberglass inner fender liners, an aluminum intake manifold, a low-restriction air cleaner, and a hot long-duration camshaft. A fiberglass hood with two functional scoops replaced the more traditional Olds under- or through-the-bumper air induction setup. The hood also featured built-in hood tie-downs. The W-30 was an impeccable performer, combining Oldsmobile luxury with supercar acceleration. It could reach ETs in the 13s at more than 100 mph (161kph), even with an automatic transmission.

Of course, 1970 was the beginning of the end for the 4-4-2 as well. The drop in compression from 10.5:1 to 8.5:1, plus increasingly detuned carburetors and ignitions, meant horsepower fell to 340 and torque to 460 on the base 455. W-30s were rated 10 horsepower higher.

For '72, GM switched to net horsepower ratings, which were substantially lower on paper than the older gross ratings. The 4-4-2 became an option package once again, and it wasn't tied to a particular engine. It was listed as a handling and appearance package. The 350 2-barrel Oldsmobile engine with 180 horsepower was the standard powerplant, and two 455s were optional—270 horse and 370 lbs.-ft. of torque for the first, 300 horsepower and 410 lbs.-ft. for the W-30. The latter was the last great Oldsmobile, and though the name soldiered on for years, it was never the torque or horsepower monster it was in its prime.

Oldsmobile Rallye 350

This was a car that was conceived by but never credited to Hurst. Starting with an F-85 Sports Coupe, a Cutlass Sports Coupe, or a Cutlass S Holiday, it was a clever combination of attention-grabbing styling and small-block muscle and was reminiscent of the GTO Judge in its execution. All Rallye 350 cars were painted bright Sebring Yellow with body-colored urethane-covered bumpers (a first for Oldsmobile); accent stripes on the sides, hood, and rear; and yellow wheels that made it hard to miss. The grille was blacked out, and there were dual outside mirrors painted the body color. A decklid spoiler was optional.

The 325-horsepower 350-cubic-inch W-31 engine (with a functional fiberglass ram air hood) was the only powerplant available. The ram air hood, called W-25, was optional on any 4-4-2 in 1970–1972 and was standard equipment on the W-30, W-31, and the Rallye. The FE-2 handling suspension with front and rear sway bars and G70x14-inch (35.5cm) bias belted tires was standard, as were a 3.23 rear gear and a rear bumper notched for trumpet-style dual exhaust tips. Like the Judge, the wheels came sans trim rings.

A custom 4-spoke sport steering wheel with "leather-like, non slip (sic) grip" gave the driver something to hold on to. "Dr. Oldsmobile scores again with a new action look," boasted the ads, referring to the psychedelic spokesman the division used back then. The car was "the boldest scene stealer that ever toured Main Street."

Vince Piggins

When Chevrolet wanted to participate in stock car racing in the 1950s, one of its best moves was to hire Vince Piggins in the fall of 1956. Piggins was an engineer who worked for Hudson before moving to Chevrolet, where he reorganized its stock car racing program.

Piggins had been recommended for the job by Henry "Smokey" Yunick, recognized then as the premier race car builder in the South. Yunick knew Piggins from his days at Hudson, since Yunick had built many of the dominating Hornets in NASCAR's early years. At Hudson, Piggins was put in charge of its new Severe-Usage Parts Program, where tough new "stock" parts were developed. They developed the first reinforced wheels for NASCAR (with Kelsey-Hayes), as well as larger-diameter rear axle shafts, improved spindles, and super heavy-duty steering arms.

After the Automobile Manufacturers Association racing ban took effect in 1957, Chevrolet went underground with its motorsports efforts. It continued to develop parts and supply teams with parts, but it did so in a clandestine fashion. It was Piggins who ran this part of Chevrolet, funneling the right parts and cars to the teams that needed them.

In the '60s, Piggins was still the performance boss, in charge of what was then called the Product Promotion group. Piggins is considered the father of the Camaro Z/28, which he had developed for the Sports Car Club of America's Trans-Am series. Originally he proposed it with a 283-cubic-inch engine, but general manager Pete Estes suggested sticking a 283 crank in a 327 block to create the soon-to-be-legendary 302. Piggins also launched a short run of L72 427 Chevelles in '69 to make them legal for National Hot Rod Association drag racing.

Above: Located behind the steering wheel on the left side of the Polara's instrument panel are the push-button controls for the TorqueFlite transmission. The last year for push-button transmissions was 1964.

Polara

Polara was an unlikely name for a muscle machine, but in the early '60s it offered enough horsepower to make other pseudo-supercars run for cover. It was the top trim level for downsized Dodges from 1962 until 1964. As it was the Polara had such niceties as full carpeting, bucket seats, dual exhausts, and special exterior trim.

More importantly for muscle car fanciers, the Polara came with the potent 413 or 426 Ramcharger V8s (the 426 was first offered in '63). If the 400-plus-horsepower versions of these engines with their multiple carb setups and solid-lifter camshafts were too much for you, the always popular 383 (330 horsepower) was available as well.

When Dodge revived the Coronet name in 1965 and attached it to the intermediate lineup, the Polara moniker was fitted to the larger-size models formerly known as the 880 series. Its days as a muscle car were a mere footnote to the era, but one worth a mention.

Above: The grille was slightly reworked on 1963 Dodges, but the styling remained controversial.

Left: The 1962 Dodges are considered to be among the most oddly styled cars of all time. This is a '62 Polara 500.

Ramchargers

The first factory drag racing team? Back when the factories believed that racing victories translated into improved engineering and sales, the Ramchargers were formed. This was a drag team begun in 1958 composed of graduates of the Chrysler Institute of Engineering, and at first it was just a club. The Ramcharger Club included the likes of Tom Hoover, Dick Maxwell, Jim Thornton, Herm Mozer, and Mike Buckel. They concentrated on their own cars but eventually put out a one-car effort, called the High and Mighty, a '49 Plymouth Business Coupe that set the C-Altered Class circuit record and won the Altered class at its first national event, the 1959 U.S. Nationals.

The High and Mighty was one of the most bizarre-looking race cars ever. To aid traction, the suspension was extensively modified and the bottom of the door sat nearly 2 feet (61cm) off the ground—that's where the "High" part of the name came from. The "Mighty" referred to its powerful 354 early Hemi engine that was modified with (among other things) an extremely tall intake manifold that was in many ways the prototype of the tunnel ram intake. The top of the air scoop sat higher than the roof of the car.

When that engine blew up, the team was stranded without any spare parts and the club approached Chrysler management about getting enough backing to go Super Stock racing. Dodge, which was completely without a performance image on the street at the time, gave the program the green light and supplied a '61 Dart with a 413 long-ram engine. With fellow Mopar men Frank Wylie and Don Nichols, the Ramchargers began racing with that Dart.

In '63 the team got a second car, a '63 Dodge called Ramcharger II. Both cars used the 426 Max Wedge. One was fitted with the push-button TorqueFlite and used 4.56 gears, while the other ran on a stick shift. This way the cars could compete in both SS/Sa and SS/S classes. It was at this time that the cars got their now-famous candy-stripe paint job—and the nicknames Candymatic and Candymatic Too.

Eventually, the Ramchargers raced every class from Super Stock to Pro Stock and Funny Car, and for the most part they were very successful. These influential engineers made their presence known on and off the drag strip; Ramcharger members like Tom Hoover and Dick Maxwell were in the thick of everything—drag racing, stock car racing, and engine development. In fact, Maxwell is considered the father of the modern Hemi engine.

Ranchero

The Ford Ranchero was the original Cowboy Cadillac, debuting in 1957. A car up front and a pickup truck out back, the Ranchero beat the Chevy El Camino to the market by two full years. By the early '60s, the car switched from the full-size Ford platform to the compact Falcon chassis until finally settling on the midsize Fairlane chassis in 1967.

It was after the Ranchero became Fairlane-based again in 1967 that big-block engines started appearing under the hood. The first was a 390 with 320 horsepower—not the most potent powerplant, but full of torque.

Eventually, the 428 and 429 Cobra Jet engines were offered, but they sold in very limited numbers. From 1968 to 1969, you could get the 428 Cobra Jet with either a 4-speed or a C-6 automatic—you could even get ram air in 1969. In '70 and '71, the 429 Ranchero Cobra Jet with ram air was an option. So were hidden headlamps on the Ranchero GT during '70 and '71.

Hot Rod wrung out the mid-year '68 Ranchero CJ with a C-6 transmission and got a 15.6 at 91.8 mph (147.5kph)—obviously weight was an issue.

This '71 Ranchero is equipped with a 429 Cobra Jet and a Shaker hood.

After 1971, Ford killed all its big-block performance engines. You could still get a 429 (and later a 460) in the Ranchero, but that was a simple passenger-car engine. While Mustang fanatics could get a decent 351 in their Mach 1, the low-performance 351s were the only ones offered in the Ranchero. The Ranchero name continued until 1979.

Randall American 401 Gremlin XR

Randall American was, in the early '70s, the largest AMC dealer in the Southwest. Located in Mesa, Arizona, it was also heavily involved in road racing, drag racing, and street performance. In 1972, AMC offered the compact Gremlin economy with a 304-cubic-inch 2-barrel engine. Randall saw this as an opportunity, since the 401 AMC engine had the same external dimensions. It wasn't long afterwards that Randall began offering compact muscle cars.

The 401 Gremlin XR (as Randall called it) started life as 304 Gremlin X (this was the first subcompact of the era to offer a V8). When you ordered the car with the optional 2-barrel V8, it came from the factory with a heavy-duty front sway bar, 10-inch (25.5cm) drum brakes, stiffer front coil springs, higher rate leaf springs in the rear with 4.5 leaves (versus 3.5), and a larger rear axle housing with an 8.88-inch (22.5cm) ring gear.

In '72 the engine was a low-compression mill that featured a forged steel crankshaft and rods, cast-aluminum dished pistons, and a hydraulic-lifter valvetrain. The heads had 2.02-inch (50mm) intake and 1.68-inch (40mm) exhaust valves. A single 4-barrel carb fed the engine, and tubular exhaust headers were standard.

Like all AMCs, the XR used the Chrysler TorqueFlite automatic transmission, though a 4-speed swap was available. Naturally, there was a traction device—a torque link running from the top of the axle housing forward to the mounting point on the frame. Heavy-duty Javelin shocks were standard, while Konis were optional; gear ratios from 2.87:1 to 5.59:1 were available with the optional Twin-Grip differential. After this, Randall allowed you to option out the car any way you wanted to, including a 650-cfm Holley carb, a blueprinted race engine, wheels and tires—you name it.

Super Stock & Drag Illustrated tested a Holley-equipped XR in its August '72 issue, and the automatic-equipped Gremlin ran a best of 13.56 at 103 mph (165.5kph). With the headers opened and new spark plugs, the XR ran a best of 13.22 at 105.76 mph (170kph).

While the 401 Gremlin XR isn't the most well-known car from the muscle car era or very noteworthy in terms of sales volume, it was an interesting vehicle nonetheless.

Rebel Machine

As far as midsize muscle cars were concerned, American Motors had absolutely nothing to offer until the 1970 Rebel Machine. Technically, the Machine was a product of AMC's relationship with Hurst Performance. Unlike the one-year-only '69 Hurst SC/Rambler and Hurst AMX S/S projects, the Rebel Machine wore only AMC badges.

The Rebel rode on a 114-inch (289.5cm) wheelbase and for 1970 was new from the rear quarter panels back. The car was introduced to the general public at the NHRA race in Dallas in October 1969. It included plenty of standard features, including high-back bucket seats, power front disc brakes, a ram air hood, a handling package, a heavy-duty cooling system, 15×7-inch (38×18cm) steel wheels, E60×15-inch (38cm) fiberglass belted tires with raised white letters, and a 4-speed shifter with Hurst linkage.

The first thousand cars came in white with patriotic red and blue stripes, including a wide blue treatment on the hood and along the lower rocker molding. There was even a red, white, and blue treatment in the lower grille opening. Later cars could be ordered in solid colors and used a blacked-out hood with silver pinstripes. In keeping with the style of the day, the rear of the car was purposely raised higher than the front. A total of 2,326 were produced.

Motivation came from a 390 AMC V8 with 10.0:1 compression, a single 4-barrel carburetor, and 340 horsepower. The functional ram air hood was said to be worth 15 horsepower. Standard was a 3.54:1 Twin-Grip axle, and a tachometer was built into the rear of the hood scoop.

In its advertising, AMC bragged that the Machine was slower than a Hemi but "faster than your old man's Cadillac." Regardless of this odd marketing pitch, the Rebel Machine was powerful enough to run with most supercars of the era with similar displacement and was a lot faster than most Fords with the same-size engine. Both *Motor Trend* and *Super Stock & Drag Illustrated* tested Rebel Machines. In its November '69 issue, *Motor Trend* reported a strong 14.4 at 99 mph (159.5kph), while in its January 1970 issue, *SS&DI* was one-tenth quicker at the same speed.

Riviera GS

This is another entry that some might consider hard to justify in *The Encyclopedia of American Muscle Cars*. The Buick Riviera was first and foremost a personal luxury car. But in 1965, Buick saw fit to introduce the Gran Sport option on its high-style flier. This meant, among other things, a standard dual-quad intake manifold on a 425-cubic-inch Super Wildcat V8. It produced 360 horsepower and 465 lbs.-ft. of torque; despite the Riviera's curb weight of more than 4,000 pounds (1,816kg), you could propel the massive Buick to mid-15-second quarter-mile times at speeds faster than 90 mph (145kph).

In '66, the dual quads remained, but the GS option returned on a completely restyled Riviera. It was a beautiful car—low and wide with a futuristic design. The only engine was a 425 that produced 340 horsepower, same as the base Riviera. The following year, all Rivieras enjoyed the use of an all-new, modern V8 engine displacing 430 cubic inches. It made 360 horsepower and 475 lbs.-ft. of torque, but there was an awful lot of car to move around. The GS option continued for years but, unlike in 1965, would never amount to much more than an options package on a very likable personal luxury car.

Road Runner

While Mopar's muscle cars never lacked for power, until 1968 they lacked a certain personality. The Pontiac GTO had it, the Mustang had it, and so did the new Camaro and Firebird. The Mopars could dominate the street and the strip, but sales were never great. That changed in 1968 with the introduction of the Plymouth Road Runner. The idea for the car is commonly credited to journalist Brock Yates of *Car and Driver*, who suggested that Chrysler put its raging 440 in a no-frills, inexpensive intermediate.

Chrysler took the 440 GTX's cam, cylinder heads, intake, carburetor, and exhaust manifolds and attached them to the short-stroke 383 big-block. The result was rated at 335 horsepower at 5200 rpm and 425 lbs.-ft. of torque at 3400. The only optional engine was the 425-horse Hemi. At the beginning of the model year, Road Runners were available only in a pillared coupe body style. A hardtop was offered as a mid-year option. The interior of the car was as sparingly equipped as possible. Standard was a bench seat, a column shift (if you ordered the automatic), and no carpeting. As you would expect in a taxicab, the floor was covered with a large rubber mat. The back windows did not roll down; they popped open from the rear.

As great as the no-frills approach was, there was still nothing out of the ordinary from a sales point of view. The secret to the Road Runner was, of course, its name and its connection to the popular Warner Bros. Saturday-morning cartoon series. The car's name has been credited to Gordon Cherry, who worked for Chrysler/Plymouth product planning manager Jim Smith. Legend has it that Cherry was struck with the idea while watching cartoons with his children.

The best part was that Plymouth really had Warner Bros. over a barrel. Warner Bros. wanted Chrysler to pay beaucoup bucks for the rights to use the cartoon character in the car's emblems and advertising. Plymouth could have called its new car the Road Runner without paying any fee—it was just the name of a bird of the Southwest, after all. Of course, without the cartoon character and trademark "beep-beep" horn, the Road Runner might have just been another powerful muscle car.

Joel Rosen

Known as Mr. Motion, Joel Rosen was (and is) the owner of Motion Performance in Baldwin on Long Island, New York. He was the man who teamed up with Baldwin Chevrolet to produce the Baldwin-Motion specialty cars, including the Phase III Camaro and Corvette, the Corvette Manta Ray, and 427 Chevelles.

Although it was Rosen who had approached Baldwin Chevrolet about selling new cars with speed parts already installed, the idea grew to the point where they were combining to sell new cars with completely different engines and upgraded suspensions, cosmetics, and wheels.

While Motion is best known today for its wild Chevrolets, it is a little-known fact that the shop campaigned one of the rare Shelby Dragonsnake Cobras. Today, Rosen is still working behind the counter at Motion Performance on Sunrise Highway. Motion offers custom fiberglass body parts for late-model Mustangs. Among Rosen's other ventures after the end of the muscle car era were breeding and selling exotic pets and building custom military models.

Below: A muscle car in the truest sense, the 1968 Hemi Road Runner had the most powerful engine in the lightest body that could be fit in on a factory assembly line.

Left: The Road Runner concept proved so successful that Plymouth added a hardtop model in 1968 and a convertible in 1969. This is a 1970 Road Runner convertible, the second and last year it was offered.

Eventually, Warner Bros. relented, accepting a pittance of $60,000, and the rest was history.

There were, of course, other factors in the car's success. The Road Runner was a legitimate 14-second supercar that cost just about $3,000. This was big news in a time when the price of most muscle machines was escalating faster than the war in Vietnam. A total of 44,599 were sold that first year, making it Mopar's most successful muscle car to date.

Hot Rod tested a 4-speed-equipped '68 and raved about its power and handling. The car turned a 14.74 at 98 mph (157.5kph) on stock tires at Madison Township Raceway Park in Englishtown, New Jersey. The ET was good, but the speed indicated the car's true potential, not to mention the adhesion limits of the stock tires.

For '69, Plymouth added a convertible to the lineup, but the hardtop still accounted for most of the sales. The engine lineup remained the same until the middle of the model year, when the 440 Six-Barrel was added. This was the ultimate street racer package. A lightweight fiberglass hood with a huge functional scoop fed a trio of Holley carburetors on an aluminum Edelbrock intake manifold. To make it even more powerful, there was a special camshaft, plus valves, springs, and rockers.

The flat-black hood was held down by four NASCAR-style pins and lifted right off—there were no hood hinges. But that was only part of it. There were no hubcaps—just painted-black wheels with chrome lug nuts and red-stripe tires. A bench seat was standard, as was a drag race–oriented 4.10 Dana rear.

Plymouth bragged in its ads that the Six-Barrel Road Runner could turn a quarter mile in 13 seconds flat at 111 mph (178.5kph), which was a bit optimistic, but not too much. It (and its cousin the Dodge Super Bee Six-Pack) was one of the ultimate straightline warriors of the era. *Super Stock & Drag Illustrated* claimed 13.65 seconds at 104.04 mph (167.5kph), *Popular Hot Rodding* printed a 13.56 at 106.5 mph (171.5kph), and *Hot Rod* scored a blistering 13.47 at 106.63 mph (171.5kph). Sales of all Road Runners exploded, to 86,292, outselling the fabled GTO by nearly 10,000 units.

BEEP! BEEP!
COYOTE DUSTER
440-6

Asa "Ace" Wilson Jr.

Ace Wilson was the owner of Royal Pontiac in Royal Oak, Michigan, the leading high-performance Pontiac dealership and Pontiac's de facto racing arm. Pontiac ad executive Jim Wangers approached Wilson with the concept of forming a relationship between the two businesses. The idea was to set up a program where racers and enthusiasts could buy Pontiac's new line of Super Duty parts and get their powerful Ponchos serviced.

Wilson embraced the idea wholeheartedly. Royal stocked the parts, trained special salespeople to sell the parts and/or the cars with the parts already installed, and got a couple of top-notch technicians to handle the cars when they came in for service. The plan worked amazingly well. Royal was involved in parts, sales, racing, and moving a ton of cars and speed goodies.

In 1961, a new concept, the Royal Bobcat, was born. The Royal Bobcat was a specially set-up Catalina that you could purchase from the dealership. The name also became attached to the package's high-output tune-up for the 389. The Royal Bobcat treatment consisted of (among other things) thinner head gaskets to raise compression, progressive carb linkage for the Tri-Power, a recurved distributor, and a special rocker arm adjustment to allow for more lift. In '62, you could get the treatment on the 421 as well.

As the muscle car movement progressed, favorable treatment by the press was imperative, so Wangers had Royal give the cars handed out to the media the Royal Bobcat treatment (often without revealing so). In some cases, these were just tuned-up cars; in others it could mean a hotted-up 421 or 428 in a GTO test car. The writers marveled at the incredible power, not realizing that the cars actually purchased by consumers were never that hot without additional tweaking.

Eventually, Royal went into the mail-order business, shipping parts all over the country. In 1969, the Royal Racing Team was sold to John DeLorean's younger brother, George, who was a racer. The Royal Racing Team withered after it was no longer part of the dealership.

"Fuselage" styling was all-new for 1971 Plymouth intermediates. The Road Runner's popularity was starting to wane, despite the hot new design. The 1971 model on the left is wearing non-stock aftermarket rims. Notice the hood pins on the 1972 model on the right. The Road Runner cartoon theme carried over under the hood, to the graphics on the air cleaner lid (inset).

The Road Runner got a slight face-lift in 1970, receiving an updated grille with a kick up in the bottom, new taillamps, and side scoops. Large, round parking lights, located on either side of the license-plate area, were far more prominent than on earlier models. There was also a triple stripe treatment on the hood, one fat lone stripe flanked by two thinner ones. Plymouth brought back the same three body styles, though this was the last year for the convertible.

The powertrains remained the same, but there were some changes. First, the 440 Six-Barrel now employed a cast-iron version of its three-deuce intake manifold. It had the same horsepower but was a few pounds heavier. Also hurting performance was the redesigned hood, which was no longer a lift-off fiberglass piece. The new hood was virtually the same heavy steel piece used on other Beepers; only the placement of the new-for-1970 Air Grabber scoop was different. The Air Grabber was a pop-up scoop that operated via an electric solenoid/vacuum arrangement. With the flip of a switch, the Air Grabber rose from the center of the hood, replete with sinister eyes and sharp-teeth graphics. Those who ordered the Hemi got a hydraulic-lifter camshaft for easier maintenance.

Chrysler's line of intermediates was completely redone for 1971, and the Road Runner came away with a new look, a new engine, and one last season of unbridled performance. Dodge and Plymouth went to what was dubbed "fuselage" styling, which was thoroughly modern with rounded fenders, a shorter tail, and bulging sides. The nose was reminiscent of the '70 but could be ordered with Elastomeric bumpers, a rubberized material that was resistant to dents, and painted the same color as the body.

Wheelbase decreased from 116 to 115 inches (294.5 to 292cm), while overall length shrunk slightly less than 1 inch (25mm). The interiors were all-new and bore a strong family resemblance to those introduced a year earlier on the E-body Barracuda and Challenger.

The 383 was still the base engine in the Road Runner, but it was downrated to 300 horsepower. Compression, which had dropped one-half of a point, from 10:1 to 9.5:1, in 1970, went down another point in '71. This contributed plenty to the missing ponies. On a positive note, the compression ratio on the 440 Six-Barrel remained at 10.5:1, though it was now rated at 385 horsepower, down 5. The year 1971 was the last stand for the race-bred 426 Street Hemi. It remained the top dog until the end, with 425 horsepower and 490 lbs.-ft. of torque.

The only addition to the powerplant list was the 275-horsepower 340, used earlier in the 'Cuda and Duster. It had plenty of compression and excellent breathing and made peak power at 5000 rpm, although it was probably better suited to a lighter car. The thought of an engine less than 383 cubic inches in the Road Runner probably seemed like heresy to some, but this solution dodged some of the high insurance premiums that accompanied big-block muscle cars.

It was also a sign of things to come. The 340 was one of three performance-oriented engines offered in 1972, and at 8.5:1 it had the highest compression. It made 240 net horsepower in '72 at 4800 rpm and 290 net lbs.-ft. of torque at 3600. A 400, which was basically a bored-out 383, was another hi-po Road Runner mill. With a ThermoQuad 4-barrel carb, it gave you 255 horsepower. A little-known fact about the 400 is that, from 1972 to 1974, if you ordered it with a 4-speed you got a steel crankshaft.

The 440 hung in there as well, with a single 4-barrel carb and 280 horsepower, but came in a model that was the combination of two cars—it was called the Road Runner GTX. This combination lasted until '74 and was considered the last of the real Road Runners. For '75, the name was attached to a weak Fury intermediate; in '76 it was desecrated again, placed on the lowly Plymouth Volare.

Royal Pontiac

The original high-performance car dealership, Royal Pontiac was located outside Detroit in Royal Oak, Michigan. Owned by Asa "Ace" Wilson Jr., it became the main purveyor of Pontiac's high-performance factory racing parts. Pontiac was barging its way into stock car and drag racing in 1959 and needed a special dealership to test the concept of selling its high-performance parts, not to mention to support the image of Pontiac as a purveyor of special automobiles.

This union was quite successful. Royal Pontiac gained a reputation as the place to go if you wanted your Poncho to be competitive on the street or strip. From the very beginning, Royal Pontiac advertised in car magazines, selling a host of factory Super Duty parts, not to mention tuning kits. If you got a Royal Bobcat kit for your Pontiac, you'd be running hard very quickly.

The Royal Bobcat treatment offered you thinner head gaskets, which increased compression; a special distributor advance kit; progressive linkage for Tri-Power cars' blocked intake heat riser gaskets (to keep the intake manifold cooler for improved performance); and special lock nuts for the rockers, which allowed you to adjust the valves so that the engine could turn a high rpm. Royal went so far as to install these Bobcat kits on some of its new cars.

Thanks to Royal's connection with Pontiac advertising executive Jim Wangers, who successfully campaigned a Royal Bobcat Catalina, many of Pontiac's press cars went out with the Royal Bobcat treatment—or more—for performance tests. It was no secret that the measured performance in a magazine road test could increase sales. Wangers was not about to leave test performance to chance, hence the "Bobcatted" press cars. In extreme cases, the cars went equipped with engines larger than the factory offered when they were sent to journalists. It was nearly impossible to distinguish a 421 Pontiac engine from a 389, so some GTOs were delivered to the media so equipped.

Like some of the Chevrolet dealerships, Royal found it necessary to sell its GTOs with engines larger than the 400 mandated by the factory. In 1968, *Car and Driver* tested a Royal Bobcat 428 GTO and lavished praise on it. The car turned a

13.8 at 104 mph (167.5kph), yet it maintained all the civility the GTO was known for. Even more remarkable is that this time was achieved in a fairly well-optioned car with an automatic transmission, street tires, and 3.55 gears. In another test, *Car and Driver* wrung out a 1969 Royal Bobcat Grand Prix. This one was equipped with a 4-speed transmission and a reworked 428 HO. The best time was a 13.98 at 102 mph (164kph)—remarkable for a car that weighed more than 4,000 pounds (1,816kg).

Other dealers tried to emulate Royal Pontiac, with varying degrees of success. Myrtle Motors in New York, Gay Pontiac in Texas, and Knafel Pontiac in Ohio did well, while others faltered. The original, however, was the most successful and fully documented; Royal Pontiac's cars are worth a premium with collectors. The dealership was sold in the early 1970s and the building was torn down in the mid-1980s.

R/T

See *Coronet*.

Satellite and Savoy

These two members of the Plymouth Belvedere lineup, the Satellite and the Savoy, were at opposite sides of the automotive spectrum. The Savoy, at the low end of the line, was a no-frills post car and the lightest of the "full-size" Plymouth cars for 1962, which were smaller and some 300 pounds (136kg) lighter than the full-size models from GM and Ford. In contrast, at the other end was the Satellite, introduced in 1965 and slated as Plymouth's top-of-the-line model (replacing the Sport Fury, which was now based on the larger C-body platform). For '65, the Satellite was considered an intermediate-size car.

Being the lowest-line model, the Savoy was a natural place for the largest, most powerful engine during the heyday of the muscle car era. A limited number of 413 Max Wedge Golden Commando

The 1965 Satellite two-door hardtop was available with up to 365 horsepower, thanks to the 426-S engine. The car shown here has the Race Hemi hood, which was not available on this body style and was added at some point in this car's history.

Carroll Shelby

Long before he built the Cobra sports car that bore his name, Carroll Shelby was a very successful race car driver, one whose career included victories in Cadillac-powered Allards, Maseratis, and Ferraris. The Texan who raced wearing bib overalls was twice named *Sports Illustrated*'s Driver of the Year.

Born Carroll Hall Shelby in Leesburg, Texas, on July 11, 1923, he drove his first road race in 1952 behind the wheel of an MG-TC. He was

victorious that day and on his way to international acclaim. In 1959, he and codriver Ray Salvadori piloted an Aston Martin DBR1/300 to victory in the 24 Hours of Le Mans, the most prestigious of all sports car races. After a number of race victories in 1960, Shelby won the United States Auto Club driving championship. That same year, he was diagnosed with angina pectoris and after the season was over, he gave up race driving for good.

In September 1961, Shelby learned that AC Cars of England had lost the source for its 6-cylinder engine, and he fired off a letter to the company suggesting it send him the chassis and bodies so that he could build a sports car powered by an American V8. At this time, Shelby learned of the new small-block Ford V8. He eventually struck a deal with Ford and its 260 V8 was initially used in the British cars.

Legend has it that the Cobra name came to Shelby in a dream and that he jotted it down on a notepad he kept by the side of his bed. The name stuck, and in February 1962 the first Shelby Cobra was on the road, powered by a high-performance 260. A month later, Shelby had a production facility up and running in Venice, California, and a pearl yellow Cobra was shipped to New York for display at the 1962 New York Auto Show.

After initial startup problems due to the extensive revisions that had to be made to the AC chassis to handle the V8, Shelby American started selling cars and entering races. The Shelby Cobra lost its first race, the Los Angeles Times Grand Prix, when a rear hub failed, but it was plain to everyone in attendance that the Cobra was faster than the Corvette that won the event. In its first year, the Cobra dominated the Chevrolet sports car and won the Sports Car Club of America A-production national championship.

Shelby is a maverick and a visionary, a larger-than-life character who has legions of loyal followers. After a twenty-year layoff, his company began building Cobra "continuation" cars again in 1989. In June 1990, Shelby received a heart transplant and less than a year later was the driver when a Dodge Viper—a sports car designed to be a modern interpretation of the 427 Cobra—paced the Indianapolis 500.

In addition to his many business ventures (including a Texas chili mix), Shelby is devoted today to the Carroll Shelby Children's Foundation. According to its website (www.shelbychildrensfoundation.org), Shelby was moved to start the foundation following years of heart-related difficulties, which finally culminated in his successful heart transplant. The foundation is dedicated to providing assistance for acute coronary and kidney care to indigent children.

Shelby lives in Las Vegas, home of the new Shelby American headquarters.

engines found their way into the Savoy in '62 and the 426 Golden Commando in 1963–1964.

The Belvedere Satellite could be ordered with a number of different engines in '65, but the most important to high-performance enthusiasts were the 330-horsepower 383 and the 426-S. The latter made 365 horsepower at 4800 rpm and was a fierce rival for most factory cars at the time. *Motor Trend* reported a 15.2 quarter-mile time for a Satellite fitted with a 426-S, despite being hampered by a fuel economy–minded 2.93:1 rear axle ratio. So equipped, the car turned out a top speed of 130 mph (209kph).

After 1966 the Satellite's status as a true muscle car was never questioned again, for this was the year the mighty Street Hemi engine joined the option list. If that 425-horsepower engine was too much for you, a 325-horse 383 4-barrel could be ordered in the Satellite.

These same two powerhouse engines returned for '67 and '68, although the 383 was rated at 330 horsepower with a 4-barrel carb. It was not the same 383 that was available in the then-new Road Runner, which was rated 5 horsepower higher. A new model, the Sport Satellite, was introduced in '68 and its differences were little more than black-out trim, different brightwork, body accent stripes, and a standard 318 engine.

After '68, the Hemi was relegated to GTXs, and to Road Runners only in the intermediate lineup.

The top engine was the 330-horse 383. For 1971, a new designation, Satellite Sebring, appeared. The 383 remained as the top engine, but its power rating was down to 300 horsepower. In '72, the Satellite Sebring was available with a 400-cubic-inch version of the B engine, which was basically an overbored 383 with low compression. The engine was rated at 255 horsepower; the bore was increased from 4.25 to 4.34 inches (108 to 110mm) to add the cubic inches.

This page: In its Hemi Satellite road test, *Car and Driver* faulted the car's conservative appearance, but loved its performance—14.5 at 95 mph (153kph) in the quarter-mile. This '66 Hemi Satellite is wearing 1967-vintage wheels.

Larry Shinoda

Detroit is a long way from Manzanar, the infamous World War II Japanese interment camp in California, but Larry Shinoda overcame this early setback in his life and went on to become one of the most famous automotive designers of his time.

A graduate of the Art Center College of Design in Los Angeles and the Douglas Aircraft Technical School, he had a job with the doomed Studebaker-Packard company before moving to General Motors in 1956. It was Shinoda who designed the bat-wing fins of the '59 Chevrolet. By 1959, he was working on Bill Mitchell's Sting Ray Sports Racer project, the body of which would become

the inspiration for the 1963 Corvette Sting Ray. He stayed with Chevrolet long enough to help style this Corvette, the much-heralded 1965 Corvair, and the dramatic 1968 Corvette, but left to join Ford Motor Company at the behest of Semon E. "Bunkie" Knudsen, who quit GM to become Ford's general manager.

While at Ford, Shinoda was in charge of all high-performance production cars, show vehicles, displays, and exhibits. It was Shinoda who designed the exterior graphics package for the 1969–1970 Boss 302 Mustang, including the sports slats for the rear window and the front spoiler and rear wing, as well as the same-vintage Boss 429, Cyclone Spoiler and Spoiler II, and Torino Talladega.

When Knudsen was unexpectedly and unceremoniously fired by Henry Ford II, it became clear that Shinoda's days at Ford Motor Company were numbered. Indeed, Shinoda was dismissed only eighteen months after he started there. He worked on a wide range of vehicles after that—everything from motor homes to diesel trucks (his streamlined White tractor revolutionized the trucking industry). Later he started Shinoda Designs in Livonia, Michigan, where he worked on numerous projects for the auto industry, including the Rick Mears Special Edition Corvette and the Boss Shinoda body kit and stripe package for 1994 and newer Mustangs.

Shinoda died from complications of kidney failure in 1997.

Shelby GT350 and GT500

Carroll Shelby's Cobra roadster, the combination of an old English roadster and brute American horsepower, dominated sports car racing in the 1960s from virtually its first race. Beginning in 1962, it annihilated the Corvette—and every other sports car in the world—in competition. Buoyed by this success, Shelby turned his attention to Ford's ponycar. Once again, the union was perfect.

When Ford approached Shelby about creating a series of high-performance Mustangs, it was a natural extension of their current relationship. Shelby, by now a legend in racing circles (he had been a successful driver until heart problems caused him to give up his seat), knew how to make cars perform magical feats.

Remarkably, it didn't take much for him to transform the Mustang 2+2 from a fun, sometimes powerful car to a road racing terror in the SCCA's B-production class. Cars were delivered from Ford's San Jose, California, plant to Shelby's production facility in Los Angeles, where they went through the transformation process. The cars were named Shelby GT350, and though many theories are given to how the name was chosen, it appears to have been a random selection. The "GT" part (meaning Grand Touring) was a standard part of the automotive

The 1967 Shelby GT500 was powered by a dual quad version of the 428 Police Interceptor engine. It produced 355 horsepower. Cast aluminum Shelby 10-spoke wheels (shown) were one of three wheels used in '67 by Shelby.

This page: Optional parts for the 1966 Shelby GT350 included a center dash-mounted gauge pod and Weber carburetors.

lexicon. But the "350" part was a mystery—it didn't represent the amount of horsepower, the torque, the engine's cubic-inch displacement, or the length of any race it might be entered in. It was just a number. Regardless, it sounded good.

The Mustangs that arrived in L.A. were all 271-horse 289 fastbacks, which minimized the number of modifications that needed to be made. An aluminum high-rise intake manifold with a 715-cfm Holley 4-barrel replaced the stock parts, and a set of tubular Tri-Y headers carried away the exhaust through high-flow mufflers and pipes that exited on the side of the car just aft of the doors. The cam was also changed to a somewhat radical 306-degree duration, 0.457-inch (11.5mm) lift grind. So equipped, horsepower rose to 306 at 6000 rpm.

To handle the rigors of racing, Kelsey-Hayes 11-inch (28cm) ventilated disc brakes were used up front, with sintered metallic linings for the 10-inch (25.5cm) rear drums. A set of functional fiberglass scoops was added to direct cool air to the rear brakes. Removing the rear seat and adding a functional scooped fiberglass hood reduced the weight by a total of 120 pounds (54.5kg). Most were painted white with LeMans-blue stripes running the length of the body.

Handling was, of course, a major priority. The cars were lowered and fitted with Koni adjustable shocks. The inner pivot of the upper control arm was moved down 1 inch (25mm) to increase negative camber. The stock 0.75-inch (19mm) anti-roll bar was replaced with a 1-inch (25mm) piece. An added Monte Carlo bar and cowl brace tied the shock towers together and improved bracing to the underhood area. The steering ratio was quickened for better response. Putting the power to the pavement was a Detroit Locker differential, and aluminum wheels with speed-rated Goodyear tires kept the car on the road.

The interior came with a large tachometer and smaller oil-pressure gauge. The spare tire was relocated on top of the shelf to improve weight distribution, and a 16-inch- (40.5cm) diameter wood-and-aluminum steering wheel replaced the stock piece. Three-inch- (75mm) wide competition seat belts superseded the factory items. All cars were delivered without radios, though dealers could add them later.

About 515 Shelby GT350s were produced for the street in 1965, but as wonderful as they were, the best were 36 special Competition models built, which succeeded in taking the SCCA B-production national championship away from the Vette in 1965. Each Competition model came without a front bumper; in its place was a fiberglass lower valence with a large opening to duct air to the radiator. The engine was modified further to produce 350 horsepower, although there was an option for four Weber carburetors that pushed it to 390 horsepower and a modified version of that which rang up 395 ponies.

The Competition models came with a race-style instrument cluster, stripped interiors, and Plexiglas side and rear windows, but without a rear bumper. It was a dominant race car as delivered. (In some racing circles, the GT350 Competition model has

Early 1967 Shelby Mustangs had their driving lights mounted together in the center of the grille. When this was found to run afoul of the lighting laws in some states, the driving lights were moved to the outer extremities of the grille cavity, as shown here.

been erroneously referred to as the GT350 R model, with the "R" specifying "race.")

In 1966, Ford civilized the GT350s a bit to make them more appealing to a wider audience. The noisy Detroit Locker was gone and the backseat returned. An automatic transmission was optional. Five new colors were added, including Guardsman Blue, Raven Black, and Candyapple Red. Hertz (of rental car fame) ordered one thousand GT350s for its fleets, almost all of which received the automatic transmission. This helped to increase Shelby production to 2,380 for '66.

The GT350s were impressive drag cars, too. *Car and Driver* reported a quarter-mile time at 14.9 seconds running 95 mph (153kph), while *Car Life* and *Road & Track* both ran 14.7 at 90 mph (145kph) with '65 models. *High Performance Cars* claimed a 14.5 at 98 mph (157.5kph) for a '66 model with a 4-speed, while *Car and Driver* tested a GT350H (for Hertz) with an automatic and ran 15.2 at 93 mph (149.5kph).

A rare and interesting option for '66 was a Paxton supercharger. The ball-driven centrifugal unit forced compressed air through the Holley carb to bring the horsepower up to 390. *Motor Trend* ran a blistering 14.0 at 102 mph (164kph) in its tester, while *Popular Hot Rodding* went 14.15 at 102.51 mph (165kph). This was not an inexpensive car, but it was the match for virtually anything on the road short of a Hemi car, 427 Cobra, or similarly engine-sized Corvette.

When Ford redesigned the Mustang for 1967 and made the engine compartment wide enough to accept a big-block, Shelby introduced the GT500 (again, the number was picked for no apparent reason, although at least in racing circles "500" meant something). It was stuffed full with a Shelby-ized 428, one stout enough to produced 355 horsepower at 5400 rpm and 420 lbs.-ft. of torque at 3200 rpm.

The 428 engine was an impressive piece. A pair of 600-cfm Holley 4-barrels sat atop an aluminum medium-rise intake manifold. A special hydraulic-lifter cam opened and closed the valves, and a dual-point distributor helped provide the spark. Compression was 10.5:1. For the right price, Shelby built a 427 GT500, but these were extraordinarily rare.

As for the GT350, the engine lineup was carried over from '66. More amenities were available in the Shelby Mustangs than ever before, taking them one more step away from their racetrack roots, getting closer than ever to grand touring machines. Shelby engineers tweaked the suspension to make it more compliant and less punishing than it had been. Much of this could be credited to softer, adjustable Gabriel shocks, which replaced the expensive, race-bred Konis, and stiffer springs.

To further distinguish the Shelby Mustangs from their standard Ford counterparts, Shelby had

Shelby teamed up with Hertz in 1966 to produce the Shelby GT350H. The program was dropped after one year because the cars were frequently abused or raced in actual competition.

For 1968, Shelby switched from dechromed 1967 Cougar taillights to 1966 Thunderbird taillamps.

designers Chuck McHose and Pete Stacey add visual excitement. The nose was extended 3 inches (75mm) and the headlight buckets were altered. The grille-mounted driving lights could be either center-mounted or outboard (but still inside the grille surround), depending on state law where the car was to be delivered. A new twin-scooped fiberglass hood ducted fresh air to the carburetor(s) and looked even more aggressive than the one used on earlier cars.

But there was more. The rear deck received a spoiler and fiberglass tail panel with dechromed Cougar taillights. Side scoops similar to those on the 1965–1966 GT350s were standard, too. These cars were pure sinew.

The best news was that, while the 390 Mustangs were no match for 396 Camaros and 400 Firebirds, the GT500s could hold their own against virtually anything from GM or Chrysler. They were capable of mid- to high-13-second quarter-mile times with good tires. Most magazine tests showed low-14-second times, often at 101–102 mph (162.5–164kph), on the standard tires.

More big changes marked the '68 Shelby Mustangs. Ford took over production of the cars in Michigan and completed their transformation from racetrack escapees to grand touring machines. Air

Early 1968 GT500 Shelbys used a single 4-barrel Police Interceptor 428 engine. Later cars were designated GT500KR and had 428 Cobra Jet powerplants.

conditioning became an option, and the automatic transmission was much more readily available. A convertible was a regular production model for the first time. Another face-lift gave the car a blunter nose with hood scoops that extended to the leading edge of the hood to more effectively pick up air. Rectangular foglights replaced the large, round driving lights of '67. Out back, '65 Thunderbird taillights replaced the Cougar units.

Under the fiberglass hood were numerous changes, depending on the engine you ordered. The 306-horse, solid-lifter 289 was replaced by a passenger-car 302 with a 4-barrel carb on an aluminum intake. It was rated at just 250 horsepower, although the Paxton supercharger was still an option; this raised horsepower to 335 at 5200 rpm and torque from 318 to 325 lbs.-ft.

Those ordering a GT500 in the first half of the year got a 428, which came with a single 4-barrel carb instead of dual quads, although it was now rated at 360 horsepower. Later cars were called the GT500KR (for King of the Road). These monsters were the recipients of Ford's new 428 Cobra Jet engine. So equipped, *Hot Rod* ran 14.01 at 102.73 mph (165.5kph) with a 4-speed fastback model and 14.58 at 97.71 mph (157kph) in a convertible with the optional C-6 automatic.

It could be said that Ford went off the deep end with the 1969 Shelby Mustangs. The cars came with fiberglass nose pieces that did not resemble other '69 Mustangs in any way (although they did hint at what the '71 Mustang would look like). The only body parts shared were the doors, roof, and rear quarters. In all, twenty fiberglass parts were used. The fiberglass hoods came with five NACA ducts—one for directing air to the carburetor and four for venting the underhood area. Along with the fenders, they knocked 70 pounds (32kg) off the front end, a definite plus.

Fastbacks and convertibles differed slightly. The nonfunctional side scoops on the fastback were situated where the faux scoops on the Mach 1 were, while those on the convertible could be found in their customary place, just ahead of the rear wheels. The tail treatment was similar to that of the '68 Shelbys, but there were rectangular exhaust tips that exited together beneath the license plate. Wheels and tires were unique to the Shelbys. Fifteen-inch (38cm), 5-spoke mags carried F60×15-inch (38cm) Goodyear tires.

With the emphasis now on luxury more than performance, *Car and Driver* called the GT350 "a garter snake in Cobra trim." *Super Stock & Drag Illustrated* called it "a lot of beautiful car going places slowly." Thanks to the success of the Mach 1, interest was waning in the Shelby Mustangs. Still, *SS&DI* got its hands on a 4-speed

G.T. 500

EAGLE GT II
GOODYEAR
EAGLE GT II
GOODYEAR

These pages: The 1969 Shelby Mustangs like the GT 500 (left) were a radical departure from Ford's lesser offerings. The hood, front fenders, and other body parts were made of fiberglass. A functional ram air hood was standard and it fed a hungry 428 Cobra Jet (top inset) that was identical to the one used in all other Mustangs that year. Interiors, in contrast to the race-bred, bare-bones 1965 GT350s, were bordering on the opulent. Note the optional automatic transmission (bottom inset).

GT500 in its September 1969 issue and ran a very good 13.87-second quarter mile at 104.52 mph (168kph).

Just 3,150 Shelby Mustangs were built in 1969, and only 601 left the lot in 1970. In actuality, 789 of the '69 models were re-titled by Ford as '70 models and were given updated serial-number plates, different hood stripes, and front spoilers.

Skylark

See *Gran Sport*.

Super Bee

What Plymouth has, Dodge wants, and vice versa: this was a long-standing way of doing business at Chrysler Corporation, so when the Mayflower division announced it was building a low-budget supercar called the Road Runner, Dodge wanted a piece of the action. It was dubbed Super Bee and came complete with a cartoon bee replete with helmet, engine, and racing tires for an emblem. All it lacked was a horn that went "buzz buzz."

The Super Bee was based on the midsize Coronet, Dodge's B-body, and received the same two engines as the Road Runner—the 383 B motor was the base powerplant and was fortified with the high-flow cylinder heads, camshaft, exhaust manifold, intake, and carb from the GTX and R/T 440. The engine produced 335 horsepower at 5200 rpm and 425 lbs.-ft. of torque at 3400 rpm. The monster 425-horse Hemi was the only optional mill. Unlike the Road Runner, which was available from the beginning of the model year, the Super Bee arrived in late February.

One body style was offered in the beginning, the coupe, and for economy reasons the back windows popped out rather than rolled down. It wore a bubble hood and had bumblebee stripes across the decklid and down the sides of the rear fenders. Unlike the Road Runner, which came standard with a heavy-duty 3-speed manual gearbox, the base transmission in the Bee was a synchromesh 4-speed Chrysler A-833 stick with a Hurst Competition Plus floor shift. Optional was a column-mounted TorqueFlite automatic.

Heavy-duty springs and shocks were used on all four wheels, which wore redline tires (F70×14-inch [35.5cm] Goodyears), while a 0.94-inch (24mm)

This 1969 440 Six-Pack engine has the air cleaner removed, exposing the trio of Holley 2-barrel carbs. The intake was cast in aluminum in 1969 and in iron after 1970.

This page: The 1969 440 Six-Pack Super Bee (and its near twin, the 440 Six-Barrel Road Runner) was the ultimate street racer's special of the '60s. Remove the four NASCAR-style hood pins and the lightweight fiberglass hood lifted off to reveal a 390-horsepower RB engine with a trio of Holley 2-barrels on an aluminum Edelbrock intake (below). The interiors came with bench seats and the wheels had no hubcaps at all—not even poverty caps.

front sway bar improved handling. Self-adjusting 11-inch (28cm) drum brakes stopped it, but front discs were optional. Like all the B-bodies in '68, the Super Bee was an extremely handsome automobile, although the grille was a bit pedestrian for a muscle car. This was rectified in 1969, when the Bee's nose went in for surgery. When it came out, it was one of the toughest-looking muscle cars yet.

More evil still was the midyear intro, the Super Bee Six-Pack. For some, the stock 383 was too little, the 426 Hemi too much. Enter the 440 RB engine wearing an aluminum Edelbrock intake and three Holley 2-barrel carbs. Powered by 390 horses and 490 lbs.-ft. of torque, this Super Bee took a backseat to no one when it came to performance. The bottom end was fortified to keep it together under even the most extreme conditions.

To improve performance, the Super Bee Six-Pack was even more stripped down than the base 383 Super Bee. The car did not have wheel covers whatsoever on its 15-inch (38cm) steel cop car rims. Only chrome lug nuts dressed it up. A fiberglass hood with an enormous molded-in air scoop took weight off the nose; better still, it was held on with four NASCAR-style hood pins—it had no hinges or locking mechanism. So what if you needed to place the entire hood on the roof or the ground every time you changed the oil? This was a street racer's dream. Even a 4.11:1 gear was standard in a heavy-duty 9.75-inch (25cm) Dana rear. Except for tubular exhaust headers and slicks, it needed nothing extra to be a successful drag car.

Magazines of the day flipped for its performance. *Car Life*, which used the most conservative test methods, went 13.8 seconds in the quarter mile at 104.2 mph (167.5kph). *Popular Hot Rodding* screamed to a 13.4 at 105.26 mph (169.5kph). This was Hemi-car performance for a mere $468.80 more than the price of a 383 Super Bee.

The last year for the Coronet-based Super Bee was 1970. The grille was freshened again, and the end result was somewhat controversial. Some liked it; others said it was reminiscent of twin horse collars laid side by side. The standard hood was a nonfunctional twin scoop affair; optional was the Ramcharger which came standard with the Hemi. To increase sales, Dodge tried lowering the base price on a 383 Bee by $64, to $3,074. "A triumphantly backward idea since most performance car prices have gone up," Dodge boasted in its advertising. Of course, nothing is free. To get the price down, Dodge made the 3-speed manual the base gearbox; the 4-speed became an extra-cost option. This didn't help, as sales collapsed by nearly 50 percent. This was not a good time to be selling muscle cars.

In '71, all two-door Dodge intermediates were called Chargers, all four-doors and wagons Coronets. Thus, the Super Bee became an option on the Charger, which was all-new for this year. The wheelbase had been shortened from 117 to 115 inches (297 to 292cm), side glass was ventless, and there was a new semifastback roof. The Charger was similar in shape to the Plymouth Satellite, Road Runner, and GTX, but the car's design was smoother and, some believed, cleaner.

In the Charger Super Bee model, a bench seat, a defanged 383 (300 horsepower), and a 3-speed transmission were standard; optional was the 340. Most of the lost power was the result of a much lower compression ratio (8.7:1) and milder carb and ignition tuning. The Bee had a bulge in the hood and exposed headlamps. For the last time, the 440 Six-Pack (now rated at 385 horsepower) and 426 Hemi (still 425 horsepower) were available, but few buyers cared enough to actually order them. They were all strong performers, but the Super Bee, 440 Six-Pack, and Hemi did not return in 1972.

These pages: The Super Bee line was switched from the Coronet to the Charger line in 1971, the year Dodge began calling all its two-door intermediates Charger. The Ramcharger was part of the Hemi option, which was not offered after '71 either.

To lure Richard Petty back to Plymouth from Ford, Plymouth decided to build its version of Dodge's NASCAR aero-warrior, the Charger Daytona. Though they look similar, the Road Runner Superbird and the Daytona have different nose cones, front fenders, and rear wings. The examples shown here date from 1970.

Superbird (Super Bird)

This was Plymouth's answer to the aerodynamic Dodge Charger Daytona of 1969. When stock car king Richard Petty found out that Plymouth wasn't getting a version of the Daytona, he wanted to switch to driving a Dodge. When Chrysler refused, he switched to Ford and won a championship with a Torino Talladega. In an effort to woo him back (and at the same time become more competitive in NASCAR racing), Plymouth relented and built its own aero warrior based on the Road Runner.

While the Superbird (or Super Bird, depending on your source) bore a strong resemblance to the Charger Daytona, the cars were quite different. The Superbird used a unique nose cone with a different grille opening, a different wing, and its own backlight. Because the rear window was a deviation from stock, the Superbird needed a different plug to fill in the area between the window and the decklid. Also, to keep from having to hand-finish the body at the roof, vinyl tops were specified for all Superbirds. This covered the battle scars that resulted from fitting the window into the Road Runner.

There was also a problem getting a nose cone that could line up with the Road Runner's front fenders, so Coronet pieces were employed. The vertical fins on the Superbird were more swept back than those of the Daytona. Like the Dodge, the vertical fins were tall enough so that you could open the trunklid all the way.

Under the hood, the Superbird certainly did not lack for power. Like the regular Road Runner, you had three choices. You could order a 375-horsepower 440 Super Commando engine with a 4-barrel carb. Next up was the 390-horsepower 440 Six-Barrel. At the top of the heap, naturally, was the Hemi. Basic bench seats were standard and bucket seats were an option.

Just how many Superbirds were produced remains a mystery. Chrysler Historical claims 1,935. Others say 1,971 or 1,920. Regardless, the car helped Plymouth regain its competitive edge in NASCAR. The Superbird won twenty-one races in 1970, and eight of the victories came on superspeedways, where its aerodynamic edge played a more pivotal role.

Super Charger

This fascinating 1970 Dodge show car was an updated version of 1969's Topless Charger. It had a cut-down, 10-inch- (25.5cm) high windscreen, a Superbird-style nose cone, an integrated rear spoiler that automatically adjusted based on vehicle speed, and sidepipes. Other interesting features were vacuum-operated hood vents and twin flip-open gas caps.

It was built as a two-seater with Ford Thunderbird Sports Roadster–style fairings behind the driver and passenger seats. It was painted Fire Orange with a black hood and black bumblebee stripes. Power came from a 375-horsepower 440 Magnum engine, which was coupled to a 727 TorqueFlite automatic.

Super Duty Pontiacs (including Swiss Cheese racers)

When the AMA, a group composed of representatives from Ford, General Motors, and Chrysler, voted on June 6, 1957, to ban their own active participation in auto racing, Pontiac general manager Semon E. "Bunkie" Knudsen and Pontiac chief engineer Pete Estes tried to find a way around the edict. Knudsen was certain that participation in racing was a critical part of Pontiac's much-needed turnaround.

What they did was begin development of parts that would be sold over-the-counter "for off-road use only" for Pontiac's 389 engine. Sure enough, from 1959 until 1961, Pontiac became synonymous with performance, thanks to its successes in drag racing and NASCAR competition. Most notable was the combination of driver Glenn "Fireball" Roberts and mechanic Smokey Yunick—they won more stock car races during that three-year period than anyone else. Pontiac's thirty-one victories in 1961 is a total matched only once, by Ford in '64, and surpassed only by Ford's 48 victories in '65.

One of the top developments of the Super Duty parts program was the cylinder heads that ended up on the 421 Super Duty engine in 1962. They had much larger ports and bigger valves than standard 389 heads. For drag racing, 421 Super Duty mills had dual Carter 4-barrel carbs for improved breathing, while NASCAR had limited every car to a single 4-barrel. Pontiac rated the dual quad mill at 405 horsepower at 6000 rpm. Meanwhile, engineer Mac McKellar was designing a series of outstanding camshafts (both the NHRA and NASCAR required stock cams).

For 1962, Pontiac built a number of Super Duty Catalinas. They had aluminum front ends (including bumpers), which saved more than 200 pounds (91kg) for drag racing. They came without sound-deadening material and with aluminum exhaust manifolds. (NASCAR versions got stamped-steel headers because the aluminum versions would melt with extended use.) Another odd fact is that Pontiac built fifteen Super Duty Grand Prixs in 1962, only one of which is known to exist today.

In 1963, the Super Duty cars got a new cam, modified cylinder heads with bigger valves, and an increase in compression from 11.0:1 to 12.0:1 and 13.0:1. Dual valve springs were used to increase redline from 6000 to 6400 rpm. Despite all the added improvements, Pontiac raised horsepower only slightly, to 390 for a single 4-barrel with 12.0:1, 405 with two 4-barrels and 12.0:1, and 410 with dual quads and 13.0:1 squeeze.

The Super Dutys were lightened even further with the incorporation of Plexiglas side windows and aluminum trunklids, bellhousings, tailshafts, and rear axle center sections. Finally, Pontiac engineers showed how serious they really were by drilling lightening holes into the frame rails. The cars were so riddled with holes that they became known as Swiss Cheese cars.

Despite the success of the Super Duty cars, GM's corporate honchos clamped down once and for all on all racing activity in 1963, and the Super Duty program died a premature death.

Bob Tasca Sr.

The owner of Tasca Ford in East Providence, Rhode Island, Bob Tasca Sr. was the driving force behind one of Ford's leading high-performance car dealerships in the 1960s and early '70s. He claims to be the person who coined the phrase "Win on Sunday, sell on Monday," to emphasize the correlation between a successful race program and new-car sales.

His dealership was heavily involved in racing in the 1960s, and its 1963 427 Fairlane laid the groundwork for the legendary factory Thunderbolt effort. Tasca also built a high-output 428 Mustang in 1967, the progenitor of the 428 Cobra Jet cars of 1968. The Tasca Mustang was a virtual blueprint for the 1968 Cobra Jet—including a 428 Police Interceptor short-block, 427 cylinder heads, a 390 GT cam, and a 427 exhaust system. The dealership also sponsored A/Factory Experimental Mustangs and nitromethane-burning Mustang Funny Cars. Tasca Racing has included or been associated with such Ford notables as Bill Lawton, John Healy, Carroll Shelby, Bob Glidden, and Roy Hill.

More recently Tasca flexed his corporate muscles and helped bring Ford Motor Company together with the John Force Racing Team. Force switched to Ford Mustang bodies in 1998 and Force's cars are the most successful the sport has ever seen. Tasca is as passionate about racing and auto sales today as he was in the '60s.

Mickey Thompson

In his lifetime, Mickey Thompson did it all. He drag raced Funny Cars, set land-speed records at Bonneville, promoted races, and owned his own aftermarket parts company.

Thompson set more speed and endurance records than any other man in the world, with 295 records at Bonneville alone. An inductee of the Motorsports Hall of Fame of America, he was the first American to unofficially break the 400-mph (644kph) speed barrier. He also ran the first 6-second Funny Car, designed and drove the first slingshot dragster, and was the first to build and qualify a stock block rear-engine car for the Indianapolis 500.

According to the Motorsports Hall of Fame, Thompson developed the signal-starting and foul-light systems for drag strips, the Wide-Oval tire, and nitrogen gas shocks in the United States.

In his lifetime, Thompson helped make off-road racing one of the most popular forms of auto racing and also brought it indoors to stadium crowds. Tragically, Thompson and his wife were murdered outside their home in southern California in 1988.

Talladega

Ford's commitment to "Total Performance" in the 1960s and its attempt to dominate all arenas of racing resulted in the development of some rather interesting street cars. For devotees of midsize muscle cars, the most interesting was the Torino Talladega. Named after NASCAR's fastest superspeedway in Alabama, the Talladega was built to counter Dodge's Charger 500 in Grand National competition.

A slippery aerodynamic shape is one of the keys to winning on the track—it helps cornering, increases top speed, and improves stability at high speeds. While the standard Torino SportsRoof worked fairly well by the standards of the day, the 500 was a big improvement over the standard Charger and the Torino. Designed specifically for improved aero, the Charger 500 had a flush grille with exposed headlights and a backlight that eliminated the street car's tunnelback roofline, which was found to hinder aerodynamics.

To counter, Ford had newly acquired designer Larry Shinoda revise the nose, the grille, and the lower body on the Torino fastback for improved aerodynamics. This wasn't just a marketing ploy. Back then, you had to actually build street versions of the cars you raced in NASCAR.

Shinoda extended the snout about 5 inches (12.5cm) and angled it down to reduce frontal area. As Dodge had done with the 500, he reworked the grille and headlights so that they were flush with the front of the beak. He also tucked in the lower edge of the body and used the rear bumper from a regular Torino up front.

On the superspeedways, the Talladegas were about 5 mph (8kph) faster than the 500s, which gave them a huge advantage, so much so that Dodge revised the Charger once again and introduced the Daytona.

For the street, Ford offered the cars in Wimbledon White, Royal Maroon, and Presidential Blue. The hood scoop common on other Torinos and the Fairlane Cobra was omitted, and all hoods were painted matte black. The cars came with bench seats, column shifters, and manual windows, but such niceties as air conditioning and bucket seats were not offered. The only option was an AM radio. Standard were the heavy-duty suspension, 428 Cobra Jet, and automatic transmission.

One exception, however, was built for then-Ford president Semon E. "Bunkie" Knudsen. Knudsen had given the Talladega race car project the green light and had the factory build him a yellow one with a white bucket seat interior, a floor shifter, air conditioning, and power windows. It is said that he loved cruising Detroit's Woodward Avenue in the car (at the time, Woodward Avenue was the street racing mecca of the Motor City).

For the 1969 stock car racing season, Ford assembled perhaps the greatest driving roster ever—Richard Petty (who had defected from the Mopar camp when he was told he couldn't switch to a Charger Daytona); David Pearson, who had already won two Grand National championships; Lee Roy Yarbrough; and Donnie Allison. Pearson won his third championship in '69, and his 105 career victories remain second on the all-time list behind Petty's 200. Also driving for Ford that year were Bennie Parsons and A.J. Foyt, who won the season opener on the road course at Riverside, California, in a regular Torino.

These were heady days at Ford, and interestingly enough the engine that powered the Talladega to all these race victories was never available in the street car. The Boss 429 semi-hemi, which had replaced the 427 wedge, was available only in the Mustang.

After '69, Petty switched back to Plymouth, driving its new aero warrior, the Superbird, and the Talladega was retired in favor of the new '70 Torino SportsRoof, which the ads bragged was "shaped by the wind." The reality is that the '70 body style, while sleek-looking, was far less aerodynamic than its predecessor.

Thunderbolt

See *Fairlane/Torino*.

Torino

In Italy, Torino (or Turin) is the epicenter of the automobile industry. This was the new name attached to the top-of-the-line trim level for the Ford Fairlane. It superceded the Fairlane 500, which became the midlevel line.

The Torino had all the goodies of the Fairlane 500, but added special emblems, lower body moldings, interior trim, and the like. The body of the Fairlane was all-new for '68 and the fastback model was one of the sportiest in the industry, but the name "Fairlane" was a bit lacking in pizzazz for the era of free love and psychedelics. Torino designers were determined to make the car a lot sportier. It should be noted that the Torino was available as a two-door hardtop, fastback, and convertible, not to mention the four-door and wagon versions.

Helping its sporting nature were the optional powerplants. The 320-horse 390 was still hanging in there, the 427 with 390 horses was technically listed as an option though it is believed none was built, and the top dog was the 335-horsepower 428 Cobra Jet (available midyear). All of the engines were available with Ford's Toploader 4-speed or C-6 automatic transmission. These were real runners, even though they were saddled with a few hundred pounds more than the Mustang. *Popular Hot Rodding* reported a 14.34-second ET in quarter mile at 100.3 mph (161.5kph) in stock trim, cutting that figure to 13.27 at 108.3 mph (174.5kph) with headers, slicks, and improved tuning.

Except for the Torino Talladega (see separate entry), the '69 Torino was virtually carried over from the year before. Taillights and trim were altered ever so slightly, but the two cars were difficult to distinguish. This was the first year for the Torino GT, which had the 302 V8 and bucket seats as standard equipment, as well as the Fairlane Cobra, which gave you the 428 Cobra Jet and Toploader 4-speed as standard equipment. Ram air was an option on the 428 Cobra Jet, as it had been the year before.

Ford completely redesigned its intermediates in 1970, and the Torino's shape was now sleek with curved fender contours. The full-width grille had

This page: The 1964 Thunderbolt was the ultimate factory Ford drag car. It drew air into the carburetors through the holes vacated by the high beam headlights, vented air through the teardrop scoop on the fiberglass hood, and got its motivation from a specially prepared 427 high-rise engine.

two headlights per side, and hideaway headlights were optional. The SportsRoof, which Ford claimed was "shaped by the wind," was the fastback model, though in actuality it was less slippery than the 1968–1969 version. (In NASCAR, the Mercury Cyclone, which came with only a standard, nonSportsRoof, was far more successful in racing.)

For this year, the Torino name was becoming more and more prominent, with the Fairlane name relegated to the lower trim levels and rarely used in advertising. The Torino was now the intermediate trim–level Fairlane, with the Torino GT as the sport model and the Cobra as the muscle car. The GT included twin sport mirrors, a hood scoop, 15-inch (38cm) wheels, and a 351 2-barrel V8 among its standard equipment.

The Cobra took this a step forward. Standard was the new 429 Thunder Jet with 10.5:1 compression, a single 4-barrel carburetor, and 360 horsepower. This was the first time a Cobra Jet engine was not standard in the Cobra, though the carburetor-mounted Shaker hood scoop was standard. Optional was the 429 Cobra Jet (370 horsepower with a Rochester 4-barrel) or the Super Cobra Jet (375 horsepower with a Holley 4-barrel) with or without the ram air. The VIN distinguishes between flat hood and ram air, however, there was no VIN to indicate the SCJ option, so technically, the SCJ is not considered a different engine.

The Torino's 429 Cobra Jet was based on the new 385-series Ford engine, whereas the 428 Cobra Jet from the year before sprung from FE roots. The

429 used canted valves, which allows the use of larger valves (among other bonuses). Standard on both the 429 CJ and SCJ were large ports, screw-in rocker studs, and pushrod guide plates. The Cobra Jet got a hydraulic-lifter cam, while the SCJ employed a mechanical stick. Both engines used the same-size valves and the same intake, but the CJ used a Rochester 4-barrel while the SCJ had a Holley. Compression was 11.3:1, and the SCJ option included an external oil cooler (needed because all SCJs came with the 3.91 or 4.30 gears). Cars equipped with the SCJ engine were equipped with Ford's Competition suspension setup for improved cornering. These cars were capable of high-13-second elapsed times at about 101–102 mph (162.5–164kph) in the quarter mile.

The same basic lineup returned for 1971, although the optional 351-Cleveland was downgraded to 285 horsepower (it had 300 horsepower in '70). The Cobra got some rather gaudy trim, including a blacked-out taillight panel, iridescent strobe stripes, and rear window louvers, although the latter two were extra-cost options.

This was the last year for the good engines from Ford. The big-blocks hung around a little longer, but without the good cams, high compression, and big carburetors.

Two Percent cars, Two Percenters

See *Altered Wheelbase Mopars*.

Opposite, Top, Middle & Bottom: This is a rarity—a 1971 Ford Torino Brogham complete with factory brocade interior and powered by a ram air 429 Super Cobra Jet engine.

Below: Ford added wild iridescent tape stripes to the Torino in 1970. This is a Cobra model with the ram air Cobra Jet engine.

This page: Some consider the 1961 Ventura to be the most beautiful Pontiac ever. This one has a 421, a 4-speed, and the optional 8-lug aluminum wheels.

Ventura

Back when Pontiac was openly supporting racing and its 389 and 421 engines were winning, the Ventura was one of the best cars to own. At the dawn of the muscle car era, in 1960, the Ventura was available with Pontiac's 333- and 348-horsepower 389s. The Ventura nameplate disappeared after the 1961 model year, although the Ventura name would soldier on as a trim option. The Ventura was replaced in the '70s by Pontiac's version of the compact Nova, but it was hardly a muscle car by then—even when equipped with the GTO option.

W-30

See *Oldsmobile 4-4-2*.

W-31 (RamRod)

While the Olds 4-4-2 could be ordered as a fire-breathing muscle machine, which turned on the kids, its performance and reputation turned off a lot of insurance companies. For those who didn't need 400-cubic-inch engines and were still interested in performance, in 1968 Oldsmobile created the RamRod 350, which would later become known as the W-31 package for the intermediate Cutlass.

In reality, the W-31 was not its own model; rather, it was (like the original GTO and 4-4-2) an option group consisting of a unique engine and specially tuned suspension. The engine was a true surprise. Starting with the low-block Olds 350 V8 (and small-port 350 heads), engineers added larger intake valves and a long-duration (308-degree) cam with 0.470-inch (12mm) lift and different valve springs. An aluminum intake manifold took some of the weight off the nose.

Feeding the single 4-barrel carb was the under-the-bumper ram air setup used on the mighty W-30 cars. Remarkably, the car revved above 6000 rpm without floating the valves with a hydraulic camshaft. It produced excellent horsepower per cubic inch, 325 total ponies at 5400 rpm and 360 lbs.-ft. of torque at 3600. Part of the package included a high-stall-speed torque converter if you ordered the automatic. A set of 3.91:1 cogs were also part of the purchase price. If there was a downside, it was that the long-duration cam didn't give enough vacuum, so power brakes could not be ordered.

The only external identification that first year was a small RamRod 350 logo decal on the front fenders, composed of a set of V-shaped pistons on connecting rods. It was barely the size of the side marker lights, making the W-31 RamRod a true sleeper. *Car Life* put one through its paces that year and found an inexpensive car that could run 14.9 seconds in the quarter mile at a remarkable 96 mph (154.5kph)—all for just $205 more than the price of a base Cutlass.

The RamRod engine continued until 1971, when it was replaced by a low-compression 455.

W-32

In 1969, when you ordered an Oldsmobile 4-4-2, the engine you received had a different camshaft, depending on whether you ordered a manual or automatic transmission. The 400 with a 4-speed was rated at 350 horsepower, while the automatic had 325. The W-32 changed that. It gave you the stick shift engine/cam combination with the automatic transmission. Further, the package included the W-30's under-the-bumper ram air induction system (but without the W-30's red inner fenders). The W-32 package was very rare in 1969.

Oldsmobile offered the W-32 option again in 1970, but not on the 4-4-2. In fact, the W-32 package was not necessarily the successor to the '69 version sharing the same code. Surprisingly, the W-32 was available only on the Cutlass SX model, which was not ordinarily considered a muscle car. The other major difference was that the ram induction setup no longer took its air from under the bumper. For 1970, Olds went with a more conventional (though less effective) functional twin-scooped hood.

Jim Wangers

P.T. Barnum had nothing on Jim Wangers. An executive for Pontiac's advertising agency at the start of the muscle car era, Wangers was one part carnival barker and one part drag racer, as well as an excellent copywriter.

Wangers worked at MacManus, John & Adams in 1958 on the Pontiac account. This was about the same time that Pontiac was transforming itself from a stuffy, conservative car division into the Wide-Track division, one steeped in racing and excitement on the street.

But Wangers was more than just a huckster. He was an accomplished drag racer—that's Wangers behind the wheel of Royal Pontiac's 1963 Swiss Cheese Catalina in the photo below—who brought Pontiac tons of good ink by winning Top Stock class honors in a Catalina at the U.S. Nationals in 1960. When the GTO came out in the fall of 1963, Wangers did everything in his power to promote the car, from placing it on TV shows to a GTO shoe promotion with Thom McAn and, of course, ads that were guaranteed to get the blood boiling in anyone under the age of thirty.

Perhaps Wangers' most enduring contribution to the success of the GTO, aside from his stirring ad copy and beautiful dealer brochures, was ensuring that all GTOs that were to be tested by the media were blazingly fast. Most were tuned by Royal Pontiac of Royal Oak, Michigan, which meant they got the Royal Bobcat treatment for added power. Wangers was also responsible for helping the legendary Hurst shifter become standard equipment on every stick shift GTO sold.

Today, Wangers owns his own automotive consulting firm and a magazine called *Pontiac Enthusiast*.

Right: One of the rarest of all—a 1968 Yenko 427 Camaro. The wheels are Pontiac Rally IIs with Yenko emblems on the center caps.

Below: For a budget supercar, Yenko created the Deuce, a 1970 Nova powered by a 360-horse Camaro Z/28 350. To an insurance agent, it appeared to be just another economy car.

Yenko Chevrolet

Located in Canonsburg, Pennsylvania, Yenko Chevrolet was the preeminent high-performance Chevrolet car dealer in the country. Owner Don Yenko got his start building the Corvair Stinger, a car designed to go road racing (which it did quite successfully). Yenko used the Central Office Production Order (COPO) to specially order the cars, which allowed him to spec them out differently than standard production options would allow (see *COPO* for complete details).

His program was so far-reaching that by 1970 there was a network of dealerships involved in selling Yenko Sports Cars: Dale Chevrolet in Waulkesha, Wisconsin; Broadway Chevrolet in Green Bay, Wisconsin; Lou Bachrodt Chevrolet in Rockford, Illinois; Fend-Tufo Chevrolet in Glendale Heights, Illinois; Sokensen Chevrolet in Waukegan, Illinois; and Mancuso Chevrolet in Skokie, Illinois.

By 1967, the muscle car movement was going full bore, and when Chevrolet introduced the Camaro without a 427 engine option, Yenko saw the opportunity to build conversion cars. A total of fifty-four 425-horsepower 427 Camaros were assembled that first year, a pretty high number considering the retail price and work involved.

In fact, it became apparent that he would need some factory support to continue the program. Using his connections at Chevrolet (GM president Ed Cole was a personal friend of Yenko's father), Yenko had the factory build his L72 Camaros in '68; the condition was that he had to keep it a

Top: In 1968, Yenko Camaro offered an optional wheel.

Above: Also offered was Yenko Deuce identification, seen here on a 1970 Nova.

Left: The 425-horsepower 427 of a 1968 Yenko Camaro is highly prized.

This page: A 1969 Yenko Nova fitted with a 427 engine was more than most insurance companies would handle.

secret. Ergo, the cars were said to be converted by Yenko's technicians. The engines had a special code so that they could be tracked during servicing—the idea being to see if it could be a viable regular production option or something that should be done on a limited basis. The '68 cars wore Pontiac Rally II rims, special hoods, and heavy-duty suspensions. Supposedly seventy-one L72 engines were shipped to the Norwood, Ohio, assembly plant, but the number of cars built is usually quoted at sixty-eight.

Thanks to the success of the 1968 program, COPO numbers 9561 and 9562 were born. The former was the number used to order L72 427 Camaros in 1969, the latter L72 427 Chevelles. Both were low-13-/high-12-second cars in the quarter mile, even on the mediocre street tires of the era. Yenko ordered the cars and added special striping on the hoods and sides (many came with the Z/28's front and rear spoilers). He called these cars Yenko Super Cars, and they even came with *sYc* emblazoned on the headrests. The retail was $4,295 for either the M22 "rock crusher" 4-speed or Turbo 400 automatic.

Super Stock & Drag Illustrated had the opportunity to put a Yenko Super Car through its paces in its July 1969 issue. For the test, the car's Doug Thorley headers were fully opened, and it was fitted with 8-inch (20.5cm) -wide M&H drag slicks. With 4.10 gears, the car rolled to a best of 11.94 seconds in the quarter mile at 114.5 mph (184kph).

There is some controversy surrounding the number of COPO cars Yenko built in 1967. The numbers most commonly quoted have been 201 and 199, but most recently sources believe it could be 221. Jim Mattison, who worked for General Motors at the time, remembers it quite differently. He recalls seeing paperwork for 500 or so Yenko COPO Camaros that year, but there is nothing to back up this claim.

The Chevelles were equally deadly. While they were hampered by extra weight (there was more weight over the rear wheels), the exhausts were probably less restrictive. It is believed some 323 COPO Chevelles left the Baltimore assembly plant in 1969, and 99 of them went to Canonsburg, Pennsylvania.

While the COPO Chevelles were deadly in a metaphoric sense, the 427 Novas built by Yenko could be that way in a literal sense. Overpowered and lightweight, they had the same powerplants as the Camaros and Chevelles. So potentially lethal were the Yenko-built 427 Novas that many insurance companies refused to write policies for them.

This convinced Yenko to come up with one of his best packages yet—the Yenko Deuce of 1970. Using the tried-and-true COPO format (number 9010), Yenko sold 176 LT-1 350-powered Novas (two other COPO LT-1 Novas went to Canada). The LT-1 was a 360-horsepower small-block whose only applications were the Camaro Z/28 and Corvette (in which it was rated with 10 more horsepower). It had the best goodies ever offered on a small-block—solid-lifter camshaft, free-flowing cylinder heads, 11.0:1 compression, and a large Holley 4-barrel. Peak power came in at 6000 rpm, and there were 380 lbs.-ft. of torque at 4000. An M-21 4-speed was standard, but an automatic was optional and fitted with a Hurst Auto Stick 1 shifter.

The Yenko Deuces had the other good stuff as well—F41 heavy-duty suspension, 4.10:1 gears in a 12-bolt Positraction rear, and front disc brakes. Inside, they were strippers with vinyl bench seats, roll-up windows, and rubber floor mats instead of carpeting, although aftermarket gauges were optional (Stewart-Warner early in the year, Rac later). A bright silver Yenko sticker from 3M was affixed to the doors.

The optional tachometer on the 1969 Yenko Nova maxes out at 8000 rpms.

All cars came with a special black hood-mounted tachometer. The exteriors were spruced up with wild stripes incorporating the Yenko Deuce name on the rear fenders and "LT/1" decals on the hood. Yenko replaced the stock 14×7-inch (35.5×18cm) steel rims and replaced them with 5-spoke Super Sport wheels, minus the stainless trim rings. A set of flush-fit, twin rear spoilers was listed as an option in the brochure, but it never made production. A hood scoop that incorporated this tach was planned as well, but it too was stillborn.

The Deuce lasted just one year.

With Chevrolet selling 454 Chevelles in 1970 and the muscle car market thinning out, Yenko turned down the heat. In '71, the dealership produced some 400-cubic-inch stroked small-block Camaros, and there were flirtations with turbocharged Vegas. The last truly interesting Yenko car came in 1981, when he marketed the special Yenko Turbo Z.

As the name implies, this was a turbocharged Z/28 Camaro. It came in two levels, Stage 1 and Stage 2. The engine was the same in both, but the latter came with Koni shocks, different stabilizer bars, aftermarket aluminum wheels, and Goodyear Wingfoot tires. Supposedly, they were good for 13-second quarter-mile times.

There is still plenty of mystery surrounding the cars built and sold by Yenko Chevrolet. Unfortunately, Don Yenko died in a private-plane crash on March 5, 1987, and he took the answers to many questions with him that day.

Appendix

Production Numbers for American Muscle Cars, 1960–1974

Following is the definitive list of high-performance cars and engines manufactured during the American muscle car era (1960–1974). The cars for American Motors Corporation, Buick, Chevrolet, Dodge, Ford, Mercury, Oldsmobile, Plymouth, Pontiac, and Shelby are listed in chronological order and in sequence from base model to specialty model. The production numbers have been divided by body style and engine type. In some instances, the production numbers by body style will include domestic and foreign production. In all instances, only high-performance engines are listed (excluding economy engines), so the body production numbers may not add up to the engine production totals. A single asterisk (*) next to a production number reflects a combined production figure for a respective engine. (For example, in 1969, there were 9,440 Mustang fastbacks with the 390 engine. This number includes standard fastbacks, the GT fastbacks, and the Mach I.) Please note that all horsepower ratings after 1971 are net, not gross.

While every effort has been made to establish the correct the numbers in these categories, not all production figures were available because of inadequate company records and conflicting sources.

American Motors Corporation

Year	Model/*Optional Engine Package*	Body Style	Production Number by Body Style	Engine (cid/hp)	Engine Code	Production Number by Engine
1967	American	all		343/280	Z	
1968	Javelin	coupe	29,097	343/280	Z	2,524
				390/315	W	12
	Javelin SST	coupe	26,027	343/280	Z	8,954
				390/315	W	871
	AMX	coupe	6,725	290/225	N	1,009
				343/280	Z	1,317
				390/315	W	4,399
1969	Javelin	coupe	17,389	343/280	Z	957
				390/315	W	53
	Javelin SST	coupe	23,286	343/280	Z	4,480
				390/315	W	4,099
	AMX	coupe	8,293	290/225	N	918
				343/280	Z	1,572
				390/315	W	5,803
	SS/AMX	coupe	53	390/340	Y	53
	SC/Rambler	hardtop	1,512	390/315	W	1,512
1970	Javelin and SST	coupe	28,210	360/290	P	n/a
				390/325	X	n/a
	Mark Donahue	coupe	2,501	360/290	P	n/a
				390/325	X	n/a
	Trans Am	coupe	100 est.	390/325	X	100 est.
	AMX	coupe	4,116	360/290	P	1,583
				390/325	X	2,533
	Rebel Machine	hardtop	2,326	390/340	Y	2,326
1971	Javelin and SST	coupe	24,812	360/290	P	n/a
				401/330	Z	n/a
	Javelin AMX	coupe	2,054	360/290	P	n/a
				401/330	Z	n/a
1972	Javelin SST	coupe	22,964	360/220	P	n/a
				401/255	Z	n/a
	Javelin AMX	coupe	3,220	360/220	P	n/a
				401/255	Z	n/a
1973	Javelin	coupe	25,195	360/220	P	n/a
				401/255	Z	n/a
	Javelin AMX	coupe	5,707	360/220	P	n/a
				401/255	Z	n/a
1974	Javelin	coupe	22,556	360/220	P	n/a
				401/235	Z	n/a
	Javelin AMX	coupe	4,980	360/220	P	n/a
				401/235	Z	n/a

Buick

Year	Model/*Optional Engine Package*	Body Style	Production Number by Body Style	Engine (cid/hp)	Engine Code	Production Num by Engine
1965	Skylark Gran Sport	coupe	2,282	401/325		2,282
		hardtop	11,351	401/325		11,351
		convertible	2,147	401/325		2,147
	Riviera Gran Sport	hardtop	3,354	425/360		3,354
1966	Skylark Gran Sport	coupe	1,835	401/325		1,835
		hardtop	9,934	401/325		9,934
		convertible	2,047	401/325		2,047
	Riviera Gran Sport	hardtop	5,718	425/360		179
	Wildcat Gran Sport	hardtop	164	all 425s		n/a
		(Custom)	852			n/a
		convertible	41	all 425s		n/a
		(Custom)	198			
1967	GS 340	hardtop	3,692	340/260		3,692
	California GS	coupe	1,577	340/260		1,577
	GS 400	coupe	1,014	400/340		1,014
		hardtop	10,659	400/340		10,659
		convertible	2,140	400/340		2,140
1968	GS 350	hardtop	8,317	350/280		8,317
	GS California	coupe	4,831	350/280		4,831
	GS 400	hardtop	10,743	400/340		10,743
		convertible	2,454	400/340		2,454
1969	GS 350	hardtop	6,305	350/280		6,305
	GS California	coupe	3,574	350/280		3,574
	GS 400	hardtop	7,602	400/340		6,346
	Stage I			400/345		1,256
		convertible	1,776	400/340		1,564
	Stage I			400/345		212
1970	GS 350	hardtop	9,948	350/315		9,948
	GS 455	hardtop	8,054	455/350		5,589
	Stage I			455/360		2,465
		convertible	1,416	455/350		1,184
	Stage I			455/360		232
	GSX	hardtop	678	455/350		278
	Stage I			455/360		400
1971	GS	hardtop	8,268	350/260		5,986
				455/315		1,481
	Stage I			455/345		801
		convertible	902	350/260		656
				455/315		165
	Stage I			455/345		81
	GSX	hardtop	124	350/260		n/a
				455/315		n/a
	Stage I			455/345		n/a
1972	GS	hardtop	7,723	350/195	K	5,896
				455/225	U	1,099
	Stage I			455/270	V	728
		convertible	852	350/195	K	645
				455/225	U	126
	Stage I			455/270	V	81
	GSX	hardtop	44	350/195	K	n/a
				455/225	U	n/a
	Stage I			455/270	V	n/a
1973	Century Gran Sport	coupe	6,637	455/225	U	979
	Stage I			455/270	V	728
1974	Century Gran Sport	coupe	3,355	455	U	438
	Stage I			455	V	478

Chevrolet

Year	Model/*Optional Engine Package*	Body Style	Production Number by Body Style	Engine (cid/hp)	Engine Code	Production Number by Engine
1961	all			348/340		n/a
				348/350		n/a
				409/360		142
	Impala SS	hardtop and convertible	456	n/a		n/a
1962	full-size	all		327/300		n/a
				409/380		15,019*
				409/409		15,019*
1963	full-size	all		327/300		n/a
				409/340		16,902*
				409/400		16,902*
				409/425		16,902*
		Z11	57	427/430		57
1964	full-size	all		327/300		50,150
				409/340		5,640
				409/400		3,044
				409/425		1,997
	Chevelle	all		327/300		n/a
1965	full-size	all		409/340		2,086
				409/400		742
				396/425		1,838
	Chevelle	all		327/350		6,021*
	SS396 Z16	hardtop	201	396/375		201
	El Camino	pickup	27,965	327/350		6,021*
1966	full-size	all		427/390		3,287
				427/425		1,856
	Chevelle SS 396	hardtop	66,843	396/325		44,362*
				396/360		24,811*
				396/375		3,099*
		convertible	5,429	396/325		44,362*
				396/360		24,811*
				396/375		3,099*
	El Camino	pickup	30,234	396/325		44,362*
				396/360		24,811*
				396/375		3,099*
	Nova/*L79*	all		327/350		5,481*
1967	full-size	all		427/385		2,213*
	Impala SS 427	hardtop	2,124	427/385		2,124*
		convertible	2,124	427/385		2,124*
	Chevelle SS 396	hardtop	59,685	396/325		45,218*
				396/350		17,176*
				396/375		612*
		convertible	3,321	396/325		45,218*
				396/350		17,176*
				396/375		612*
	all Chevelle exc. SS	all		327/325		4,048*
	El Camino	pickup	30,769	327/325		4,048*
				396/325		45,218*
				396/350		17,176*
				396/375		612*
	Nova	all		327/325		6 est.
	Camaro SS	hardtop and convertible	34,411	350/295		29,270
				396/325		4,003
				396/375		1,138
	Camaro Z/28	hardtop	602	302/290		602
	Camaro SS/RS pace car	convertible	200 est.	350/295		n/a
				396/325		n/a
				396/375		n/a
	Yenko Camaro	hardtop	54 est.	427/450		54 est.
1968	Impala	all		427/385		4,071*
				427/425		568*
	Impala SS 427	hardtop, coupe, and covertible	1,778	427/385		4,071*
				427/425		568*
	Chevelle SS 396	hardtop	55,309	396/325		45,553*
				396/350		12,481*
				396/375		4,751*
	L89 aluminum heads			396/375		n/a
		convertible	2,286	396/325		45,553*
				396/350		12,481*
				396/375		4,751*
	L89 aluminum heads			396/375		n/a
	all Chevelle L79 exc. SS	all		327/325		4,082*
	El Camino SS	pickup	5,190	396/325		45,553*
				396/350		12,481*
				396/375		4,751*
	El Camino		32,772	327/325		4,082*
	Nova L79 exc. SS	coupe		327/325		1,274
	Nova SS	coupe	5,571	350/295		4,670
				396/350		234
				396/375		667
	Camaro SS	hardtop and convertible	30,695	350/295		12,496
				396/325		10,773
				396/350		2,579
				396/375		4,575
				396/375		272
	Camaro Z/28	hardtop	7,199	302/290		7,199
		convertible	1	302/290		1
	Yenko Camaro	hardtop	65	427/450		65
1969	full-size	all		427/390		5,582*
				427/425		546*
	Impala SS 427	hardtop, coupe, and covertible	2,455	427/390		5,582*
				427/425		546*
	Chevelle SS 396	hardtop, coupe, and covertible	87,030	396/325		59,786
				396/350		17,358
				396/375		9,486
	L89 aluminum heads			396/375		400*
	Chevelle COPO	hardtop		427/425		323 est.
	El Camino SS	pickup		396/325		59,786*
				396/350		17,358*
				396/375		9,486*
				396/375		400*
	Nova SS	coupe	17,564	350/300		10,355
				396/350		1,947

Chevrolet (continued)

Year	Model/*Optional Engine Package*	Body Style	Production Number by Body Style	Engine (cid/hp)	Engine Code	Production Number by Engine
				396/375		4,951
	L89 aluminum heads			396/375		311 est.
	Yenko Nova	coupe		396/375		9
				396/425		28
	Camaro SS	hardtop and convertible	34,932	350/300		22,339*
				396/325		6,752*
				396/350		2,018*
				396/375		4,889*
	L89 aluminum heads			396/375		311*
	Camaro Z/28	hardtop	20,302	302/290		20,302
	Camaro SS/RS	convertible	3,675	350/300		22,339*
	Pace Car			396/325		6,752*
				396/350		2,018*
				396/375		4,889*
	L89 aluminum heads			396/375		311*
	Camaro COPO/L72	hardtop		427/425		500-1000 est.
	ZL1			427/430		69
	Yenko Camaro	hardtop		427/425		221 est.
1970	Chevelle SS	hardtop, convertible, and El Camino	62,372	402/350		51,437
				402/375		2,144
				454/360		4,298
				454/450		4,475
	L89 aluminum heads			454/450		18
	all Chevelle exc. SS	all		402/330		9,338*
	Monte Carlo	hardtop	142,152	402/330		9,338*
	Monte Carlo SS 454	hardtop	3,823	454/360		3,823
				454/450		0 est.
	Nova SS	coupe	19,558	350/300		13,991
				402/350		1,802
				402/375		3,765
	COPO Nova	coupe		350/360		2
	Yenko Nova		175	350/360		175
	Camaro SS	hardtop	12,476	350/300		10,012
				402/350		1,864
				402/375		600
	Camaro Z/28	hardtop	8,733	350/360		8,733
1971	Chevelle and SS	hardtop and convertible		402/300		17,656*
	Chevelle SS 454	hardtop and convertible	9,502	454/365		9,502
	El Camino and SS	pickup		402/300		17,656*
	El Camino SS 454	pickup		454/365		9,502
	Heavy Chevy	hardtop	6,727	402/300		17,656*
	Monte Carlo SS454	hardtop	1,919	454/365		1,919
	Nova SS		7,016	350/270		7,016
	Camaro SS	hardtop	8,377	350/270		6,844
				402/300		1,533
	Camaro Z/28	hardtop	4,862	350/330		4,862
1972	Chevelle and SS	hardtop and convertible		402/240		20,031*
	Chevelle SS 454	hardtop and convertible	5,333	454/270		5,333*
	El Camino and SS	pickup		402/240		20,031*
	El Camino SS 454	pickup		454/270		5,333*
	Heavy Chevy	hardtop	9,508	402/240		20,031*
	Camaro SS		6,526	350/200		5,556
				402/270		970
	Camaro Z/28		2,575	350/255		2,575
1973	Chevelle SS	coupe	28,647	454/245		22,528†
	El Camino		28,647	454/245		n/a
	Camaro Z/28	hardtop	11,574	350/245		11,574

* Combined production number includes the total number of engines regardless of body styles for that year.

† This is an engine total for all Chevelles for 1973.

Dodge

Year	Model/*Optional Engine Package*	Body Style	Production Number by Body Style	Engine (cid/hp)	Engine Code	Production Number by Engine
1961	all	all		383/330		n/a
				383/340		n/a
				413/350		n/a
				413/375		n/a
1962	all	all		383/343		n/a
				413/380		n/a
	Max Wedge			413/410		n/a
	Max Wedge			413/420		n/a
1963	all	all		383/343		n/a
	Max Wedge			426/415		n/a
	Max Wedge			426/425		n/a
1964	all	all		426/365		n/a
	Max Wedge			426/415		n/a
				426/425		n/a
	Hemi			426/415		n/a
	Hemi			426/425		n/a
1965	Coronet	sedan	n/a	383/325		33
				426/365		16
	Coronet Deluxe	sedan	13,252	383/325		239
				426/365		175
	Coronet 440	hardtop	27,714	383/325		1,765
				426/365		585
		convertible	2,786	383/325		137
				426/365		31
	Coronet 500	hardtop	29,577	383/325		4,704
				426/365		1,169
		convertible	3,168	383/325		474
				426/365		124
	Coronet S/S	sedan	101	426/425		101
	full-size	all	n/a	426/365		n/a
1966	Coronet	sedan	n/a	383/325	G	38
				426/425	H	34

Year	Model/*Optional Engine Package*	Body Style	Production Number by Body Style	Engine (cid/hp)	Engine Code	Production Number by Engine
		4-door sedan	1,753	426/425	H	2
	Coronet Deluxe	sedan	12,751	383/325	G	92
				426/425	H	49
	Coronet 440	hardtop	42,822	383/325	G	2,976
				426/425	H	288
		convertible	3,493	383/325	G	192
				426/425	H	5
	Coronet 500	hardtop	42,512	383/325	G	7,298
				426/425	H	339
		convertible	3,626	383/325	G	640
				426/425	H	21
	Charger	fastback	37,344	383/325	G	12,328
				426/425	H	468
	Dart	all exc wagons	29,777	273/235	D	163
	Dart 270	all exc wagons	n/a	273/235	D	431
	Dart GT	hardtop and convertible	n/a	273/235	D	2,856
	"D-Dart"	hardtop	n/a	273/275	D	n/a
1967	Coronet Deluxe	all exc wagons	n/a	383/325	H	370
				426/425	J	n/a
	Coronet 440	hardtop	38,551	383/325	H	1,678
				426/425	J	n/a
	Coronet 440 "WO23"			426/425	J	55
		convertible	1,982	383/325	H	1,678
				426/425	J	n/a
	Coronet 500	hardtop	30,328	383/325	H	3,268
				426/425	J	n/a
		convertible	2,252	383/325	H	3,268
				426/425	J	n/a
	Coronet R/T	hardtop	10,109	440/375	L	9,826
				426/425	J	283
		convertible	628	440/375	L	9,826
				426/425	J	283
	Charger	fastback	15,788	383/325	H	4,840
				440/375	L	660
				426/425	J	117
	Dart	all	n/a	273/235	E	91
	Dart 270	all	n/a	273/235	E	764
	Dart GT	hardtop	34,496	273/235	E	2,645
		convertible	3,729	273/235	E	2,645
	Dart GTS	hardtop	34,496	383/280	H	457
		convertible	3,729	383/280	H	457
1968	Coronet Deluxe	coupe	21,587	383/330	H	n/a
	Super Bee	coupe	7,841 US	383/335	H	7,716
				426/425	J	125
	Coronet 440	coupe	n/a	383/330	H	72
				426/425	J	2
		hardtop	49,760	383/330	H	1,201
	Coronet 500	hardtop	21,179	383/330	H	2,736
		convertible	2,527	383/330	H	343
	Coronet R/T	hardtop	10,280	440/375	L	9,734
				426/425	J	219
		convertible	569	440/375	L	519
				426/425	J	9
	Charger	hardtop	74,886	383/330	H	19,013
	Charger R/T	hardtop	17,584	440/375	L	17,109
				426/425	J	475
	Dart GTS	hardtop	8,295	340/275	P	5,513
				383/300	H	2,112
	Mr. Norm's GSS			440/375	M	48
	Hurst Hemi Dart	Race Hemi			M	80
		convertible	450	340/275		315
				383/300	H	80
1969	Coronet Deluxe	coupe	6,185	383/330	H	9
	Super Bee	coupe	8,202	383/335	H	7,122
				440/390	M	420
				426/425	J	91
		hardtop	19,644	383/335	H	16,709
				440/390	M	1,487
				426/425	J	165
	Coronet 440	coupe	2,886	383/330	H	26
		hardtop	42,937	383/330	H	605
	Coronet 500	hardtop	18,308	383/330	H	2,027
		convertible	1,944	383/330	H	246
	Coronet R/T	hardtop	6,755	440/375	L	6,351
				426/425	J	97
		convertible	483	440/375	L	416
				426/425	J	10
	Charger	hardtop	69,142	383/330	H	17,308
	Charger R/T	hardtop	20,057	440/375	L	18,344
				426/425	J	432
	Charger 500	fasttop	580	440/375	L	n/a
				426/425	J	100 est.
	Charger Daytona	fasttop	503	440/375	L	433
				426/425	J	70
	Dart Swinger 340	hardtop	n/a	340/275	P	16,637
	Dart GTS	hardtop	6,285	340/275	P	3,645
				383/330	H	1,272
				440/375	M	640
		convertible	417	340/275	P	272
				383/330	H	73
1970	Coronet Deluxe	coupe	2,978	383/330	N	13
	Super Bee	coupe	3,966	383/335	N	3,431
				440/390	V	196
				426/425	R	4
		hardtop	11,540	383/335	N	9,404
				440/390	V	1,072
				426/425	R	32
	Coronet 440	coupe	1,236	383/330	N	19
		hardtop	24,341	383/330	N	355
	Coronet 500	hardtop	8,247	383/330	N	689
		convertible	924	383/330	N	93

Dodge (continued)

Year	Model/*Optional Engine Package*	Body Style	Production Number by Body Style	Engine (cid/hp)	Engine Code	Production Number by Engine
	Coronet R/T	hardtop	2,319	440/375	U	1,948
				440/390	V	194
				426/425	R	13
		convertible	296	440/375	U	219
				440/390	V	16
				426/425	R	1
	Charger	hardtop	n/a	383/330	N	996
	Charger 500	hardtop	n/a	383/330	N	7,027
				426/425	R	1 known
	Charger R/T	hardtop	10,337	440/375	U	8,574
				440/390	V	684
				426/425	R	112
	Dart Swinger 340	hardtop	13,781	340/275	H	10,382
	Challenger Deputy	coupe	n/a	383/330	N	6
	Challenger (including Deputy)	hardtop	53,337	340/275	H	6,933
				383/330	N	1,480
		convertible	3,173	340/275	H	264
				383/330	N	122
	Challenger SE	hardtop	6,584	383/330	N	814
	Challenger R/T	hardtop	14,889	383/335	N	8,939
				440/375	U	2,802
				440/390	V	1,640
				426/425	R	287
		convertible	1,070	383/335	N	684
				440/375	U	163
				440/390	V	99
				426/425	R	9
	Challenger R/T-SE	hardtop	3,979	383/335	N	2,506
				440/375	U	875
				440/390	V	296
				426/425	R	59
	Challenger T/A	hardtop	2,400	340/290	J	2,400
1971	Charger	hardtop	46,183	383/300	N	625
	Charger 500	hardtop	11,948	383/300	N	1,615
	Charger SE	hardtop	15,811	383/300	N	3,962
				440/370	U	616
	Charger Super Bee	hardtop	5,054	383/300	N	3,858
				340/275	H	320
				440/370	U	26
				440/385	V	99
				426/425	R	22
	Charger R/T	hardtop	3,118	440/370	U	2,504
				440/385	V	178
				426/425	R	63
	Dart Swinger 340	hardtop		340/275	H	50 est.††
	Demon 340	coupe	10,089	340/275	H	7,981
	Challenger	coupe	n/a	383/300	N	16
		hardtop and coupe	23,088	340/275	H	1,226*
				383/300	N	520
		convertible	2,165	340/275	H	1,226*
				383/300	N	167
	Challenger R/T	hardtop	4,630	383/300	N	2,509
				340/275	H	1,078
				440/385	V	246
				426/425	R	70
1972	Charger	coupe	7,803	340/240	H	163
				400/255	P	95
				440/280	U	39
				440/330	V	n/a
	Charger	hardtop	45,361	340/240	H	1,364
				400/255	P	2,025
				440/280	U	785
				440/330	V	n/a
	Charger SE	hardtop	22,430	400/255	P	3,082
				440/280	U	755
	Charger Rallye	coupe	460	all		n/a
		hardtop	3,431	all		n/a
	Demon 340	coupe	10,222	340/240	H	10,222
	Challenger	hardtop	18,535	340/240	H	1,267
	Challenger Rallye	hardtop	8,128	340/240	H	5,012
1973	Charger	coupe	11,995	340/240	H	394
				400/260	P	111
				440/280	U	26
	Charger	hardtop	45,415	340/240	H	2,811
				400/260	P	2,020
				440/280	U	713
	Charger SE	hardtop	61,908	400/260	P	6,940
				440/280	U	1,627
	Charger Rallye	coupe	985	all		n/a
		hardtop	6,019	all		n/a
	Dart Sport 340	coupe	11,315	340/240	H	11,315
	Challenger	hardtop	32,596	340/240	H	8,435
	Challenger Rallye	hardtop	n/a	340/240	H	n/a
1974	Charger	coupe	8,876	360/245	J	13
				400/250	P	25
				440/275	U	14
	Charger	hardtop	29,101	360/245	J	165
				400/250	P	520
				440/275	U	208
	Charger SE	hardtop	36,399	400/250	P	2,376
				440/275	U	834
	Charger Rallye	coupe	336	all		n/a
		hardtop	105	all		n/a
	Dart Sport 360	coupe	3,314	360/245	J	3,314
	Challenger	hardtop	16,437	360/245	J	n/a
	Challenger Rallye	hardtop	n/a	360/245	J	n/a

* Combined production number includes the total number of engines regardless of body styles for that year.

†† Available in Canada only.

Ford

Year	Model/*Optional Engine Package*	Body Style	Production Number by Body Style	Engine (cid/hp)	Engine Code	Production Number by Engine
1960	full-size	all		352/360	R	n/a
1961	full-size	all		390/375	Q	n/a
				390/401	Z	n/a
1962	full-size	all		390/330	P	n/a
				390/375	Q	n/a
				406/385	B	n/a
				406/405	G	n/a
		lightweight	10	406		10
1963	full-size			390/330	P	n/a
				406/385	B	n/a
				406/405	G	n/a
				427/410	Q	n/a
				427/425	R	n/a
		lightweight		427		50
	Fairlane	all		289/271	K	n/a
1964	full-size	all		390/330	P	n/a
				427/410	Q	n/a
				427/425	R	n/a
		lightweight		427		n/a
	Fairlane	all		289/271	K	n/a
		Thunderbolt	100	427/425	R	100
	Mustang	hardtop and convertible	121,538	289/271	K	n/a
1965	full-size	all		390/330	P	n/a
				427/410	Q	n/a
				427/425	R	n/a
	Fairlane			289/271	K	n/a
	Mustang and GT	all	559,451	289/271	K	n/a
1966	full-size	all		427/410	W	180*
				427/425	R	180*
	7-Litre	hardtop	8,705	428/345	Q	8,669
				427/425	R	36
		convertible	2,368	428/345	Q	2,366
				427/425	R	2
	Fairlane 500	hardtop	75,947	427/425	R	57
	Fairlane GT	hardtop	33,015	390/335	S	33,015
	and GT/A	convertible	4,327	390/335	S	4,327
	Mustang and GT	all	607,568	289/271	K	n/a
1967	full-size	all but 7-Litre		427/410	W	77 est.*
				427/425	R	77 est.*
	7-Litre	hardtop	813	428/345	Q	803
				427/410	W	2
				427/425	R	8
		convertible	255	428/345	Q	253
				427/410	W	0
				427/425	R	2
	Fairlane	sedan	10,628	427/410	W	1
				427/425	R	35
	Fairlane 500	coupe	8,473	427/410	W	1
				427/425	R	10
		hardtop	70,135	427/410	W	11
				427/425	R	92
	Fairlane 500XL		14,871	427/410	W	7
				427/425	R	72
	Fairlane GT	hardtop	18,670	390/320	S	18,670
		convertible	2,117	390/320	S	2,117
	Mustang	hardtop	356,324	289/271	K	120*
				390/320	S	7,878*
		fastback	71,062	289/271	K	319*
				390/320	S	17,350*
		convertible	44,821	289/271	K	50*
				390/320	S	2,181*
	Mustang GT	hardtop	6,545	289/271	K	120
				390/320	S	7,878*
		fastback	16,212	289/271	K	319*
				390/320	S	17,350*
		convertible	2,341	289/271	K	50
				390/320	S	2,181*
1968	Fairlane	hardtop	44,683	427/390	W	n/a
	Cobra Jet			428/335	R	n/a
	Fairlane 500	hardtop	33,282	427/390	W	n/a
	Cobra Jet			428/335	R	22 est.
		fastback	32,452	427/390	W	n/a
	Cobra Jet			428/335	R	n/a
		convertible	3,761	427/390	W	n/a
	Cobra Jet			428/335	R	n/a
	Torino	hardtop	35,964	427/390	W	n/a
	Cobra Jet			428/335	R	n/a
	Torino GT	hardtop	23,939	390/325	S	n/a
				427/390	W	n/a
	Cobra Jet			428/335	R	n/a
		fastback	74,135	390/325	S	n/a
				427/390	W	n/a
	Cobra Jet			428/335	R	n/a
		convertible	5,310	390/325	S	n/a
				427/390	W	n/a
	Cobra Jet			428/335	R	n/a
1969	Fairlanes	hardtop	44,683	428/335	Q	n/a
	Cobra Jet Ram Air			428/335	R	n/a
	Fairlane Cobra	hardtop	n/a	428/335	Q	n/a
	Cobra Jet Ram Air			428/335	R	n/a
		fastback	n/a	428/335	Q	n/a
	Cobra Jet Ram Air			428/335	R	n/a
	Fairlane 500	hardtop	28,179	428/335	Q	n/a
	Cobra Jet Ram Air			428/335	R	n/a
		fastback	29,849	428/335	Q	n/a
	Cobra Jet Ram Air			428/335	R	n/a
		convertible	2,264	428/335	Q	n/a
	Cobra Jet Ram Air			428/335	R	n/a
	Torino	hardtop	20,789	428/335	Q	n/a
	Cobra Jet Ram Air			428/335	R	n/a
	Torino GT	hardtop	17,951	390/320	S	n/a
	Cobra Jet			428/335	Q	n/a

Ford (continued)

Year	Model/*Optional Engine Package*	Body Style	Production Number by Body Style	Engine (cid/hp)	Engine Code	Production Number by Engine
	Cobra Jet Ram Air			428/335	R	n/a
		fastback	61,319	390/320	S	n/a
	Cobra Jet			428/335	Q	n/a
	Cobra Jet Ram Air			428/335	R	n/a
		convertible	2,552	390/320	S	n/a
	Cobra Jet			428/335	Q	n/a
	Cobra Jet Ram Air			428/335	R	n/a
	Torino Talladega	fastback	754	428/335	Q	754
	Mustang	hardtop	150,637	351/290	M	5,225*
				390/320	S	858*
	Cobra Jet			428/335	Q	105*
	Cobra Jet Ram Air			428/335	R	138*
		fastback	134,440	351/290	M	35,939*
				390/320	S	9,440*
	Cobra Jet			428/335	Q	12,896*
	Cobra Jet Ram Air			428/335	R	12,896*
		convertible	14,744	351/290	M	1,225*
				390/320	S	251
	Cobra Jet			428/335	Q	122*
	Cobra Jet Ram Air			428/335	R	122*
	Mustang Grande	hardtop	22,186	351/290	M	5,225*
				390/320	S	858*
	Cobra Jet			428/335	Q	37
	Cobra Jet Ram Air			428/335	R	0
	Mustang GT	hardtop	1,483	351/290	M	5,225*
				390/320	S	858*
	Cobra Jet			428/335	Q	105*
	Cobra Jet Ram Air			428/335	R	138*
		fastback	4,084	351/290	M	35,939*
				390/320	S	9,440*
	Cobra Jet			428/335	Q	12,896*
	Cobra Jet Ram Air			428/335	R	12,896*
		convertible	1,127	351/290	M	1,225*
				390/320	S	251*
	Cobra Jet			428/335	Q	122*
	Cobra Jet Ram Air			428/335	R	122*
	Mach I	fastback	72,458	351/290	M	35,939*
				390/320	S	9,440*
	Cobra Jet			428/335	Q	12,896*
	Cobra Jet Ram Air			428/335	R	12,896*
	Boss 302	fastback	1,628	302/290	G	1,628
	Boss 429	fastback	849	429/375	Z	849
1970	Fairlane 500	hardtop	70,636	351/300	M	n/a
	Cobra Jet			429/370	C	n/a
	Cobra Jet Ram Air			429/370	J	n/a
	Torino	hardtop	49,826	351/300	M	n/a
	Cobra Jet			429/370	C	n/a
	Cobra Jet Ram Air			429/370	J	n/a
		fastback	12,490	351/300	M	n/a
	Cobra Jet			429/370	C	n/a
	Cobra Jet Ram Air			429/370	J	n/a
	Torino Brougham	hardtop	16,911	429/370	C	n/a
	Cobra Jet Ram Air			429/370	J	n/a
	Torino Cobra	fastback	7,675	429/360	N	3,213
	Cobra Jet			429/370	C	974
	Cobra Jet Ram Air			429/370	J	3,488
	Torino GT	fastback	56,819	351/300	M	n/a
				429/360	N	n/a
	Cobra Jet			429/370	C	n/a
	Cobra Jet Ram Air			429/370	J	n/a
		convertible	3,939	351/300	M	n/a
				429/360	N	157
	Cobra Jet			429/370	C	30
	Cobra Jet Ram Air			429/370	J	64
	Mustang	hardtop	96,151	351/300	M	1,903*
	Cobra Jet			428/335	Q	31*
	Cobra Jet Ram Air			428/335	R	39*
		fastback	87,551	351/300	M	20,992*
	Cobra Jet			428/335	Q	755*
	Cobra Jet Ram Air			428/335	R	2,617*
		convertible	7,820	351/300	M	582
	Cobra Jet			428/335	Q	14
	Cobra Jet Ram Air			428/335	R	33
	Mustang Grande	hardtop	13,583	351/300	M	1,903*
	Cobra Jet			428/335	Q	31*
	Cobra Jet Ram Air			428/335	R	0
	Mach I		40,975	351/300	M	20,992*
	Cobra Jet			428/335	Q	755*
	Cobra Jet Ram Air			428/335	R	2,617*
	Boss 302	fastback	7,014	302/290	G	7,014
	Boss 429	fastback	500	429/375	Z	500
1970.5	Falcon	sedan	26,071	351/300	M	n/a
				429/360	N	n/a
	Cobra Jet			429/370	C	n/a
	Cobra Jet Ram Air			429/370	J	n/a
1971	Torino	hardtop	37,518	351/285	M	n/a
	Cobra Jet			429/370	C	n/a
	Cobra Jet Ram Air			429/370	J	n/a
	Torino 500	hardtop	89,966	351/285	M	n/a
	Cobra Jet			429/370	C	n/a
	Cobra Jet Ram Air			429/370	J	n/a
		fastback	11,150	351/285	M	n/a
	Cobra Jet			429/370	C	n/a
	Cobra Jet Ram Air			429/370	J	n/a
	Torino Brougham	hardtop	8,593	351/285	M	n/a
	Cobra Jet			429/370	C	n/a
	Cobra Jet Ram Air			429/370	J	2
	Torino Cobra	fastback	3,054	351/285	M	n/a
	Cobra Jet			429/370	C	n/a
	Cobra Jet Ram Air			429/370	J	n/a
	Torino GT	fastback	31,641	351/285	M	n/a
				351/280	Q	n/a

Ford (continued)

Year	Model/*Optional Engine Package*	Body Style	Production Number by Body Style	Engine (cid/hp)	Engine Code	Production Number by Engine
	Cobra Jet			429/370	C	n/a
	Cobra Jet Ram Air			429/370	J	n/a
		convertible	1,613	351/285	M	n/a
				351/280	Q	n/a
	Cobra Jet			429/370	C	n/a
	Cobra Jet Ram Air			429/370	J	n/a
	Mustang	hardtop	83,108	351/285	M	2,008*
				351/280	Q	32*
	Cobra Jet			429/370	C	33*
	Cobra Jet Ram Air			429/370	J	53*
		fastback	60,453	351/285	M	16,955*
				351/280	Q	108*
	Cobra Jet			429/370	C	310*
	Cobra Jet Ram Air			429/370	J	1,427*
		convertible	6,121	351/285	M	590
				351/280	Q	5
	Cobra Jet			429/370	C	10
	Cobra Jet Ram Air			429/370	J	32
	Mustang Grande	hardtop	17,406	351/285	M	2,008*
				351/280	Q	32*
	Cobra Jet			429/370	C	33*
	Cobra Jet Ram Air			429/370	J	53*
	Mach I	fastback	36,498	351/285	M	16,955*
				351/280	Q	108*
	Cobra Jet			429/370	C	310*
	Cobra Jet Ram Air			429/370	J	1,427*
	Boss 351	fastback	1,805	351/330	R	1,804
1972	Mustang	hardtop	75,395	351/266	Q	1,041*
				351/275	R	19*
		fastback	43,297	351/266	Q	8,677*
				351/275	R	366*
		convertible	6,401	351/266	Q	531
				351/275	R	13
	Mustang Grande	hardtop	18,045	351/266	Q	1,041*
				351/275	R	19*
	Mach I	fastback	27,675	351/266	Q	8,677*
				351/275	R	366*
1973	Mustang	hardtop	76,754	351/259	Q	1,064*
		fastback	46,260	351/259	Q	10,526*
		convertible	11,853	351/259	Q	968
	Mustang Grande	hardtop	25,274	351/259	Q	1,064*
	Mach I	fastback	35,439	351/259	Q	10,526*

* Combined production number includes the total number of engines regardless of body styles for that year.

Mercury

Year	Model/*Optional Engine Package*	Body Style	Production Number by Body Style	Engine (cid/hp)	Engine Code	Production Number by Engine
1962	Monterey Custom	hardtop	2,772	390/330	P	n/a
	S-55			390/375	Q	n/a
				406/385	B	n/a
				406/405	G	n/a
		convertible	1,315	390/330	P	n/a
				390/375	Q	n/a
				406/385	B	n/a
				406/405	G	n/a
	full-size	all		390/330	P	n/a
				390/375	Q	n/a
				406/385	B	n/a
				406/405	G	n/a
1963	S-55 Marauder	fastback	2,317	390/330	P	n/a
				406/385	B	n/a
				406/405	G	n/a
				427/410	Q	n/a
				427/425	V	21
		hardtop	3,863	390/330	P	n/a
				406/385	B	n/a
				406/405	G	n/a
				427/410	Q	n/a
				427/425	V	21
		convertible	1,379	390/330	P	n/a
				406/385	B	n/a
				406/405	G	n/a
				427/410	Q	n/a
				427/425	R	21
		all exc. full-size		390/330	P	n/a
	S-55			406/385	B	29
				406/405	G	64
				427/410	Q	25
				427/425	R	37
1964	Comet	all		289/271		n/a
	Cyclone	hardtop	7,454	289/271		n/a
	full-size	all		390/330	P	n/a
				427/410	Q	n/a
				427/425	R	n/a
1965	Comet	all		289/271		n/a
	Cyclone	hardtop	12,347	289/271		n/a
	full-size	all		390/330	P	n/a
				427/410	Q	n/a
				427/425	R	19
1966	Cyclone	hardtop	6,889	390/335	S	n/a
		convertible	1,305	390/335	S	n/a
	Cyclone GT	hardtop	2,158	390/335	S	2,158
		convertible	13,812	390/335	S	13,812
	S-55	hardtop	2,916	428/345	Q	2,916
		convertible	669	428/345	Q	669
	full-size	all		428/360	P	n/a
				427/425	R	n/a
1967	Comet 202	coupe	14,251	427/410	W	0

Mercury (continued)

Year	Model/*Optional Engine Package*	Body Style	Production Number by Body Style	Engine (cid/hp)	Engine Code	Production Number by Engine
				427/425	R	22
	Capri	hardtop	11,671	427/410	W	1
				427/425	R	6
	Caliente	hardtop	9,966	427/410	W	0
				427/425	R	4
	Cyclone	hardtop	2,682	390/320	S	n/a
				427/410	W	8
				427/425	R	19
		convertible	431	390/320	S	n/a
	Cyclone GT	hardtop	3,419	390/320	S	3,419
		convertible	378	390/320	S	378
	Cougar	hardtop	123,684	390/320	S	3,122
	Cougar GT		5,791	390/320	S	5,791
	Cougar XR-7	hardtop	27,209	390/320	S	993
	Cougar XR-7 GT		2,653	390/320	S	2,653
	Monterey S-55	hardtop	570	428/345	Q	570
		convertible	145	428/345	Q	145
1968	Cyclone	hardtop	1,034	390/325	S	n/a
				427/390	W	n/a
				428/335	R	n/a
		fastback	6,165	390/325	S	n/a
				427/390	W	n/a
				428/335	R	n/a
	Cyclone GT	hardtop	6,105	390/325	S	n/a
				427/390	W	n/a
				428/335	R	n/a
		fastback	334	390/325	S	n/a
				427/390	W	n/a
				428/335	R	n/a
	Cougar	hardtop	81,032	390/325	S	1,547
	Cougar GT		995	390/325	S	1,547
				428/335	R	113
	Cougar GT-E		115	427/390	W	101
				428/335	R	14
	Cougar XR-7	hardtop	32,709	390/325	S	3,308
	Cougar XR-7 GT		1,845	390/325	S	3,308
				428/335	R	94
	Cougar XR-7 GT-E		279	427/390	W	256
				428/335	R	23
1969	Cyclone	fastback	5,882	351/290	M	n/a
				390/320	S	n/a
				428/335	Q	n/a
	Cobra Jet Ram Air			428/335	R	n/a
	Cyclone Cobra Jet	fastback	3,261	428/335	Q	n/a
	Cobra Jet Ram Air			428/335	R	n/a
	Cyclone Spoiler	fastback	196	351/290	M	n/a
				390/320	S	n/a
				428/335	Q	n/a
	Cobra Jet Ram Air			428/335	R	n/a
	Cyclone Spoiler II	fastback	323	351/290	M	323
	Cougar	hardtop	66,351	351/290	M	7,076
				390/320	S	931
				428/335	Q	145
	Cobra Jet Ram Air			428/335	R	508
	Boss			429/375	R	2
	Eliminator		2,250	351/290	M	n/a
				390/320	S	n/a
				302/290	G	169
				428/335	Q	n/a
	Cobra Jet Ram Air			428/335	R	n/a
		convertible	5,796	351/290	M	970
				390/320	S	124
				428/335	Q	13
	Cobra Jet Ram Air			428/335	R	23
	Cougar XR-7	hardtop	23,914	351/290	M	6,803
				390/320	S	1,562
				428/335	Q	172
	Cobra Jet Ram Air			428/335	R	504
		convertible	4,024	351/290	M	1,216
				390/320	S	438
				428/335	Q	46
	Cobra Jet Ram Air			428/335	R	127
1970	Cyclone	hardtop	1,695	429/360	N	n/a
				429/370	C	n/a
	Cobra Jet Ram Air			429/370	C	n/a
	Cyclone GT	hardtop	10,170	351/300	M	n/a
				429/360	N	n/a
				429/370	C	n/a
	Cobra Jet Ram Air			429/370	C	n/a
	Cyclone Spoiler	hardtop	1,631	429/370	C	1,631
	Cougar	hardtop	49,479	351/300	M	3,499
				428/335	Q	156
	Cobra Jet Ram Air			428/335	Q	302
	Eliminator		2,267	351/300	M	n/a
				302/290	G	469
				428/335	Q	n/a
	Cobra Jet Ram Air			428/335	Q	n/a
		convertible	2,322	351/300	M	213
				428/335	Q	5
	Cobra Jet Ram Air			428/335	Q	2
	Cougar XR-7	hardtop	18,567	351/300	M	4,021
				428/335	Q	146
	Cobra Jet Ram Air			428/335	Q	163
		convertible	1,997	351/300	M	549
				428/335	Q	29
	Cobra Jet Ram Air			428/335	Q	37
1971	Cyclone	hardtop	444	351/285	M	n/a
				429/370	C	n/a
	Cobra Jet Ram Air			429/370	J	n/a
	Cyclone GT	hardtop	2,287	351/285	M	n/a
				429/370	C	n/a
	Cobra Jet Ram Air			429/370	J	n/a

Mercury (continued)

Year	Model/Optional Engine Package	Body Style	Production Number by Body Style	Engine (cid/hp)	Engine Code	Production Number by Engine
	Cyclone Spoiler	hardtop	353	351/285	M	n/a
				429/370	C	n/a
	Cobra Jet Ram Air			429/370	J	n/a
	Cougar	hardtop	34,008	351/285	M	1,695
				429/370	C	14
	Cobra Jet Ram Air			429/370	J	12
		GT	787	351/285	M	741
				429/370	C	15
	Cobra Jet Ram Air			429/370	J	31
		convertible	1,722	351/285	M	139
				429/370	C	2
	Cobra Jet Ram Air			429/370	J	18
	Cougar XR-7	hardtop	25,417	351/285	M	4,941
				351/280	Q	1
				429/370	C	172
	Cobra Jet Ram Air			429/370	J	157
		convertible	1,717	351/285	M	529
				429/370	C	14
	Cobra Jet Ram Air			429/370	J	13
1972	Cougar	hardtop	23,731	351/266	Q	566
		convertible	1,240	351/266	Q	69
	Cougar XR-7	hardtop	26,802	351/266	Q	2,557
		convertible	1,929	351/266	Q	368
1973	Cougar	hardtop	23,731	351/259	Q	313
		convertible	1,240	351/259	Q	44
	Cougar XR-7	hardtop	26,802	351/259	Q	2,485
		convertible	1,929	351/259	Q	436

Oldsmobile (continued)

Year	Model/Optional Engine Package	Body Style	Production Number by Body Style	Engine (cid/hp)	Engine Code	Production Number by Engine
	Cutlass S Rallye 350	coupe		350/310		160
		hardtop		350/310		2,367
	Cutlass SX	hardtop	6,404	455/365		n/a
		convertible	793	455/365		n/a
1971	4-4-2	hardtop	6,285	455/340		5,475
	W-30			455/350		810
		convertible	1,304	455/340		1,194
	W-30			455/350		110
	Cutlass SX	hardtop	1,820	455/320		1,820
		convertible	357	455/320		357
1972	Cutlass 4-4-2	hardtop	751	350/180		n/a
				455/270		n/a
	W-30			455/300		17
	Cutlass S 4-4-2	coupe	123	350/180		n/a
				455/270		n/a
	W-30			455/300		19
		hardtop	7,800	350/180		n/a
				455/270		n/a
	W-30			455/300		623
	Cutlass Supreme 4-4-2	convertible	1,171	455/270		n/a
	W-30			455/300		113
	Hurst/Olds	hardtop	279	455/270		n/a
	W-30			455/300		n/a
		hardtop sunroof	220	455/270		n/a
	W-30			455/300		n/a
		convertible	130	455/270		n/a
	W-30			455/300		n/a

Oldsmobile

Year	Model/Optional Engine Package	Body Style	Production Number by Body Style	Engine (cid/hp)	Engine Code	Production Number by Engine
1964	F-85 4-4-2	coupe	148	330/310		148
		4-door	3	330/310		3
	F-85 Deluxe 4-4-2	4-door	7	330/310		7
	Cutlass 4-4-2	coupe	563	330/310		563
		hardtop	1,842	330/310		1,842
		convertible	436	330/310		436
1965	F-85 4-4-2	coupe	1,087	400/345		1,087
	Cutlass 4-4-2	coupe	5,713	400/345		5,713
		hardtop	14,735	400/345		14,735
		convertible	3,468	400/345		3,468
1966	F-85 4-4-2	coupe	647	400/350		490
	L69			400/360		132
	W30			400/360		25
	F-85 Deluxe	hardtop	1,217	400/350		1,039
	4-4-2/*L69*			400/360		170
	W30			400/360		8
	Cutlass 4-4-2	coupe	3,787	400/350		3,404
	L69			400/360		378
	W30			400/360		5
		hardtop	13,493	400/350		12,322
	L69			400/360		1,155
	W30			400/360		16
		convertible	2,853	400/350		2,613
	L69			400/360		240
1967	4-4-2	coupe	4,750	400/350		4,621
				400/360		129
		hardtop	16,998	400/350		16,625
				400/360		373
		convertible	3,079	400/350		3,079
1968	4-4-2	coupe	4,726	400/325-350		4,411
	W-30			400/360		315
		hardtop	26,772	400/325-350		25,346
	W-30			400/360		1,426
		convertible	5,142	400/325-350		4,972
	W-30			400/360		170
	F-85/*W-31*	coupe		350/325		38
	Cutlass S/*W-31*	coupe		350/325		674
		hardtop		350/325		30
	Hurst/Olds	coupe	64	455/390		64
		hardtop	451	455/390		451
1969	4-4-2	coupe	2,984	400/325-350		2,788
	W-32			400/350		25
	W-30			400/360		171
		hardtop	22,560	400/325-350		21,216
	W-32			400/350		247
	W-30			400/360		1,097
		convertible	4,295	400/325-350		4,149
	W-32			400/350		25
	W-30			400/360		121
	F-85/*W-31*	coupe		350/325		212
	Cutlass S/W-31	coupe		350/325		106
	W-31	hardtop		350/325		569
	W-31	convertible		350/325		26
	Hurst/Olds	hardtop	912	455/380		912
		convertible	2	455/380		2
1970	4-4-2	coupe	1,688	455/365		1,426
	W-30			455/370		262
		hardtop	14,711	455/365		12,137
	W-30			455/370		2,574
		convertible	2,933	455/365		2,669
	W-30			455/370		264
	4-4-2 pace car	convertible	268	455/365		266
				455/370		2
	F-85/*W-31*	coupe		350/325		207
	Cutlass S/*W-31*	coupe		350/325		116
	W-31	hardtop		350/325		1,029
	F-85 Rallye 350	coupe		350/310		1,020

Plymouth

Year	Model/Optional Engine Package	Body Style	Production Number by Body Style	Engine (cid/hp)	Engine Code	Production Number by Engine
1961	all	all		383/330		n/a
				383/340		n/a
				413/350		n/a
				413/375		n/a
1962	all	all		383/343		n/a
				413/380		n/a
	Max Wedge			413/410		n/a
	Max Wedge			413/420		n/a
1963	all	all		383/343		n/a
	Max Wedge			426/415		n/a
	Max Wedge			426/425		n/a
1964	all	all		426/365		n/a
	Max Wedge			426/415		n/a
				426/425		n/a
	Hemi			426/415		n/a
	Hemi			426/425		n/a
1965	Belvedere I	sedan	56,843	383/325		227
				426/365		128
	Belvedere II	hardtop	77,492	383/325		3,099
				426/365		544
		convertible	1,921	383/325		141
				426/365		13
	Satellite	hardtop	25,201	383/325		5,288
				426/365		800
		convertible	1,860	383/325		290
				426/365		65
	Belvedere S/S	sedan	101	426/425		101
	Barracuda	fastback	61,523	273/235		10,062
1966	Belvedere I	sedan	9,381	383/325	G	22
				426/425	H	136
	S/S			426/425	H	50
	Belvedere II	hardtop	36,644	383/325	G	3,268
				426/425	H	531
		convertible	2,502	383/325	G	254
				426/425	H	10
	Satellite	hardtop	35,399	383/325	G	7,795
				426/425	H	817
		convertible	2,759	383/325	G	489
				426/425	H	27
	Valiant 100	all exc. wagon	n/a	273/235	D	173
	Valiant 200 & Signet	all exc. wagon	n/a	273/235	D	446
	Barracuda	fastback	38,029	273/235	D	1,917
	Barracuda Formula S	fastback	38,029	273/235	D	3,702
1967	Belvedere I	all exc. wagon	n/a	383/325	H	831
		sedan	4,718	426/425	J	n/a
	Belvedere II	hardtop	34,550	383/325	H	3,701
				426/425	J	n/a
	RO23			426/425	J	55
		convertible	1,552	383/325	H	3,701
				426/425	J	n/a
	Satellite	hardtop	30,328	383/325	H	3,725
				426/425	J	n/a
		convertible	2,050	383/325	H	3,725
				426/425	J	n/a
	Belvedere GTX	hardtop	12,010	440/375	L	11,277
				426/425	J	733
		convertible	680	440/375	L	11,277
				426/425	J	733
	Valiant 100	all	n/a	273/235	E	101
	Valiant Signet	all	n/a	273/235	E	245
	Barracuda	hardtop	28,196	273/235	E	4,890
		fastback	30,110	273/235	E	4,890
		convertible	4,228	273/235	E	4,890
	Barracuda	all	n/a	273/235	E	5,352
	Formula S			383/280	H	1,841
1968	Belvedere	coupe	15,702	383/330	H	n/a
	Road Runner	coupe	29,240	383/335	H	28,138

Plymouth (continued)

Year	Model/*Optional Engine Package*	Body Style	Production Number by Body Style	Engine (cid/hp)	Engine Code	Production Number by Engine
				426/425	J	840
		hardtop	15,359	383/335	H	15,166
				426/425	J	169
	Satellite	hardtop	31,180	383/330	H	1,038
		convertible	1,771	383/330	H	51
	Sport Satellite	hardtop	21,014	383/330	H	3,307
		convertible	1,523	383/330	H	182
	GTX	hardtop	17,914	440/375	L	16,673
				426/425	J	410
		convertible	1,026	440/375	L	881
				426/425	J	36
	Barracuda	hardtop	1,119	340/275	P	867
	Formula S			383/300	H	252
		fastback	3,820	340/275	P	2,857
				383/300	H	963
	Hurst Hemi	Race Hemi			M	70
		convertible	258	340/275	P	193
				383/300	H	64
1969	Belvedere	coupe	7,063	383/330	H	48
	Road Runner	coupe	37,743	383/335	H	31,397
				440/390	M	615
				426/425	J	356
		hardtop	48,549	383/335	H	45,629
				440/390	M	797
				426/425	J	421
		convertible	2,128	383/335	H	1,880
				426/425	J	10
	Satellite	hardtop	38,323	383/330	H	594
		convertible	1,137	383/330	H	42
	Sport Satellite	hardtop	18,807	383/330	H	1,341
		convertible	918	383/330	H	85
	GTX	hardtop	14,902	440/375	L	13,866
				426/425	J	197
		convertible	700	440/375	L	540
				426/425	J	11
	Barracuda	coupe	12,757	340/275	P	280
		fastback	17,788	340/275	P	686
		convertible	1,442	340/275	P	42
	Barracuda	coupe	12,757	340/275	P	325
	Formula S			383/330	H	98
		fastback	17,788	340/275	P	1,431
				383/330	H	603
		convertible	1,442	340/275	P	83
				383/330	H	17
	Cuda 340	coupe		340/275	P	98
		fastback		340/275	P	568
	Cuda 383	coupe		383/330	H	83
		fastback		383/330	H	378
	Cuda 440	coupe		440/375	M	360
		fastback		440/375	M	360
1970	Belvedere	coupe	4,717	383/330	N	n/a
	Road Runner	coupe	15,716	383/335	N	14,057
				440/390	V	651
				426/425	R	74
		hardtop	24,944**	383/335	N	20,216
				440/390	V	1,130
				426/425	R	75
		convertible	824	383/335	N	621
				440/390	V	34
				426/425	R	3
	Superbird	hardtop	1,935	440/375	U	1,084
				440/390	V	716
				426/425	R	135
	Satellite	hardtop	28,200	383/330	N	298
		convertible	701	383/330	N	27
	Sport Satellite	hardtop	8,749	383/330	N	680
	GTX	hardtop	7,748	440/375	U	6,398
				440/390	V	678
				426/425	R	71
	Barracuda	coupe	n/a	383/330	N	4
		hardtop	25,651	383/330	N	1,118
		convertible	1,554	383/330	N	59
	Gran Coupe	hardtop	8,183	383/330	N	1,088
		convertible	596	383/330	N	82
	Cuda	hardtop	18,880	383/335	N	4,595
				340/275	H	6,032
				440/375	U	952
				440/390	V	1,755
				426/425	R	652
	AAR Cuda			340/290	J	2,724
		convertible	635	383/335	N	209
				340/275	H	262
				440/375	U	34
				440/390	V	29
				426/425	R	14
	Duster 340	hardtop	22,117	340/275	H	21,799
	Sport Fury GT	hardtop	666	440/350	T	605
				440/390	V	61
1971	Road Runner	hardtop	14,218	383/300	N	11,682
				340/275	H	1,681
				440/385	V	246
				426/425	R	55
	Sebring	hardtop	30,579	383/300	N	n/a
	Sebring Plus	hardtop	10,700	383/300	N	n/a
	GTX	hardtop	2,942	440/370	U	2,538
				440/385	V	135
				426/425	R	30
	Barracuda	coupe	n/a	383/300	N	10
		hardtop	9,459	383/300	N	169
		convertible	1,014	383/300	N	19
	Gran Coupe	hardtop	1,615	383/300	N	97
	Cuda	hardtop	6,228	383/300	N	1,739

Plymouth (continued)

Year	Model/*Optional Engine Package*	Body Style	Production Number by Body Style	Engine (cid/hp)	Engine Code	Production Number by Engine
				340/275	H	3,300
				440/385	V	237
				426/425	R	107
		convertible	374	383/300	N	128
				340/275	H	140
				440/385	V	17
				426/425	R	7
	Duster 340	hardtop	12,886	340/275	H	10,478
	Sport Fury GT	hardtop	375	440/370	U	375
1972	Road Runner	hardtop	7,628	340/240	H	2,360
				400/255	P	3,828
	GTX			440/280	U	672
				440/330	V	n/a
	Satellite	hardtop	10,507	400/255	P	n/a
	Sebring	hardtop	34,353	400/255	P	n/a
	Sebring Plus	hardtop	21,399	400/255	P	n/a
	Duster 340	hardtop	15,681	340/240	H	15,681
	Barracuda	hardtop	10,622	340/240	H	390
	Cuda	hardtop	7,828	340/240	H	5,864
1973	Road Runner	hardtop	19,056	340/240	H	5,384
				400/255	P	2,740
	GTX			440/280	U	749
	Satellite	hardtop	13,570	400/260	P	n/a
	Sebring	hardtop	51,575	400/260	P	177
	Sebring Plus	hardtop	43,628	400/260	P	1,731
	Duster 340	hardtop	15,731	340/240	H	15,731
	Barracuda	hardtop	11,587	340/240	H	626
	Cuda	hardtop	10,626	340/240	H	6,583
1974	Road Runner	hardtop	11,555	360/240	H	1,688
				400/255	P	1,109
	GTX			440/280	U	386
	Satellite	hardtop	n/a	400/250	P	n/a
	Sebring	hardtop	n/a	400/250	P	n/a
	Sebring Plus	hardtop	n/a	400/250	P	n/a
	Duster 360	hardtop	3,879	340/240	H	3,879
	Barracuda	hardtop	6,745	340/240	H	125
	Cuda	hardtop	4,989	340/240	H	1,191

** Includes Superbirds.

Pontiac

Year	Model/*Optional Engine Package*	Body Style	Production Number by Body Style	Engine (cid/hp)	Engine Code	Production Number by Engine
1961	full-size	all		389/333		254
				389/348		1,933
				389/368		n/a
				421/373		n/a
1962	full-size	all		389/333		875
				389/348		2,407
	Super Duty			389/385		13
				421/320		72
	Super Duty			421/405		200
1963	full-size	all		421/320		981
				421/353		1,051
				421/370		2,071
	Super Duty			421/390		13
	Super Duty			421/405		59
	Super Duty			421/410		5
	Catalina/Super Duty	sedan		421		14
	Super Duty	hardtop		421		42
	Grand Prix/Super Duty	hardtop		421		3
	Tempest/Super Duty	coupe		421/405		2
	Super Duty	wagon		421/405		6
	LeMans/Super Duty	coupe		421/405		6
1964	full-size	all		389/330		3,235
				421/320		3,064
				421/350		997
				421/370		1,345
	2+2	hardtop and convertible	7,998	389		n/a
				421		n/a
	GTO	coupe	7,384	389/325		21,942
				389/348		8,245
		hardtop	18,422	389/325		21,942
				389/348		8,245
		convertible	6,644	389/325		21,942
				389/348		8,245
1965	full-size	all		389/338		1,915
				421/338		13,623
				421/356		1,753
				421/376		1,836
	2+2	hardtop and convertible	11,521	421/338		13,623
				421/356		1,753
				421/376		1,836
	GTO	coupe	8,319	389/335		54,934
				389/360		20,547
		hardtop	55,722	389/335		54,934
				389/360		20,547
		convertible	11,311	389/335		54,934
				389/360		20,547
1966	full-size	all		421/338		9,201
				421/356		1,531
				421/376		1,082
	2+2	hardtop and convertible	6,383	421/338		9,201
				421/356		1,531
				421/376		1,082
	GTO	coupe	10,363	389/335		77,698
				389/360		12,236
				389/360		185
		hardtop	73,785	389/335		77,698

Pontiac (continued)

Year	Model/*Optional Engine Package*	Body Style	Production Number by Body Style	Engine (cid/hp)	Engine Code	Production Number by Engine
				389/360		19,063
				389/360		185
		convertible	12,798	389/335		77,698
				389/360		19,063
1967	full-size			428/360		5,967
				428/376		1,457
	2+2	hardtop and convertible	1,768	428/360		n/a
				428/376		n/a
	GTO	coupe	7,029	400/335		64,177*
				400/360		12,236*
	Ram Air			400/360		695*
		hardtop	65,176	400/335		64,177*
				400/360		12,236*
	Ram Air			400/360		695*
		convertible	9,517	400/335		7,520
				400/360		1,591
	Ram Air			400/360		56
	Firebird HO	hardtop	67,032	326/285		6,111*
		convertible	15,528	326/285		6,111*
	Firebird 400	hardtop	67,032	400/325		18,604*
	Ram Air			400/325		64*
		convertible	15,528	400/325		18,604*
	Ram Air			400/325		64
1968	full-size	all		428/375		6,294
				428/390		495
	GTO	hardtop	77,704	400/350		64,586
				400/360		9,337
	Ram Air			400/360		940
	Ram Air II			400/366		246*
		convertible	9,980	400/350		8,207
				400/360		1,227
	Ram Air			400/360		114
	Ram Air II			400/366		246*
	Tempest/LeMans/350 HO	all		350/320		5,822
	Firebird HO	hardtop	90,152	350/320		6,422*
		convertible	16,960	350/320		6,422*
	Firebird 400	hardtop		400/330		18,714*
				400/335		2,099*
	Ram Air			400/335		413*
	Ram Air II			400/340		110*
		convertible	16,960	400/330		18,714*
				400/335		2,099*
	Ram Air			400/335		413*
	Ram Air II			400/340		110*
	Ram Air and *Ram Air II*	hardtop		400		511
	Ram Air and *Ram Air II*	convertible		400		12
1969	full-size	all		428/360		101,191
				428/390		751
	Grand Prix	hardtop	112,486	400/350		90,544
				428/370		19,944
				428/390		1,131
	GTO	hardtop	64,851	400/350		54,776
	Ram Air III			400/366		1,701
	Ram Air IV			400/370		403
		convertible	7,436	400/350		6,800
	Ram Air III			400/366		259
	Ram Air IV			400/370		54
	GTO Judge/*Ram Air III*	hardtop		400/366		6,428
	Ram Air IV			400/370		297
	Ram Air III	convertible		400/366		103
	Ram Air IV			400/370		5
	Tempest/LeMans/350 HO	all		350/330		4,255
	Firebird HO	hardtop	75,362	350/330		5,127*
		convertible	11,649	350/325		5,127*
	Firebird 400	hardtop		400/330		11,522*
				400/335		1,125
	Ram Air IV			400/345		85
		convertible		400/330		11,522*
				400/335		144
	Ram Air IV			400/345		17
	Trans Am	hardtop	689	400/335		634
	Ram Air IV			400/345		55
		convertible	8	400/335		8
1970	GTO	hardtop	32,731	400/350		27,496
	Ram Air III			400/366		4,356
	Ram Air IV			400/370		767
				455/360		3,733
		convertible	3,621	400/350		3,059
	Ram Air III			400/366		288
	Ram Air IV			400/370		37
				455/360		396
	GTO Judge	hardtop	3,629	400/366		n/a
	Ram Air IV			400/370		n/a
				455/360		14
		convertible	162	400/366		n/a
	Ram Air IV			400/370		n/a
				455/360		3
	GT-37	coupe and hardtop	1,419	400/330		n/a
				400/330		n/a
	Firebird Formula 400	hardtop	7,708	400/330		7,019
				400/345		689
				400/370		0
	Trans Am	hardtop	3,196	400/345		3,108
				400/370		88
1971	GTO	hardtop	9,497	400/300		8,432
				455/325		534
	HO			455/335		531
		convertible	661	400/300		587
				455/325		43
	HO			455/335		31
	GTO Judge	hardtop	357	455/335		357
		convertible	17	455/335		17
	T-37	coupe	7,184	400/300		20
				455/325		4
	HO			455/335		11
		hardtop	29,466	400/300		58
				455/325		4
	HO			455/335		15
	GT-37	hardtop	5,802	400/300		572
				455/325		15
	HO			455/335		54
	LeMans	coupe	2,734	400/300		10
				455/325		1
	HO			455/335		0
		hardtop	40,966	400/300		153
				455/325		9
	HO			455/335		6
	LeMans Sport	hardtop	34,625	400/300		570
				455/325		40
	HO			455/335		22
		convertible	3,865	400/300		220
				455/325		50
	HO			455/335		17
	Firebird Formula	hardtop	7,802	400/300		n/a
				455/325		350
				455/335		321
	Trans Am	hardtop	2,116	455/335		2,116
1972	GTO	coupe	134	400/250	T	119
				455/250	Y	5
	HO			455/300	X	10
		hardtop	5,673	400/250	T	4,803
				455/250	Y	235
	HO			455/300	X	635
	LeMans	coupe	6,855	400/250	T	n/a
				455/250	Y	n/a
	HO			455/300	X	9
		hardtop	80,383	400/250	T	n/a
				455/250	Y	n/a
	HO			455/300	X	46
		convertible	3,324	400/250	T	280
				455/250	Y	34
	HO			455/300	X	26
	LeMans GT	hardtop	8,766	400/250	T	614
				455/250	Y	24
	HO			455/300	X	14
		convertible	114	400/250	T	31
				455/250	Y	2
	HO			455/300	X	7
	Firebird Formula	hardtop	2,429	400/250	T	2,429
	HO			455/300	X	276
	Trans Am		1,286	455/300	X	1,286
1973	GTO	coupe	494	400/230	T	469
				455/250	Y	25
		sport coupe	4,312	400/230	T	3,793
				455/250	Y	519
	Firebird Formula	hardtop	10,166	400/230	T	4,622
				455/250	Y	730
	Super Duty			455/310	X	43
	Trans Am	hardtop	4,802	455/250	Y	n/a
	Super Duty			455/310	X	252
1974	GTO	coupe	5,335	350/200	K	5,335
		hatchback	1,723	350/200	K	1,723
	Firebird Formula	hardtop	14,519	400/225	T	n/a
				455/250	Y	n/a
	Super Duty			455/290	X	58
	Trans Am	hardtop		400/225	T	n/a
				455/250	Y	n/a
	Super Duty			455/290	X	943

* Combined production number includes the total number of engines regardless of body styles for that year.

Note 1: For 1970, Ram Air Judge production numbers are included in regular GTO production numbers. An estimated 398 Judges came with Ram Air IV.

Note 2: For 1971, 12 more 455HO GT-37s were built in Canada.

Shelby

Year	Model/*Optional Engine Package*	Body Style	Production Number by Body Style	Engine (cid/hp)	Engine Code	Production Number by Engine
1965	GT-350	fastback	515	289/306	K	515
1966	GT-350	fastback	1,370	289/306	K	1,370
		convertible	6	289/306	K	6
	GT-350H	fastback	1,000	289/306	K	1,000
	GT-350S	fastback	n/a	289/400	K	n/a
1967	GT-350	fastback	1,175	289/306	K	1,175
	GT-500	fastback	2,048	428/355		2,048
1968	GT-350	fastback	1,253	302/230		1,253
		convertible	404	302/230		404
	GT-500	fastback	1,140	428/360		1,140
		convertible	402	428/360		402
	GT-500KR	fastback	1,053	428/335	R	1,053
		convertible	518	428/335	R	518
1969	GT-350	fastback	826	351/290	M	826
		convertible	136	351/290	M	136
	GT-500	fastback	1,154	428/335	R	1,154
		convertible	245	428/335	R	245
1970	GT-350	fastback	261	351/290	M	261
		convertible	58	351/290	M	58
	GT-500	fastback	380	428/335	R	380
		convertible	90	428/335	R	90

Note: The total production for all 1969–70 Shelbys is 3,150 (which does not include three pilot cars).

Bibliography

Antonick, Michael. *The Camaro White Book.* Osceola, Wis.: Michael Bruce Associates, 1993.

Boyce, Terry V. *Chevy Super Sports, 1961–1976.* Osceola, Wis.: MBI Publishing, 1981.

Campisano, Jim. *American Muscle Cars.* New York: Metrobooks, 1995.

———. *Mustang.* New York: Metrobooks, 1997.

Consumer Guide, ed. *Muscle Car Chronicle.* Lincolnwood, Ill.: Publications International, 1993.

DeMauro, Thomas A. *Firebird Decoding Guide, 1967–1981.* Saddle Brook, N.J.: CSK Publishing, 1997.

———. *Original Pontiac GTO.* St. Paul, Minn.: MBI Publishing, 2001.

Donohue, Mark, and Paul Van Valkenburgh. *The Unfair Advantage.* Cambridge, Mass.: Robert Bentley Inc., 2000.

Friedman, Dave. *Trans-Am, The Ponycar Wars.* Osceola, Wis.: MBI Publishing, 2001.

Gabbard, Alex. *Fast Chevys.* Lenoir City, Tenn.: Gabbard Publications, 1989.

———. *Fast Fords.* Los Angeles: HP Books, 1988.

———. *Ford Total Performance, 1962–1970, the Road to World Racing Domination.* New York: HP Books, 2000.

Golenbock, Peter, and Greg Fielden, eds. *The Stock Car Racing Encyclopedia, The Complete Record of America's Most Popular Sport.* New York: Macmillan, 1997.

Huntington, Roger. *American Supercar.* Tuscon, Ariz.: HP Books, 1983.

Old Cars Publications, ed. *The Standard Catalog of American Cars, 1946–1975.* Iola, Wis.: Krause Publications, 1987.

Riggs, D. Randy. *Flat-Out Racing, An Insider's Look at the World of Stock Cars.* New York: Metrobooks, 1995.

Sessler, Peter C. *Mustang Red Book, 1964 1/2–2000.* Osceola, Wis.: MBI Publishing, 2000.

Wangers, Jim, and Paul Zazarine. *Glory Days, When Horsepower and Passion Ruled Detroit.* Cambridge, Mass.: Robert Bentley Inc., 1998.

Young, Anthony. *Chrysler, Dodge & Plymouth Muscle.* Osceola, Wis.: MBI, 1999.

Photo Credits

©Dale Amy: pp. 11, 33, 34–35, 41, 45, 48, 50–51, 59, 97 top, 97 bottom, 98 bottom, 99, 116–117, 118, 119 top, 119 bottom, 122 inset, 122–123, 123 inset, 124, 124 left inset, 124 right inset, 125, 126, 126 left inset, 126 right inset, 128, 135, 135 inset, 152 bottom, 154–155, 155 inset, 162, 162 inset, 163, 167, 172 left inset, 172–173, 189, 194 bottom, 198–199, 199 inset, 202 left, 203 right, 216 top, 216 middle, 216 bottom, 223 top, 223 bottom, 224, 225 top, 225 bottom, 232 top, 232 middle, 232 bottom

©Neil Bruce: pp. 8–9, 87 right, 101

©Neil Bruce/Peter Robert Collection: pp. 6–7 (background), 98 top, 100 top left, 100 top right

©Jim Campisano Collection: pp. 136, 137, 172 right inset, 182, 217

©John A. Conde Collection: pp. 67, 69 right

Corbis: pp. 93, 131, 132, 134, 179 bottom, 212 top, 212 bottom

©Richard Cummins: pp. 28, 80, 152 top

©T. DeMauro: p. 62

©Jerry Heasley: pp. 18, 21, 27 top, 27 bottom, 29 top, 36, 37 top, 43, 49, 68 left, 68–69, 70, 71 top, 71 bottom, 74 top, 75 top, 85 right, 88, 89 top, 89 bottom, 92 top, 92 bottom, 94, 95 top, 95 bottom, 109, 112, 113 top, 114, 129, 130, 138, 139, 141, 151 inset, 160 inset, 161 top, 164, 165, 171, 178 top, 181 bottom, 187 top, 190 inset, 193, 200 top, 200 bottom, 201, 204, 214 left, 236 top, 236 bottom, 237 middle, 238 top, 238 bottom, 239

©Ron Kimball: pp. 2–3, 12–13, 14–15, 19, 20, 22-23, 32, 38, 39, 40, 44, 46, 52–53, 56, 61, 64–65, 73, 74–75, 76, 81, 81 inset, 82–83, 84–85, 86–87, 90–91, 102–103, 104–105, 106–107, 110–111, 120–121, 127, 133 top, 142–143, 144–145, 146–147, 148–149, 150–151, 156–157, 158–159, 160 top, 160–161, 174, 181 top, 185 top, 185 bottom, 186–187, 190–191, 192, 195, 196–197, 202–203, 206–207, 207 top, 208–209, 208 inset, 211, 214–215, 218–219, 220–221, 222–223, 228 top, 228–229, 233, endpapers

©Richard Prince: pp. 188, 219 top, 237 top, 237 bottom

©Private collection: pp. 26, 96, 113 bottom, 121 right, 153, 186 top, 197 top

©Diego Rosenberg: pp. 55 top, 55 bottom

©Zone Five Photo: pp. 16–17, 25, 29 bottom, 30–31, 37 bottom, 78 inset, 78–79, 105 top, 108, 133 bottom, 170, 175, 176, 177 top, 177 bottom, 178 bottom, 179 top, 194 top, 213 top, 213 bottom, 226, 227, 231 top, 231 bottom, 234 top left, 234 top right, 234 bottom, 235

Index

Page numbers in bold refer to main *Encyclopedia* entries; those in italics refer to tables and photos.

H

I

J

K

L

M